SURVIVAL IN THE SOUTH PACIFIC

SURVIVAL IN THE SOUTH PACIFIC

A Lost Airman's Desperate Rescue amid the Maelstrom of War

ROBERT RICHARDSON

CASEMATE
Pennsylvania & Yorkshire

Published in the United States of America and Great Britain in 2024 by
CASEMATE PUBLISHERS
1950 Lawrence Road, Havertown, PA 19083, USA
and
47 Church Street, Barnsley, S70 2AS, UK

Copyright © 2024 Robert Richardson

Hardcover Edition: ISBN 978-1-63624-415-0
Digital Edition: ISBN 978-1-63624-416-7

A CIP record for this book is available from the British Library

All rights reserved. No part of this book may be reproduced or transmitted in any form or by any means, electronic or mechanical including photocopying, recording or by any information storage and retrieval system, without permission from the publisher in writing.

Printed and bound in CPI Group (UK) Ltd, Croydon, CR0 4YY
Typeset in India by DiTech Publishing Services

For a complete list of Casemate titles, please contact:

CASEMATE PUBLISHERS (US)
Telephone (610) 853-9131
Fax (610) 853-9146
Email: casemate@casematepublishers.com
www.casematepublishers.com

CASEMATE PUBLISHERS (UK)
Telephone (0)1226 734350
Email: casemate@casemateuk.com
www.casemateuk.com

Front cover: Mt. Turi (Author's collection); Douglas C-47D cockpit at the National Museum of the United States Air Force (U.S. Air Force photo).
Back cover: Aviation Cadet Leonard G. Richardson (Richardson Family Archives); C-47 (Author's collection).

Contents

Acknowledgements		vii
Prologue		ix
Preface		xi
Introduction		xv

1	The Approaching Storm	1
2	Early Months of the War in the Pacific	11
3	America Begins to Respond	23
4	North to Espiritu Santo	37
5	The New Hebrides and its People	49
6	Espiritu Santo Becomes Critical	61
7	Santo and Guadalcanal	79
8	Advance Base Button	89
9	A New Garrison Force for Espiritu Santo	103
10	Richardson Arrives in the South Pacific	115
11	The 403rd Arrives in the South Pacific	131
12	Air Echelon on the Move	139
13	Flight Operations from Santo	149
14	September 5, 1943	161
15	Survival	171
16	Tan Pants	193
17	Lieutenant Richardson's Private War	211

Epilogue: Back to Espiritu Santo	221
Appendix 1: The 64th's Rescue Team and Their Casualties	241
Appendix 2: The 129th Combat Team	251
Appendix 3: The 64th Troop Carrier Squadron	259
Endnotes	271
Bibliography	311
Index	313

This book is for the ni Vanuatu, and especially for my friends Douglas Dick, Thomas Tavuli, Mark Tome and Pascal Tome.

And for Leslie, with thanks for your loving support and patience.
And for Rose and Sam, in whom I see strong reflections of their grandfather.

Acknowledgements

As a work of historical non-fiction, *Survival in the South Pacific* has as its overarching goal the straightforward, factual, and verifiable narration of events occurring in the early fall of 1943 on the small island of Espiritu Santo in the New Hebrides. Creating that narration has required the contributions of many scores of individuals, organizations and institutions, and to each I wish to express my sincere gratitude.

Foremost among the individual contributions are the four contemporaneous memoires shared by the families of key participants in the story that follows. These four documents provided independent corroboration of the myriad military reports, communications, orders and studies on which this narration is based. The contributors include the Jack Roessell family (Jack and Sandi Roessell), the Morris Naudts family (John Averett), Curtis Craver and family (Carolyn and Ashley Craver), and the Leonard Richardson family. My sincere thanks to the late authors of those memoires, and to their families.

Special recognition is due to the families of those servicemen who crewed C-47 # 42-23711 in the fall of 1943: the Robert Healy family (Irene Healy), the Augustus Miller family (Nancy Hueur), the Harry Wlodarsky family (Lynda Katz, John Wlodarsky), and the family of Joe O'Connell (Veronica Connelly).

Thanks also to the families of Alfred Richwine (Linda Richwine Horton), Kenneth Kidd (Kate Reed and Nancy Marchioni), and James P. Moyle (Jim Moyle). And sincere thanks to Matthew Spriggs, to Renata Netaf, and to John Anderson for their input and perspectives.

In the current age of digitalization, the material available for historical research has become astonishing in both depth and breadth. And for research materials not yet rendered in electronic form, the capabilities of mainline archives and repositories has reached a very high level. Each of the following are deserving of special recognition.

For their contributions related to the history of the 129th Infantry Regiment, my special thanks to the Illinois State Historical Society, the Illinois State Archives, the Illinois National Guard Command Historian, the Ohio History Connection and the 37th Division Veterans Association (Mandy Oberyszyn).

Among Army institutions, the U.S. Army Center for Military History (Kate Richards), the Army Military Enterprise at CMH (Sarah Forgey), the Army Heritage and Education Center (Marlea D. Leljedal and Stephen Bye), and the Ike Skelton

Combined Arms Research Library (Elizabeth Dubuisson and Rusty Rafferty) have been exceptionally helpful. My thanks to the following Navy institutions: the Naval History and Heritage Command (Heidrun Perez and Megan Casey), the National Naval Aviation Museum (Jared Galloway), and the Naval War College (Elizabeth Delmage). And thanks also to the Marine Corps History Division (Alyson Mazzone). Among Air Force institutions, special recognition and thanks to Tammy Horton and Maranda Gilmore at the Air Force Historical Research Agency (AFHRA), and to the Air Mobility Command History Office (Jeffrey Michalke).

Among U.S. government sponsored museums and archives, special recognition is due the Textural Records and Still Pictures Branches of the National Archives (College Park, San Francisco), and to the Smithsonian National Air and Space Museum (Dr. Roger Connor, Dr. Elizabeth Borja). Among foreign government sponsored museums and archives, my thanks to the National Library of Australia, the National Library of New Zealand (Jared Davidson), the Australian War Memorial Research Centre (Chris White), and the Nederlands Instituut voor Militaire Historie (Welmoed Bons). And special thanks to privately sponsored museums and archives, including the South Pacific World War II Museum (James Carter, Brad Wood), the Pima Air & Space Museum, the Wisconsin Veterans Museum (Beverly Phillips), and the 64th Troop Carrier Association (Janis Hayes et al.). Private research organizations and archives have also contributed significantly in the preparation of this book and a special note of recognition and thanks to USNavyResearch.com (Jerry Leslie), Redbird Research (Lori Miller, NPRC), Sam Askew (NARA College Park), Sydney Soderberg (Presidential Libraries and NARA Institutions), George Cully (AFHRA), and Military Research Service (John Thatcher).

Among U.S. universities and colleges, the Cushing Memorial Library & Archives at Texas A&M University, the Institute on World War II and the Human Experience, Florida State University (G. Kurt Piehler), the University of Nebraska—Lincoln (Erick Saxon), the South Carolina Library (Nicole Molyneux), and Norwich University (Nick Connizzo). Among foreign universities, thanks to University of Otago, Dunedin, New Zealand (Stuart Broughton and Jacinda Boivin). Special thanks is due to Mark Seiderman at the National Oceanic and Atmospheric Administration's National Centers for Environmental Information. The Spokane Public Library has been of exceptionally helpful in securing many dozens of interlibrary loans, and my thanks extend to their partner ILL institutions for their generosity in providing those important loans.

Prologue

When Strength Endures, Hope is Alive

He had crawled for five days through jungle soil turned slick by the daily rains. Slimy, ochre-colored clay encrusted his tattered flight suit and smeared his skin and hair, creating a perfect camouflage against the jungle foliage. Only his blue eyes, peering from his mud-stained face, distinguished him from a fallen log. Lying quietly across a faint trail, he heard them coming.

"*Hem i ledaon longwe. Long lefsaed. Long tri ya. Hem i no muv. Ating i ded finis.*" [He's lying there. On the left. Next to the tree. He hasn't moved. Maybe he already died.]

"*Bubu, mi luk hem. Yu stanap long ples ya, mo yu no muv.*" [I see him, old woman. Stay here, and be still.]

Tome slowly, silently, approached, not knowing if what he saw lying on the trail was the ghost of a long-dead ancestor, a foe from another clan, or a dead man dropped from the metal birds that flew overhead.

He neared, and paused.

"Hey! Over here!"

The man lying there croaked weakly, slowly raising his arm, as if that small effort was all he could manage, then rolled onto his back.

Shaken, but pushing against his shock, Tome eased forward slowly. Standing over the nearly lifeless man, he spoke softly: "*Yu karekil? Nem blong mi Tome, mo hemia famle blong mi. Bambae mifala i save helpem yu.* [Are you hurt? I am Tome from Butmas, and these are my family. We can help you]."[1]

The young second lieutenant, lying broken and bleeding on the jungle floor, understood nothing beyond the empathy and concern on the face of the man who spoke. For the second time since his ordeal began, the words "Thank God" came to his lips.

Two weeks earlier, the aircraft in which the lieutenant served as navigator had nearly completed a routine 1,300-mile mission to deliver supplies and equipment from one small South Pacific Island to another, returning with a load of spent aircraft engines for rebuilding. He had, once again, successfully brought his plane, his crewmates, and their cargo to the head of the island on which they were based—five minutes from wheels down and the prospect of a hot meal and much-needed sleep.

Eighteen months earlier, before the events at Pearl Harbor, the young lieutenant had been a high school science teacher. Tome had lived quietly in the village of Butmas in the wild remotes of the New Hebrides, only slightly aware of the changes that had swept over his island and utterly oblivious to the inconceivable war-making capacity of the combatants.

Along that still jungle trail, on that small island in the remote South Pacific, and in the midst of unprecedented industrial warfare, these two men had found each other. Their coming together held no significance to the conflict going on around them, and would go almost unnoticed.

Preface

My siblings and I know our father's story like we know our own. Our earliest memories include him nursing his injured leg; having to descend steps canted a bit sideways to favor his weaker right leg; seeing him lying on the couch with his leg elevated; often a bit of fever; a bit of drainage that continued off and on his whole life; the mass of tissue atop his right shin; and occasional injections delivered by his wife, his former nurse, our mother. All of us held that he was brave, that he had been lucky, and that with a stronger pharmaceutical industry in 1943, he would have recovered from his wounds completely.

His body was a patchwork of scars, mostly from where tissues had been removed and transplanted to his leg as part of the more than thirty surgeries he'd endured. As kids he told us those scars were left when he was run over by a tractor. We thought he must have been tough to have survived being run over by a tractor.

Our father would speak about the crash, his crawl down the mountain, and his rescue, but only as his children grew older, never in great detail, and only when asked.

As my father, Leonard Richardson, neared the end of his life, he wrote a short narrative entitled *The Crash of '43*. In it, he briefly described his arrival to the South Pacific, the unit to which he was assigned, his experiences on the island of New Caledonia, and his flights out of Espiritu Santo. He wrote in some detail about the events of September 5, the crash, his efforts to save himself, and his rescue.

For us, his was a heroic story; to us he was a hero. We were never embarrassed at his disability, never apologetic about his limp. And, on the few occasions when he would reach out for a shoulder to lean on, it was an honor to be the one whose shoulder it was. Sons and daughters will respond to their heroes, and we all surely did, each in our own ways.

As with many of the Baby Boomer generation, among his children Leonard's passing summoned thoughts of conversations they might have had, but never did, and of the details of his war service about which they knew very little. After a time, his family began, tentatively, to look for more details about his life and his service during the war.

This book is the result of 12 years of research to provide the context to Leonard's own narrative, to create an understanding of what role the man played in the vast industrial war that was in full cry in the South Pacific in 1943, and to explain how he and the victims of the crash came to be in that aircraft at that time and in that place.

His service trunk yielded records that detailed his enlistment, his flight training, and his embarkation to the South Pacific. Much was also learned from the Missing Air Crew Report his commander, Maj. Jack Roessell, had filed on September 7, 1943 when Richardson's aircraft failed to return to base as scheduled. This electrifying three-page document identified the crewmen who lost their lives in the crash, and deeply personalized the research that would follow.

Further important details came to light from the Individual Deceased Personnel Files (IDPF) for each of the four men killed in the plane crash on Mt. Turi. These records included the initial telegram to each family that their sons and husbands were missing. Also included was a second telegram that contained the terrible confirmation their loved one had been killed. The "Crash of '43" began to encompass much more than Leonard's story.

Though limited in scope, within each of those IDPFs, amid quite a lot of unhelpful Army documentation, was recorded the location of the crash site: the north side of Mt. "Terrin," "Tourin," or "Turin." A quick look at a map of Espiritu Santo revealed Mt. "Turi," about thirty air miles northwest of Leonard's home base at Pekoa Airfield.[1] An advertisement was placed in the national Vanuatu newspaper in an unsuccessful attempt to elicit local information about the events of September 5, 1943. Eventually, with archival records yielding only limited information, a personal visit to the island of Espiritu Santo was planned. Accordingly, in 2011 I travelled to Espiritu Santo to learn more about the "Crash of '43," an endeavor that would encompass not just my father's story, but the story of the young men—boys, really—who died in the crash.

More years would follow while the work of building biographies for each of the men in the plane with Leonard, and creating a narration for their service, was undertaken. And, as further evidence that miracles do still occur in this modern age, a man was located who was a participant in actions undertaken in the days immediately following the crash, who had helped lead a small party to hack through the dense jungle to the crash site, and who later wrote a published account of those events. More importantly, that man—Curtis Craver of Raleigh, North Carolina—had, at the age of 95, a near-total recall of the events surrounding the crash. With his help, the story that follows began to unfurl more rapidly. In addition to his own first-hand knowledge of the events, Craver provided information that led to the unpublished memoir of his commanding officer and to the records of the Army unit to which they were assigned. Further research led to the similarly unpublished memoir of the commander of the Army Air Force unit to which the missing aircraft was assigned.

With these four contemporaneous accounts in hand, the account of the events leading to and following the loss of this aircraft could be written. What took much more time was chronicling the context of the event. What mission was being flown, and to where? Why was the aircraft's squadron based on Santo, what other missions had it flown, and by what process had it arrived in the South Pacific theater of operations? What military decisions had led to its deployment, what other combat was occurring during that time, and what were America's prospects in the war with Japan?

Answering those questions required reference to the vast military records of the National Archives, the Air Force Historical Research Agency, the Army's Combined Army Research Library, and many other archival sites.

The final critical element in this narrative was provided by the Command Summary of Admiral Chester Nimitz, overall commander of American forces in the South Pacific. That formerly classified information contained the exchanges between top commanders in the Pacific, including General Douglas MacArthur and Admiral "Bull" Halsey, and chronicled the timeline of events leading to the crash on Santo.

The villagers on Espiritu Santo are surely among the kindest in the world. Equally, until the turn of the 20th century, and viewed from a Western perspective, they were among the most savage. This story does not soften their history. Neither does it soften the scurrilous depictions recorded in early European chronicles following the islands' mid-17th century discovery, or the racism that marked the islanders' subsequent subjugation and exploitation. In contradiction of Aesop's admonishment that those without something good to say ought to remain silent, with regard to the natives of Espiritu Santo, and their treatment by white explorers and exploiters, this story will be factual and will rely on the reader to accept the narrative in the context of the period. My friends on Santo know how I feel about them.

Based on the above materials and research documents, the full story of the "Crash of '43" can now be told, including its aftermath and the results of the search undertaken 68 years later by the aforementioned aging and not particularly robust explorer.

Introduction

On a small mountaintop on the remotest of South Pacific islands, in the midst of a brutal clash of superpowers, came together a handful of men. They included soldiers who had traveled from the other side of the world—some who would see no combat right up until the day they were killed, others who would see the most horrendous fighting of the Pacific War—and indigenous islanders.

Their coming together was inconsequential to the vast war that had engulfed the South Pacific. Inconsequential but for the dead and near-dead, and for the families back home left with an enduring grief. Their gathering was one of innumerable unforeseen events following countless diplomatic and military debates, many quite contentious, and of many daring decisions. It resulted from months and months of mobilization, planning, training, and combat. Bold, even desperate actions had already been undertaken, often with not enough time and too few resources, all serving as prelude for the events on the island of Espiritu Santo in the fall of 1943.

Unpacking those conferences, decisions, and actions provides a context without which the commitments and sacrifices of those young men would be poorly understood. Without proper context, for example, how can it be explained that a shoe salesman in Chicago could, in a very short time, become a seasoned combat reconnaissance scout. And, for the head man in the most primitive of villages in the most alien of cultures, what acts of diplomacy or elements of military strategy could lead to his playing a part—however slight—in the maelstrom of industrial war that had swept over the entire South Pacific?

Japan, in its drive to Empire, believed the Pacific War was desirable, inevitable, and ultimately winnable, and while it is now known Japan was never going to win the war, in 1942 the outcome was utterly in doubt. The story that follows recounts America's desperation in the early months of the war with Japan, and relates the actions and consequence in the first critical months in the South Pacific theater that ultimately foretold the defeat of Japan.

The story is set in the New Hebridean archipelago[1] that, seemingly overnight, became a vast base for Navy, Army, and Air Force operations in the South Pacific. And, on their arrival, U.S. forces immediately faced an aspect of the New Hebrides that was to shape the conduct of war more significantly than anything else—the scourge of endemic malaria. America found itself utterly unprepared to deal with the terrible consequences of the disease for its military forces.

Over this narrative looms the dreadful saga of the Guadalcanal campaign, a fight Japan would quite likely have won had it just a few more days of preparation. Throughout the early years of the war, time and timing determined many of the failures and successes that befell both Japan and the Allies.

World War II is too immense for any but the most dedicated historian to completely comprehend. To bring the war into a comprehensible scale, most published works adopt a "30,000-foot" perspective, with strategy, action, and consequence described in necessarily broad strokes. Other works parse the war into individualized stories—stories from a ground-level perspective, from a ship's bridge, or from a cockpit; stories that demonstrate the resilience of the American spirit, and the triumph of faith and courage over despair.

The story that follows does both—stories of individuals at war are presented within the vortex of world war that had taken them from their homes and swept them to the remotest places on the globe, serving their country in ways impossible for them to have imagined in their peacetime lives.

Even from ground level, action means much less if its consequences remain unknown. In the case of those few troops who met on that remote mountaintop, chronicling their subsequent combat deployments, and the heavy losses they endured, gives proper meaning to their service—meaning that has been little noted in broader war narratives, but which has been included in this story.

The same is true for the indigenes of Espiritu Santo. The history of the villagers of that region reflected what had become a standard arc for similar societies in the Pacific: discovery, resource extraction, disease and resultant population reductions, and the arrival of Christian missionaries. The present story describes the experiences of those peoples during the American occupation, describes the fate of those people during the 80 years since the Americans left, and concludes with an assessment of the islanders' future, giving fresh meaning to the timeless adage that oftentimes bad things happen to good people.

Woven through this narrative is the story of one man's survival in the vastness of warfare in the Pacific, a story that represents countless other tales of duty fulfilled, challenges met, and consequences endured.

"The only thing new in the world is the history you do not know." So said Harry Truman. The following narrative will, for most, represent something new, and heroic.

CHAPTER ONE

The Approaching Storm

Two great rivers converge in the western foothills of the Bitterroot Mountains, a region that had been home to the storied Nez Perce people for thousands of years before the arrival of Europeans to North America. From the south, the Snake River, known to the Nez Perce as the *Weyikespe*, drains most of Idaho. From the east flows the smaller *Koos Koos Kia*—the "Clearwater." For millennia, the indigenous peoples relied on these rivers for their sustenance and plied the rivers deep into the interior to hunt and gather, or on trading missions or war parties.

The nearly exhausted Lewis and Clark expedition visited the region in 1805 on its outbound leg to the Pacific. By the 1860s, the area began to attract gold miners and white settlers: the town of Lewiston would be founded on the eastern bank of the Snake at its confluence with the Clearwater; its sister city Clarkston on the western bank.[1] These were extractive communities, yielding ores and timber and producing rich crops courtesy of the area's extended growing season in the sheltered Snake River valley. Despite the arrival of whites, with their innovations and technologies, in the early 20th century the region looked much as it did in the fall of 1805.

Identical twin brothers Leonard and Norman Richardson came to the valley at the age of three when their parents emigrated from Saskatchewan in 1920. The brothers were bred tough and raised Christian by a dominant father and an industrious mother. They developed the ethos: "I don't have to like it; I just have to do it."

They completed high school in Clarkston and in the process joined every club and played every sport. They excelled at football, sang in the glee club, and played in the orchestra: Leonard the clarinet; Norman the tuba.

"Fighting was one of the activities typical of our existence. Normally if one of us couldn't whip the other guy, two of us could." Regardless of the odds, they always had each other's back, and tangled in ways that were pugnacious, but not meanspirited. But when foes were scarce they would sometimes take on each other. Norm had the size advantage, and Leonard later observed, "I won only moral victories—Norm used to pulverize me."[2]

Leonard and Norman as young boys, circa 1924. (Richardson Family Archives)

Norman, Leonard, and their pals ranged the hills west of Clarkston and the basalt cliffs overlooking the Snake, and fished for sturgeon and carp along the shoreline in the shadow of those cliffs. They spent many hot summer hours at the City Beach and at the "Highland Hole," their high school's secluded hangout. They swam across the Snake effortlessly, drifting down with the main current until sweeping out on an eddy to the opposite shore. Sometimes they would snitch a watermelon from a local grower, floating with it down to the rapids by which time it would be wonderfully cooled. Other times they hiked upriver to shoot the rapids astride a log.

The family camped often in the Idaho Bitterroots and in the corrugated hills of the Salmon River watershed. On one trip to Dixie, the twins and their father caught hundreds of fish from the nearby rivers and Leonard's mother and sister preserved them in salt they bought from the old-timer at the Dixie post office. They all picked huckleberries and canned them over an open fire. The family fished but never hunted, and owned no guns.

At that time and place, lives were focused on family, church, school, and work. Radio, newspapers, and school sports provided all the diversions needed, and the young grew to understand the merits of hard work and the value of knowing what was right and fair and what was not.

Both went by "Ritchie," and their high school annual attests to their cockiness. Norman's senior photo is captioned "I am a self-made man, and I love my maker." Leonard's was "One side, Professor, let me show you how."

A small airstrip east of Lewiston had been in operation since at least 1914 and local newspapers kept residents informed—perhaps titillated—with the latest aviation news. In the years following the end of World War I, aviation had captivated the American imagination. The "Age of Flight," arriving roughly contemporaneously with automobiles, stretched perspective into a third dimension, into the heavens. The danger in early aviation was compelling and the barnstorming heroics of early pilots and wing walkers were electrifying. The twin communities of Lewiston and Clarkston were as swept up in aviation enthusiasm as everyone else in the country. Inevitably, many young boys in this era were enthralled by flight, not least among them, Leonard Richardson, who noted in his autobiography:

> Clarkston now had an airport, and the Gooch brothers were the pilots. One was a sober businessman trying to establish aviation in Clarkston. The other, Roy, was alcoholic, and the things he did with that airplane I will never forget. He would hedgehop with passengers, and then his crowning achievement was to loop the Lewiston Clarkston Bridge. I witnessed this several times. He was eventually grounded by the aviation authorities. Bert Zimmerly took over the operation of the airport and had it for several years until he was killed in a plane crash near Pullman.

The twins and their parents were aware of the military and diplomatic tensions in both Asia and Europe. War, rumors of war, and heightened international militarism were daily headlines. They read and listened to reports of the Japanese invasion of Manchuria in 1931, and of Germany's rearmament in contravention of the Treaty of Versailles during the early 1930s. They were witting of the diplomatic wrangling between Britain and Italy that presaged the Italian invasion of Abyssinia (now Ethiopia) in October 1935.

But, for the people of America, as alarming as the news from Europe was, it remained a European war and the opinions in favor of neutrality continued to run strong. In 1938, polls reported two-thirds of American men would not be willing to fight overseas if the United States was to become involved in a European war. But that same poll clearly showed the strong patriotism of those questioned: 90% would be willing to fight if American territory was attacked.[3]

Norm and Len both enrolled at Whitworth College in 1935, roomed together in each of their four years there, and each majored in History. They sang in the choir, served in student government, and generally cut a wide swath through the campus social scene. They anchored both sides of the line for the Pirates football team and resembled each other so closely that when Norm was named to the Little All-American football squad, Len went on stage to accept his award with no one the wiser. They worked throughout summer. In Weippe, they were brush pilers and "road monkeys"; in Moscow, they shoveled rock. At the Mayview tramway,

Leonard and Norman, burly young men working tough summer jobs, 1936. (Richardson Family Archives)

Leonard and Norman nearing graduation, 1939. (Richardson Family Archives)

they stacked 140-lb sacks of wheat, and were "grunts" for the Washington Water Power. They grew as familiar with a pickaxe and shovel as they were with American history or the books of the Old Testament.

As they neared graduation, they became increasingly concerned by the ominous reports coming from both Asia and Europe, and of Germany and Japan's intensified military aggression. By the time Leonard and Norman graduated in the spring of 1939, Japan had invaded China, Hitler had been appeased at Munich, and Germany, Italy, and Russia had all occupied neighboring territories. For the Richardson twins, knowing their futures would be affected—perhaps determined—by their government's war policies, the daily war news took on a new sharpness.

American leaders, reflecting the prevailing sentiments of the populace, adamantly maintained neutrality and passed four separate Neutrality Acts between 1935 and 1940 to prevent the supply of arms and war materials to belligerents. As the 1930s gave way to 1940, the American public largely held to the belief that events in Asia and Europe need not embroil the United States in armed conflict.

But an awareness of the mounting tensions within America and a knowledge of the war that was engulfing Europe and China did not prepare the American public, including the Richardson family, for what lay ahead or for the awful consequences global war would soon bring to their doorsteps:

During this time we saw the rise of the Nazis under Hitler in Germany, Mussolini in Italy, and the Japanese were known as the "Yellow Peril" in the Far East. The labor movement was taking hold during those years. We were blissfully unaware of the seriousness of the situation, and went about our everyday lives.

It is strange to compare the seriousness of the events in Europe and the detachment that permeated their family and their community. For example, on May 23, 1939, the morning of their college graduation, the *Spokane Daily Chronicle*'s headline read "Axis Powers Sign Military Accord" with an accompanying report describing the dangerous new economic and military alliance forged by Germany and Italy. But their commencement speaker's inspirational address later that same day was largely disassociated from current events. Seattle Mayor Arthur Langlie enjoined them: "You have a wide field and a great frontier ahead ... Leadership is lacking in the nation today. We need young men and women who understand the vital principles of it."[4] In his address, the mayor never referred to the ominous developments in Europe, or to the possible impact those events would have on the lives of the young people seated before him.

This seeming unconcern was also evident in Whitworth's student newspaper. At a time when other college campuses were loudly denouncing any potential American involvement in a European war, the *Whitworthian* was utterly silent on American diplomacy or military developments in Europe. But both Spokane daily newspapers were rife with reports from Europe, the rise of American military mobilization, and the dangers of both German and Japanese diplomatic and military initiatives.

In the spring of 1939, Americans remained staunchly opposed to entering the European war and believed their president when he repeatedly assured them the country would remain neutral. Still the drumbeats continued. In the late 1930s, European events remained daily front-page news, culminating in German's invasion of Poland in September, and Great Britain and France's declaration of war. By the spring of 1940, the German *Blitzkrieg* was in full cry. Belgium, the Netherlands and Luxembourg had all been overrun; France was under siege. In late May, British and French troops began evacuating continental Europe at Dunkirk and, by the end of June, France had fallen. In the early fall of 1940, Japan invaded French Indochina and had entered into the "Tripartite Pact" with Germany and Italy. America responded initially with an embargo of shipments of aircraft and aviation gasoline to Japan, and later expanded the export bans to include oil, iron, and steel. And just as the Snake surged on the strength of spring snowmelt, so too did the frightening news from Europe swell tensions within the American home front to palpable levels.

Norman Richardson remained at Whitworth to earn a post-graduate secondary teaching certificate. Leonard landed a teaching position with the Asotin County school district for the 1940–41 academic year, teaching math and science in Clarkston's junior high school. As they prepared to begin their teaching careers, the United States continued its war mobilization skillfully orchestrated by President Roosevelt and, in September, the Selective Service Act was implemented—the first peacetime draft in American history. All men between the ages of 21 and 45 were required to register, essentially creating a "pool" from which individuals could be selected for service. More than sixteen million young men did just that, including Norman and Leonard Richardson.

On the cusp of beginning his teaching career, Leonard was earning $35 a week, had an active social life and a bit of money set aside. Each day, however, he read of the worsening violence in Europe, North Africa, and in the Atlantic, Japan's mounting aggression in Asia, and America's failing diplomatic efforts and increasing military mobilization. He knew that if America entered the war his future would be largely out of his control, but he also knew that by making decisions early he could influence where and how he would serve; for Leonard, being decisive was a part of his nature.

His thinking about military service was shaped by his early interest in aviation and, in December 1940, midway through his first year of teaching, he applied for admission into the spring cohort of Lewiston's Civilian Pilot Training (CPT) Program.[5]

The CPT Program was developed by the Civil Aeronautics Authority (CAA) in 1938 to boost the flagging civilian aviation industry—particularly small flying schools, light plane manufacturers, and fixed-base operators—and to serve as a vocational training program for American youth. The program to which Leonard had been accepted had been approved by the CAA in late 1939. By 1940, with the disturbing news coming from Europe, the American military recognized the value of creating a pool of trained civilian pilots.[6]

The Army Air Corps was playing catch up. Germany had been increasing its air force since 1933 and had reaped enormous experience through its combat operations during the Spanish Civil War. Concurrently, Japan was also greatly increased its air arms. As early as 1930, the Imperial Japanese Navy began a flying crew training program that was unequaled anywhere in the world, and also benefitted from combat operations in Manchuria and China.[7] In early 1941, American air power was in an extremely disadvantaged position.

The CPT Program bought no airplanes, rented no classrooms, and hired no instructors. Its genius was in fostering *consortia* from academic institutions, private flight schools, and general aviation airfields already in operation. In the Lewiston CPT, that consortium consisted of the Lewiston State Normal School, a teacher-training institution, and the well-established Zimmerly Flying School. The Asotin County Airport, located along the southern bank of the Snake River just below its confluence with the Clearwater, met the minimum standards set by the program for length, width, and prevailing winds, and became the third component of the CPT triad.

Together with 19 other students, Leonard shelled out $40 for a life insurance policy and physical examination, and entered the CPT's Preliminary Flight Program.[8] He intended to complete both the Preliminary and Secondary aviation courses with CPT, making him eligible to enter the Army Air Corps' pilot training program.

For the Preliminary Course, the Normal school delivered most of the required 72 hours of ground instruction, with topics including the history and theory of flight, civil air regulations, meteorology, and navigation. Classes began at Lewiston Normal on February 22 and were held in two-hour sessions, three evenings a week.

Additional ground instruction of an entirely different type was provided by the Zimmerly Flying School at the Asotin County Airport. Zimmerly's ground instruction was decidedly practical and included familiarizing the student with the airplane's flight controls and instrumentation, engine start up and shutdown, and warnings—the danger of propellers, the difference between ground speed and airspeed, parking a plane during a strong wind, and running an engine with no one in the cockpit.

Flight training for Leonard and his fellow flight students began on March 22. Bert Zimmerly supplied all aircraft and flight instructors for the program and delivered a minimum of thirty-five hours of flying instruction to each cadet, including at least fourteen solo hours.[9] Cadets flew the 65-horsepower Piper J-3C Cub and, in the initial phase of instruction, focused on taxiing, take-offs and landings, spins and stalls, forced landings, and "air work"—level flight, gentle climbs and turns, 70-degree turns, and landing approaches.[10]

J3C Piper Cub. A 65 hp aircraft with a top speed of 87 mph, a ceiling of 11,500 feet, and a range of 220 miles. Most pilot trainees had their first flights in Cubs, soloed in Cubs, or were certificated in Cubs. (Wikimedia Commons)

The young men in the flight program may never have flown before, but they all knew what the twin cities of Lewiston and Clarkston looked like from above. The highway to Spokane ran north, climbing the steep, 2,000-foot Clearwater Escarpment via the 64-turn Spiral Highway—eight tortuous miles of twisting, unbanked road through the desiccated, folded hills above the Snake River before topping out at a spectacular south-facing vista—Lewiston and Clarkston below and fertile orchard and farmland land extending to the foothills of the Blue Mountains. The young men often had occasion to look down on their hometowns from this overlook, following the westerly flow of the Snake after its confluence with the Clearwater. What they couldn't see looking south across the rivers was the massive expanse of the Palouse Hills behind them, to the north. The "Palouse," 18,000 square miles of the most fertile and productive farmlands in the United States, and surely the country's most picturesque, could only be fully appreciated from the altitude the new student pilots would reach in their cross-country flights.[11] From the air, the innumerable hills and swales of the Palouse resembled nothing so much as ocean waves stacking up on shallow water before crashing to shore.

The final phase of the Preliminary course focused on precision landings, power turns, figure eights around pylons, stalls, spins and slips, and power landings. As students neared the completion of the program, they were required to complete a two-hour solo cross-country flight of fifty miles minimum distance, including two full-stop landings at different airports. As summer approached, the days grew long, twilight not coming until nearly 9:00 pm, leaving many hours for the student pilots to log solo hours and longer flights.

Leonard Richardson, private pilot, June 1941. (Richardson Family Archives)

On June 13, Leonard passed the flight test for his private pilot's license and was issued Private Pilot Certificate No. 86852.[12] He immediately applied for admission to the Secondary Civilian Pilot Training Program, also offered at the Zimmerly Flying School, and reported for the requisite physical exam on June 26.[13]

The Secondary CPT course was of great interest to these young pilots because it offered the opportunity of a much more intensive ground school and a flight course of up to fifty hours in a higher-performing aircraft—the low-wing Howard DGA-18, with a powerplant double the size of the Piper Cubs.[14]

Since the CPT did not shield its aviation students from the draft, Leonard received his first draft card on June 27, 1941, classifying him I-A "until further notice."[15] At the same time, he also received word from the CAA that he had failed his physical for the Secondary CPT course; to his great surprise, he learned that at the time of his physical he was suffering from diplopia—he was seeing double.[16] The CAA suggested, in a very courteous letter, that it might be in his best interest to voluntarily surrender his private pilot's license, rather than the CAA institute revocation proceedings. Knowing the CPT pathway to service with the Army Air Corps had come to an end, the genuinely disappointed Richardson surrendered his license on September 29, 1941.[17] Until this point, Richardson had excelled at everything he had attempted and had attained every goal he had set for himself, including the mastery of flight. In many ways his life had been exceptional, and in considering the war he knew was coming, Richardson wanted his service to be similarly exceptional. He was unafraid, felt himself equal to any challenge, and was surrounded by other young men who felt the same way. But now they might fly, and he would not. At age 24, at the apex of personal vigor and sensing the limitless options available to him, he was stymied by a condition about which he was completely unaware. Perhaps college football had left its mark. During games he occasionally tossed his leather football helmet to the sidelines to impress the coeds with his toughness and demonstrate his disdain for the competition. He might have taken a blow that still endured.

In 1938, President Roosevelt had seen that America was ill-prepared to defend itself in the event of war and had been taking action to rearm the military and shepherd the country away from its keen isolationist tendencies. In July 1941, Roosevelt had asked his Secretary of War for an assessment of the overall industrial production the country would need to defeat its potential enemies—how many men, and what munitions, would be needed if the United States was drawn into the war as an active belligerent. The resultant report was completed in late September 1941 by the Joint Army Navy Board and soon become known as the "Victory Plan."

It was immediately evident the American armed services were not within a cannon shot of the recommendations in that report.[18] The Army had just over one million six hundred thousand men in uniform, organized into 37 divisions (only 17 of which were considered technically ready for combat), and there was only enough ammunition available to support one division.[19] In the event of war, Army ground forces would need 215 divisions (infantry, armored, motorized, airborne, mountain, and cavalry), and a total of 6.7 million officers and men.[20] The Army Air Corps was equipped with just 560 medium and heavy bombers and roughly one thousand modern fighters. The Victory Plan estimated the AAC would need just over two million men, eight thousand five hundred bombers, and not less than twenty thousand fighters to fight a simultaneous war with Germany and Japan.[21] The Victory Plan estimated the Navy would require 3,649 vessels of all types in the coming war, of which 850 would be combat vessels—aircraft carriers, cruisers, destroyers, and submarines.[22] By September 1941, the Navy was in fair proximity to the requirements estimated in the Victory Plan, with ships on hand or under construction totaling 2,289, of which 853 were warships,[23] but it would still need to recruit and train 1.2 million men and would need 21,000 more aircraft and crews to fly them. The Marine Corps would need to triple in size and add two Marine air wings and 13 defense battalions.[24] Finally, due to the dependence of the armed forces on troop and cargo shipping. the merchant fleet would have to increase by 18 million tons—roughly two thousand six hundred ships.[25]

America's first draft began as a trickle in 1940, with just 18,633 young men selected for service, but in the nation's second draft lottery, held in July 1941 and fully five months before the surprise attack at Pearl Harbor, that trickle became a torrent, with over nine hundred thousand men called to service. With one eye on the Draft Board, most young men at the time were ambivalent about military service, though many were actively considering their options.[26]

When Leonard received a new teaching contract for the '41–42 academic year at Charles Adams High School, his draft classification was amended to "2-A." He would not be among the first to be drafted, but the new classification was valid for just six months. Leonard was an unmarried, physically fit young man and knew his deferment would only temporarily excuse him from the draft. Like countless thousands of other men his age, with heightened urgency he began to finalize his plans for military service. With CPT no longer available to him, Leonard, then 25, was nearing the age when some service options would no longer be available to him, in particular, aviation. He was not inclined to let his local draft board determine his fate and, with the enormous mobilization then sweeping the country, many other service options were available. And his 2-A status provided a sliver of time for him to make his selection.

And then, four months into his second teaching term, came Pearl Harbor. Leonard's draft status abruptly reverted to "1-A."[27]

CHAPTER TWO

Early Months of the War in the Pacific

Japan's best hope for the defeat of the United States was an overwhelming opening assault, the rapid occupation of critical territories, a short war, and a negotiated peace that would leave its newly expanded Empire intact. Its first necessary step was the defeat of America's two primary Army–Navy–Air Force bases in the Pacific—the long-established bastion in Hawaii and the growing defensive forces in the Philippines. Constrained by limited resources and industrial capacity, Japan's military leadership knew precisely how long it could afford to fight. The genius who planned the Pearl Harbor attack, Admiral Isoroku Yamamoto, had earlier advised his superiors they must force America to come to terms with Japan within four months of Pearl Harbor or Japan's defeat was inevitable.

Japan's attack in Hawaii, its devastating assault on the American forces in the Philippines, and its lightning advances in the western and southern Pacific were executed with great precision and led to a stunning series of victories. By the end of that *single* day,[1] in addition to the surprise attack in Hawaii, Japan had invaded Siam (Thailand) and launched coordinated air attacks across a wide swath of the Pacific, including on the Philippines and the islands Wake and Guam. Japanese air forces attacked British-held Singapore and Hong Kong, and its naval forces shelled Midway. At Shanghai Harbor, Japan sank 41 British cargo ships. Eight other Allied ships were sunk in the Pacific, and one American troopship was captured.[2]

By the end of day three of the war in the Pacific, Britain's naval mainstays in the Pacific—the battleship HMS *Prince of Wales* and the battlecruiser HMS *Repulse*—were attacked and sunk by Japanese aircraft off the coast of Malaya. Japanese forces began coming ashore on the Philippine island of Luzon.

By the end of the first week, Guam had fallen and, by the end of December, Wake Island was taken, Hong Kong had surrendered, Imperial Japanese Army troops were ashore in Burma and British Borneo, and had occupied New Britain and New Ireland to the east of New Guinea. American naval forces evacuated the Philippines, and Army forces on Luzon began retreating to the Bataan peninsula.[3]

In late December, 14 days after the attack in Hawaii, President Roosevelt, British Prime Minister Winston Churchill, and their advisors met at the First Washington Conference—codename *Arcadia*—to hammer out the much-needed joint war plan for the Pacific, Mediterranean, and European theaters. On the agenda: confirming overall strategy; identifying military measures required immediately; and the allocation of forces in light of the Japanese advances.[4] The strategists were forced to cope with a military situation that was in constant motion: over the two weeks of the conference, Japanese forces took both Hong Kong and Manila, drove British troops in Malaya southward toward Singapore, and landed at several points in Borneo and on Celebes. In the Mediterranean, the British had more than they could handle with German Field Marshal Erwin Rommel, his *Afrika Korps*, and the Italians.

The conference concluded that "Germany First" remained the overriding grand strategic policy and Allied assets would predominantly be devoted to defeating the Axis Forces in the Mediterranean and Europe.

For many years, Army leadership had strongly advocated for a defensive posture in the Pacific in the event of war with Japan, protecting the Alaska–Hawaii–Panama "strategic triangle." In contrast, Navy leadership ardently promoted an aggressive, offensive-minded war policy. The prevailing American war plan—*Rainbow 5*—had somewhat accommodated these two diametric strategic philosophies, but, as Japanese gains continued, the shape of the war in the Pacific started coming into sharper focus.

Pre-war, military strategists believed the remote American outposts in the Philippines, Wake, and Guam could be supported through a mid-Pacific supply line. But the sweeping Japanese victories had not been anticipated, and the central Pacific was now solidly Japanese and too dangerous for surface ships. The United States was forced to consider a more southerly track for supply vessels and troopships.

This critical "Southern Supply Line" began on the west coast and extended over eight thousand miles through Hawaii, Christmas and Canton Islands, the Samoa and Fiji island groups, and terminated in New Caledonia, New Zealand, and the east coast of Australia. This impossibly long line of communication was "indispensable to maintenance of an air route to Australia, and as a screen for vital seaways." Tonga, the Society Islands, and the New Hebrides Islands were nearly adjacent to this supply line and were also considered critically important.[5]

The events in the Pacific had forced American military and civilian leadership back to square one in war planning. In an impossibly short time, a new war plan would be developed that addressed the key factors of leadership, strategy, intelligence, tactics, and logistics in the global war America now faced.

In the Pacific Theater, *Arcadia* again confirmed the U.S. Navy's role would remain defensive—stopping further Japanese advances in the Hawaii–Midway corridor and maintaining lines of communication from the U.S. to Alaska, Hawaii, Australia, and the Far East with the now-critical Southern Supply Line.

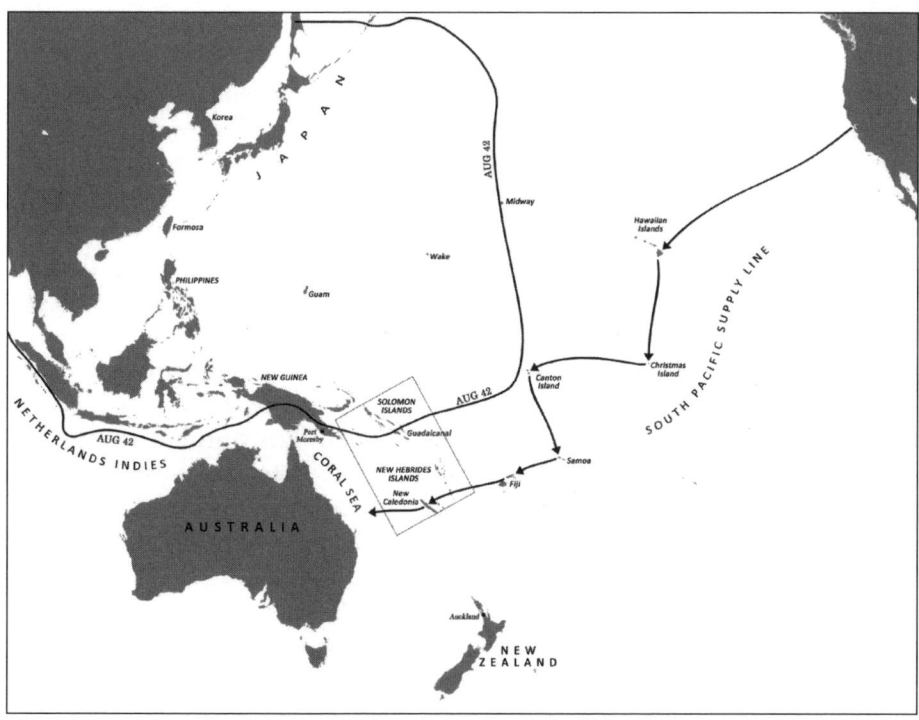

Japanese Territorial Expansion and the all-important Southern Supply Line to Australia (Yosemite Productions)

While Allied operations in the Pacific would be primarily defensive, *Arcadia* was specific as to the Southern Supply Line: "The security of these routes involves ... holding and capturing essential sea and air bases" and that "only such positions in the Pacific theater as will safeguard vital interests ... points of vantage from which an offensive against Japan can be eventually developed must be secured."[6] In so stating, *Arcadia* acknowledged that within the overall defensive posture for the Pacific, some limited offensive actions might also be required. Fleet Admiral King would later describe this as the Defensive–Offensive Phase of War in the Pacific.

One can easily imagine the consternation within naval hierarchy. Leaving *Arcadia*, they would still have the same overall strategy for the Pacific Theater—a defensive one—but they now had fewer warships to command, were operating with far less British participation, with fewer Pacific bases at their disposal, and with much of the Pacific no longer accessible to them.

One point had become glaringly obvious—the strategic importance of New Caledonia. Its position in the South Pacific made it a key locale in the Southern Supply Line connecting Australia and the United States. Should it fall to Japan, Australia would be isolated and vulnerable to invasion from the west, the north, and east. Additionally, New Caledonia's extensive nickel resources were critical for munitions manufacture, and the island could serve as a base from which an early Allied offensive could be mounted against Japan.

The conference produced an accurate assessment of available military assets in the Pacific and identified the forces that would be required for the region. It was apparent to all that the entire South Pacific had little with which to defend itself. All air assets—just 53 aircraft—were based on Samoa and Fiji. New Caledonia, Canton, Christmas, and Bora Bora were essentially undefended.[7]

The conference recommended the allocation of 22,000 troops for New Caledonia and other islands along the Supply Line, and the commitment of 250 fighter aircraft and 143 medium and light bombers for the region.[8]

Arcadia also led to the formation of the American Joint Chiefs of Staff (JCS) to implement the operational strategy in all theaters and to coordinate operations between the Army and Navy Departments, and with their British counterparts.[9] Admiral William Leahy was the presiding officer of the Joint Chiefs; all individual service chiefs operated under his authority. The Navy was represented by the Commander in Chief of the U.S. Fleet (COMINCH), Adm. Ernest King. He would also soon be designated the Chief of Naval Operations (CNO). Possessed of a ferocious temper, King was later described as "hostile, tactless, arrogant, and sometimes disrespectful or even subordinate."[10] However, he was tough, he was brilliant, he was insightful, and he was dynamic. Army Chief of Staff Gen. George Marshall represented the Army on the Joint Chiefs. He was previously assigned to the Army's War Plans Division (WPD) and was deeply knowledgeable about the current *Rainbow 5* War Plan and its development over the prior three decades. General Henry Arnold, who had learned to fly from the Wright Brothers and served in the US Army since 1907, represented the Army Air Forces (AAF) on the Joint Chiefs.

It fell to the Joint Chiefs to decide how to deliver and employ these new Army and AAF units to the Pacific, and under what command structure. A sharp interservice debate raged for three months, with the Army and Navy clearly expressing their views and with neither especially keen to concede.

In brief, the Navy held that *Arcadia* expected future offensives to be launched once strongpoints were established along the Southern Supply Line. In King's parlance: "hold what you've got and hit them when you can."[11] The Army argued "only the minimum of force necessary for the safeguarding of vital interests in other theatres should be diverted from operations against Germany."

By the end of January, Japan had swept further into southeast Asia, invading the Dutch East Indies, Java, and Celebes and occupying the Samarinda oil fields in Borneo. Its forces had overrun the small Australian garrison force at Rabaul and had come ashore on New Ireland in the Bismarck Archipelago, on Bougainville in the northern Solomon Islands, and at Java in the Dutch East Indies. Japan's forces were arrayed across a 4,000-mile east–west expanse, creating an isolating corridor just north of Australia.

Japan's successes were so stunning that, as early as January 1942, it began putting plans in motion for a second phase of offensive operations—extending its frontier to Midway in the east and New Caledonia in the south.

After two months of war, Japan had achieved its most important military objectives. In occupying the Dutch East Indies, it had secured the critical oil resources it needed and had attained undisputed control of the sea lanes extending from those oil fields back to the Japanese home islands. It had protected its western flank by occupying Singapore and Burma, and its eastern flank through its attack at Pearl Harbor and by seizing Guam and Wake Island. It had strengthened its position against Chinese forces by threatening the critical Burma Road, had pushed far to the east in the Central Pacific with forces established in the Marshall and Gilbert Islands, and was at the doorstep to the South Pacific.

Japanese military leaders believed they had set the U.S. Navy back 10 months and that prospects for a negotiated settlement of hostilities in the Pacific had become considerably brighter.[12] Japan was now poised to either invade Australia or to isolate it from American aid by controlling the seaways connecting it to the American west coast, a feat its forces could accomplish with one final dash into the South Pacific.

Japan's next actions indicated it would exercise both options. On March 7, the threat to Australia intensified when Japanese forces occupied Lae and Salamaua on the northeastern coast of New Guinea, just 300 miles from the Australian mainland. As Japan had amply demonstrated, 300 miles of open water was no obstacle at all. And, nearly concurrently, Japan moved in a slightly different direction toward the Solomon Islands. In doing so, it further threatened the critical sea route through which Australia would be resupplied and American forces would arrive in the South Pacific. Success in this two-pronged offensive would virtually guarantee a ceasefire in the Pacific and bring America and Great Britain to the negotiating table.

Nothing better suited Japanese plans than the Solomon Islands. They were oriented in precisely the direction Japanese forces would advance to seize New Caledonia and the geography provided the excellent harbors required by the Navy and flat terrain needed by the Army for the development of airfields to support land-based fighters and bombers.

By the end of March, Japanese forces advanced southward to positions in the northern Solomons and were now 350 miles closer to New Caledonia. With just one more jump into the southern Solomons, all of the New Hebrides would be within range of Japanese bombers and Japan would be in position to make the final move—to New Caledonia.[13]

***

Realizing the tremendous threat from Japan's unprecedented advance and knowing the emphasis placed on the Allied Atlantic strategy, Admiral King began an unflagging request for more men and *matériel*. He based his arguments, in part, on the terms of the *Acadia* Conference's "Grand Strategy" which included a requirement for the Navy to maintain air routes from the United States to Australia and from Australia to the Philippines.

The Japanese capture of Rabaul on New Britain particularly troubled King: "The capture of Rabaul so clearly forecast further enemy expansion to the southwest that immediate planning to contain the Japanese advance in that direction became imperative."[14]

In mid-February, with Army reinforcements now committed to the South Pacific, King had strongly suggested to his counterpart, General Marshall, that the Army establish additional garrisons along the lightly-held Southern Supply Line—including Fiji, Canton, Christmas, New Caledonia, and Palmyra, and most particularly, on Tongatabu (Tonga, codename *Bleacher*) and Efate (New Hebrides, codename *Roses*). King was particularly interested in defending Efate since doing so "will serve to deny a stepping stone to the Japanese if they moved South from Rabaul, New Britain" and would provide American forces with a base "from which a step-by-step general advance could be made through the New Hebrides, Solomons and Bismarcks."[15]

King believed early offensive actions could be staged from these expanded garrison and aviation forces. In this he had the support of key Army and Navy commanders in the South Pacific, Gen. Douglas MacArthur and Adm. Chester Nimitz.[16]

But the Army–Navy contretemps, with roots extending back to the turn of the century, continued. King's chief adversary within the Army was the formidable Gen. Dwight Eisenhower, at the time the Chief of the Army's War Plans Division, and a staunch advocate of the "Germany First" policy. Eisenhower felt King's preferred approach to the war in the Pacific—an island-by-island advance—would be "slow, laborious, and indecisive."[17]

Eisenhower went further in clarifying his position regarding the war in the Pacific when he issued a report on February 28, which included in part: "The United States interest in maintaining contact with Australia and in preventing further Japanese expansion to the Southeastward is apparent ... but ... they are not immediately vital to the successful outcome of the war." While not discounting the criticality of the South Pacific, in the same report he stated: " ... we must differentiate between those things ... necessary to the ultimate defeat of the Axis Powers, as opposed to those which are merely desirable because of their effect in facilitating such defeat."[18] Among those things Eisenhower considered "merely desirable" was the defense of the bases west and southwest of Hawaii, that is to say, the Southern Supply Line. Eisenhower cast an unmistakable shadow over King's hopes for the region.

General Marshall was aware of the clear restrictions on force commitments *Arcadia* had stipulated and was extremely wary of anything that smacked of offensive initiatives in the Pacific. In responding to King's requests, Marshall noted that sending additional troops to the Pacific would have "far-reaching implications." He requested further clarifications from King and reminded King that operations in the Southwest Pacific must be "limited to the strategic defensive" so far as air and ground forces were concerned. In closing, he noted King's request amounted to a change in the already-approved—and long-standing—basic strategy for the war, and that "the entire situation must be reconsidered before we become involved more seriously in the build-up of Army ground and air garrisons in the Pacific Islands."[19]

King had waited two weeks for Marshall's response; during that time the strategic situation in the Pacific had worsened dramatically and Japanese advances in the southwest Pacific shattered any illusion Allied forces in the region could provide anything like an effective defense.

During the *Arcadia* Conference, the Allies had agreed to the formation of the American–British–Dutch–Australia Command (ABDACOM) in order to create an overall command structure for forces remaining in the Pacific. At the time, the sea communications between the Indian Ocean and the Pacific—what was termed the "Malay Barrier"—were still open, and the mission of ABDACOM was to keep that region open and to protect the western approaches to Australia. Failure to do so would effectively split Allied forces: British forces would be confined to the Indian Ocean and American forces would be limited to the Pacific with no possibility of concerted action against the Japanese.[20]

But as King and Marshall debated the strategy, British forces surrendered Singapore, and MacArthur evacuated the Philippines. Japanese reconnaissance seaplanes overflew Hawaii and Melbourne, Australia, two dropping bombs on Oahu. And on February 19, Australia itself came under severe attack when a Japanese carrier task force hit the large concentration of Allied vessels in the harbor at Darwin with a combined force of carrier-based aircraft and land-based medium bombers, with devastating results.[21]

Worse still, Japan cut the Burma Road and completely controlled the Malay Barrier, eliminating any possibility of combined British–American operations in the region. ABDACOM, barely a month old, ceased to exist, leaving the Dutch East Indies and the western approaches to Australia utterly exposed. Japan had again completely changed the war landscape.[22]

And in February alone, Allied forces fought four naval battles in the Pacific, all engagements intended to delay the seemingly inexorable Japanese advance; each ended in Allied defeat, having had little effect on Japan's offensive initiatives and leaving a good portion of the Allied naval fleet resting on the bottom of the Java Sea.[23]

***

Even before the *Arcadia* Conference had identified the force requirements required for the Pacific, and with the Pacific war strategy likewise still in play, the rapid advances by the Japanese in the direction of the South Pacific made evident the need for a robust garrison on New Caledonia. On January 12, the War Department General Staff hastily commissioned "Task Force 6814" (TF 6814), a consortium of Army units for the defense of New Caledonia (codename *Poppy*).[24] Initial plans for the task force envisioned a roughly division-sized ground force of one reinforced infantry regiment, one fighter squadron, field and coastal artillery regiments, two engineering battalions, a medical regiment, and many other smaller support units and detachments. Totaling nearly seventeen thousand officers and men, TF 6814 would be an Army undertaking: later task forces would be joint Army–Navy enterprises.

The diverse units assigned to TF 6814 were hastily plucked from Army forces located in thirteen different states, with the selection of units based in part on what New Caledonia's defense required, but also reflecting what units were immediately available. A later retrospective notes: "In some ways, Task Force 6814 might have looked a bit like an infantry division but, for the most part … it was nothing but an odd conglomeration of spare parts, a wartime military stew of men and equipment."[25]

The men and women of the Task Force, together with a portion of their equipment and supplies, assembled at the New York Port of Embarkation in mid-January and began loading aboard seven troop transports. In the chill early morning darkness of January 23, just 47 days after Pearl Harbor, the first ships set to sea in convoy.[26] Eleven unescorted cargo ships delivered the balance of the task force's equipment, sailing from west coast ports between February 12 and March 10.[27]

TF 6814 was one element in a tsunami of American forces that embarked for the Pacific theater between January and March. Some seventy-nine thousand troops would be sent to the Pacific Theater in early 1942, nearly four times the number sent into the Atlantic Theater. These forces minimally bolstered other key points along the Southern Supply Line: Fiji, Bora Bora, and Christmas and Canton Islands. Strung along an expanse of 4,000 miles and unable to offer mutual support, the term "outpost" aptly described these remote positions.[28]

On March 2, shortly before TF 6814 would take up station in New Caledonia, King repeated his earlier proposal to establish ground garrisons in the South Pacific but this time limited his request to just two islands—Efate and Tongatabu.[29]

King did not wait for a formal reply from JCS. Instead, he pled his case directly to President Roosevelt, issuing a letter on March 5 that generally followed his missive to JCS outlining his vision for the conduct of war in the Pacific, given the circumstances that existed at the time. He referred to the four "strong points" being developed in the South Pacific—Samoa, Fiji, New Caledonia, and Tonga—and noted two additional strong points were being considered at Efate in the New Hebrides and at the Ellice Islands, north of Fiji.

His pitch to the president was: "When the foregoing 6 'strong points' are made reasonably secure, we shall not only be able to cover the lines of communications

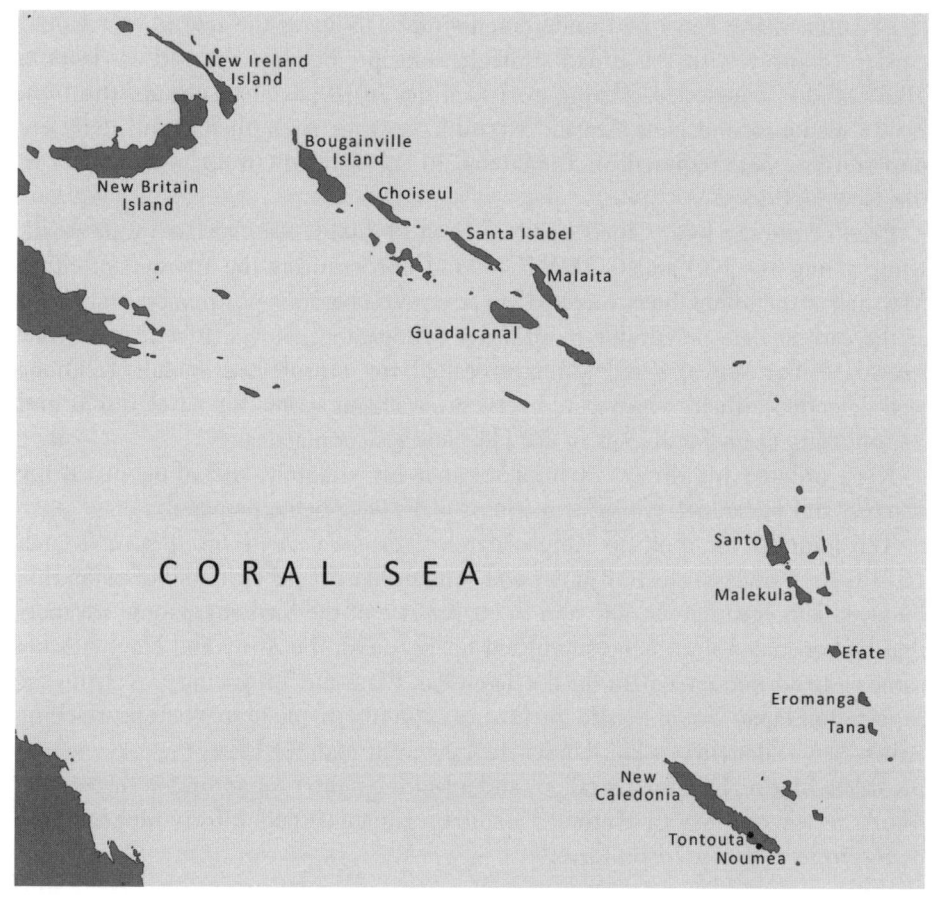

The Northern New Hebrides and Southern Solomon Islands (Yosemite Productions)

... but we can drive northwest from the New Hebrides into the Solomons ... (in the same) step-by-step advances that the Japanese used in the South China Sea."[30] King cogently summarized his recommendation: Hold Hawaii—Support Australasia—Drive northwest from New Hebrides.

These forceful requests to the president by Admiral King might have seemed an "end run" by the Army and the Joint Chiefs. But that point aside, King was the commander of all naval forces in the Pacific and, entirely apart from what General Marshall and the Joint Chiefs might or might not agree to concerning joint operations or increased ground and air force commitments to the Pacific, King felt unconstrained regarding the Navy's responsibilities in the Pacific. He pressed Navy planners for the development of other advanced *naval* positions he knew would be required to provide logistical support for the naval forces under his command in the Pacific; naval positions akin to what was then in the works for Bora Bora.

20 • SURVIVAL IN THE SOUTH PACIFIC

In January, the Navy had undertaken studies to assess the resources it would need to comply with the broad strategic concepts being developed at *Arcadia*. Those studies concluded existing port facilities in the Samoan Group, the Fijis, New Caledonia, and New Zealand would have to be strengthened and that new port stations were required on Tongatabu, in the Tongan Group, and at Efate in the New Hebrides.[31]

Even before the Joint Chiefs had convened to discuss King's March 2 proposal, King, acting as CNO and COMINCH, and not requiring the approval of either Marshall or the Joint Chiefs, directed "an advanced operating position be established at the earliest date practicable to Bleacher (Tongatabu), Roses (Efate), and Straw (Samoa)." For Roses, King's directive called for a protected anchorage and a well-defended airfield which could serve as a staging point for naval vessels and a supporting point for aircraft in the Fiji-New Caledonia area.[32]

King ordered his directives implemented immediately, including procuring *matériel* and personnel, while formal joint plans were being prepared.

The Joint Chiefs took up King's March 2 proposal at its meeting on March 16—its sixth since its creation at *Arcadia*. And unlike the debate and indecision that followed King's earlier request, and in cognizance of the further Japanese advances that had occurred since King submitted his proposal, the Army and Navy quickly came to an ad-hoc agreement for the defense of Efate and Tongatabu, largely on the expectation Japan would invade the former as an intermediate step before attacking either New Caledonia or Fiji. Under the new joint plan for Efate, the Navy would provide a Marine Defense Battalion, and a Marine fighter squadron for air defense. The Army agreed to send a reinforced infantry regiment—roughly forty-nine hundred men—to serve as a garrison force.[33]

***

In the five weeks since the start of the war, the news from North Africa and the Pacific went from bad to worse, and an anxious Leonard Richardson remained unsure about which service he would join, or whether he would just let the draft board decide for him.

Although his vision problems prevented him from entering the Secondary Civilian Pilot Training (CPT) Program, Richardson, as a college graduate, was qualified for many of the officer-candidate programs within the armed services. In late January 1942, he contacted the Navy Department to enquire about the V-7 United States Naval Reserve Midshipmen's School—a four-month program leading to commissioning as a Navy ensign and likely assignment to the Pacific Theater.

In his initial letter to the Navy, he acknowledged he did not meet one of the requirements for admission to the V-7 program; he was not born in the United

States. After review, the U.S. Navy Recruiting Station in Portland denied his request for a waiver of that requirement.[34]

Richardson continued to explore other possibilities for service and, a month later, applied for the Army Air Corps Aviation Cadet Program. He took his first qualifying physical examination at Geiger Field in Spokane.

The physical exam went considerably beyond a routine enlistment examination. Candidates were tested to confirm "a stable equilibrium, a sound cardio-vascular system, a well-formed, well-adjusted, and coordinated physique, and an integrated and stable central nervous system." Hearing was much more carefully evaluated. The board also examined applicants to confirm they possessed the personal and character traits "suitable to a person who may become a commissioned officer." It identified 37 "disqualifying defects," including a history of rheumatic fever, syphilis, kidney stones, malaria, asthma or hay fever, sleepwalking, fainting, amnesia, and more.[35]

Richardson knew the medical exam would include a detailed eye examination, including a color-perception evaluation and a procedure to evaluate depth perception. His eyes had failed him during the entry physical for the Secondary CPT Program, and so it was with great relief that he learned his diplopia had apparently been a transient condition, and that he had passed the Army's eye examination.

He was found "physically qualified for Aviation Cadet Processing." He was 5 feet, 7 inches tall, with a 33-inch waist. Evaluators found his 175-lb weight—15 lbs above the maximum allowable—was not considered a problem because of his muscular build.[36]

Richardson next sat for the Aviation Cadet Qualifying Examination (ACQE), a three-hour test given by the Army Air Corps to measure general aptitude and to identify applicants who were "sufficiently alert and intelligent to be capable of learning an air-crew assignment and who could measure up to the intellectual and leadership standards required of officers in the Army."[37]

The ACQE was a three-part "threshold test." Applicants with passing grades could eventually become pilots, navigators, flight engineers, or bombardiers; they would receive a specific assignment at a classification center during their first weeks in the Aviation Cadet Program.[38]

The first part of the ACQE test, the "mental" examination, would today be referred to as an IQ, or mental-acuity test. The test included vocabulary, reading comprehension, practical judgment, mathematics, alertness to recent developments, and mechanical comprehension. High reading comprehension, mathematics, and judgment scores were strong indicators of an applicant's suitability for pilot training. Mathematics was the strongest indicator of suitability for navigator training; those cadets who eventually became navigators had, on average, the highest ACQE scores. The test takers themselves had different ideas about how the Army used these test scores, claiming:

> The classification tests sorted cadets into three bins: pilots were chosen from those who gave quick and correct answers; bombardiers were chosen from those who gave quick and erroneous answers; navigators were those who gave slow and correct answers.[39]

The second part of the examination was a psychomotor test to measure hand–eye coordination, visual acuity, reflexes, and the ability to perform under pressure.

The third part of the test program was a psychological evaluation, which was the most difficult to administer. The line of inquiry included family history and environment, personal achievements, mental stability, "sociality," and the applicant's philosophy of life—"the principles by which the individual lives."

Richardson passed all three sections of the ACQE and was accepted into the Aviation Cadet Program, one of over one hundred and twenty-two thousand applicants who took the ACQE during the first three months of 1942. The flow of flight personnel into the Army Air Forces was beginning to swell.

Under rules passed just a month earlier, the War Department required all successful flight candidates to enlist in the U.S. Army. Should they fail to complete the flight-training program, the cadets reverted to the rank of private and could be reassigned "according to the needs of the service."[40]

Richardson reported for enlistment on March 19, 1942,[41] and in doing so became Private Leonard G. Richardson, Army serial number 19033109. His service was for "war duration plus 6 months."[42] Just as he had often been swept downstream by the strong Clearwater current, now his future would be determined by a much stronger and potentially more lethal tide.

Richardson was granted a short furlough that allowed him to complete the school year at Adams High School; he was to report for the first phase of his aviation training by June 8. The timing of his report date worked out well for both Leonard and his brother Norman. On June 6, Norm and his college sweetheart Jan Peterson were married. Their best man was, naturally, Leonard.

Word that he was headed for military flight training quickly spread among Leonard's students. The Adams High School yearbook for 1942 includes many notes from his students wishing him good luck in the Army Air Corps. Student Patty Way: "I hope you can get a glimpse at one of those yellow Japs and knock down a couple for me."[43]

CHAPTER THREE

America Begins to Respond

With the Pacific war in its fourth month, America's command structure for the Pacific had yet to be determined and had become a critical priority. But, on March 30, after strenuous debate, the Joint Chiefs established two Pacific theaters of operations, named the commanders for American operations in those theaters, and assigned their missions. General MacArthur, as expected, was appointed Supreme Commander of the Southwest Pacific Area—a title he himself changed to Commander in Chief. Admiral Nimitz, given the dual capacity as fleet and area commander, was designated Commander in Chief of the Pacific Fleet and Commander in Chief of the Pacific Ocean Areas (CINCPAC–CINCPOA).

The Joint Chiefs further divided Nimitz's Pacific Ocean Area command into three subordinate areas. Nimitz retained direct control over the Central and North Pacific. For the third subordinate area, the South Pacific, Nimitz designated Vice Adm. Robert Ghormley as Commander South Pacific (COMSOPAC), with command of all base and local defense forces then assigned or to be assigned to the South Pacific islands.[1] Rear Admiral John McCain was designated Ghormley's Commander Aircraft South Pacific Force (COMAIRSOPAC) and assumed operational control of all shore- and tender-based aircraft. Under this organization, the Navy (Nimitz, Ghormley, et al.) controlled various subordinate Army headquarters and units in the Central and South Pacific Areas while, conversely, the Army (MacArthur, et al.) exercised highest jurisdiction over Navy headquarters and units in the Southwest Pacific Area.

With his theater almost surrounded by Japanese forces, MacArthur's mission as determined by the Joint Chiefs remained primarily defensive and included only the injunction to "prepare to take the offensive."[2] The Joint Chief's directive to Admiral Nimitz was also primarily defensive. He was explicitly ordered to hold island possessions between the United States and the South Pacific necessary for the security of the line of communications. But the directive also included a strongly offensive component, instructing Nimitz to "prepare for the execution of major amphibious offensives against positions held by Japan, the initial offensives to be launched from the South Pacific Area and Southwest Pacific Area."[3]

***

Task Force 6814 (TF 6814) had arrived at Noumea, New Caledonia, on March 12, well before the Joint Chiefs had confirmed the command structure for the Pacific.[4] The orders to the task force's commander could not have been more succinct: "In cooperation with the military forces of the United Nations, hold New Caledonia against attack."[5]

The huge influx of men and *matériel* soon swamped the inadequate onshore facilities at the port of Noumea. Equally inadequate was the Army's advance logistical planning for the task force: "Thousands of tons of supplies piled up on and around the docks … there was no way to protect the material from the weather … food and equipment [lay] massed in huge piles under the burning sub-tropical sun."[6] The weeks-long task of sorting and storing the huge quantities of material was later termed the "Battle of Noumea."

Fearful Japan could jump to the south at any time, the War Department's overall defensive plan for New Caledonia included the directive that an advanced position be established on the island of Efate in the New Hebrides, 328 miles north of Noumea, reasoning that an occupying force there might give early warning of a further Japanese advance to the south and serve as a bulwark for the Southern Supply Line. The location of the New Hebrides—east of the Coral Sea, west of Fiji, and south of the Solomon Islands—was critical to both America's defensive plans and Japan's offensive strategies.

Efate would "serve as an outpost for supporting both New Caledonia and the Fijis, and subsequently, to serve as a minor advanced air and naval base for future offensive operations."[7]

Responding to the Army's directive, and as "a temporary measure, pending the establishment of a permanent garrison," TF 6814 "calved off" a smaller detachment to occupy Efate, a unit referred to as "Force A."[8] Included in the cohort were two companies from the 3rd Battalion of the 182nd Infantry Regiment—L Company, a rifle unit, and M Company, a heavy weapons unit. Also included were detachments from the 182nd's Medical Department and Headquarters Detachment and a detachment of 37 men—the Eliott Detachment—from the 57th Engineering Combat Battalion. In total, it was a force numbering some five hundred officers and men under the command of Brig. Gen. William R. Rose.[9] The command of General Rose on the island, given its codename *Roses*, would inevitably result in confusion among wartime historians.[10]

Force A left Noumea on March 16, just four days after the main task force had disembarked at New Caledonia, and with a good deal of the supplies and equipment for the Task Force still strewn across the piers. Transport to Efate was courtesy of the Australian and New Zealand Navies: so small was the detachment that it embarked aboard a single ship, the armed merchant cruiser *Westralia*. Two light Kiwi cruisers, the HMNZS *Achilles* and *Leander* served as escorts.[11] By the 18th, Force A had disembarked the *Westralia* and began establishing itself on its new, terribly vulnerable outpost.

Owing to Efate's extremely exposed position, the Navy assigned two additional units for its defense: the 4th Marine Defense Battalion (MDB), an anti-aircraft unit, and VMF-212, a Marine fighter squadron, both based in Hawaii.[12] But with Efate having nothing resembling an airfield, the Marine fighter planes remained temporarily in Hawaii while the Forward Echelon of Marine Air Group 24 under the command of Capt. John Little—the "Little Detachment—was also ordered to Efate and tasked with carving an airstrip from the island's dense jungle. The 4th MDB and the Little Detachment loaded aboard the USS *Crescent City* and in company with the cargo ship *Castor* and the tanker *Cuyama* and Navy destroyer escorts *Henley* and *Helm*, slipped out of Pearl Harbor on March 15.

The *Crescent City* convoy arrived March 29 at Vila Harbor on Efate. On seeing the verdant slopes Efate, the blue-green water of Vila Harbor, the tall palms and native women in bright Mother Hubbards along the shore, the newly arrived troops first reckoned they'd arrived at a great place to start their war. But as exhilarated as they may have felt, they also knew that they had gone far beyond safe waters and had deadly work to perform.

> We thought we were out of school. So far away nobody would care what we did. We thought we were playing hooky. But we were the ones that were hooked. And gaffed, too. We were going to stick there month after month, in a fine, slippery, wet hell with the mosquitoes sounding off like air-raid sirens. We were right up there under Tojo's chin. If he only opened his mouth, we'd fall in. A couple of Jap destroyers could have cleaned us out almost any time. That's what it meant being a forward echelon. We were for war, all right. We were right on the edge of the falling-off place.[13]

Capt. Little's force of 152 men disembarked onto the entirely unfamiliar terrain with very limited supplies and equipment—two bulldozers, a dump truck, two light trucks, a truck crane and a small handful of assorted rolling stock. Not much, considering the task ahead. Perhaps most significantly, Little's force included a single J2F "Duck" amphibious aircraft, and a sole pilot—Tech Sergeant Sidney Woolley.[14] The first piece of equipment unloaded over the side of the *Crescent City* was the precious "Duck." Capt. Little ordered Sgt. Woolley and the detachment's photographer to photograph the coastline of Efate so that the pictures could be delivered to Hawaii on the returning *Crescent City*. And not long after, they would make a second flight to photograph the island itself in order to find a suitable site for the airfield they had been sent to construct.

General Rose reportedly took early advantage of having an amphibious aircraft at his disposal. On April 27, he was flown by Sergeant Woolley to the Segond Channel on the southern shore of the island of Espiritu Santo, the northernmost island of the New Hebrides, with the purpose of exploring the feasibility of an airfield on the island. Getting there by seaplane was Rose's only option—there was at that time nothing remotely resembling an airstrip on Espiritu Santo, and no large agricultural areas or grasslands on which any sort of aircraft could land.[15]

On arrival, Rose met with Tom Harris, a New Zealander who managed a store in Luganville for the Australian firm of Burns-Philp and who was well-familiar with the island and its locals. Harris, who epitomized many of Santo's long-term European residents, was a planter, an island banker, and a confirmed bachelor in addition to his store duties. He was described as "grizzled, unkempt, but actually pleasant."[16]

Back at Efate, Capt. Little settled on a site located on the property of the estimable Madame Bladiniere, a woman whose "heart was so big and her patriotism so perfect that she never complained about the wholesale destruction of her property or attempted to get a price for her land."

Force A was not entirely alone in the northern New Hebrides. As a result of the Wellington Defence Conference of 1939,[17] aerial reconnaissance of the area between Tonga and the New Hebrides became the responsibility of New Zealand, with Australia similarly responsible for reconnaissance over New Guinea, the Solomon Islands, and the New Hebrides.

Months before Pearl harbor, with British Commonwealth forces already two years into World War II, the appearance of three German raiders in the region led to the creation of a South-West Pacific Patrol by the Royal Australian Air Force (RAAF), with frequent operations in and around Efate.[18] An Advanced Operating Base (AOB) was established at Vila Harbor on Efate with moorings for three flying boats, housing and mess facilities for up to 59 officers, enlisted personnel, and indigenes.

Throughout 1941 and into the early months of 1942, PBYs and Empire Flying Boats of the RAAF's #11 and #20 squadrons made daily reconnaissance flights into the northern Solomon Islands from bases in Gavutu (Tulagi) and Efate. But facing further Japanese advances to the south, Australian reconnaissance shifted north and operated from bases at Port Moresby on New Guinea, and from Horn Island just across the Torres Strait but continued to use the seaplane base on Efate for refueling and loading bombs.

Six months before Pearl Harbor, with Germany seen as the greatest imminent threat in the Pacific, the Australian 1st Independent Company (No. 1 Ind. Coy.) had been formed to become the defensive garrison at Kavieng on New Ireland in the Bismarck Archipelago, immediately north of the Solomon Islands. And much as had been done with American forces in Task Force 6814 at Noumea, No. 1 Ind Coy dispatched smaller detachments to provide a minimal defensive capability at other locations in the region, including at Tulagi on Guadalcanal, the Buka Passage on Bougainville, and at Vila on the island of Efate in the central New Hebrides islands.

By December 5, the Vila detachment, consisting of two officers and 28 enlisted personnel had arrived at Vila Harbor with the principal task of providing a local defense of the Royal Australian Air Force (RAAF) Advance Operating Base (AOB) already in place at Vila Harbor. At the time the RAAF AOB consisted of a Camp Site, a high-frequency Direction Finding Station, a Transmission Station, and moorings for four "flying boats".[19]

The British and French Resident Commissioners on Efate had previously been ordered to raise a 130-man native infantry company—the Home Guard—with white officers and non-commissioned officers, a supplemental garrison force of 12, and

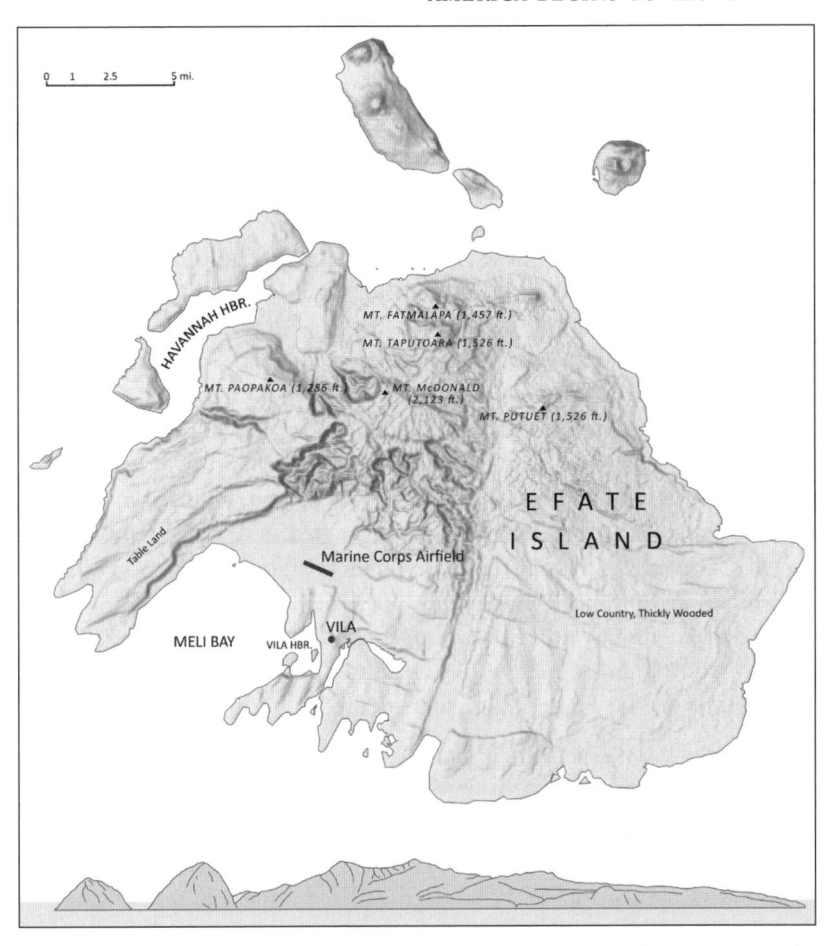

Northern Approach and Topographic Views, Efate Island, New Hebrides, 1942 (Yosemite Productions)

a militia force of 30,[20] with the Vila detachment from No. 1 Ind. Coy. providing organization and training for the volunteer force, and coordinating the local defenses of the local RAAF station.[21]

***

All was not roses at Roses. In its earlier occupation of Efate, the American military came face-to-face with an unseen force that would shape both Japanese and Allied war efforts for the duration of war in the Pacific. Malaria, "the greatest single destroyer of the human race," was endemic in the New Hebrides and Rose and his men had stepped into its gaping maw.[22]

Perhaps they were unaware of a warning posted by the British Foreign Office in 1920: "The islands are on the whole unhealthy for Europeans, and this is especially true of the larger islands where many marshes give ideal conditions for the breeding of mosquitoes. Malarial fevers and dysentery are common."[23] Historical reports are rife with reports of the devastation caused by malaria to combat troops. The British commander in Burma noted: " ... for every man evacuated with wounds we had one hundred and twenty evacuated sick ... (at this rate) in a matter of months my army would have melted away. Indeed, it was doing so under my eyes."[24]

General MacArthur's troops also suffered miserably, and he would lose over ten million man-days to malaria.[25] MacArthur once commented to a Marine physician: "Doctor, this will be a long war if for every division I have facing the enemy I must count on a second division in hospital with malaria and a third division convalescing from this debilitating disease!"[26]

Efate was the most malaria-ridden island to be occupied in the South Pacific, and troops arriving there in mid-March 1942 were the hardest hit. Force A came with an insufficient supply of bed nets ("mosquito bars"), were required to work at night when mosquitoes were most active, and bivouacked near native labor camps that were heavily "seeded" with malaria. Perhaps most significantly, local commanders did not realize how serious malaria could be. The concept of "malaria discipline" was unheard of; one Army officer expressed the prevailing attitude that "We are out here to fight troops, and to hell with mosquitoes."[27]

Provost Marshal Maj Harold Tate later recalled:

> Our men were told they must take quinine every day but there is none to give them. Everybody was told they had to wear gloves but there are only gloves for vehicle drivers. Soldiers must wear headnets but there are none issued. Officers have been told to make reconnaissance but at the same time there were told not to leave the area (due to malarious regions nearby).[28]

The result was near-catastrophic: Rose's men suffered a malarial rate of two thousand seven hundred cases per one thousand troops (per annum). Essentially, every man who came ashore contracted malaria and most suffered two or three relapses in the first year.[29]

Malaria was hardly unknown to the American military, but exigencies of the war had led to the occupation of islands in the South Pacific before the level of risk and practical means of mitigation were fully understood. At the time, quinine was the only treatment option and it would be six weeks before it first became available to Rose's troops. Even then, the limited supply allowed only half the troops to receive daily doses.

The men took for granted the malarial mist before their eyes and aches in their bones. But on top of the nightmare of malaria, troops suffered other natural and man-made onslaughts. Dense clouds of flies carried the stench of the latrines, covering hands and faces and flecking food with specks of feces. Drinking water was dosed with foul tasting chlorine. "Their sleeping hours became a torment. Damp tents, wet bedding, the tangle of mosquito netting. If your hand touched the netting it was covered with welts in the morning, and the men on guard duty were continually shooting at ghosts and rousing the camp. Night in the tropical jungle is not like the calm of darkness of a northern woodland. There is always a stir of life, quiet slitherings and splashings, and now and then pale gleams or sudden upflashings of phosphoresce, for in the wet heat of the jungle, life is forever building or consuming in quick decay."[30]

Fortunately, troops on Efate had caught a break in May with the onset of the dry season and a lessening of mosquito breeding; in July, insect-control measures on the island began to take hold and troops began receiving a weekly dose of the new therapeutic, Atabrine.[31] By September, only 84 new malarial cases were reported—a 97% reduction since March. While the rate would climb again sharply with the advent of the next rainy season, remediation was becoming more effective.

But in the late summer of 1942, American military strategists were planning the United States' first offensive effort in the South Pacific, an offensive against Japanese forces on other islands where malaria was unremediated, and where malaria would again exact a terrible price on ill-protected troops.

***

The occupation of the island of Efate set the standard for many similar advances in the war: a small Army contingent would first arrive as an occupying force. A much larger garrison force would follow to provide a more robust area defense, a naval construction unit would be dispatched to complete an airfield and build port and personnel facilities, and an Army Air Force or Marine squadron would be assigned to provide air cover for the island, and aerial reconnaissance.

At the time, little was known about Efate and its principal town Port Vila. Adventure traveler Beatrice Grimshaw, who visited in 1906, had this to say:

> Washington, capital of the United States, has been described as a city of magnificent distances. Vila, capital of the exceedingly disunited New Hebrides, may, in parallel fashion, be described as a city of magnificent omissions. It is principally remarkable for what is not there. Its splendid hotel, its handsome Town Hall, its pier and promenade, its public buildings—are still in the quarry. Its main street can (only) be distinguished from the surrounding bush with care and a pioneering axe ... The other streets consist of crazy lettered boards, planted about uninhabited wilds, and declaring, in the teeth of probability, that this particular section of guava bush or cottonwood scrub is the Boulevard de Something, or the Avenue de Something Else. That is Vila.[32]

Force A on Efate, however insignificant it might have appeared, was now the farthermost Allied defensive force in the Pacific. And however disorganized the harbor at Noumea continued to be, with these actions, the island of New Caledonia was at least minimally defended. As TF 6814 and its junior partner, Force A, began consolidating their positions, other reinforcements also began moving to the Pacific Theater.

***

At the outset of the war, the American intelligence community already had a rich history of espionage, spying, and code breaking, often with spectacular results. The code used by the Imperial Japanese Navy (IJN) in early 1941 was "JN-25," used for high-level command and control, including vessel movements and planning operations. Following Pearl Harbor, code-breaking efforts within the American military intensified. The task of deciphering the IJN code and, later, the Imperial Japanese Army codes fell to a Hawaii-based detachment codenamed HYPO. HYPO's progress was agonizingly slow, but with great effort by March 1942 the cryptanalysts had begun to intercept and decypher messages related to Japanese troop and ship movements that hinted of action to come in the South Pacific. By April—a very critical point in the Pacific war—HYPO had begun to show results. HYPO code breakers first reported a large naval force from Rabaul would target Australian-controlled areas of New Guinea. By early April, further intercepts and intelligence analysis confirmed the targets would be Port Moresby in New Guinea and the northern Solomon Islands, that a carrier strike force based in Truk would support the operation, and that Japanese naval forces would be concentrated in the Coral Sea to the east of Australia's Cape York. British code breakers in Ceylon intercepted and decrypted the final piece of the puzzle, informing Nimitz that two of Japan's first-line carriers would participate in the operation.[33]

On May 1, it was reported that "The preliminaries of the Japanese offensive in the Southwest Pacific are underway. There are indications that the main first objective is Port Moresby. The Solomons are to be attacked also. To keep our forces from interfering the Japanese ... may raid as far east as Roses, Noumea, Fiji, and Samoa. Evacuation was started from Tulagi today."[34]

In April, the Japanese Imperial General Headquarters set in motion Operation *Mo*, the invasion of Port Moresby, to bolster the defensive forces protecting their large military bastion at Rabaul. The war directive also called for the occupation of Tulagi in the lower Solomon Islands in order to defend the eastern flank of Japanese forces as they moved toward Port Moresby, and to serve as an additional base for operations in the Coral Sea.[35]

Following the occupation of Port Moresby and Tulagi, Japan planned to launch Operation *FS*—the broad expansion of forces further to the south intended to overwhelm the lightly defended New Hebrides and to occupy important points in New Caledonia, Fiji, and Samoa. If successful, Operation *FS* would cut the supply and communication lines between Australia and the United States, and would reduce or eliminate Australia as a threat to Japan's newly acquired positions in the South and Southwest Pacific.

These plans reflected Admiral Yamamoto's conviction that the United States would have to be brought to the negotiating table within four months of Pearl Harbor if Japan was to win the war. Launching Operation *Mo* in early May put Japan a month behind Yamamoto's timetable, but if both Operation *Mo* and *FS* went according to plan, Japan's overall war strategy of securing a negotiated settlement with America and its Allies, leaving Japan with new territories in the Dutch East Indies (Indonesia) and French Indochina, would be much closer to a reality.[36]

On May 3, Japanese forces landed unopposed at Tulagi but U.S. Naval intelligence had alerted the Pacific Fleet of this impending action, giving American commanders time to position two carrier task forces just 150 miles to the east.[37]

The decisive Battle of the Coral Sea began when the aircraft carrier USS *Yorktown* launched a series of three air strikes, commencing in the early morning hours of May 4. Despite having taken the Japanese occupiers by surprise, and with 60 dive- and torpedo-bombers in the attacking force, the results of the raid were disappointing, and those attacks confirmed to the Japanese that American aircraft carriers were in the vicinity. Sensing an opportunity, the Japanese naval commander abandoned the Port Moresby invasion force and turned south toward the Coral Sea to locate, engage, and destroy the Allied carrier fleet, hoping to finish the job it had begun in the attack on Pearl.

After Japanese and American air reconnaissance sorties located their opposing forces, each carrier force launched airstrikes on May 7; intense aerial attacks continued through May 8.

At the end of the day, the U.S. Navy lost three ships, including the carrier USS *Lexington*. Japanese bombers had so damaged the carrier *Yorktown* that it was forced to limp back to Pearl for repairs. The Japanese lost five ships, including one light aircraft carrier, and seven ships were damaged, including a large fleet carrier.

The Battle of the Coral Sea was the first action between aircraft carriers and the first naval engagement in which the opposing ships neither sighted nor fired directly upon each other. And the engagement settled, at least for a time, the question about which naval asset would be of greatest value in the war in the Pacific: at the Battle of the Coral Sea, no battleships were employed by either side.

More importantly for the conduct of war in the Pacific, with two of their carriers badly damaged and so many carrier aircraft lost in battle, Japanese commanders had insufficient forces to provide air cover for the landings at Port Moresby, so the invasion was cancelled.[38]

***

For the South and Southwest Pacific regions, April 1942 had been relatively quiet. The Japanese had established new positions in the northern Solomons, but had not ventured farther south. Following the overwhelming military offensives of the prior four months, the calm of April comforted no one—it was clear the war in the Pacific was in the eye of a hurricane, with much to follow that was unpredictable and potentially momentous.

The quiescence in the southern stretches of the Pacific did not apply elsewhere. During April, Allied troops at Bataan had surrendered, and the Dutch East Indies and Burma had fallen. The number of Allied troops surrendering to the Japanese was staggering: seventy-eight thousand officers and men in the Philippines. In Singapore, eighty-thousand. In the Dutch East Indies, one hundred thousand. In Malaya, fifty thousand. Japan had bombed Australia and invaded New Guinea, and British naval forces were defeated decisively in the Indian Ocean with the loss of an aircraft carrier, two heavy cruisers and several smaller warships. Audaciously, the U.S. Army Air Force (USAAF) flew 16 B-25 medium bombers from the deck of the carrier USS *Hornet* to raid the Japanese homeland—the Doolittle Raid.

At the time, American strategic plans for the Pacific lacked clarity but it was evident fast action would be needed to blunt Japanese advances toward New Caledonia. The island of Efate, now occupied and minimally defended by Force A from TF 6814, would need a much stronger garrison force to bolster the island's defense, and if Efate were to serve as a jumping-off point for future American military advances, it would need a complete base infrastructure—airfields, hospitals, sanitation facilities, fuel storage, and the like. First priority was constructing an aerodrome to bolster the island's defense, enable USAAF reconnaissance operations, and support the already anticipated future offensive operations in the region.

On March 20, with Force A still settling into Efate, the Joint Chiefs issued the Joint Plan for the Occupation and Defense of Efate, New Hebrides. The Joint Plan led to the creation of Joint Task Force 9156 (JTF 9156), roughly half the size of New Caledonia's TF 6814.[39]

The Joint Plan committed an Army force of nearly 5000 officers and men for the island's defense, including the 24th Infantry Regiment, the 4th Field Artillery battalion, the 515th Engineer Combat company, a large Naval hospital, a detachment of the 1st Construction Battalion, an Inshore Patrol Squadron equipped with OS2U amphibious aircraft, and other support and service units. The 24th Infantry Regiment already had a rich history. It was one of the African American units active in the Indian Wars, was retained within the segregated Army after World War I, and was the first Black infantry regiment sent overseas during World War II. Of the Army troops to come ashore at Efate with the task force, over half were Black—some thirty-four hundred officers and men.[40]

The Navy's role within the Joint Plan was four-fold: (1) to construct, administer, and operate a naval advance base, seaplane base, and harbor facilities; (2) to support Army forces in defense of the island; (3) to construct an airfield and at least two outlying dispersal fields; (4) to provide facilities for the operation of VPB-type seaplanes.[41]

This task force represented a stiffening of American positions in the South Pacific and a commitment to an "active" defense in the region. This new advanced base—soon designated Advanced Naval Base Roses—would become the first of Admiral King's steppingstones northward out of the South Pacific.[42]

In further compliance to the stipulations of the *Arcadia* Conference, the Joint Chiefs also implemented defensive and base construction plans for other key outposts on the highly vulnerable Southern Supply Line. Shortly after TF 6814 departed New York for New Caledonia, similar joint forces embarked for Bora Bora, Tonga, and Samoa.[43]

***

In building these new advanced bases at remote and undeveloped sites, every nail, bag of concrete, or metal sheet would have to be brought from America. But the more vexing issue confronting the Navy at the start of the war was that it lacked what it needed most for advanced base development—someone to build the bases. In peacetime, the Navy used civilian contractors for construction projects at home and abroad. But a prewar change in international law made it illegal for any civilian workforce to resist enemy attacks. The Navy was loathe to send a construction unit abroad that could not defend itself and reckoned it would need to create a new type of naval construction specialty.

The Navy acted quickly to cobble together and embark construction teams to the critical South Pacific islands.[44] The Navy's 1st Construction Battalion (CB), the "Seabees," was assembled at the Naval Air Station at Quonset Point, Rhode Island, in January, just a month after the war in the Pacific started. Active-duty military personnel skilled in one or more fields of construction were given additional military training for their defense; "Thus was sown the seed that was to grow during the years that lay ahead into the great program of advance-base development in the Pacific."[45]

In aggregate, a "regular" construction battalion consisted of 33 commissioned officers and 1,081 enlisted personnel, organized into four construction companies plus a headquarters company. The enlisted men in each construction company represented 60 different trades. The headquarters company included 176 men who served as office workers and specialists who made it possible for the battalion to operate as a self-contained unit.[46]

Facing the exigencies in the Pacific, the Navy split the 1st CB into three detachments and assigned each its own advance base to build. The first detachment, codename *Bobcat*, joined the joint force headed for Bora Bora. The second, codename *Bleacher*, was part of the joint force sent to Tongatabu in the Tongan Group.

The third detachment, the *Roses* Detachment, was initially assigned to New Caledonia. Reflecting the fluid nature of the war in its early days, however, and as Japanese advances began moving southward in the Solomon Islands, the unit was incorporated into JTF 9156 headed for Efate in the New Hebrides, 300 miles closer to the Solomons.[47]

That the Seabees did not exist before January 5, and had, by mid-April, assembled, classified, partially trained, equipped, and embarked three construction units—and delivered to them the necessary materials and supplies—is a most remarkable achievement.

As part of JTF 9156, the *Roses* Detachment was assigned a long project list, including installing six 6-inch shore defense guns and constructing an entire seaplane base at Havannah Harbor to include wharves and piers, lighters, and barges. It would also build a runway and two dispersal fields for heavy bombers near the principal town of Vila, a power supply and electrical distribution system, a 400,000-gallon above-ground gasoline tank farm, a water-supply system, a 600-bed hospital, housing, and cold and dry storage facilities.[48]

The Seabees had been given about a month to prepare plans, procure materials, equipment, and supplies, and to assemble at the San Francisco port of embarkation. A Seabee historian would later record their entire construction plan was based on a single Navy hydrographic chart, "plus an illustrated article from the National Geographic magazine that indicated that there was a small port (and) a small town. There were no topographic charts." The base layout would have to be determined "by reconnaissance," after arrival.[49] That is to say: " … look around when you get there and sort out where everything will fit." They were also provided with a short vocabulary of Polynesian dialects.

At the time of its embarkation with JTF 9156, the *Roses* Seabee Detachment included just 12 officers and 508 enlisted men. Later in the war, a construction team of as many one thousand five hundred men would be assigned to complete similar construction projects. Relatively "seasoned," the average age of the officers in the *Roses* Detachment was 28; the average age of the enlisted men, many of whom were successful contractors and skilled tradesmen and all of whom were volunteers, was 32.[50]

At that time, fast decisions and immediate action by the American war leadership were not the norms. But, on April 12, about a month after General Rose's Force A had landed at Efate and just three weeks after being created by Joint Chiefs directive, JTF 9156—the *Roses* Convoy—departed San Francisco.

> In our holds and on our decks were trucks and jeeps, parts of Quonset huts that would become hospital wards, operating rooms and administrative buildings, knocked-down seaplanes, bulldozers, seacoast defense guns, fire pumps, radio stations, typewriters, small boats … refrigerators, barges for unloading ships, a 90-day supply of food for 6,400 men, and ammunition—all the many items needed for an advanced military base.[51]

So hurried were the preparations that freight trains were still pulling into the supply depot with supplies intended for the Roses Seabees as the ships pulled away from the docks. The historian for the 1st CB would later comment: "[As the convoy left San Francisco] the whole ship carried an atmosphere of tenseness; it was not the operatic movie version of men off to war. It was the real thing."[52]

A day later, a second reinforcement convoy departed San Diego with destination "Strawsack" (Samoa). When the two convoys rendezvoused in the eastern Pacific it consisted of five troopships and three cargo ships. On the 28th the Samoan-bound vessels left the convoy, which continued to Roses under the watchful escort of a five ships, most of which were New Zealand naval vessels.

In committing forces into this deeply unsettled theater, Admiral King and his peers with the Joint Chiefs were driven by a factor utterly out of their control.

> Time is working against us. The Japs will now continue to strengthen their defenses in Burma, Indo-China, Malaya and China as well as their Pacific bases and concentrate on the development, with all possible speed, of the many natural resources it acquired in the early months of the War (oil, tin, rubber, iron, coal, etc.). Japan, the one world power which lacked raw materials, now has them. It can therefore be seen that the longer our offensive against Japan has to be delayed the more difficult it will become.[53]

That Japan would surely continue to press its advantages, move to further advanced positions, and sharpen its advances to sever the Southern Supply Line were self-evident and accepted by all. The key questions were when and where would Japan strike next.

In the morning hours of May 4, 1942, Efate residents observed an approaching fleet on the horizon off Melee Bay. Some residents fled to the hills, not knowing if the ships were American or Japanese. Others gathered on the shore. "In an hour we'll know if we'll live or die."[54] To their great relief, it was Gen. Harry Chamberlin arriving with JTF 9156, including the much-needed *Roses* contingent of the 1st CB. With its destroyer escorts maintaining station outside Vila harbor, the ships of the convoy disembarked the Seabees who immediately set to work on the airfield that had been started by Force A of TF 6814.

General Chamberlin's JTF 9156 joined General Rose's Force A as the sharp end of the Allies' defense in the South Pacific. Nothing but a scattering of islands and long stretches of easily traversed ocean separated the men on Efate from the Japanese to the north.

CHAPTER FOUR

North to Espiritu Santo

Among the first ashore at Efate when Joint Task Force 9156 (JTF 9156) arrived on May 4 were Lt. H. N. Wallin, officer in charge of the *Roses* Seabee detachment, and his executive officer, Lt. Sam Mathis. The latter, who would gain fame in the Pacific for his airfield-building prowess, recorded his thoughts: "It was a picture-book May morning when we reached the harbor at Vila. The blue water, green foliage and red-topped buildings reminded you of a technicolor movie … We moved 506 officers and men ashore, took charge of the airstrip and began setting up our camp."[1]

The historian of the 1st Construction Battalion (CB) would later record:

> The beauty of the Harbor itself, and the size and serenity of Port Vila were a pleasant surprise in comparison to what was expected by most of the crew. Instead of an enemy-held cannibal island completely covered by jungle, there was a friendly harbor, a pleasant town with commercial and government establishments, and private residences on the hills sloping down to the water.[2]

It was ironic that on the day before Wallin and his men came ashore at Efate, 800 miles to the north the Japanese had come ashore at Tulagi, with similar purpose. These two construction forces—one American, one Japanese—of roughly equal size and neither of which were intended for combat duty, and each of which would rely on indigenous labor, would shape the course of war in the Pacific.

The process of preparing for the work ahead took the better part of two weeks. Material was unloaded and stored, campsites and the detachment mess and medical unit were built. Construction equipment was retrieved from the ships' holds and prepared for use.

As Wallin may have anticipated, the hurriedly prepared base layout plan developed before leaving the United States was rubbish:

> The first few days after arrival were spent in adjusting the base development plan to fit actual terrain conditions. The entire base layout plan had to be discarded because of the great disparity between actual conditions on the ground with those assumed by the planners. For example, the gasoline and fuel oil tank farm were shown on the base layout plan were in fact where the French Hospital was located.[3]

But the Seabees, seeing that General Rose's Force A team had selected a good location for the airfield, began work as soon as their equipment was unloaded. "It was funny to look out there on that field, and see them working. We had natives, soldiers, Marines, Marine pilots and Seabees all working together. The Seabees were running the machines, and the rest of them were doing the unskilled work."[4]

The New Hebridean labor force was essential to the construction effort on Efate and was recruited from Efate, Tanna, and the Shepherd Islands. Labor recruits signed on for three-month tours of duty, were organized in gangs of 25 men who spoke the same dialect, were fed well, and paid $.25–$.50 a day ($7.50 a month)—pay rates that were "purposely kept low at the insistence of the British and the French … (fearing) postwar wage inflation."[5]

In addition to their airfield and road construction work, the local laborers worked as stevedores, on mosquito-abatement crews, in military hospitals, and in the transportation unit.

The Marine unit Mathis mentioned was an advance construction echelon of Marine fighter squadron VMF-212—the Marine squadron committed to Efate's defense. Under the command of Captain J. Little, this 150-man unit had arrived from Hawaii on March 29 to locate and construct the airfield their pilots would use in the coming action. When JTF 9156 arrived, Little's detachment had cleared, graded, and partially surfaced with coral about 1,800 feet of the runway. But Captain Little's construction team had entered the same malarial miasma as had greeted Force A, and the airfield work slowed when his men became badly infected with malaria.

The Seabees divided themselves into construction teams and began working— mostly simultaneously—on 17 different construction projects on the island, most urgently the airfield, to which one officer and 35 enlisted personnel were assigned.

In addition to coping with the severe malaria epidemic, the Seabees on Efate were the first to encounter ground conditions that would plague their future construction efforts elsewhere in the Pacific: the rich but lightweight tropical humus found on most islands—up to two feet in thickness—had to be removed to reach the clay underlayment on which roads and airfields could be built. But the clay—very hard when dry—became a soft, greasy "gumbo" when wet which led to serious construction problems during the long rainy season of the South Pacific.

And the work being done by the Little Detachment and the newly arrived Seabees only heightened the risk for the American forces on Efate. Every tree removed or road built increased the chance that Japanese reconnaissance flights would detect this new American presence, and could potentially lead to a Japanese assault before the island was equipped to defend itself.

> Under these conditions the building of the field went forward in a nightmare of effort and illness. … For twenty-nine days there had been rain with few intermissions, rain so thick it made a sensible burden on the shoulders of a man walking through it, rain that washed away the air needed for breathing.[6]

With Captain Little's construction echelon already hard at work on Efate, the balance of VMF-212 and their Grumman F4F Wildcats had loaded aboard the carriers USS *Enterprise* and USS *Hornet* at Pearl Harbor and departed on April 29. Steaming southwest in a task force that included three cruisers, seven destroyers and two tankers, after 12 days at sea the squadron's aircraft launched from the carriers for Noumea, about 400 miles away. The original destination had been *Roses*, but the *Enterprise* group commander had determined the airfield at Efate was still unsatisfactory.

The long flight to Noumea was nearly too long for the Wildcats on this day. The green Marine pilots would be making their first carrier take-offs and would launch from both the Enterprise and the Hornet. Squadron CO Bauer's diary entry the day prior would not have imbued his pilots with confidence: "It won't be long now! I hope we all get off O.K. ... " He later alluded to delays in assembling the twenty-one plane flight formation once aloft, leading to higher-than-planned fuel consumption. Most planes landed at Tontouta with nearly dry tanks, and one plane ditched just south of the airfield because of a broken fuel line.[7]

On May 15, four days after arriving at Noumea, squadron commander Joseph "Indian Joe" Bauer left by patrol boat for Efate to inspect the progress of the airfield construction. He found it too narrow, too soft, and too short, and gave General Rose and the Seabee engineers his specifications for the airfield: 400 feet wide × 4,000 feet long for fighters, and 6,000 feet long for bombers. He estimated the construction force would need another 20 days to get the airstrip into operating condition for fighters, much longer for bombers.

But, by May 27, the combined construction team, working day and night, and with Seabee leadership and skilled Seabee equipment operators, had extended the airfield to 2,800 feet—just long enough for an experienced fighter pilot—and on that day, Bauer and two other pilots left Noumea and became the first to land at Efate. They began patrol flights immediately. Two additional fighters had been lost by the squadron in operational accidents, but by June 8, all 18 of the VMF-212's Wildcats had arrived at Efate, to be followed by a two-seat SNJ utility aircraft and a J2F Duck amphibious biplane.[8]

For the first three weeks of flight operations the fighter squadron was living in the dark. The radar system that had been installed at Efate could not be made to work properly, and the only reliable reconnaissance information came from visual observations by Bauer's pilots, or by occasional reports from the Royal Australian Air Force. Reliable aerial intelligence was supplied by Sergeant Woolley in the Duck. "(He) ranged from Noumea to Guadalcanal and the Santa Cruz Islands, across many hundred miles of extra-salty sea that he had to fly by dead reckoning, without navigational aids and without a scrap of armament to put up a fight if an enemy scout made a pass at him."[9]

Concurrent with their work on the main airfield, the Seabees of the 1st CB detachment had also been working on a seaplane base at Havannah Harbor on Efate and completed the construction soon after the Navy fighters arrived at the Efate airfield. PBY Catalina flying boats began operations almost immediately from the new base, flying reconnaissance and bombing missions against Japanese positions in the Tulagi vicinity.

As evidenced by Gen. Rose's visit of April 27, it had become apparent to both Army and Navy commanders that the occupation of the large New Hebridean island just to the north—the island of Espiritu Santo—would improve Efate's defense.[10] And that occupation would also need to include an airfield for defense and to support further air reconnaissance to the north.

General Rose's reconnaissance capabilities were greatly enhanced with the arrival on May 4 of the Navy's In-Shore Patrol Squadron VS-5-D-14 and its contingent of eight OS2U *Kingfisher* single-engine float planes stowed aboard the cargo vessels of JTF 9156.[11] On May 12 Army Brig. Gen. W. I. Rose boarded one of those *Kingfishers* to make the 182-mile flight from Efate to Espiritu Santo to continue his assessment of its potential for advanced Air Force bomber and fighter fields.[12]

Rose again sought out Tom Harris, who took the general to meet Pascal Michel, operator of the Bencoula Plantation near Pallikulo Bay. Guided by Harris and Michel, Rose spent four days on the island and inspected several potential airfield sites, including Michel's plantation. He quickly recognized the suitability of Santo for airfields.

The island's eastern half is a low plateau of upraised coral with an average elevation of 300–600 feet. The only topographic feature of any consequence was Mt. Turi, located well to the northwest of any potential airfield site and rising to just 1,837 feet.[13] Rose knew construction units then arriving at Efate could make an immediate start on the airfields at Espiritu Santo and that Marine air units on Efate could at least minimally support the island.

The island of Espiritu Santo was populated by roughly four thousand indigenous New Hebrideans, plus a thousand or so Tonkinese (Vietnamese), a handful of Chinese and Japanese traders, fishermen and small businessmen, and roughly a thousand French and 250 British citizens. The main town of the island, Luganville, was a "small, sleepy port town serving an underdeveloped plantation economy beyond the fringes of the colonialist world."[14] Luganville was situated along the Segond (Segund) Channel which separated Espiritu Santo from the island of Aore, just to the south. Though General Rose, as an Army officer, might not have appreciated it, the nine-mile-long channel was one of the finest natural harbors in the South Pacific, and was the ideal location for a Navy base. On the gently rising ground to the north of the channel, several large Frengh plantations were candidate sites for airfields, and there was ample space for shops, warehousing, magazines, hospitals, and harbor-defense facilities.

As heartening as the news was from the Coral Sea, and as welcome as the arrival of JTF 9156 to Efate was, the American commanders now knew Japanese forces were ashore at Tulagi, just 800 miles to the north. Admiral King believed Japan would attack Efate and New Caledonia within a month. The once insignificant island of Espiritu Santo now became the focus of nearly everyone's attention.

Japan had taken the "long view" in its expansion of empire. As early as 1910, Japanese surveyors were reportedly at work on and near Espiritu Santo, recording land measurements and interviewing natives. They reportedly told the natives "The Japanese were coming to the New Hebrides in the near future and that they would run the white man out of the island."[15]

In May, the commanding general on Efate dispatched a small team to make a further sea-based reconnaissance of the Segond Channel area of Espiritu Santo. Led by the Army's assistant intelligence officer on Efate, 1st Lt. Ritchie Garrison, and including two officers from the New Hebrides Defense Force, the team was to determine if there were any signs of Japanese reconnaissance of the area, and to further investigate potential sites for airfields, piers, and the like.[16]

General Rose returned to Santo on May 12. Garrison's report confirmed the Segond Channel would an excellent anchorage, could accommodate a large number of ships, and its adjacent shoreline was suitable for deepwater piers. Garrison further noted the adjoining plantation areas could accommodate headquarters, troop areas, and supply depots, and that there was no sign of a Japanese presence or reconnaissance on the island.

On returning to Efate, General Rose briefed his commanding officer, Brig. Gen. Harry D. Chamberlin, US Army commander at Efate. On May 19, Chamberlin sent the following message to General Patch, the commander of all Army forces in the South Pacific at the time, and to the Commander in Chief of the Pacific, Admiral Nimitz:

> Recommend occupation ESPIRITU SANTO NH which possess excellent harbor, seaplane base, and airfield sites in 2nd [Segond] channel areas. If authorized shall send small force including reconnaissance detachments, infantry, engineers, to initiate work on airfields. ...[17]

Admiral Ghormley, overall commander of forces in the South Pacific Theater, lent his support to the proposal, messaging Nimitz the next day:

> In my opinion relatively small force can deny ESPIRITU SANTO ISLAND to Japs advance if not in force. Importance of ESPIRITU SANTO to US cannot be over accentuated. If Japs occupy this island, defense of lines of communications and positions (at) ROSES and (at) POPPY made most difficult.[18]

Nimitz approved the occupation of Santo on May 23, but withheld authorization of the airfield construction, cautioning: "Army not prepared to furnish additional troops from US therefore airfield not be to constructed until adequate defense is assured." Nimitz was confirming that no Army units were available to provide a defensive garrison force for Espiritu Santo equal in capability to those dispatched for the defense of New Caledonia and Efate. His caution was rooted in the fear that a Japanese invasion of Santo could lead to the capture of an airfield, which could then be used against Efate and, ultimately, New Caledonia.

But by mid-May Commander in Chief Admiral King was becoming increasingly concerned about the strength of the South Pacific bases, particularly in light of the Japanese occupation of Tulagi. He believed Japan would strike at New Caledonia and Efate sometime after May 25.[19]

The prospect of constructing another airfield came when the Seabees at Efate already had their hands full. With the airstrip on Efate still at least a week from being able to receive aircraft, it now appeared that, upon completion of that airfield, they might have to undertake a new field at Espiritu Santo. But the new assignment at Santo would be different in two important respects: unlike their work on Efate, there were no facilities or services, of any sort, on Santo; and the Seabee unit dispatched for the airfield construction would be very small, since the new assignment on Santo did not relieve the Seabees of the construction projects they had yet to complete on Efate.

Two weeks after his May 12 inspection tour of Espiritu Santo—with Generals Chamberlin, Patch and MacArthur, and Admirals Nimitz, Ghormley and McCain all eager for an American occupation of the island—General Rose was directed to assemble another small Army detachment to secure the island, an advance much like his occupation of Efate just two months earlier. Rose's mission was twofold: to occupy the island before Japan did and to improve its defensive and reconnaissance capabilities by constructing an airfield.

At the same time, General Chamberlin made an urgent request for two more infantry regiments to support the defensive forces on Efate, a request that reflected his fear a Japanese offensive against the New Hebrides and New Caledonia was imminent.[20] Chamberlin's request for more troops was in line with Admiral King's belief of a late-May Japanese offensive. These troops would have to be in place before Admiral Nimitz, who shared King's concern about the likelihood of a Japanese move to the south, would support the development of an airfield.[21]

General Rose and a mixed detachment taken from Force A loaded aboard the New Zealand light cruiser HMNZS *Leander* and departed Vila Harbor in the late evening of May 27, escorted by the American destroyer USS *Whipple*. A second American destroyer, USS *Alden*, had left Vila earlier in the day to conduct an anti-submarine patrol in the seaway to Santo.[22]

The small convoy arrived at Santo at 4:30 on the morning of the 28th. Notwithstanding Lt. Garrison's report from earlier in the month that the Japanese had not occupied the island, Rose's men arrived fully prepared to fight their way ashore. With *Whipple* and *Alden* conducting anti-submarine patrols, *Leander* disembarked Rose's small force.

General Rose established a command center on a plantation near the shores of Surundu Bay on Espiritu Santo, just north of the Pallikulo plantation he had earlier inspected in company with Tom Harris. He immediately set his men into motion unloading arms, supplies, and gear, and appealed to the French plantation operators in the area to contribute their plantation laborers to the effort. Within hours, hundreds of native workers were on hand.

Since Santo had no piers or port facilities, USS *Alden* carried lighters and towing craft to land Rose's troops and equipment. Along with these small craft, every available boat, barge, or punt along the Segond Canal was volunteered or commandeered to help with the offload. All day, in driving rain, the small delivery fleet plied to and from shore, under constant threat of enemy air attack and with no American air cover. Some gear was floated in, and some was swum ashore by the native helpers.[23]

Rose's force included most of the Force A troops and equipment that had first moved to Efate just 71 days earlier. In rough numbers, about four hundred officers and men.[24]

In an operation that was at once agonizingly slow and overwhelmingly vulnerable, by late afternoon the Army force was ashore. The two Navy destroyers departed for Tonga, leaving the small Army contingent to its fate. Rose's force had become the most advanced American unit in the Pacific—the spearpoint representing America's hopes and the military's desperate plans. It was evident to every man in the detachment that should the Japanese take an interest in the island, no friendly force could arrive in time to help.[25]

The Navy's Inshore Patrol Squadron, VS-5D14 equipped with eight OS2U Kingfisher amphibious aircraft, had been conducting short range reconnaissance missions in the northern New Hebrides since arriving in early May. In order to boost the aerial reconnaissance further northward, in mid-June two Kingfishers arrived at the Segond Channel, thus becoming the first air unit to be stationed on Santo, and the northernmost American air unit in the South Pacific.[26]

Their first task was to sustain themselves on the island; the troops began erecting their own tents and setting up mess facilities and sanitation stations. Their next task was to develop defensive positions for the rifle company and for the men and armament of the heavy weapons company. Only after completing that task, and pending authorization of the airfield from General Rose's superiors, would the small occupying force turn to the construction of an airfield.

The sequence of Rose's command assignments thus far in the war is fascinating. Aboard the convoy bringing the massive Task Force 6814 to Noumea, Rose temporarily commanded the entire enterprise—nearly seventeen thousand officers and men. Shortly after arrival at Noumea, Rose took the much smaller Force A to defend Efate. Now, landing on Santo, Rose had at his immediate command just 400 infantry troops and was heavily reliant on native labor. Far from being a reflection of his competence, this new assignment was a testament to his ability to create a potent defense from almost nothing. The size of the advance force in no way reflected the criticality of the station at Santo to the security of the Southern Supply Line. It was simply all that could be afforded at the time.[27]

The site selected for the future airfield was adjacent to Pallikulo Bay on the southeasternmost tip of Santo, 644 miles southeast of Guadalcanal, and 160 miles closer to Japanese positions than the base on Efate. The initial airfield plans encompassed just over four thousand acres—about 6½ square miles—part of which was a stately palm plantation, but most of which was dense virgin bush. The original airfield design called for a 4,500-foot runway with an 8-inch coral base.

While not yet authorized to construct the airfield, Rose's force was not idle and began clearing and grading for roads the base would require.[28] But like their assignment at Efate, Rose's force was an occupying force, not an airfield construction force, and was scantily equipped for the work that lay ahead. Working day and night without the benefit of heavy grading equipment, the Army construction team had just six small tractors, two scrapers, one grease truck, one gas wagon, three weapon carriers and a single 50-kw generator.[29] "We had numerous small bulldozers, but they won't push over a cocoanut [sic] tree, nor will they do the heavy work that the big bulldozer [D8 type] has to do in that type of country."[30]

Rose learned more about Santo than where to place an airfield.

In mid-summer 1942, the island was a backwater, "nearly invisible to most world powers, and of scant importance even to those who administered it."[31] The local populace consisted of a thousand or so Tonkinese, a handful of Chinese and Japanese traders, fishermen, and small businessmen, roughly 1000 French and 250 British citizens, and roughly four thousand native New Hebrideans. Santo had no telephone system, police force, municipal water supply, dock or pier, and the first electric lights had been installed just before the Allies arrived. Transportation inland was by bullock cart. Christian missions operated the only schools and health care was limited to a few small government clinics and the Catholic hospital. The main town of the island, Luganville, more reasonably described as a village, was situated along the Segond Channel west of the Sarakata River.[32]

Apart from the widely scattered plantation operators, the island expatriate community was concentrated in two small clusters of buildings: halfway down the Segond Channel were the French delegation and the Catholic mission and hospital; a mile to the east was an assortment of warehouses at the mouth of the Sarakata River. Plantations filled the gap between, and the island's dozen or so motor vehicles plied the island's only dirt road between these two hubs. There were no bridges of any sort. A cable barge provided passage across the Sarakata River; the Renee River, the second largest in the southern region of Santo, was crossed only by boat.[33]

***

The shape of war in the Pacific had again changed while Pvt. Leonard Richardson ended his leave and prepared to report for flight training in the spring of 1942. Army garrison forces and U.S. Army Air Force bomber and fighter units had departed from west coast ports and airfields to bolster the defenses of many critical

South Pacific island positions, including New Caledonia and Efate. Colonel Jimmy Doolittle had led an audacious bomber raid over Tokyo, and MacArthur's forces in the Philippines were defeated. Japanese forces had landed in the southern Solomon Islands, threatening New Caledonia and Australia, but had been thwarted in their attempt to seize Port Moresby in New Guinea by a combined Allied fleet at the Battle of the Coral Sea.

Time must have moved very slowly for Richardson in the remaining two months of the school year as he witnessed the frenzy evident in the Pacific. Both he and the Army had made their decisions about his service, and he doubtless was ready to get on with it. But while he bided his time in Clarkston, significant and deeply guarded strategic decisions and troop deployments were made that would eventually have a huge effect on his service and his life.

The training process aviation cadets followed included Preflight school (essentially ground school) and three levels of flight instruction: Primary, Basic, and Advanced. The entire program could be completed in 35 weeks, though some cadets were advanced more quickly through the program, depending on the immediate needs for aircrew.

Richardson first reported for Preflight training at the Santa Ana Army Air Base (SAAAB), California, on June 8, 1942. He received a second physical exam there on June 18 and again met the physical requirements for aviation training.

Richardson was among the first to report to SAAAB and arrived to find the base still under construction. The military's ramp up of aviation crew training led to the hurried creation of many flight training centers like SAAAB. Just three months before the first cadet cohort arrived, Santa Ana was little more than bean and tomato fields, but in 90 days the camp went from bare dirt to a nearly complete training center. It included four classroom buildings, 10 administration buildings, mess halls, a gasoline station, a post office, theaters, chapels, and a 151-bed hospital. Newly arriving cadets were housed in tents while additional barracks were constructed. By the war's end, it had grown to over eight hundred buildings, with a teaching and training contingent of twenty-six thousand.[34]

Richardson et al. at SAAAB. (Richardson Family Archives)

Aviation Cadet Arthur Driedger, who was undergoing Preflight instruction at the same time at a base in San Antonio, later reported:

> The commander made a welcome speech, and in that speech, he told us to look to the man on our right, the man on our left, the man in front of us and the man behind us. He informed us that in one year one of these men would be dead, not from enemy action but from operational flying accidents.[35]

During the first week in Preflight training, the cadets underwent "Classification" where the Army decided whether the cadet would train as a navigator, bombardier, or pilot. Candidates were also given yet another physical, and those who failed to meet aviation standards were returned to the regular Army. Richardson was elated to be classified for pilot training.

Preflight training at Santa Ana continued for nine weeks; during the first five weeks, cadets received instruction in military regulations, drill, military courtesy, and other basic military and officer training. In the latter weeks, cadets received classroom instruction in customs and courtesies of the service, chemical-warfare defense, small-arms familiarization, aeronautics, theory of flight, aircraft design, and related military subjects. Physical conditioning was one of the major purposes of Preflight. Calisthenics, in varying amounts, were mixed with competitive sports, cross-country hikes, and obstacle courses.[36]

There was no airfield at Santa Ana—it provided basic ground training before the cadets' advancement to one of the Primary aviation schools for initial flight training. But as part of Preflight, cadets received 10 hours of instruction in the Link Trainer, a simple but ingenious flight simulator in which the cadet could practice navigation, altitude flying, and spin recovery, and learn how to maintain airspeed and attitude using the "needle and ball" (flight instruments) alone.

With General Rose's busy small force securing the forgotten and malaria-riddled island of Espiritu Santo in the far South Pacific, and Aviation Cadet Richardson nearing completion of the first step in the Army's flight training program, a new Japanese initiative, one involving unimaginably larger forces and with barely conceivable consequences for the United States, began looming 3,000 miles to the north in the mid-Pacific.

At the Battle of the Coral Sea, the Allies had blunted a major Japanese advance for the first time since the start of the war, and Japan's movement into the South Pacific had been unexpectedly suspended. It was evident to Japan's primary military strategist, Admiral Yamamoto, that aircraft carriers were the principal threat to the overall Japanese Pacific campaign, and he set plans in motion to correct the salient error of Pearl Harbor—the failure to destroy the American Pacific carrier fleet.

Yamamoto selected the island of Midway, northernmost island of the Hawaiian archipelago, as the center point of his next action. He correctly reasoned the Americans would consider Midway a vital outpost of Pearl Harbor and would commit significant naval forces for its defense. A sea and air battle there would allow Japan to engage the American carriers with superior numbers.

Even after its losses in the Coral Sea, Japan held a formidable naval superiority in the Pacific, but it was also mindful of the huge naval construction program underway in America and Yamamoto knew the death blow to the Pacific carrier fleet would have to happen quickly if it were to happen at all.[37]

Victory at Midway would carry enormous consequences for Japan. American naval forces would have to withdraw to defensive positions in Hawaii, Alaska, and the continental west coast, and with America unable to repeat its previous interdiction in the Coral Sea, Port Moresby would fall. Japan could then advance in strength, largely unopposed against Fiji, the New Hebrides, and New Caledonia. Its forces would then threaten New Zealand and make the job of maintaining any supply line from the U.S. to Australia exceedingly difficult. Any thoughts MacArthur might have for an offensive against Japan and a return to the Philippines would not receive a second glance from the Joint Chiefs, and Allied forces on Australia would become increasingly ineffectual.

Victory would significantly advance Japan's hope for a negotiated settlement by mid-summer.

Like many Japanese military plans, the initiative at Midway—Operation *MI*—was characteristically complex. Yamamoto's carefully choreographed plan incorporated two strike forces, over two hundred ships, and seven hundred aircraft, all disposed over hundreds of miles of open sea. But, on the eve of battle, the immense Japanese strike force had reached a point of great vulnerability: by mid-March the American cryptology program HYPO had cracked the Imperial Japanese Naval operational code—JN-25—and each day the U.S. military leadership became more aware of Japanese plans.

These intelligence reports were hardly verbatim, and many transmissions were missed. But, during the month of May, HYPO had identified the carriers that Japan would deploy at Midway, their approximate locations, the direction from which the attack would come, and the plan of attack. By the end of the month, the most critical piece of intelligence—the date of the attack—had been ascertained: the diversionary attack in the Aleutians would come on June 3 and at Midway on June 4. Even before the first bomb was dropped, the odds were tipped significantly in the direction of the Americans.[38]

Sailors aboard ships, flight crews sitting in cockpits, gun crews at their stations on Midway, and military strategists at their desks—all felt the immense tension of the moment and looked to what fate would soon befall the American forces. In Washington, Admiral King referred to it as "the start of what may be the greatest sea battle since Jutland. Its outcome, if as unfavorable to the Japs as seems indicated, will virtually end their expansion."[39] King's Pacific commander, Admiral Nimitz, noted on the morning of the 3rd: "The whole course of the war in the Pacific may hinge on the developments of the next two or three days."[40]

In the early morning hours of June 4, American reconnaissance aircraft pinpointed the Japanese fleet and within a few hours the U.S. fleet had itself been located by Japanese surveillance aircraft. Strike and counterstrike ensued all that day and the next, with many aircraft from both sides lost in bombing and torpedo attacks or in defensive efforts to intercept attacking aircraft. In the end, the U.S. Navy lost the carrier USS *Yorktown*, but by midday on the second day of battle four Japanese fleet carriers had been attacked and sunk and what was left of the Japanese fleet withdrew.

"[Nimitz] was able to satisfy all three of Clausewitz's 'principles of warfare': decision, concentration, and offensive action. ... Without a doubt these were major contributions to a truly decisive American victory, a victory of the magnitude of Salamis in 480 B.C. and Jutland in 1915 ..."[41]

The Japanese defeat was both stunning and decisive. King would note: "It was the first decisive defeat suffered by the Japanese navy in 350 years ... it put an end to the long period of Japanese offensive action, and restored the balance of naval power in the Pacific."[42] Victory at Midway was the turning point in the war in the Pacific: "At one blow—in a single day's fighting—the advantaged gained (by the Japanese) at Pearl Harbor had been lost and parity in carrier power was restored in the Pacific."[43]

In the awful calculus of war, the loss of life in the battle was light relative to World War II battles yet to come: Japanese casualties totaled 3,057 killed and 37 captured; American losses were 307 killed. But for Japan, *matériel* losses were staggering. By the time the two naval forces disengaged, Japan had lost four carriers—all of which had participated in the attack on Pearl Harbor five months earlier—plus 248 aircraft and a heavy cruiser. American losses included the carrier *Yorktown*, the destroyer USS *Hammann* and 150 aircraft.[44]

The Japanese leadership saw the defeat at Midway as a disaster and a national embarrassment but not a crippling blow to their overall plans. The Pacific War remained principally naval, and Japan still held a numerical advantage over the U.S. Pacific Fleet in every category of warships, and it held an advantage in the number of aircraft, land-based airfields, and naval bases. Overall, Japan was still in a strong position to prosecute the war.

But it was also true that with Japan's carrier force greatly diminished and the loss of hundreds of experienced pilots in the battles in the Coral Sea and at Midway, Japan would have to look increasingly at shore-based airfields for its further offensives in the Pacific. Japan and the United States now shared a common interest in any small island in the Pacific large enough to accommodate an airfield.

CHAPTER FIVE

The New Hebrides and its People

> For all involved ... one of the biggest events of human history was being enacted on some of the world's smallest islands in its largest ocean. Many islands were the most isolated in the world ... and they were the least developed. The built environment was negligible ... a few wharves, a couple of warehouses, short filaments of roads wisping out tentatively from small port towns to jungle dead ends ... the native inhabitants (were), in terms of familiarity with the wider world, among the least sophisticated; most were illiterate.
>
> —JUDITH BENNETT, *NATIVES AND EXOTICS*

Roughly three thousand years ago, as Europe entered the Bronze Age and the great Mayan civilization began to emerge, primitive man first reached the South Pacific. These people, the Lapita, eventually reached the New Hebrides, New Caledonia, Tonga, Fiji, and Samoa, and their appearance marked "the beginning of the last major human dispersal to unpopulated lands."[1] Spanish explorer Pedro Fernandez de Quiros was the first European to reach the New Hebrides in 1606 during his expedition to discover, claim and settle the "great south land," *Terra Australis*.[2] De Quiros and his expedition remained at Big Bay on northern Espiritu Santo for 38 days; each encounter with the indigenous peoples, from the first to last, was marked by bloodshed and unspeakable atrocities.

The first scientific assessment of the islands is credited to Royal Navy Captain James Cook, who was first to recognize that the island group was an archipelago, christened it the "New Hebrides," and devoted considerable time to charting many of the islands during the 46 days he remained in the region.[3] Cook's encounters with the indigenous was no less violent than his predecessors. Every encounter resulted in arrow and stone attacks, musket and cannon fire from the Europeans, and the death of villagers.[4]

These earliest explorers had encountered a civilization that, compared to European culture, could only be described as Stone Age. Tools, implements, and weapons were constructed of stone, earth, and shells. Clothing and ornaments were of found materials. Other than pigs, no animals were domesticated. Apart from primitive pottery, no significant artisan crafts had developed, no communities existed above the level of village, and no written language existed.

At the time of Cook's expedition, Europe was at the mid-point in what is now called "The Age of Enlightenment," but on both sides of the Atlantic white domination of people of color was viewed as entirely compatible with natural rights and government. Their journals reflect the cultural superiority that was the hallmark of this era of exploration, and were patently racist and even scurrilous.[5]

It quickly becomes tedious to read about the New Hebrideans as being primitive. The earliest chroniclers, de Quiros, Cook, and others, clearly, abjectly, and unabashedly reflected the prevailing notions of the day based on the inherent superiority of the white race. The islanders' disdain for these white intruders, and their innate ferocity, was no less apparent. When Cook and his party landed on Tanna in 1774, he attempted to disrupt a group of encroaching natives with a round of non-lethal musketry, which resulted in a strong show of force by the islanders. One especially bold warrior "shewed (sic) us his backside, in a manner which plainly conveyed his meaning," a display which precipitated a broadside of cannon fire but which left an indelible impression on the Europeans.[6]

***

Save for clearing garden sites, the indigenes of the New Hebrides had little effect on the islands. Quite the reverse, it was the island's environment that dictated how people would live, who would thrive, and who perish. Stunningly beautiful, incredibly harsh, lethal and fecund; the environment of the New Hebrides invites description but defies comprehension except at ground level.

Most plant and animal species in the New Hebrides originated from islands to the north—New Guinea, New Britain, and the Solomon Islands. Windblown, borne on ocean currents, or carried by birds, over uncounted eons the blackened volcanic islands began to green and teem with life. But because of its isolation, only a relatively limited number of plant and animal species reached the New Hebrides compared to the lands from which these species originated, resulting in a relatively limited biodiversity in the archipelago.

But what the New Hebrides biome lacks in diversity is more than compensated for by its abundance, and the pejorative "jungle" has often been used to describe the overwhelming flora found on the islands.

But "jungle"—implying a dark, unforgiving, and unenlightened environment—is a misnomer; the more precise term for the flora of the New Hebrides is "tropical rain forest," which more accurately connotes tall, solemn canopies, green cathedrals filled with dappled sunlight, and brilliant songbirds.

Observers have extolled the beauty and serenity of tropical islands like Espiritu Santo for hundreds of years: "In their greenness and freshness, the islands conjure up visions of unending youth and a heavenly paradise ... encapsulated by the jubilant embrace of delightfully cool prevailing trade winds."[7] But experientially, the lyric qualities of the rainforest are soon overwhelmed by the realities of the dense ground-level vegetation, what is referred to by locals as "dak bus" (dark bush).

The nearly impenetrable bush reaches five feet in height, pierced with enormous parasols of taro leaves reaching higher than a man, and ferns growing from both the ground level and epiphytically on the branches of the taller trees. Clumps of bamboo rise above the undergrowth, and lianas hang everywhere. But with limited sunlight reaching the rich humus of the forest floor, very little herbaceous growth occurs at ground level.

> Various climbing plants, some of which extend to the uppermost canopy, form an undergrowth that is difficult to penetrate except along established trails. Off the trails in the jungle, where it is necessary to hack a way through the undergrowth with machetes, a half-mile per hour is considered a rapid march speed. Even along trails, rapid movement is impossible because of the slippery footing, obstructing roots, and the long, whiplike extensions of the rattan palm that hang across the trails and grasp at clothing or flesh with sharp, stout, recurved spines.[8]

No better description of the Santo bush exists than that recorded by Felix Speiser in 1913, a record that might suggest Speiser had been too long in the *dak bus*:

> These woods have none of the happy, sensuous luxuriance which fancy lends to every tropical forest; here is a harshness, a selfish struggle for the first place among the different plants, a deadly battling for air and light. Giant trees with spreading crowns suppress everything around, kill every rival and leave only small and insignificant shrubs alive. Between them, smaller trees strive for light. Around and across all this wind the parasites, lianas, rotang, some stretched like ropes from one trunk to another, some rising in elegant curves from the damp mouldy ground, where leaves rot and trunks decay, and where it is always wet, as never a sunbeam can strike in so far.
>
> ... it is sad in the forest, and strangely quiet, as in a churchyard, for not even the wind can penetrate the green surface. It passes rushing through the crowns, so that sometimes we catch an upward glimpse of bright yellow sunshine as though out of a deep gully. Moisture and lowering gloom brood over the swampy earth; one would not be surprised if suddenly the ground were to move and wriggle like slimy snakes tightly knotted around each other.
>
> ... a white man would be lost in this wilderness without the native, whose home it is. As the white man finds his way about a city by means of street signs, so the savage reads his directions in the forest from the trees and the ground, and describes the least suggestion of a trail. He sees everything, every track of beast or bird, and finds signs on every tree and vine, peculiarities of shape or grouping. He knows every plant and its uses, the best wood for fires; he knows when he may expect to find water, and which liana makes the strongest rope.[9]

British adventurer Beatrice Grimshaw, writing in 1907, was astounded at a friend's suggestion of taking a four-mile walk through the Santo rainforest:

> Four miles! What is that to a healthy Briton? A mere stroll ... But four miles in the New Hebrides is something else. To begin with, there are no roads. There is usually a track, some few inches wide, but one cannot keep to it without a guide, and it is generally slippery and boggy ... Then there is no level ground. Either you are struggling up the side of a slope so steep that you have to use your hands, or you are sliding with clenched feet and fingers down into a pit

of destruction. Also, there is little air, and not much light to speak of, because the overhanging canopy of densely knitted leaf and liana shuts off both. Then it is hot—a good deal hotter than the orchid-house at Kew, and a good deal moister.[10]

Author James Michener, writing cogently and much less lyrically, opines that for those venturing into the interior of Espiritu Santo, "jungle" is an altogether appropriate descriptor:

> ... there is another kind of rain forest that is neither inspiring nor majestic, and the vast forests of Espiritu Santo are in that category. Here each tree is burdened with parasites. The sky is never seen, the ground never free of crawling growth. Malignant vines clutch at the intruder. Extensive swamps suck down his feet, and the atmosphere is rank.
> Thin feelers of the lawyer cane, sometimes forty feet long, tore at them with inverted fish hooks. There were prickly vines, itch plants, poisonous leaves. If they stepped upon a fallen log, it crumbled into dust. If in stumbling they scratched themselves on the rotten wood, the sore festered in six hours and might not heal for six months.[11]

Just as referring to the dense impenetrable jungle on Santo as a "temperate rainforest" seems inadequately descriptive, so too is referring to its climate as "tropical." The weather in the New Hebrides, hot and humid throughout the year, is the least seasonal in the world. According to Navy records in 1943, the average high temperature for the year was 88° F, with a variance in the high temperature of only two degrees throughout the year, and humidity is never less than 75%. Rains were a near constant: "For six months it rains, and then the wet season starts."[12] Southeastern Santo received 117 inches of rain in 1943; rainfall could be torrential.

But in 1943, Santo's weather was not entirely lacking in variety. Just an inch of rain fell in August in southeastern Santo and, coupled with southeast winds reaching 28 mph, the effect was a temporary desiccation of the island: "(Santo) is one of the few places in the world where a person can be up to his knees in mud and still have dust blowing in his face." So recorded Lt. Dalibor Kralovec in his superb *Naval History of Espiritu Santo*. That August respite was short-lived—October rainfall totaled over 19 inches.

And as if volcanism and earthquake aren't enough, the New Hebrides is the most cyclone-prone region in the South Pacific; on average, every other year cyclones engulf one or more islands in the group, often causing widespread devastation and loss of life.[13]

***

Researchers hoping to find detailed ethnographic information about the New Hebrides from the reports of the earliest European explorers would be disappointed. Those expeditions had two objectives: locating and claiming new lands for their sponsoring nations; and spreading the Christian faith to the native peoples of those lands. Their interest in the indigenes was determined mainly by the degree to which the natives would advance or retard the expedition's first objective— whether they would provide food and water to the ship's depleted stores, and how much military force would be needed to secure the needed supplies.

About the native peoples of Espiritu Santo, de Quiros wrote of his 1606 discovery of Espiritu Santo that "the natives generally seen here are corpulent [i.e., heavy-set], not quite black nor mulatto. Their hair is frizzled. They have good eyes. They cover their parts with certain cloths they weave. They are clean, fond of festivities and dancing ... It is, to all appearance, a people courageous and sociable ... "[14] He added "the natives of that bay continued to be hostile, owing to the bad treatment they had received ... "[2]

Captain Cook's journals added:

> [The islanders] were naked, except having some long grass, like flags, fastened to a belt, and hanging down before and behind, nearly as low as the knee. Their colour was very dark. Some had black short frizzled hair, but others had it long, tied up on the crown of the head, and ornamented with feathers like the New Zealanders. Their other ornaments were bracelets and necklaces; one man had something like a white shell on his forehead, and some were painted with a blackish pigment.[15]

Martin Johnson arrived at Santo in 1917 after having spent considerable time on the island of Malekula. On his experience with the residents of a northern region of Santo, he recorded:

> We found the men of Santo ... quite different in type from the Malekula bush savages. They were smaller and more gracefully built. They wore flowers and feathers in their hair. They had a curious custom of removing part of the bone that divides the nostrils so that the bridges of their noses fall in and they appear to be always scowling. To enhance their fierceness still further, they put sticks through their noses.[16]

Author John Baker mirrored some of Johnson's views:

> I doubt whether the reader would consider the natives ... as handsome ... by our standards; but any facial defects are atoned for by the perfection, in many cases, of the physique of the rest of their bodies. ... The heathen natives, both male and female, hold themselves very erect, and the men generally stride along lightly with an appearance of vigour and self-confidence.[17]

In 2002, anthropologist and Oxford Professor Jeremy MacClancy wrote: "It is difficult to speak of 'tribes' in Vanuatu since there does not appear to have been social and political organisation [*sic*] on such a large scale." Rather, their societies were largely organized in clans. Clansmen might live in one or more villages, villages might include one or more clans, and a community might consist of one or more villages and several clans.[18] And in each village, every clan would have its own men's meeting house (the *nakamal*) and ceremonial ground (the *nasara*).

The village of Butmas, located a few miles northwest of Mt. Turi in central Santo, typifies the social organization of the island. It is home to the families of six local clan lineages numbering around one hundred indigenes, all of whom

Indigenes of New Hebrides. (Alamy images)

speak the local dialect Butmas-Tur. Each clan occupies its own land—termed "man ples"—and each has its own head man. The head man of the clan which possesses the ground on which the village proper is located has traditionally been considered the village leader.

The arrangement in Butmas reflects one of the most important aspects of New Hebridean culture—the criticality of the land itself. The land is a living connection between the villager's past and their future. It contains the bones of their ancestors and effortlessly and reliably produces the food on which their children grow. Men call each other "Brothers," because the same soil has nurtured each. Clans own the land and families have individual holdings. But in a deeper sense, the clan is inseparable from the land: "A clan *was* its land and *man ples*, the indissoluble identity of a man and his land."[19]

As a people, the indigenous of the New Hebrides were traditionally prone to intense violence. First observed by French explorer Bougainville in the 18th century: " ... around us there were a great number of people, all of whom appeared to be of a miserable disposition. Perhaps this was because they constantly engage in internecine war ... Inter-tribal war in these parts is a cruel and constant scourge."[20]

While relations within the clan were normally harmonious, those with the people from another clan or a nearby village were often troubled. MacClancy described the often-violent exchanges between villages:

> People in the next valley, who most likely spoke a different dialect, if not a different language, were regarded with permanent suspicion and antagonism. To have wandered unannounced into their territory was to invite death.
>
> Most villages waged war on others. These "wars" were not set battles with two groups of warriors attacking one another in formation but surprise ambushes by the men of one village against the people of another. The intention was not to kill as many men as possible, but one man. Having been insulted in such a fashion, the enemy village prepared for a counter attack to avenge its loss.[21]

While the violence was on a small scale, it was pervasive and unrelenting. "These processes of attack and counter attack ... meant that, theoretically, wars never stopped."[22]

Following a successful attack, the victors normally feasted on the vanquished. The human meat—termed "long-pig" by the islanders—was often roasted and eaten by the village men, and pieces of the corpse—an arm or a leg—were shared with the men of other friendly villages.

In the years leading to the war in the Pacific, reports of cannibalism in the New Hebrides became commonplace. An article in the October 1900 edition of *New Hebrides Magazine* contains this anecdote: "One Sunday morning, the catechist explained the story of John the Baptist. 'And when the girl had placed the head of John on a plate, what did she do with it?' he asked. A small boy answered without hesitation: 'She ate it!'"[23]

In 1903, visiting artist George Collingridge proposed a new postage stamp commemorating Espiritu Santo and the New Hebrides. Designed in jest, the now-infamous "Presbyter Coccidus" (Cooked Missionary) amused many and offended others.

Writing in 1937, noted explorer, journalist and ethnologist Tom Harrisson reported, "There are still full-blooded cannibal heathens in the unvisited mountains. Three thousand of them within ten miles of a wireless station, hospital, Government post and three sects of missionary."[24]

Postage stamp designed by George Collingridge.

Writing in 1942, Marine Corps Maj. Robert Heinl recorded the partiality to "Long-Pig." "At the time of our arrival, Santo was the least civilized spot in the new Hebrides archipelago. While cannibalism was something of a laughing matter to units in the southern New Hebrides, it was anything but that in the north. As recently as the 1920s white men had been ambushed and slain."[25]

Just after the turn of the 20th century, contemporary traveler and writer Beatrice Grimshaw, reflecting the prevailing sense of *noblesse oblige* and the lack of consideration for the indigenous people, wrote:

> At present, the islands are in the most uncomfortable and unsettled state it is possible to conceive. There is no other place in the world where an uncivilized coloured [*sic*] race is to be found in an entirely self-ruling condition, owning no real master, and not even "protected" by any of the great Powers.[26]

From its discovery in 1606 until the arrival of the Americans in World War II, Europeans, explorers, anthropologists, and ethnographers had applied the most defamatory and denigrating terms to describe the inhabitants of the New Hebrides. Writers of the age, even those kindly disposed to the residents, used words like "ape-like," heathen, savage, and brutish.

Explorers and writers in the 19th and early 20th century were, at times, less harsh in their descriptions of the indigenous peoples of the islands than the earliest European explorers, but even they often seemed to revel in the "base" societies they observed.

Grimshaw also wrote, "The New Hebredean, in his native state, is neither more nor less than a murderous, filthy, and unhappy brute," and allowed that he was tolerable only after having been "tamed, cleaned, and restrained from slaying his acquaintance either wholesale or retail."[27] Her writing continued at some length in the same vein, although she did take time to record the unfailing honesty of the New Hebridean—theft, at least of white possessions, was virtually unheard of. Her later writings also mirrored the prevailing notions of the racial and cultural superiority of the developed world and none of the awareness of later cultural anthropologists.

By 1914, the rhetoric had softened somewhat.

> All of them ... are mere children in character and disposition. They are cruel unconsciously and kind intuitively. They are happy in temperament, but subject to sudden fits of anger or sulking; they forget injuries as easily as they forget kindnesses. They represent one of the lowest rungs in the ladder of the human race.[28]

Even the most charitable, Christian, and open-minded anthropologists and explorers have struggled with commenting on the culture and society of the New Hebrides in a manner that is not patently demeaning or evidencing racially superior. "The Melanesians have been widely considered as among the lowest people in the world. And the New Hebrideans [*sic*] as the lowest, most primitive Melanesians."[29]

Many of the practices of the New Hebridean societies appear to outsiders as barbaric in the extreme, and the societies themselves not yet fully formed.

Editor Margaret Jolly noted the rhetoric of French explorer Dumont d'Urville, who in 1826 described the peoples of the region in the most scurrilous and Eurocentric terms, claiming that "institutions (of this region were) still in their infancy." But some commentators have recognized that the societies of the New Hebrides were of long-standing duration. These stable and growing populations, if glimpsed before the arrival of Europeans, could themselves define a successful society, however repugnant some of their practices might have been to European sensitivities. In fact, the institutions derided by d'Urville had been in place longer than those of his home country.[30]

The most difficult task facing social scientists has been not the description of the unsettling practices of the peoples of the New Hebrides, but rather characterizing the nature of the individuals apart from what they considered to be brutish societal practices. They attempted to separate the person from the person's behavior, and in some cases were unsuccessful. Describing the indigenous peoples of the New Hebrides as lacking in industry or unable to tame their violent tendencies is akin to denigrating a beehive for failing to produce wine or a lion for being unable to fly.

***

By the end of the 19th century, European imperialism was making significant inroads throughout Melanesia. The Dutch had established positions in western Melanesia—now known as Indonesia. The British and French were active in eastern Melanesia, and the Germans took more northerly positions in the Bismarck Archipelago. The result of imperialism was much like that in China: extraction of resources, development of local markets for European goods, and the introduction of missionaries.

Europeans began to acquire land and plant crops in the New Hebrides by the late 1860s, exporting cotton at good prices until the market's collapse in 1873. Settlers then diversified into other crops, growing and exporting more traditional tropical crops, notably coffee, maize, vanilla, cocoa, bananas, and, most successfully, coconuts.

The extreme topography of Santo made it unsuitable for large-scale agriculture except for coconuts, and coconut plantations began to dominate the southeastern corner of the island. Santonian labor was cheap but unproductive and, in an ironic departure from the decades-old practice of "Blackbirding," plantation owners began to import labor from the Tonkin region of French Indo-China, just south of the Chinese provinces of Yunnan and Guangxi. The Tonkinese were legendary in their capacity for work and soon a thriving community developed. The pattern of plantation ownership also changed with French settlers becoming the majority by the turn of the 20th century.

The New Hebrides would have been of marginal interest to the French had it not been for its proximity to New Caledonia, a land annexed by France in 1853 and about which the French were keenly interested. New Caledonia possesses nearly every precious and semi-precious metal and was an important element in France's commercial imperialism at the turn of the century. Just 300 miles distant, the New Hebrides possessed many more safe harbors than New Caledonia, produced significant grain crops needed by France, and was positioned much closer to new trading routes that had emerged with the completion of the Panama Canal. Further, it was envisioned the New Hebrides could serve as a resettlement point for ex-convicts released from their New Caledonian prisons. Of particular concern to France, annexation of the New Hebrides by any other country would leave New Caledonia surrounded by non-French colonies.

As with many imperialistic ventures, France sought to maintain control over both New Caledonia and the New Hebrides without the expense of colonization. France's support extended to subsidizing the traders, settlers, and steamer companies of the archipelago, and from time to time, as native unrest peaked and as the French settlers demanded, France would send a warship to the islands, lob a few rounds into the bush, and consider their obligations to their citizens satisfied.

Equally demanding for protection and support were the British subjects who had formed settlements and operated commercial ventures in the islands. Great Britain, while recognizing the value of the New Hebrides due to its proximity to Australia and New Zealand, was much less passionately disposed toward annexation and even less toward colonization.

Land ownership, and the transfer of ownership, became problematic. Without governance, the expatriates had no way to regulate or validate land transfers, a point of great concern to settlers intent on investing heavily in plantation crops. Within the principles of Kastom,[31] the islanders could neither own nor sell the land. For them, land transactions permitted white settlers only to use the land and take its harvest, a view not shared by the settlers.

In 1878, the British and French governments agreed that neither would annex the New Hebrides without the agreement of the other. In 1888, under pressure from their citizen-settlers, the two countries agreed to provide for the protection of their respective citizens by establishing a Joint Naval Commission. The limited scope of that arrangement served the expatriates but did not provide for any type of colonial administration of the islands—not for the expatriates, and certainly not for the indigenous, who remained effectively stateless and largely voiceless:

> ... By not providing any civil authority in the islands, and by refusing to oversee properly the actions of the settlers, [this agreement] indirectly allowed a state of anarchy and lawlessness to develop in Vanuatu, one that was to characterize white settlement for the next four decades.[32]

At the turn of the 20th century, the expatriate population in the New Hebrides was still low—just 151 French settlers and 55 British. But, within a few years, a substantial influx of expatriates occurred and by 1906 there were 401 French settlers and 228 English, and roughly half the land area of the New Hebrides had come under French ownership.[33]

***

The loss of so many men and women through indentured labor came at a time when the islands of the New Hebrides were experiencing a steep decline in population from other causes.

One of the last places on earth visited by white men, the archipelago suffered the same fate as so many other indigenous people following the European "Age of Discovery." In Africa, in the Americas, and in the eastern Pacific, regions utterly isolated for millennia, the arrival of explorers, whalers, sandalwooders, traders, labor recruiters, and missionaries brought more than western ways, trade goods, and religion with them—they brought germs to which the natives were not immune.

Villagers died by the thousands as wave after wave of epidemics swept the islands: pneumonia, dysentery, tuberculosis, influenza, smallpox, scarlet fever, mumps, chickenpox, measles, meningitis, diphtheria, and whooping cough. Neither the village spirits nor traditional medicine could stop the deaths and the white man's God was equally powerless.

The death rate due to disease is mind-numbing. Captain Cook's botanist, Johann Forster, noted the region of Big Bay was densely inhabited and estimated the population of Santo in 1774 at 200,000. Felix Speiser, coming to Santo in 1910, estimated the populace at 12,500—a 94% decline in population. Allies arriving at Espiritu Santo in 1942 estimated that only 4,000 natives remained on the island, and that huge swaths of the island were essentially depopulated.[34]

Writing of his time on Santo in 1937, Alan Marshall recorded:

> Everywhere one goes there are poignant reminders of a former huge population. Deserted gardens, crumbling stone walls … every where [sic] I went the natives spoke of the glories of the past. Those days there were plenty of men, plenty of pigs, great chiefs, big canoes, adventurous trading trips. At the termination of some thrilling reminiscence always there came the dismal, regretfully mumbled "before" … [35]

The indigenous were powerless victims. Women of childbearing age became fewer and fewer, and for those left the prospect was miserable. As one woman recalled, "Why should we have any more children? Since the white men came they all die."[36]

CHAPTER SIX

Espiritu Santo Becomes Critical

Prior to Midway, Japan had been on schedule to implement Operation *FS*—an offensive against Fiji, New Caledonia, and Samoa to sever the Allied Southern Pacific supply line, establish a staging area to support further movements to the south, and to further protect its large base at Rabaul. Now, in mid-May 1942, Operation *FS* was canceled. But Japan knew America would soon springboard from its victory at Midway with a counteroffensive and that a defensive bulwark in the South Pacific could at least temporarily keep the Americans at bay.

Japan decided to fortify the same bases it would have used offensively in Operation *FS*, hoping to deflect potential American advances and yet be able to mount new offensives to the south if the military situation permitted.[1]

The Solomon Islands perfectly suited Japanese plans to advance their forces further to the south and southeast. Composed of over nine hundred islands spread over a quarter million square miles of ocean area, the Solomons range in a generally southeastern direction, with seven main islands arrayed in a parallel chain and encompassing New Georgia Sound.[2]

Even before the events in the Coral Sea, the American Joint Chiefs (JCS) had recognized the strategic importance to Japan of the Tulagi region in the southern Solomons. The harbor at Tulagi—enclosed by the small islands of Tulagi, Gavutu, and Tanambogo—was deep and spacious, and airfields for land-based aircraft could be quickly developed on nearby Guadalcanal to provide air cover for the harbor. A base in the Tulagi–Guadalcanal region could be supported and defended by the Japanese stronghold at Rabaul, just 650 miles distant, and from a series of even more proximal bases in the southern Solomons and New Georgia; importantly, Japan also knew the nearest American bomber and fighter forces were on New Caledonia, out of reach of Tulagi.

As early as February—months before the battles of the Coral Sea and Midway—Admiral King had become aware of the rapid strengthening of the Japanese forces at Rabaul and recognized the Solomons could serve as "stepping-stones" for Japanese movements southward, but could equally support American plans to resist those advances and launch their own counterstrike to the north.

The *Arcadia* Conference had given the aggressive-minded Admiral King all the authority he needed for offensive operations in the region by directing that " ... points of vantage from which an offensive against Japan can be eventually developed must be secured."

King's directives to Nimitz following *Arcadia* were abundantly clear: "Current operations ... should be directed toward preventing further advance of enemy land airplane base development in the direction of Suva and Noumea.[3] Nimitz was directed to prepare "a strong and comprehensive offensive to be launched soon against exposed enemy naval forces and the positions he is now establishing in the Bismarcks and Solomons."[4]

Now, in early June, feeling the tailwind created by the decisive victory at Midway, the Joint Chiefs recognized that, for the first time in the Pacific War, and in fact for the first time in any theater, America could dictate where and when the next battle would take place. For a very brief period, and only with prompt action and only in the South Pacific, America could take the initiative.

"Each side held a rear base, Rabaul for the Japs and New Hebrides for the Americans, upon which its South Pacific defense swung. Loss or neutralization of either base would mean the defeat of the side depending on that base, in the battle for the South Pacific." But for a brief time, the opposing forces were at a stand-off: Japanese air forces at Rabaul could not reach American assets in the New Hebrides or New Caledonia, and were themselves out of range of American air forces. It was the middle ground—accessible by both combatants—that held the greatest strategic value, and where the immense forces were set to collide.[5]

Both countries were considering options for more forward airfields. For America, it was Efate and Espiritu Santo. The flat plain on the northern coast of Guadalcanal—just opposite Tulagi—was the obvious choice for Japan.

A well-developed and strongly defended aerodrome on Guadalcanal could serve as the launch point for bomber attacks on American positions to the south—the New Hebrides and New Caledonia; Allied military planners could not let this happen.[6]

And reflecting the strategic thinking of Admiral King, the obverse was also true for the United States. From established American airfields in the Tulagi region, the Japanese stronghold at Rabaul—and its myriad supporting and ancillary bases—could be reached by long-range B-17 bombers.[7]

As a major Army retrospective would later report: "If the Americans were going to blunt the Japanese advance into the South Pacific, Guadalcanal would have to be the place ... [8]

But while a military advance into the southern Solomons held great advantages for both parties, any action in the Tulagi region, whether offensive or defensive, and whether initiated by Japan or America, would be a most challenging undertaking. As historian James Smith would note, "The region lay at the intersection of the furthest ranges of the two combatants' land-based airpower, and was accessible only through dauntingly long lines of communication and supply." For either side, with the significant distances involved, the southern Solomons region would be a "border march."[9]

Author H. P. Willmott would later note that, after the Japanese defeat at Midway, " ... the strategic initiative in the Pacific War was like a gun lying in the street: it was there for either side to pick up and use."[10]

For Japan, timing was critical. America's massive industrial and manpower recruitment and training capabilities continued to ramp up, making replacements of losses possible. Conversely, Japan's own industrial base was less able to absorb material and manpower losses, and its war-making capacity was markedly diminished.

***

In late May, the airfield on Efate became ready for fighter operations and the "Hell Hounds" of VMF-212, under the command of Major Harold Bauer, began flying their Grumman F4F Wildcat fighters from the new airfield—later known as Bauer Field.[11] But by the end of June, the work of building an airfield on Espiritu Santo had still not been authorized.

With the war in the Pacific nearly six months old, and sensing a real but fleeting opportunity in the South Pacific, the United States' military leadership was finally coming to a consensus for the strategic objectives of America's initial offensive operations: clearly the reduction of Rabaul was most critical. Achieving that objective would involve a concerted effort by both the Army and Navy and would require intermediate operations leading to a final assault. With the immediate strategic objectives settled, what remained was developing a detailed plan, and deciding under whose command the plan would be implemented.

General MacArthur responded first with a proposal submitted to the Joint Chiefs on June 8. His scheme was viewed as too expansive and too aggressive, but it served to galvanize Army–Navy positions and generated considerable debate within the services, and within the Joint Chiefs.

King and his planning staff, having contributed to the demise of MacArthur's plan, used this brief period of debate within the Joint Chiefs and theater commanders to alert Admiral Nimitz of possible impending action. In a flurry of messages in the last week of June, King notified Nimitz of the nature of the debate within JCS, identified Tulagi as the primary target, gave a general plan for the likely joint Army–Navy–Marine operations, and indicated a starting date as "about August 1st."[12] Keeping the Joint Chiefs and the War Department fully informed on his preparations, King directed copies of his dispatches to Nimitz be delivered to General MacArthur in Australia, and copies to be hand delivered to General Marshall.[13]

On June 25, with his forces on high alert, King came to the Joint Chiefs with a counterproposal to MacArthur's expansive and unrealistic plan of June 8. King's proposal was essentially a restatement of his earlier suggestions for Pacific war strategies, first expressed in February, and again repeated in early March in a direct appeal to the president. His plan was based on the development of "strong points" along the South Pacific line of communications. With that accomplished, American forces could take the initiative.

King's strategic planning recommendations had been consistent for months: "Hold Hawaii—Support Australasia—Drive northwest from New Hebrides."

The day following his proposal to the Joint Chiefs, King upped the ante by bluntly telling General Marshall the Navy was prepared to launch an offensive in the South Pacific "even if no support of Army forces in the Southwest Pacific is made available."[15] It now fell to Army Chief of Staff General George Marshall to mediate an awkward compromise from which a larger offensive plan could develop.

Marshall's very measured proposal to Admiral King came three days later—an eternity considering the volcanic natures of the parties involved and the critical military situation in the South Pacific. He proposed the Navy, specifically Admiral Ghormley (COMSOPAC), would be in command of initial operations against Tulagi and adjacent areas in the southern Solomons, and that General MacArthur would assume control of subsequent operations, including those in the central and northern Solomons, leading to the capture of Rabaul.

The first phase of Marshall's plan called for the capture of the Santa Cruz Islands, Tulagi, and "adjacent positions," with Admiral Ghormley in command. Among those adjacent positions was Guadalcanal (codename *Cactus*); among the tactical objectives

ADM Ernest J. King (COMINCH), center, ADM Chester W. Nimitz (CINCPAC-PAO), left and ADM William F. Halsey (COMSOPACFOR) right. (Naval History & Heritage Command, NH 62645)

General Douglas MacArthur, Supreme Commander, Allied Forces, Southwest Pacific Area, and General George C. Marshall, Chief of Staff, U.S. Army (right) late 1943. (Photograph from the Army Signal Corps Collection in the U.S. National Archives. SC 183951)

was the occupation of sufficient terrain on Guadalcanal to construct airfields and to initiate construction of same.

The plan was accepted by the Joint Chiefs and, on July 2, 1942 it issued the "Joint Directives for Offensive Operations in the Southwest Pacific Area," ordering that an offensive be mounted at once.[16] Admiral King immediately sent a long, three-part message to Nimitz, MacArthur, and Ghormley—"Handle this with utmost secrecy"—describing the overall plan and setting August 1 as the target date. When it later became evident the troop transports carrying the Marine landing force would be delayed in arriving from New Zealand and that weather was likely to cause further delays, "D-Day" for the invasion of Tulagi was deferred to August 7.[17]

Understanding the criticality of effective reconnaissance and a strong bombing force, General Marshall ordered the creation of two B-17 mobile air forces, to be taken from units already in the Pacific, with each comprising at least one heavy bombardment group.

Admiral King wasted no time in notifying his theater commanders that bombers would soon arrive in the South Pacific. At the time, the only airfields between Hawaii and Australia able to accommodate the B-17s were at New Caledonia and Fiji—both too far removed to be of any value in the coming offensive. A new airfield on Espiritu Santo—the northernmost position under Allied control—became the subject of strident communications at top levels of the American command and a matter of great urgency.[18]

On the same day the Joint Chiefs issued their "Joint Directives," Admiral Ghormley ordered Rear Admiral John McCain, commander of all ground-based aircraft in the South Pacific, to "Proceed with construction bomber strip at *Button* [Espiritu Santo] using part of your construction battalion, light equipment and local transport … Report progress weekly."[19] In a separate message, Nimitz tersely added a critical deadline: "This project has highest priority. Desire field ready for operation heavy bombers not later than July 28."[20]

Twenty-four days to construct an operational airfield able to accommodate the largest aircraft then in the Army Air Forces' inventory was an impossible task. McCain received this message while at Efate and, accompanied by General Rose and Major Bauer, flew to Santo on July 4 to further evaluate sites for landing fields. McCain returned the following day and reported to Nimitz and Ghormley that several good sites had been identified.[21]

Later that morning, July 5, Bauer and Lieutenants Wallin and Mathis from the 1st Seabee detachment were called to a meeting with Admiral McCain and General Rose and were told of Ghormley's directive, including the stipulation the Seabees on Efate would have to provide the manpower, equipment, and supplies for the new Santo airfield.[22] "The situation existing at the time of this … conference was very dim from the standpoint of available Seabees. The only construction troops in the entire New Hebrides—New Caledonia area were the one-half of the First

Naval Construction Battalion (approximately one hundred seventy-seven officers and men), all of which were located at Efate."[23]

And while the first airfield at Efate was useable for Navy fighters, the Seabees were still working hard to extend the field to accommodate bombers, on top of the many other construction projects they had been assigned: maintaining the roads on the island, operating the water, power and refrigeration plants, and unloading ships. Finding troops to spare was not an easy job.[24]

All eyes were on Mathis. He had been in charge of the airfield construction on Efate and would be for the new field on Santo. He would have just over three weeks to make it happen; three weeks to assemble his team, collect the necessary equipment and materials, move everything to Santo, set up camp, and build a 6,000-foot runway.

There was not an hour to lose.

The next day the essential materials and equipment needed for the new airstrip construction were identified, and Lt. Wallin selected the construction team: one officer and thirty-seven enlisted men, of whom thirty-five were equipment operators. "Before making a decision on men to be sent they were given a chance to volunteer on the task which, it was explained to them, might be extremely hazardous. Only one man withdrew; he was then on the sick list."[25]

Within hours, men and material began flowing to waiting ships. *YP 239*, a small patrol craft formerly used as a bait boat for the Pacific tuna fleet, was laden with 30 days' rations and lumber for tent decks. With 12 of the Seabees aboard, it departed Vila Harbor at midafternoon on July 7, towing a 50-ton pontoon barge to facilitate unloading at Santo.[26]

The cargo ship *Joseph Lykes*, loaded with troops, material, and equipment, sailed at midnight. "We had one Marine AA [anti-aircraft] battery to protect us, and a company of colored Army infantry to do the unskilled work."[27]

The Navy's Seabees might have felt the Army Air Force was also nudging them forward; as they were preparing to leave Vila Harbor, they would have seen the first B-26 Marauder medium bomber land on the Efate airfield.

Bauer, Wallin and Mathis returned to Santo on July 6 to refine the site selection for the new airfield. "We flew all around spotting the likely sites, then landed to look them over from the ground. We located a particularly good one and a few alternatives."[28] They were joined by Lt. H. V. Eliott of the 57th Combat Engineers, already on Santo as part of Rose's occupation force, and Pascal Michel, a local plantation operator. The next day, the men laid out the boundaries for the new airfield. "The site was a coconut grove located near Pallikulo Bay on the southeast corner of Santo. The soil was principally coral with a few spots containing the familiar black "gumbo" clay which later had to be removed and replaced by coral.[29]

Bauer and Mathis returned to Efate while Mathis awaited the arrival of his men and material.[30] Bauer was not hopeful: "Orders were to have it by 28 July. I don't think it can be done with the men and equipment furnished."

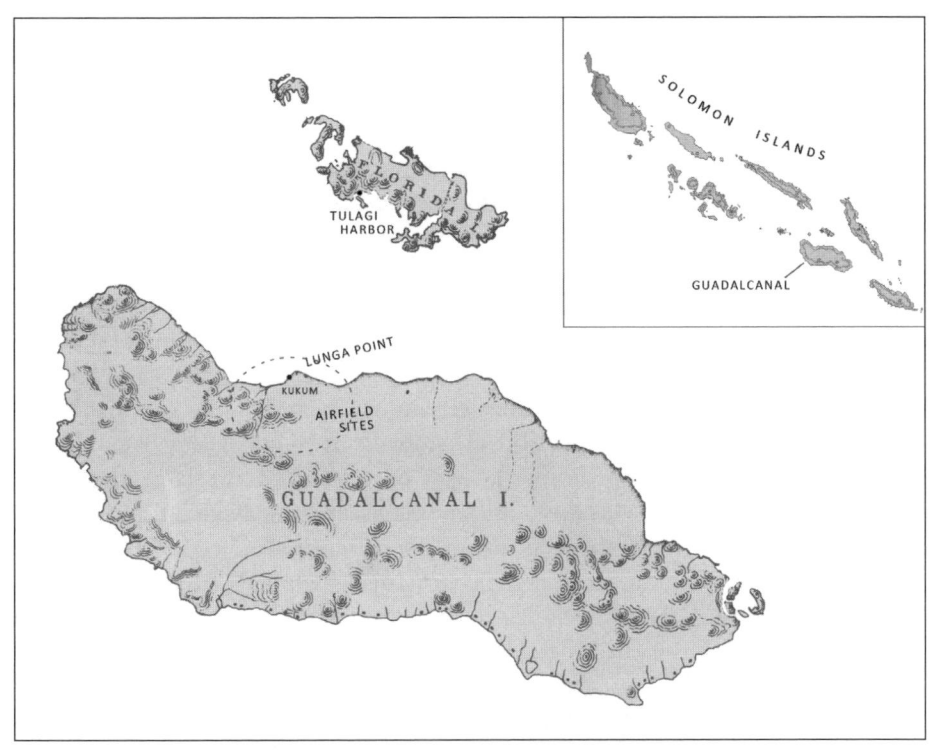

The island of Guadalcanal. (Yosemite Productions)

When *Joseph Lykes* arrived at Espiritu Santo on the afternoon of July 8, the Seabees encountered the same problem as General Rose's earlier contingent. Unloading was a tedious process that required lightering men, equipment, and supplies ashore: "We began unloading and clearing. There wasn't a damn thing there but jungle."[31]

Given the importance of the long-range B-17s to the coming offensive, completing the new airfield on Santo became critical. At that time in the war, the only heavy bombers in the Pacific Theater were B-17E models, which could carry a bomb load of 4,000 lbs over an effective range of 2,000 miles. The round-trip distance from an airfield at Efate to Guadalcanal was 1,600 miles. Under combat flying conditions, the distance was too great for safe bomber operations—the bombers would have no fighter support, no opportunity for emergency landing or refueling, and few possibilities for the rescue of downed airmen. While carrier aircraft could have undertaken limited bombing operations, the waters around Guadalcanal were far too dangerous to risk the Navy's precious remaining carriers.[32]

***

Concurrently with General Rose's occupation of Santo and the debate that raged within the Joint Chiefs about future American offensives in the South Pacific, Japanese ground forces in the Tulagi area had taken actions that made the Allied actions and decisions all the more critical.

Guadalcanal is the second largest island in the chain and roughly the size and shape of New York's Long Island, or a good-sized Texas county. Ninety miles long and 25 miles wide at its center, the island's southern half is mountainous, volcanic, and forbidding, with peaks rising steeply from the shoreline to over seventy-five hundred feet. The northwest coast of Guadalcanal—the Lunga Plain—was one of just three relatively flat areas in the Solomon Islands suitable for developing large aerodromes.

Intending to take advantage of that terrain, in mid-May, the commander of the Japanese air group stationed at Tulagi—roughly speaking, Major Bauer's direct counterpart—ordered the preliminary work on an airfield site large enough to support both fighters and Mitsubishi *Betty* bombers, and from which Espiritu Santo and the growing base at Efate could potentially be targeted. On May 27, Japanese engineers created a wildfire to clear the coarse, man-high grass from the level area on the Lunga Plain.[33] Aerial reconnaissance reports reached Admiral Ghormley in late June confirming the activity on the Lunga Plain, with the presumed intention to construct an airfield.[34]

Nearly concurrently, on June 25, the Japanese naval commander at Rabaul ordered construction units to build an airfield at the Lunga Plain. Between July 2–12, 400 naval and 1,200 civilian laborers, accompanied by an additional security force, landed on the northern shore of Guadalcanal to begin building the airstrip.[35]

Airfield construction on the Lunga Plain. (WikiCommons)

In initiating this work, the Japanese commander created the precise situation Nimitz had sought to avoid when he was first asked for permission to proceed with an airfield on Espiritu Santo—the activity on the Lunga Plain elicited an immediate reaction from the Allies.

By July 4, with American Army and Navy forces having received notification of the Solomons offensive, further intelligence, including coastwatching reports, confirmed the landing of Japanese troops and construction workers on Guadalcanal not far from Lunga Point. Nimitz's diary entry for July 5 noted, "There is the probability that [Japanese naval units]units are in the Tulagi–Guadalcanal area and that an airfield is being constructed on the north shore of the latter island."[36] On July 8, MacArthur reported that "The enemy ... is making a major effort in the development of airfields at ... Guadalcanal which will greatly facilitate the operation of its air elements throughout the area ... it appears at the present time he is installing the heavy equipment for an air base on Guadalcanal.[37]

By July 11, the Japanese labor force had completed offloading men, materials and machinery. The following week, the unit established their camp, began removing coconut trees, and continued burning slash and tall grass from the airfield site. Construction of the airstrip started on July 17.[38] The airfield was intended to provide a base for 60 Japanese naval aircraft and was initially scheduled for completion by August 15. But Japanese commanders, sensing the importance of this new airfield, soon ordered an acceleration in the construction and set a new completion date of August 7.[39]

On the same day construction of the airfield began, a B-17 based at Port Moresby made a reconnaissance flight over the Tulagi–Guadalcanal region but was unable to detect any construction, reporting: "No evidence of the existence of Japanese airfields on Guadalcanal—other than burned off areas behind Lunga Point and Tetere sectors—was observed."[40]

But naval reports 10 days later reported that "The Japs continue to consolidate their positions in eastern New Guinea and are apparently constructing two airplane fields on the North coast of Guadalcanal." On July 28, intelligence reports indicated Japan was working on not one but three airfields on Guadalcanal.[41]

It's evident that shortly after occupying Tulagi in early May, Japan's military commanders had perceived the "gun lying in the street," and were taking action to pick it up before America could.

***

Four hundred miles to the south, the beleaguered construction team on Santo was working with equal haste. Establishing a camp on Santo for new Seabees was left until later, and for several nights the men slept without tents in near-constant rain. The airfield construction team now included the Seabees, 37 men from Lieutenant

Eliott's 57th Engineer Combat Battalion, and five officers and 145 engineers from the Efate-based 4th Marine Defense Battalion. Four hundred indigenous New Hebrideans were also put to work, some from Santo, others from the nearby island of Malekula, "one of the most wild localities in the world; if they were not headhunters, they were sons of headhunters."[42]

Mathis later remembered: "We set up floodlights and worked around the clock. I had twelve Seabees who operated nine big pieces of equipment twenty-four hours a day for a month. You can figure out for yourself how much sleep they got."[43]

On July 12, having been advised that 35 Army Air Force B-17 bombers would initially be sent to the South Pacific, Admiral McCain arranged for the following disposition: two squadrons to New Caledonia and one squadron each to Fiji and Efate. But McCain intended to redeploy one of those squadrons to Santo as soon as the airfield was ready.[44]

B-26 medium bombers began making test hops to Efate in early July and, on the 15th, General Rose left Efate aboard a B-26 to overfly Santo. He reported on his return to Santo that "the field was laid out so that (the pilot) couldn't approach it." The next day, Bauer went to Santo and found that, "Sure enough, much to my consternation—it was being laid out differently than I had instructed and was consequently too difficult to approach. I had them change it." He returned three days later and recorded that "The new alignment will be O.K., although not perfect."[45]

Before Mathis had laid out the airfield boundaries, Rose's original airfield construction force apparently made more than one false start. The Seabees would later report, with an element of pique, and perhaps illustrating the occasional Army–Navy contretemps:

> The first 7 days of labor was fruitless because the Army (had) kept changing its mind about the location of the field; one start of 1000 feet was abandoned for a second start of 2000 feet of runway. The third and final location was by this time entirely clogged up with debris from the first two attempts. The value of the Army and natives in building the field was sometimes detrimental, for when trees were felled by axes, a mat of trees resembling a jack-straw puzzle actually handicapped the bulldozer operators.[46]
>
> On a typical day—say July 21—here is who we had working on the field: 295 Army infantrymen, 90 marines, 32 Seabees and 50 natives. The Seabees were running the equipment; the rest were clearing by hand.
>
> With the final airfield location settled, construction began in earnest. Equipment was in operation 24 hours a day and, despite the site's exposed position, blackouts were ignored and the field flood-lighted at night so work could continue. The skilled mechanics and equipment operators of the Seabee unit were the nucleus in directing the work and operating the construction equipment. Ground troops of the Army and Marine Corps assisted by driving trucks and doing general labor.[47]

Mathis had intended to surface the new airfield with Marston matting, but the Seabees did not wait for its arrival. "We cleared and surfaced 6000 feet of runway, but we didn't cover the runway with Marston mat. We didn't have any mat. We just graded and rolled the coral."[48]

Back at Efate, the work to extend the airstrip to 6,000 feet had been completed and the first B-17 of the 26th Bomb Squadron, 11th Bomb Group (11th BG) arrived on July 23, to be followed two days later by the remaining seven aircraft of the squadron.[49] Concurrently, the other squadrons of the 11th BG had also arrived at their South Pacific stations: the 42nd and 98th Squadrons to Plaine Des Gaiacs on New Caledonia, and the 431st to Nadi in the Fijis.[50] The Army's most lethal air forces had assembled and all would depend on the completion of the airfield at Palikulo in the coming days.

On July 25, Rear Admiral McCain issued his operation orders for the shore-based Navy and Army aircraft within his command, confirming "Dog Day" was "tentatively seven August." The specific missions McCain assigned to the 11th BG were threefold: to complete daily searches over two sectors, to track important enemy contacts, and to execute air attacks on enemy objectives as directed.[51]

McCain's plan listed the available airfields, including the airstrips at Efate and Santo. But on the date the plan was issued, neither McCain nor Rose was confident the new airfield at Santo would be ready for use; the plan indicated "1 bomber strip under construction (at Santo). Date available for use to be announced."

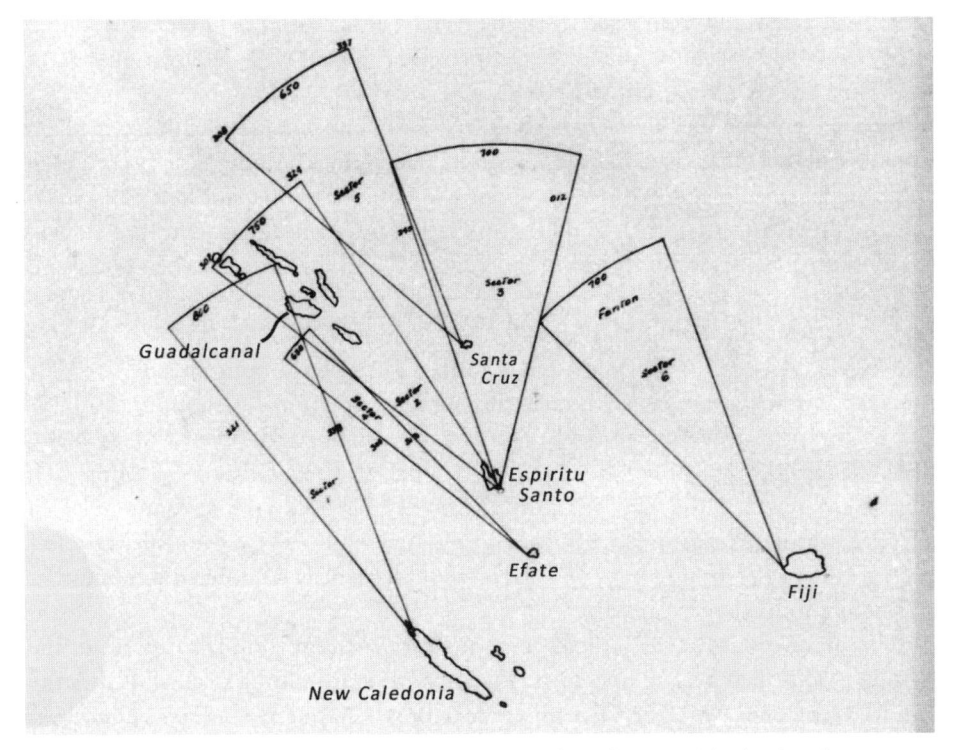

Search Sectors assigned to the 11th Bomb Group operating from the New Hebrides. (Credit to Eastern Carolina University Digital Collections)

The search area assigned to the 11th BG was of critical importance. Sector 2 was assigned to the aircraft based at Palikulo and covered the entire lower Solomons, including Guadalcanal. Sector 4 was assigned to the aircraft at Efate and included the ocean areas to the west of Santo. The reconnaissance flights over these two sectors would be critical over the next six months. The shorter-range B-26 and Hudson bombers based at New Caledonia were assigned other search sectors.

Admiral McCain, COMAIRSOPAC, directed the commander of the 11th BG, Colonel Laverne "Blondy" Saunders, to hit Tulagi and Guadalcanal "with maximum strength" in the week immediately before the Marines' landing. Given the uncertainty about the new Santo airstrip, however, and with the deadline rapidly approaching for the start of bombing operations against Tulagi and Guadalcanal, Saunders decided to launch the initial bombing sorties out of Efate. With that extra flight distance, only B-17s equipped with auxiliary fuel tanks could be used; even then, the bombers could only carry a much-reduced bomb load.

On the 28th, Saunders put out an urgent call for a quick inventory of all aircraft in the 11th BG to determine which were so equipped and learned that, out of the 35 aircraft in his command, just nine were equipped with the extra tanks: six B-17s in the 26th Bomb Squadron, one in the 42nd, and two in the 98th.[52]

As McCain would soon make clear, he needed either additional fuel tanks or an operational field at Santo. The latter was preferred since it would allow bombers to make air strikes with full bomb loads.

McCain sent not one but two urgent messages to Nimitz requesting the immediate shipment of fuel tanks from Hawaii.[53] Admiral King himself immediately responded and, possibly being quite exercised about the issue of the Japanese landing field construction on Guadalcanal, told Ghormley "It is most important that [the Tulagi–Guad operation] be not delayed beyond August 7 and that this date be anticipated if possible in order that enemy may not be given time to perfect installations now under construction in objective areas for use against us."[54]

McCain replied to Ghormley and Nimitz: "Large scale bombing planned for the 31st … must await arrival and installation (of) additional gas tank in 10 B17s [*sic*] or completion of Button field. Will attack as planned that date with as many these planes now so equipped—about 9."[55] What McCain did not say, but which all parties knew, was that the airfield on Santo had been initially recommended on May 19, but that Nimitz had withheld approval until July 4. Had the airfield project been greenlit when originally proposed, it would have been completed weeks earlier and with a much larger capacity.

Dire necessity drove the airfield construction. With exceptional leadership, the efficiency of skilled Seabee operators, the strength and stamina of unskilled Army and Marine troops, with the help of islanders for whom much of what they saw was utterly alien, and with determination by all, by July 28 the airstrip construction was complete. Twenty-one days after the ship carrying Mathis's Seabees had dropped anchor at Espiritu Santo, three fighter aircraft landed on the new airfield.

ESPIRITU SANTO BECOMES CRITICAL • 73

Bomber 1 Airfield, Pallikulo Bay, Espiritu Santo. (USAF Photo 22142 A.C.)

Major Bauer:

> Well—believe it or not—we landed the SNJ and 2 fighters at Santos today [July 28).] It could have handled B-17s in an emergency but will be completed in about 2 more days. I flew the General [Rose] in the SNJ so that he could say he was the first to land at Santos—the field which he is greatly responsible for.[56]

But the Seabees could do a lot in 24 hours, and the very next day, after Bauer's first landing at Santo, a B-17 from the 26th Bomb Squadron at Efate made its first landing there. Aboard the B-17 were General Rose, Bauer, and Lieutenant Garrison. They landed at 2:30 p.m., stayed an hour, and then returned to Efate to prepare the rest of the bomber squadron for its move to Espiritu Santo.[57] General Rose reported this critical development to Admiral McCain immediately and undoubtedly with great satisfaction.[58]

The Americans were getting much more adept carving airfields from virgin bush. The 2800 foot airstrip on Efate had been brought to a useable condition in 59 days. The bomber field at Pallikulo Bay, 6000 feet in length, was completed start-to-finish, just 61 days after Rose's advance force had arrived on Santo.

The new airfield on Santo was the absolute minimum for bomber operations. Its revetments were narrow and barely deep enough to keep the B-17s' noses off the runway. There were no lights. Jeep headlights marked the end of the runway, and bottles of oil with strips of paper for wicks marked its edges. "Invariably the prop wash extinguished the bottle flares and the next plane had to wait until the lamps were relighted."[59] The lack of taxiways and dispersal areas led the commander of the 11th BG, Colonel Saunders, to conclude he could operate just eight B-17s from the airfield—six strike aircraft and two search planes.[60]

Busy as it would be in conducting offensive operations, the base on Santo would remain "unrefined" for many weeks. General Harmon, Commanding General South Pacific, visited Espiritu Santo in early September 1942 and would later write to General Marshall that:

> ... the base was a raw new landing field, [with] inadequate dispersal and concealment; Army, Navy and Marines all mixed in the jungle; mountains of supply piling up on the beach and a roadstead full of ships; bombs and fuel drums scattered throughout ... a fine picture of war as *she is* [Harmon's emphasis] but not as it should be.[61]

Harmon's point was reinforced in a report issued by Admiral Nimitz in mid-October, which cited:

> One of the outstanding features of the War ... has been the ability of U.S. Forces to build and use air-fields, on a terrain and with a speed both of which would have been considered fantastically impossible in our pre-War days ... The Credit (belongs) not least to the Air Forces themselves, who knew well that even the best available sites in some areas would have been considered almost murderously unsafe by pre-War standards, yet who accepted the dangers as well as the inconveniences and hardships of such fields, through their strategic necessity.[62]

With no additional fuel tanks having been delivered, the first mission consisted of just nine aircraft and required careful choreography. Six B-17s from the 26th Bomb Squadron took off from Efate on the afternoon of July 30, landed at Santo, and remained overnight. These six strike aircraft took off from Santo at 6:50 a.m. on July 1 and rendezvoused with three more B-17s from the 42nd and 98th Bomb Squadrons that had departed Efate earlier that morning.

The six aircraft from the 26th were each loaded with twenty 100-lb bombs and made their drop against the supply dumps in the Lunga Point area. The other three aircraft, loaded with 500-lb bombs, hit the landing strip. As part of the mission, the north and east coasts of Guadalcanal were photographed. At the conclusion of the mission, all nine planes returned to Efate around 3:30 in the afternoon.[63] Saunders would later report "the mission was a good example of perfect execution ... "

The days following this first mission were hectic in the extreme for the airfields at both Efate and Santo. Saunders's group would launch 56 strike missions in the coming seven days, and 22 search missions. Each day, at least eleven B-17s were in action against the Japanese forces just 640 miles north of Santo. "A most creditable performance in view of the primitive conditions under which operations labored."[64]

***

Fascinating as he would have found the events in the New Hebrides in the mid-summer of 1943, Leonard Richardson had little time for distraction. He had completed his Preflight training in mid-July 1942, received his Cadet Wings, and reported to his next training assignment—Primary Flight Training—at Ryan Field, just outside of Tucson, Arizona.

In Primary, elementary flight instruction was given in private flight schools under contract to the Civil Aeronautics Authority—War Training Service. Cadets got around sixty to sixty-five flight training hours in two-seat aircraft before advancing to the next level of flight in the program—Basic Flight Training.

Aviation Cadet Richardson reported for the Primary program at Ryan Field on July 15, 1942, one of 124 cadets in Class 43-B. The cadets were further divided into one of four "flights" in the class—E, F, G or H. Richardson and 31 other cadets were assigned to "G Flight" and its cadre of eight civilian instructors. As was true for all cadets at every Primary school, Richardson was assigned a single flight instructor for his entire time at Ryan Field. Some new cadets, like Richardson, had completed all or part of the Civilian Pilot Training (CPT) Program. Others had not so much as sat in the cockpit of an airplane.[65]

The Primary flight program started fast and never slackened.[66] The program included ground instruction and flight training, and the entire day was tightly structured. Wake-up at 5:45 a.m., breakfast at 6:00, a quick inspection and classroom instruction until noon, and flight instruction every afternoon. After supper, cadets could study, attend chapel, or play sports; all returned to barracks for an evening inspection before the 9:30 taps.

The Ground School included 96 hours of instruction in a five-course curriculum, with half of that devoted to the principles and workings of the various operating systems of an aircraft.[67]

Before ever mounting their training aircraft, the cadets reviewed the four forces acting on an airplane in flight—thrust, drag, lift, and gravity—and were lectured on the plane's control surfaces: the ailerons to control movement of the aircraft around the longitudinal axis; the elevators to control its movement around the lateral axis; and the rudder to control movement around the vertical axis. Instructors reminded cadets repeatedly that the proper use of these control surfaces was essential to achieving "coordinated" flight—a smooth turn required the pilot to use the rudder and ailerons in concert. In the ground courses, the training emphasized the practical—teaching the student how to perform necessary operations—and theory was held to a minimum.

Richardson's Primary flying training included four standard phases. The pre-solo phase was essentially a refresher course for those who had first flown in the CPT program: taxiing, take-offs and landings, turns, gliding, stalls and spins, and flying in traffic. Cadets learned pilot awareness was critical—recognizing an impending stall, knowing when a stall has occurred, and being able to recover effectively were learned skills. "See it, hear it, and feel it."

In the second, or intermediate, phase, cadets learned precision of control by flying standard courses or patterns: elementary figures of 8, lazy 8s, pylon 8s, and chandelles. Cadets also practiced steep turns, maximum-performance power glides, stalls, and spins. The third, or accuracy, phase demanded high proficiency in various types of landing approaches and landings. The fourth, or aerobatic, phase required cadets to perfect loops, Immelmann turns, slow rolls, half-rolls, and snap rolls.[68]

The flight instruction used in Primary was simple but effective: when airborne, the instructor first explained, then demonstrated, each new maneuver. Students would then attempt the new maneuver, receive the instructor's critique, and then practice. Supervisors made important progress checks after 20, 40, and 60 hours of flight time. While in Primary, each cadet received 60–65 hours of flight training, half of which would be solo hours, and would make at least 175 landings. After 30 flight hours, cadets qualified for a civilian private pilot's license.

Like tens of thousands of future Army Air Force pilots, Richardson had flown a Piper J-3C Cub in the CPT Program. For his first flight at Ryan Field, he climbed into an open-cockpit Ryan PT-22 Recruit—a 160-hp two-seat trainer with a metal fuselage and fabric-covered wings. It had triple the power of the Cub, and could reach a speed of 125 mph, with a service ceiling of 15,400 feet. Nicknamed the "Maytag Messerschmitt," the PT-22 was described as "Odd looking and finicky to fly, [it] offered a challenge to cadet pilots [and] was known for its demanding ground handling characteristics."[69]

PT-22 Recruit. The United States Army Air Corps' first purpose-built monoplane trainer. (Wikimedia Commons)

During his aviation training, Richardson flew 25 different aircraft, including "94" shown below.

Under the rigorous program, cadets soon began to exhibit all the signs of exhaustion. Cadet Arthur R. Driedger Jr. commented: "Flying in an open cockpit kept one awake until he landed. After landing, almost everyone fell asleep at the table in the waiting room. I never knew whether it was the open air blowing on us, or the release of tension of flying that caused us to fall asleep, but it was a universal phenomenon."[70]

At various points in the course, cadets also learned how to bale out of an aircraft, control the descent, and avoid obstacles. Since the flight program also included at least one cross-country flight, cadets also received instruction in navigation and instrument flying.

Cadets also got a taste of Army regime—marching, ceremonies, inspections, military customs and courtesies, and vigorous PT. Cadets would first encounter the "real" Army when they reported to their next schools for Basic flight instruction.[71]

With the huge demand for qualified pilots, instructors quickly assessed a cadet's suitability as a pilot. Airsickness or poor coordination led to immediate washouts; cadets who could not catch on fast enough were also expelled. During the course of the war, over forty percent of cadets were eliminated before graduation—more than one hundred twenty thousand cadet pilots—many of whom would serve as bombardiers or navigators.

Samuel Hynes, in his book *Flights of Passage*, noted:

> I think not so much that the people they washed out couldn't learn to fly, but they couldn't learn to fly fast enough. You were expected to solo within 8 or 10 hours, and there were tests, but not like any test that I had taken at school or university. You couldn't cram for it, and you couldn't fake it. You weren't even being tested on something that you had studied, really, but

Aviation Cadet Leonard G. Richardson, Ryan Field, Class 43-B, G Flight. (Windsock, Ryan School of Aeronautics, and Richardson Family Archives)

on what you were. If you were a flier, you passed; if you weren't, you washed out. It became clear that some people were natural fliers, and some weren't. The athletes usually were; they used their bodies easily and naturally, and they seemed to make the plane a part of themselves.[72]

Primary had a high elimination rate but a relatively low casualty rate. Still, as Hynes observed: "Possibly during Primary, and certainly during Basic, the cold-blooded numbers took on visceral meaning. Few airmen ... escaped seeing or knowing about somebody who died in a training accident."[73]

Flying accidents were common: eight non-fatal accidents occurred at Ryan Field during Richardson's training, including one midair collision. Eleven fatal accidents occurred at the six other training bases in Arizona.[74]

The cadets of Class 43-B at Ryan did not suffer the dire fate predicted in the welcoming speech by the commander at San Antonio. Nonetheless, seven of the 60 would not survive the war. Two were killed in action, one flying a B-24 Liberator and one on D-Day while on a paradrop mission. Five were killed in non-combat flights, most likely in aircraft training accidents.[75]

Richardson's Pilot's Log Book records his first training flight on July 28, 1942.[76] He flew at least once each day and had soloed within a week of starting his training.

Their training had a sharpness that reflected the criticality of America's military posture in the Pacific. On the day of Richardson's first flight, the United States launched its first offensive operation in the war when bomber forces based in the New Hebrides began flying missions against Japanese positions in the lower Solomons in preparations for the Marine landings on Guadalcanal and the savage campaign that would ensue there.

CHAPTER SEVEN

Santo and Guadalcanal

Admiral Ghormley had been given roughly three weeks to create an invasion plan, assemble forces and *matériel* and rehearse the Marines' landings, and despite pleas from both him and MacArthur for more time, D-Day remained August 7. As a result, some aspects of Ghormley's plan, particularly regarding logistics, suffered from the haste of its development. As Admiral King later reported: "Because of the urgency of seizing and occupying Guadalcanal, planning was not up to the usual thorough standard," and the first American offensive action in the Pacific soon acquired the nickname "Operation Shoestring."[1]

But the southern Solomon Islands had never figured in the prewar plans of the U.S. Navy.[2] As preeminent WWII historian Samuel Morrison would later note, "If Admiral [Richmond K.] Turner's task force had been embarked on a voyage to the moon, the junior officers and bluejackets would have been only a little more ignorant of their destination than they were of Guadalcanal and the Solomons."

The tactical design included simultaneous amphibious assaults against Tulagi and Guadalcanal in a plan that was "creatively simple and incorporated limited deception ... it planned for mobility and speed of execution."[3]

***

The airfield on Espiritu Santo—designated Bomber 1—reached a point of operational readiness on August 1 and bomber operations from both Efate and Santo became near-constant. B-17 missions from both Efate and Santo carried full bomb loads since Efate-based aircraft could stop at Santo on the return leg to refuel.

Operational problems were rampant. Engines failed, missions were frustrated by weather, malaria and dengue hit the aircrews, and fuel was often scarce.[4] And the airfields were getting crowded. Major Harold Bauer, commander of the Marine air unit at Efate, noted that, on August, 3 there were over 50 aircraft on the field, of nine different types.[5]

Colonel Saunders, commander of the bomber forces, intended to maintain a striking force of nine B-17s at Santo, with a reserve strike force of 4–5, and an additional 4–9 for search missions. But launching nine bombers on a combat mission was rarely possible: there were no circulating taxiways on the airfield, and there was no lumber to build a control tower. Given the bombers' slow take-off rate, strike aircraft required more time aloft to assemble into an attack formation, leading to greater fuel consumption and ultimately smaller bomb loads. And still more time—and fuel—was needed should the bombers return to base after dark.[6]

Operations were made harder by the lack of accommodations for the air and ground crews at Santo.

> At first, things were even more primitive on Espiritu Santo than they had been on Efate. For a couple of weeks we ate K rations only and we slept on cots under the wings of our (B-17) airplanes, with the flaps lowered and bomb bay doors open to give us as much protection as possible from the rain. We did little but fly combat, refuel, bomb up, sleep and eat—and darn little of the latter two.[7]

B-17 reconnaissance missions were critically important but terribly fatiguing for the flight crews. In what would become standard practice, B-17s flew outward of Santo in a reconnaissance arc of 9 degrees in a flight that comprised 1,725 miles and covered an expanse of 50,000 square miles. But the work soon became a grinding routine; at a cruising speed of 150 mph, these missions were at least 12 hours in duration.[8]

On average, each day, 11 bombers would fly either a reconnaissance or a bombing mission, and these missions were costly. In the first four weeks of operations, the 11th Bomb Group (BG) lost 11 B-17s: one in combat, eight due to operational losses (weather, landing or take-off accidents) and two missing in action at sea.[9]

Both men and machines were rapidly wearing out. Getting spare parts, fresh engines, equipment, and supplies was a problem, as was the continuing shortage of bombardiers and navigators. On balance, though, given the high loss rate of the B-17s, it appeared the aircrews would outlast their equipment. In September, the 11th BG would begin receiving reinforcements when two squadrons of B-17s from the 5th BG arrived on detachment from Hawaii.[10]

***

Under the protective shield of severe storms and heavy cloud cover, the Allied invasion force made its final approach to Guadalcanal on the night of August 6. The next morning, 11,000 Marines of the 1st Marine Division landed four miles east of Lunga.[11]

Surprise was complete and, by the end of the second day, the Marines had secured the airfield and the nearby Japanese encampment, as well as Tulagi and adjacent islands.

As the Marines began to consolidate their positions around the airfield, a great uncertainty remained as to the strength of the inevitable Japanese response, a response that was immediate and would develop into a costly problem for Navy, Marine, and Army Air Force units committed to Guadalcanal.

On the night of August 9, forty-two hours after the American landings, Japanese warships entered the confined waters around Savo Island, immediately north of the landing beaches, a small stretch of water that would soon become known as "Iron Bottom Sound." At that point, the Japanese forces were detected and engaged by a 23-ship Allied cruiser/destroyer force—the bulk of the American Expeditionary Force's escort vessels. In this first direct naval engagement in the Guadalcanal Campaign, later termed the Battle of Savo Island, the Japanese force nearly annihilated the Allied naval forces, sinking three cruisers outright and causing a fourth, the Royal Australian Navy's HMAS *Canberra* to be later scuttled. The Japanese Navy—expert at night-fighting operations–left relatively untouched, delivering "the worst open-sea defeat in United States naval history."[12]

Following the hammering at Savo Island, Admiral Jack Fletcher, in command of the Expeditionary Force and its three carrier groups, retired from the immediate area to protect his carriers from attack by Japanese aircraft. The commander of the Amphibious Force, Admiral Turner, with four of his cruisers lost in the sea battle and without the cover of Fletcher's carriers, was forced to retire the next morning with many of his transports still not fully unloaded.

With their victory, Japan gained sea supremacy in the area north of Guadalcanal and seriously jeopardized this first offensive initiative by the Allied forces. So abrupt was this change of fortunes that a more forthright follow-up by the Japanese could have led to the defeat of U.S. ground forces on Guadalcanal and the collapse of the American initiatives in the South Pacific.

A Marine engineer battalion had begun to complete the Lunga airstrip and the first aircraft arrived on August 12. Within nine days, two squadrons of fighter aircraft from Marine Air Group 23 began operations from what was now designated Henderson Field.[13] By the end of the month, the Army Air Force's 67th Fighter Squadron also arrived at Henderson; these air assets came to be known as the "Cactus Air Force," derived from Guadalcanal codename. By the end of September, the newly arrived 6th Naval Construction Battalion had extended the airstrip to 6,000 feet and B-17s began arriving.[14] This new American air capability was a game changer and would have an immediate effect on the battle for Guadalcanal.[15]

Despite the ease with which the Marines had come ashore, the outcome was far from assured. "Not the most pessimistic old chief petty officer in the Expeditionary Force could have predicted that it would take twenty-six weeks' hard fighting by Navy, Marine Corps, Army and Air Forces to secure what had been occupied in little more than that number of hours."[16]

Overnight, the Marines' mission changed from a full offense to a cautious defense—particularly protecting the newly-captured airfield from a combined Japanese land and sea counterattack. The five-day mission now became open-ended, with no clear endgame, and while it was true the Marines had been left in a worsened position, the Japanese were in much more desperate straits. In the days immediately following the Marines' landing, Japanese forces on Guadalcanal were severely outnumbered, ill-equipped, and virtually unsupported.

By mid-August, Admiral Ghormley had grown deeply alarmed by the situation on Guadalcanal. He messaged Nimitz, King, McCain, and MacArthur: "It is my considered opinion that until ... the South Pacific area has been reinforced by air and troops ... there is a reasonable doubt whether the positions now occupied could be held."[17] If he did not get reinforcements soon, he told Admirals Nimitz and King, America stood to lose not only Guadalcanal but also other vulnerable positions in the South Pacific.

But the reinforcements Ghormley demanded would have to come by ship and, by mid-October, having fought three major naval battles in the waters of the southern Solomons, the U.S. Navy had failed to contain Japanese naval operations in the region. Nimitz reported to King: "It now appears that we are unable to control the sea in the Guadalcanal area. Thus our supply of the positions will only be done at great expense to us. The situation is not hopeless, but it is certainly critical."[18]

Three days later, after receiving King's concurrence, Nimitz replaced Ghormley as Commander South Pacific. "It was felt that Admiral Ghormley has not been successful for several reasons and that the critical situation there requires a more aggressive Commander." His replacement was Vice Admiral William "Bull" Halsey.

The Navy's inability to limit Japanese naval operations, particularly during nighttime hours in the waters north of Guadalcanal, permitted Japan to reinforce its beleaguered forces on the island. Beginning in late August, in what came to be termed the "Tokyo Express," Japan adopted a pattern of nighttime resupply and reinforcement; during the first two weeks of September alone, Japan made successful reinforcement runs on five separate occasions.

Reinforced and resupplied by intensified Tokyo Express runs, the Japanese forces on Guadalcanal launched a major effort to retake Henderson Field culminating in the Battle of Bloody Ridge (September 12–13). Coming within a whisker of succeeding, the Japanese suffered heavy casualties before breaking off the attack, but the strength of the attack confirmed the nighttime resupply runs could eventually prove successful for the Japanese.

The U.S. Navy was not able to interdict these resupply operations and, despite steadily increasing U.S. reinforcements and supplies, by the end of October the Japanese had as many men on the island as the Americans.[19]

Worse still, following these nighttime missions, Japanese naval forces would often stand off Guadalcanal and shell Marine shore positions, as occurred on the evening of October 13 when two Japanese heavy cruisers skirted Savo Island undetected and delivered a devastating bombardment on Henderson Field and its fuel dump that continued for three-and-a-half hours. So severe was the pounding that American commanders estimated the number of battleships at between four and six. "The accuracy and volume of fire were remarkable."[20]

Just as the Navy was confounded by its inability to deny Japanese ships freedom of movement in the seas north of Guadalcanal, so too did the Army Air Force find it impossible to deny Japanese aircraft freedom of operations over the southern Solomons. In the early weeks of the campaign, McCain's combined air assets faced a number of grim limitations: the Allies had no night-fighting capability; Henderson Field had insufficient fuel dumps and a too-limited maintenance and support capability; it was operating with less-than-optimum aircraft; and conditions at its most forward base, Espiritu Santo, were nothing short of primitive.

With all the flying being done, especially the long-range reconnaissance missions, the pilots were hammered with fatigue. During September, some aircrews had flown as many as seventeen consecutive days on missions of up to thirteen hours. With poor conditions at Santo, some returned from combat missions and went to bed without being fed, only to rise the next morning for yet another mission. The only good news for the aircrews was that mosquito control was effective on Santo; the bomber aircrews in September and October were little affected by malaria or dengue. That good fortune would change as the bombers moved forward to the intensely malarial Guadalcanal.

Following "Black October," with Marines ashore and the Navy fighting Japanese naval forces to the limit of their capability, the Joint Chiefs concluded the game was worth the candle and began committing more Army assets to the South Pacific:

> The race [for Guadalcanal] had been far too close for comfort. But now from November forward, the Allied potential began to show … men, ships, guns and planes reached Guadalcanal in numbers sufficient to provide a modest margin of safety.[21]

Included in the surge were all three regiments of the Army's Americal Division, which arrived on Guadalcanal between October and December. The battle-hardened but disease-wracked 1st Marine Division left Guadalcanal on December 9 and General Alexander Patch, the man who had led the first Army forces to the South Pacific with Task Force 6814, was named in overall command of the island. In less than a week, units of the Americal Division would be fighting through the thick jungle in an attack against what proved to be a Japanese stronghold on Mt. Austen.[22]

***

When the Marines landed at Guadalcanal the seas were far from safe for Allied ship traffic and it soon became apparent resupply of ground and aviation forces by air would be critical. Equally critical was the capability of evacuating badly wounded personnel to the base hospitals in New Caledonia and New Zealand.

Marine Utility Squadron (VMJ) 253, flying R4D-1 aircraft—the Navy's designation for the Army's C-47 troop/cargo aircraft—had arrived in the South Pacific in late August and made its first landing at Henderson Field on Guadalcanal on September 3. A second Marine unit, VMJ-152, also flying R4D-1s, arrived at New Caledonia a month later; both units began operating as Marine Air Group (MAG) 25. A third transport unit—the Army Air Force's 13th Troop Carrier Squadron (TCS), arrived at Plaine des Gaiacs on New Caledonia on October 10, and began operations into Guadalcanal on the 19th.[23]

By the end of October, these units had delivered 105 tons of food, medical supplies, fuel, and war *matériel* to the largely isolated marines on Guadalcanal, along with five tons of mail and 339 passengers. Small arms, grenades, bombs, and torpedoes for the U.S. Navy's PT boats were delivered, as were aircraft engines and replacement parts. Spent aircraft engines were returned by air to Espiritu Santo for rebuilding, then delivered back to Guadalcanal to keep Army Air Force and Marine air units in the fight.[24]

The aircrews of the 13th TCS became immediately aware of the dangerous flight operations they were about to undertake. On the day before the 13th's arrival, a heavily loaded aircraft from VMJ-253 took off from Tontouta on an early morning flight to Guadalcanal. Flight conditions were terrible: the ceiling and visibility were 50 feet and less than a mile respectively. The pilot, a veteran TWA airline pilot before the war, crashed into a mountain half a mile from base, killing the crew of five and the three passengers.[25] These first resupply missions from New Caledonia to Henderson Field were nearly 900-mile overwater flights in unarmed and generally unescorted aircraft. Over Guadalcanal, air superiority was still being contested, enemy fighters were often present, and the airfield itself was often shelled; transports often flew and landed under enemy fire.[26] Adding to the challenge, at that time in the region, pilots had no radio navigation aids, and every mission depended on accurate dead reckoning, celestial navigation, or by identifying ground features.

The strain on flight crews never abated during the campaign. Conventional wisdom within the Army Air Forces at the time held that five days of intensive combat was about all men could stand but if they were rested at intervals they might hold out for three weeks. Despite this, combat pilots on Guadalcanal remained in combat for six weeks or more because there were no replacements. The workload of the aircrews all across the South Pacific was staggering.

General Harmon recognized that his aircrews were almost too tired to carry on, but he could give them " … no reasonable assurance as to how long they will have to carry the ball. To them there appears no end—just on and on till the Jap gets them."[27] By November, Harmon could only describe the condition of the bomber crews as "more and more rapidly approaching the point of exhaustion."[28]

In July, before the start of the Guadalcanal Campaign, the War Department had issued a circular directing that "Combat crews be relieved after 100 to 125 hours of combat operational flying and returned to a rest area for a period not to exceed one week," but it also carried the proviso "if the local situation permits."[29] In fact, in all theaters of the Pacific War during its first year, there were far too few replacement crews to follow that rotation policy. Combat tours continued to look open-ended.

A rest camp—an "Aviatorium"—was set up in Auckland, New Zealand, in conjunction with the American Red Cross and, after roughly one hundred sixty hours of combat, aircrews received seven-day stays. In comparison, and underscoring the critical shortages of aircrews in the Pacific, bomber crews in the Eighth Air Force in England could complete their entire combat tour in as few as 150 hours and be returned home. South Pacific aircrews simply returned to combat after their short rest camp.[30]

Short leave periods could temporarily extend a man's usefulness in combat, but his efficiency nearly always reached a point where relief from combat and a return Stateside was necessary. The 23rd Marine Air Group is a case in point. It was the first aviation unit to arrive at Henderson Field on September 20; by mid-November the entire group was relieved from combat: when evacuated, all the remaining pilots in MAG 23 were incapable of rehabilitation in the SoPac and were returned to the United States.

By December, the Thirteenth Air Force Flight Surgeon estimated that, out of the entire 11th BG, fewer than 10 flying officers could pass a standard medical exam. Flight crew shortages had become critical—of the 60 bomber crews of the 11th and 5th Bomb Groups, 25 lacked navigators and 10 were without bombardiers.

For its part, the Navy's operations began to shape the Guadalcanal Campaign. Under Halsey's leadership, three more savage naval battles would be fought by year's end and the U.S. Navy established firm control of the waters of the southern Solomons.

Recognizing further efforts on Guadalcanal would be fruitless, Japan's Imperial General Headquarters ordered the evacuation of all Japanese forces from Guadalcanal. They directed a new line of defense be established on New Georgia in the northern Solomons. By the end of the first week of February 1943, after six months of intense combat, during which time scarcely a day passed without action on land, in the air, or at sea, Japan had evacuated nearly twelve thousand men from Guadalcanal. The U.S., acting on misinterpreted intelligence, did not attempt to interdict the Japanese evacuation fleet. Guadalcanal was secure.[31]

***

Both the Japanese and American initiatives at Guadalcanal had been driven by the calendar and the clock. Neither side expected, nor had prepared, for the six months of fighting that followed the American invasion on August 7.

The "shoestring" planning for the American invasion—as impressive as it was when viewed objectively—resulted in immense challenges for the Marines, the Navy, and the Army Air Force. Had time permitted better force preparation and logistics, the Guadalcanal Campaign would have been shorter and less costly. In its final report on the Guadalcanal Operation, the 1st Marine Division would report: "The decision of the United Nations [Allies] to attack was based upon ... reasons of the most compelling nature, it must be presumed, for seldom has an operation been under more disadvantageous circumstances."

With its defeat at Guadalcanal, Japan's relentless wave of victories in the southern Pacific was not just stalled, it was reversed. It abandoned plans to cut the Allies' Southern Supply Line and realized its fortress at Rabaul would soon lie within reach of Allied air power. Yet Japan still came away with a few positive, if costly, results. Perhaps most notably, the six-month campaign had slowed American initiatives in other areas and had given Japan time to strengthen key positions in the Solomon Islands, in the Bismarck Archipelago, and along the northeast coast of New Guinea. But the overall impact on Japan's military cannot be overstated: "Guadalcanal is no longer merely a name of an island in Japanese military history. It is the name of the graveyard of the Japanese army."[32]

Casualties and losses in the campaign—still somewhat ill-defined—illustrate the depth of the Japanese defeat, and the grinding attrition of the ground and naval action. The Allies suffered 7,100 dead and nearly eight thousand wounded. Japan lost over nineteen thousand troops, among which were over ten thousand non-combat losses—men who died of illness, ill-treated wounds, and starvation. Naval losses for Japan totaled 38 ships, including one light carrier and two battleships, and 683 aircraft lost. The Allies lost 29 ships, including one fleet carrier, and 615 aircraft.[33] Steep as those losses were, the casualty counts alone do not fairly represent the impact those many battles had on the war's outcome.

Ultimately, the retention and expansion of Henderson Field and the joint efforts of Allied air and naval forces led first to the denial of air and seaways to Japanese forces, and later to air and naval supremacy.

The turn of events on Guadalcanal exemplified a common theme about the War in the Pacific—the importance of time. Admiral Hart needed another ten months to complete the defensive preparations on the Philippines prior to the outbreak of the war. General MacArthur was just a week late in his New Guinea initiative—Operation *Providence*—in the summer of 1942.[34]

Perhaps most importantly, in retrospect, it is apparent that, had Japan acted a week earlier in building its airfield on Guadalcanal, or had American reconnaissance observed the airfield a week later, or had the Marine landings been delayed another week, the outcome on Guadalcanal would likely have been much different. Instead of American bombers and fighters operating out of Guadalcanal, it would have been, at least for a time, Japanese aircraft. And just as American air power on Henderson had dictated the campaign's outcome, so too would Japanese air forces, if successfully established at Henderson, have dictated the final outcome. It would have been Japanese bombers softening Espiritu Santo in preparation for a landing at Big Bay or Palikolo. Efate would be the next contested island and, after that, New Caledonia, Fiji, and Samoa.

Would such developments have led to the negotiated ceasefire Japan so much desired? That possibility has fostered endless speculation.[35]

CHAPTER EIGHT

Advance Base Button

By the end of August 1942, Leonard Richardson had completed 30 training flights and begun working on the precision-control phase of Primary, including the Pylon 8 maneuver.

This training maneuver involves flying the airplane in circular paths, alternately left and right in a "figure 8" around two pylons on the ground. The objective is to develop the ability to maneuver the airplane accurately while dividing one's attention between the flight path and selected points on the ground.

At this point in the Primary program, Richardson had nearly completed the program, with just six hours of flight training remaining. He had shown good promise as a pilot, and was the first in his flight to solo, but on September 4 he became the first to be "washed-out"; he'd completed 21 hours of dual instruction and 15 hours of solo flying.

The reason for his elimination from the aviation program is not known but the most common reasons were: insufficient progress for the amount of instruction time received; making the same mistake too many times; inability to receive and retain instruction; inability to relax while at the controls; and failure to make the necessary progress.[1]

Richardson appeared before the "wash-out board," a panel of six officers who reviewed notes from the personnel section, from his performance in ground school, and in PT. His squadron commander's evaluation was presented, and his scores from the Aviation Cadet Qualifying Examination (ACQE) were reviewed. Since he had a college degree, but was not going to be a pilot, the panel considered several options. He could become a weather officer, serve in engineering, service and supply, maintenance, or intelligence, or he could become a navigator or bombardier.[2]

In the very early months of the war, the Army urgently needed more qualified navigators, and was having a great deal of difficulty in processing enough cadets through their navigation school programs. The increase in navigator training was slower than for pilot training, and it was only in 1944 that the rate of trained navigators reached the Army's requirements. By war's end, 49,804 cadets had graduated from navigation schools and received commissions as second lieutenants.

In evaluating candidates for navigation training, arithmetical reasoning, dial and table reading, and general reading comprehension were key skills. Only those students with the highest scores in these areas had a good chance of completing their training successfully, and their selection became more restrictive than that for either pilots or bombardiers.[3]

Given Richardson's strong math scores in the ACQE tests, and in considering he had been a math and science teacher at Charles Adams High School, the panel concluded he could best serve the war effort as a navigator, and on September 14 he was relieved from duty at Ryan Field and directed to report back to the Santa Ana Army Air Base (SAAAB) for Pre-Flight Navigation School.[4] Also washing out and reporting back to SAAAB was Richardson's fellow cadet, Raymond Smith, who was reclassified as a bombardier.

The day after being assigned to the Navigator training program, Richardson returned to Santa Ana for his second round of Preflight training. The base had much improved since his initial arrival there in March. Roads and walkways were less muddy than before, and he quartered in a standard GI barracks, instead of the tent he had first occupied.

To some extent, the instruction at SAAAB was a repetition of that included in the aviation cadet Preflight pilot training, and returning to SAAAB must have been a discouragement, especially having to complete the same "military science" courses: close-order drilling, instruction in voice and command, uniform and insignia, discipline, and military conduct. And just as in the Aviation Cadet Preflight instruction, great emphasis was placed on physical conditioning.

On many Army Air Force (AAF) bombers, the navigator and bombardier also manned a defensive machine gun. So, on completion of his navigation Preflight instruction in late December 1942, Richardson's next stop was a two-month stint at the Las Vegas Army Gunnery School, based at Wendover Army Airfield. He reported there on December 23, 1942.

In late 1942, the AAF's standard gunnery course was normally five weeks in duration.[5] Trainees worked with a variety of machine guns, turrets, and sighting procedures in the familiarization phase, but the majority of training was on the .50-caliber machine gun, which had become standard equipment on American bombers.

Sixty-five hours of instruction was given in the ground-firing phase, initially using weapons as simple as B.B. guns[6] in stationary firing but soon progressing to larger-caliber machine guns. Later in the course, students manned truck-mounted machine guns and practiced against targets that were also moving.

In aerial gunnery training, cadets flew in training aircraft, such as the AT-18 Hudson gunnery trainer, and fired at targets towed by utility aircraft.[7] For final qualification, "Career" gunners—those whose sole function was as an aerial gunner—had to score 20 hits on a target plane from 100 rounds of ammunition fired. Richardson would not have qualified: in two training flights, his high score was 19.[8] But he was close, and might have qualified had his Gunnery School assignment not ended two weeks early, on January 20, 1943, possibly due to the Army's urgent need for navigators.

Along with 39 other aviation cadets, he was assigned to Class 43-7 of the Advanced Navigation School at Mather Field, about twelve miles east of Sacramento, with a report date of January 22.[9] Illustrating that every bomber needed a bombardier, but not every bomber needed a navigator, also reassigned from Las Vegas were 113 aviation cadets who were reassigned to the Bombardier School at Victorville, California.

As Richardson made his way to navigator training, the war news from the Pacific brightened considerably. U.S. Army and Navy forces at Guadalcanal were nearing the successful end of that terrible campaign. With Japanese forces preparing to evacuate Guadalcanal, the American Joint Chiefs issued an important statement of strategic intent for the coming year which clearly committed Army, Navy and AAF forces to aggressive action in the South Pacific, action that would involve most of the young men in Richardson's training cohort at Mather Field.[10]

The new navigator cadets were told in plain English that the navigator's job was two-fold: to know the aircraft's position at all times (location), and to provide the pilot with the necessary directions to fly the aircraft to the mission's intended destination (direction).

The program at Mather was 15 weeks in duration, most of which—five hundred hours or so—was spent in ground instruction devoted to teaching the various forms of navigation. Theory was reduced to a minimum in favor of practical how-to instruction.[11]

> Navigation, using the procedures practiced in WWII, was an art and not a science. However, during ideal situations, it could be reasonably accurate. The purpose of the Advanced Navigation School was to teach students to navigate accurately under those ideal conditions, and to navigate successfully under non-ideal situations.[12]

Instruction began with an introduction to the basic principles of navigation, and cadets became familiar with the tools they would use on every flight: the compass, drift meter, altimeter plotting sheet, and logbook. Ground instruction also included sections on weather and instrument calibration, as well as on military science and PT.

The training curriculum was precisely defined in every respect. For example, cadets spent 2½ classroom hours studying "Names of Constellations and the Navigational Stars"; four hours in "Theory of Radio Navigation," and four hours in "Vector Diagrams and Graphical Solutions."[13]

Beginning in the fourth week of the program, and concurrent with ground instruction, the students would make up to twenty navigation flights, often in AT-7 Navigator advanced training aircraft, applying what they had learned on the ground to real-world conditions. On these flights, generally including three trainees and an instructor, the cadets flew simulated navigation missions, and problems involving rendezvous, search, and patrol sorties. During nighttime flights, they practiced celestial navigation.[14]

Four methods of navigation were used in that era of flight, but the objective of navigation training was to qualify students as precision dead-reckoning navigators with basic proficiency in pilotage, radio, and celestial navigation.

In Dead Reckoning, navigators record the position of the airplane by keeping an accurate account of the track and distance flown over the earth's surface from the point of take-off or last-known position. It can be performed whether visibility is good or not and is normally done to some extent on all flights as a cross-check of the accuracy of other methods of determining position, and as a convenient method of maintaining the log sheet.

In Pilotage, the navigator confirms the plane's position and course by recognizing ground features—rivers, cities, mountains, etc.—and locating them on a map. Obviously, this method can only be used in conditions of good visibility and was of little value on overwater flights with no landmarks.

In Radio Navigation, a radio compass is used to detect and chart the bearings of two or more ground radio stations of known locations. This method is the least accurate because radio signals can be bent by weather conditions or topography but could be useful as a check on dead reckoning or pilotage navigation.

Navigator cadets at work. (United States Army Air Forces)

Aviation Cadet Norman C. Richardson, April 1943 (Richardson family archives)

Celestial Navigation is the most sophisticated of the methods. The navigator, having memorized the identity and location of 50 stars that might possibly be used for navigation in various parts of the world, used an octant to determine the angular elevation of a known bright star or stars. The precise locations of the stars in the heavens were tabulated and available to the navigator, and celestial navigation was accurate to within about 10 miles. On long overwater flights, such as those commonly flown in the Pacific Theater, celestial was often the only navigation method possible.[15]

The trainee had to be able to navigate by day within a course error of 1.5 degrees and a time error of 1.5 minutes per hour of flight, and to navigate in darkness by celestial means and over distances up to the full range of the training aircraft to within 15 miles of his objective.

The trainees learned that the protocol followed in a flight mission was fairly standardized and reflected the need for close communication between the pilot/s and his/their navigator. Prior to a mission, pilots and navigators reviewed the flight plan of the route to be flown, received weather reports, and confirmed their expected airspeed and altitude. During the mission, the pilot/s informed the navigator of changes in altitude, course, or airspeed.

In just under twenty weeks from the start of their training at SAAAB, 90 navigation cadets, including Richardson, were notified on May 7, 1943, that they had completed the course of instruction for navigators.[16] Richardson was given an Honorable Discharge as an enlisted man, and on May 8 was sworn into the Army Air Corps Reserve as a 2nd lieutenant, serial number O-744866.[17] At the same time, he received his Rating as Aircraft Observer (Aerial Navigator).

Richardson celebrated *Cinco de Mayo* at Mather Field as a brand-new 2nd lieutenant in the Army Air Corps—a qualified navigator ready for assignment to a combat unit.

And midway through Richardson's navigator training, he learned that his twin brother Norman had also made a decision about his military service. As a married man with a child, Norm's call-up had been deferred and he had been teaching and coaching at Prosser High School in south-central Washington State. In the 1942–43 school year he coached Prosser's football and basketball teams to league titles, but by the spring of 1943 his number was up and he enlisted in the Army. Like his brother, he applied for and was accepted into the Aviation Cadet Training Program, and was assigned to AAF Weather School in Grand Rapids, MI,[18] his robust football build probably disqualifying him from the pilot training program.

During the months in which Richardson had undergone pilot training, then gunnery and navigator training, the shape of the global war had transformed entirely. In the Pacific, Japanese forces ended their resistance on Guadalcanal in February, Admiral Halsey's forces launched campaigns against Japanese positions in the Solomon Islands to the north of Guadalcanal, and in June MacArthur launched the initial phases of his much-anticipated Operation *Cartwheel* with the invasion of New Georgia midway up the Solomon Islands chain. Russian forces began an offensive against Stalingrad, forcing its surrender two days later. General Dwight Eisenhower was given overall command of the North African Theater of Operations and, in April, Admiral Yamamoto, Commander in Chief of the Japanese Combined Fleet, was killed when his aircraft was ambushed by AAF P-38 Lightning pilots. Richardson might have felt the war was in full cry and he would be leaping onto a moving train. His brother Norman's future service with the armed forces was also clarified about the same time: in March he had enlisted in the Army and was assigned to the Plans and Training Division after basic training, and later in the year would be accepted into the AAF Cadet Program.

He was assigned temporarily to the 668th Navigation Group at Mather Field, along with four other recent graduates from the Navigation Program: Lieutenants Richard Fager, Herbert R. Kitto, Philip M. Smith, and Bryce E. Sammon. All received their standard navigator "kit": a Type A-12 Sextant, a Hamilton Master Navigator Watch, an Elgin Ground Speed "Jitterbug" watch for determining ground speed, and a Waltham Type A-11 Navigation (Hack) watch.[19]

They were still uncertain about which theater of operations they would report to, what type of unit they would be assigned to, and what type of aircraft they would fly. Bomber units were a strong likelihood, and that would have taken them into one of the most dangerous combat assignments in the war.

On May 8, they received their standard Personal Equipment, which also gave no hint as to the direction they might be going. Included in the kit were both winter and summer helmets, light and winter jackets, winter trousers, and summer suits.[20] A notation on the equipment record admonished Richardson: "This equipment is issued to you for the Duration ... You are personally responsible for its care."

Richardson was in a "holding pattern" during this time at Mather Field. As he noted in a letter home on May 16:

> They have been holding me off so long—as they have all the cadets & new officers—that it should really be a big day when I get to see you again ... I'm attached to the school that I went thru—Echelon 31 & am helping out the instructors there. Also when any planes go for a trip & need a navigator, I go along.

By May 21, he had at least a partial answer about his future assignment. He explained in a letter to his parents:

> Yesterday the Major called 6 of us in and informed us that we were being sent out immediately to Salt Lake City. Now I am all packed and am awaiting further orders. As soon as we get our special orders thru Santa Ana, we will leave.
> Of course we are all excited—as to what type of plane we'll be in—I want the new B-29— and who the rest of the crew will be. Also we'll see new country—learn lots of new things.[21]

By the spring of 1943, Richardson had been in the Army Air Forces for 14 months and undergone 11 months of flight training, navigation instruction, and gunnery school. He'd received innumerable physical examinations and been inoculated for smallpox, typhoid, and tetanus.[22] A newly commissioned second lieutenant and a fully qualified navigator, he was eagerly awaiting his next orders; he knew, with the urgent demand for navigators, he would not have long to wait.

On May 22, with nine other men from the Mather Field Navigation School, Richardson was ordered to Army Air Forces Technical Training Command in Kearns, Utah—a temporary duty assignment pending further orders.[23] While at Kearns, he was given another physical examination, and was found to be "physically qualified for Foreign Duty."[24]

At that time, flight personnel from around the country were being collected at Kearns, including from the Applied Tactics School at Orlando, the Navigation School at Mather, the West Coast Training Center at Santa Ana, and from flight-training programs at bases around the country; all assigned to temporary duty pending further assignment.[25]

His assignment to Kearns was brief: navigators were hot commodities at that time in the war, particularly by the Army Air Forces operating in the South Pacific. A week after arriving at Kearns, Richardson and 55 other officers, including six of the navigators who had accompanied him from Mather, received orders to depart Kearns immediately, to entrain to Camp Stoneman, Pittsburg, California, and to report to the San Francisco Port of Embarkation (POE) to await "further orders for water transportation to overseas destination, semi-tropical climate." Richardson's navigator friends included Bamberger, Gonder, Hauan, Sammon, Seliga, and Smith. Of his fellow officers, Richardson was best acquainted with Smith, with whom he had undergone training at the Las Vegas Aerial Gunnery School in December and January. In addition to the tropical summer clothing he would be issued, he was to receive a tube of skin ointment, a tin of shoe-waterproofing cream, a shelter half tent, a gas mask, and a first-aid packet.[26] They were assigned to shipment AJ-707-E, aboard US Army Transport (USAT) *Puebla*, taking their places among the million-and-a-half servicemen who would ship out to Pacific assignments through the San Francisco POE during the course of the war.

In their orders, the men learned the San Francisco POE would be their final point of embarkation for foreign service, and wives should not accompany them.

A big question had been answered—they all knew they were headed for the tropics—the Pacific Theater of Operations, the South Pacific, but they still did not know what they would be doing. Navigators could be assigned to a bomber unit, a troop-transport unit, or a reconnaissance unit, and, depending on the assignment, they might fly a variety of missions, including bombardment, ground attack, long-range reconnaissance, weather sorties, troop transport or cargo.

As a second lieutenant, Richardson would earn a base salary of $150 per month, plus "Additional pay for foreign service" equal to 10% of his base salary, and 50% more for flying. His total pay was $247.50 per month, about twice what he was paid in 1942 as a teacher at Charles Adams High School in Clarkston.[27]

***

With Guadalcanal secured by the end of February 1943, the Allies immediately began to develop and implement plans to occupy additional points in the northern Solomons.

In the days before Guadalcanal, with the U.S. in defensive and reaction mode, its strategies demanded one sort of logistics. But now, the expansive American offensives required a much different set of logistical plans and capabilities. Delivering and maintaining ground troops and aviation units at the point of conflict required both a strong Navy, a reliable supply chain, an array of advanced bases at which the Navy itself could be maintained and provisioned, and Army Air Force cargo transports for rapid delivery of men and materials to the battle zone, and for the evacuation of wounded. A "shoestring" approach to war would no longer do.

Pearl Harbor and Manila were considered for use as advance bases, but in the war that came, Manila, Wake, and Guam quickly fell to Japan, and Pearl rapidly became too distant to serve as either a forward base or a launch point for offensive action. It was clear to all that advance naval bases would be required, mainly in undeveloped locations well north of the Bora Bora–Tonga–Efate line.

As part of its strategic plan for advance base development, the Navy carefully defined the responsibilities of the Army and Navy. The Army was to occupy and defend the island where the base was located and to assist in the defense of ships and other bases within the operating range of aircraft of the island. This was to be accomplished in part by constructing and operating airfields, deploying an infantry regiment as a garrison force, and establishing a coastal-defense system. The Navy built and operated the naval advance base, including a PT boat facility, radio station, naval depot, seaplane base, and harbor facilities. The Navy also installed fixed naval guns, contributed to the building of airfields suitable for heavy bombardment unit operation, and assisted the Army in island defense.

Thus far, the Navy had not yet settled on base locations. Just weeks after General Rose's occupying force had arrived at Espiritu Santo, the Commander of the Pacific Fleet dispatched his confidential advisor to survey various South Pacific islands as candidates for a more northerly advance naval base site. That advisor, former polar explorer Admiral R. E. Byrd, immediately recognized the unique advantages Espiritu Santo offered for naval operations. The Segond Channel was possibly the best in the South Pacific. It was eight miles long and nearly a mile wide, with an "unlimited" depth and a sandy/coral bottom. It could accommodate a large number of naval and merchant vessels and, very importantly, its entrances were narrow and easily protected with anti-submarine nets. Other natural harbors on Santo, notably Palikulo and Turtle Bays, offered the possibility of developing ancillary port and service facilities.

Espiritu Santo was the northernmost island at which a large base could be established short of the Solomons, and conveniently fell halfway between Noumea and Guadalcanal. The southeastern region of Santo was large enough, flat enough, and well-enough drained to allow siting airfields, airplane shops and storage, magazine depots, hospitals, and harbor defensive facilities and the like. Finally, expatriate planters had already cleared many locations in Santo for palm tree plantations, and in other areas the remaining dense jungle could provide camouflage against marauding Japanese aircraft.[28]

By November 1942, Espiritu Santo was chosen as the site of the Navy's first Advance Naval Base and assigned codenamed *Button*.

It is challenging to comprehend the scale of what was being planned: the Navy intended that Base Button would be equivalent in capacity and capability to Pearl Harbor. The equipment, material, and manpower needed to effect this transformation at Santo was mind-numbing.

Equally astonishing was the timeline for this transformation. Pearl was developed over a period of 30 years, following the establishment of Naval Station Pearl Harbor in 1908. Advance Base Button would rise from nothing, with no local materials, in mere months—a phenomenal undertaking.

Just a year before, Admiral King had confided to Admiral Nimitz that "As a practical matter, the installation ... of maintenance facilities, such as shops, wharves, and dry docks, is a laborious procedure taking, under the best of circumstances, two to five years."[29]

As they had shown with the construction of Bauer Field on Efate or Bomber 1 on Santo, joint Army–Navy efforts could build a serviceable advance airfield large enough for heavy bombers with a small cadre of engineers and equipment operators, and a handful of bulldozers, in just a couple of weeks. All they needed was a safe place to work.

In October, Nimitz would comment on the speed with which the airfield was completed: "Our superiority over the enemy in air-field construction has been an outstanding element of our success so far. It is not too far-fetched to say that the American bulldozer and grader deserve a place with the American ship, plane, and gun as agencies for victory."[30]

But in the new year of 1943, timelines were long, but timing was of the essence. Surely the Navy could not wait years for advance base development—the ground offensives planned for the northern Solomons would slow to a crawl if the Navy found itself hampered by a lack of base support.

The Chief of Naval Operation's decision set Espiritu Santo's fate against the course of the war. From nothing, the island of Espiritu Santo would become a naval supply operation to rival any in the world.

While suited perfectly as the site was for a naval base, in terms of infrastructure Santo lacked everything the Navy required. But so did every other candidate site. The Navy had long realized that whatever facilities it required would have to be built from nothing, with shore installations hacked out of the dense bush or carved from local palm tree plantations.

The first Naval construction units to drop anchor at Santo were the 6th and 7th Construction Battalions (Seabees), which arrived at Santo's Segond Channel on August 11, 1942:[31]

> That first night, it rained—a cold, drenching downpour. There had been time to erect but few tents. Those who were without shelter built great coconut fires to dry and warm themselves, and slept as best they could in the open on army cots. Many of the men worked throughout the night on unloading operations, others were still aboard ship. That first afternoon and night was one of confusion and disorder; its memory conjures up a picture of disarray, of a jumbled hodgepodge of every conceivable kind of paraphernalia; or men working frantically to unload gear from small boats that threatened to swamp; of men working to clear the dock of its accumulating freight; of men deciding where things should be stowed, and shouting for someone to bear a hand: of men in coffee lines.[32]

> At this juncture, the camp would look nothing like a military base but rather like a military-tidy version of a Depression-era squatters' camp.[33]

> Difficulties in "Americanizing" this island and gearing it to the needs of modern warfare were immense. Roads were mere ruts in between the countless palm trees, there were no harbor facilities for the incoming ships to discharge vital cargo, the danger of malaria was ever present, the extreme heat together with the heavy rainfall were ever recurrent, there were no facilities for stowage or communications.[34]

Their arrival marked the beginning of the explosive development of Base Button. These Seabees were later joined by the 15th Construction Battalion (CB), which arrived at Espiritu Santo in the early morning hours of October 13, just in time for the base to be shelled by a Japanese submarine.[35] Compounding the challenges it faced on arrival at Santo, after establishing camp—tents, latrines, and field kitchen—and with its supplies streaming ashore, severe diarrhea struck all hands.[36]

In the coming few months, three more construction battalions would arrive at Santo.[37] These construction battalions were, at least on paper, equally qualified to construct an advance naval base. Each was equipped and staffed to build a bridge, a bomber base, or a bakery. They had the men to guarantee the end product would be built in the right place, to the correct design, and with the material they brought with them or could source locally. Whatever the project, they could plumb it, paint it, wire it, blow it up, burn it down, or bury it. The largely self-sustaining battalions included medical and dental units, mess and commissary, and engineering.

Sometimes working independently, other times in concert, these construction teams completed an astonishing number of projects, including three more airfields, miles of new roads, water wells, rock crushers and sawmills, six wharves and piers, utilities, warehouses and magazines, tank farms, hundreds of Quonset huts of all sizes, fuel pipelines and pumping stations, bridges, power plants, power-distribution systems, telephone, refrigeration, boilers, distribution, a concrete plant, base housing for Navy and Army personnel, hospitals, Red Cross buildings, an array of communication towers, a large seaplane base, a PT boat base, a huge crane and an enormous battleship drydock, a torpedo-overhaul shop, a mine-assembly plant, a ship-repair unit, and an aviation-overhaul base. "At every turn was improvisation and invention, made necessary by the shortages and lack of equipment and material"—a phenomenal achievement in a short period of time.[38]

The creation of the aviation-engine-overhaul base by the 36th CB is one example of the myriad of projects completed on Base Button. Located between Bomber 1 and Bomber 2, the unit provided overhaul facilities for aircraft engines, propellers, powerplant accessories, and for the major overhaul of instruments (bomb sight, radio, and radar equipment). In creating that single operating unit, the Seabees built 85 Quonset huts to house the unit's 250 officers and 1,800 enlisted men, 18 standard 40×100-foot arch-rib shop buildings, messing facilities, four Quonset huts on concrete decks for offices and instrument shops, and all necessary utilities. This one facility, unheralded in most war memoirs, was capable of overhauling 200 aviation engines a month.

As is suggested above, Santo in the summer of 1943 was in the midst of a developmental hurricane.[39]

Santo was essentially a green open field. Besides the coral mined and used for surfacing roads and runways, everything that went into this vast infrastructure was shipped to Santo from the United States. In many cases, early arrivals had to build their living quarters and work stations regardless of their rates and specialties. By the first week of January 1943—just six months after General Rose had finalized the selection of Espiritu Santo for advance airfields, the island had become a vast, functioning aerodrome complete with two bomber airfields, a fighter airfield, and all the infrastructure, equipment, and personnel to support offensive operations in the north. The units operating at Santo were ready to provide for the logistical support of a small naval task group.

During the earliest weeks of the Guadalcanal Campaign, units assigned to Santo were either strike units (like the 11th Bomb Group), construction units (like the 6th and 7th CBs), defensive forces (4th Marine Defense Battalion detachment or the elements from the 182nd Infantry Regiment) or supporting units' (hospitals, etc.). By the end of September 1942, with combat on Guadalcanal beginning to heat up, officers and men associated with these units on Santo numbered almost ten thousand.[40]

The Allies had initially tried to keep the existence of the airfield at *Button* a secret, but it was discovered on October 2, 1942, by a seaplane launched from the Japanese submarine *I-24*.[41] The submarine shelling on October 15 was not the first time and not the last time Santo would be shelled or bombed or that U.S. Navy vessels in nearby waters were attacked. In the 12-month period from October 15, 1942, to October 14, 1943, Japan attacked or overflew Santo on 16 occasions. Attacks ceased as the war increasingly turned against the Japanese in 1943.[42] The historian of the 29th Air Service Group recorded:

The sound of an air siren (sometimes it was the clanging of a tire iron against an iron ring), and the bright searchlights of the anti-aircraft battalions scattered around the island illuminating enemy planes while firing their guns, were frequent experiences ... Foxholes were dug in strategic locations in all unit areas. Huge palm tree logs were cut up and used to top off the holes which were later covered and camouflaged with palm fronds. At first this was very traumatic for practically everyone, especially when the noise of exploding bombs were heard. Later, as the incidents of raids were less frequent, some of the braver (?) men would stay outside with helmets on and watch as the lights followed the action. Foxhole safety and security was later verified when several tents were riddled by shrapnel and made believers out of everybody.[43]

Santo is a large island, but most Allied facilities were located in a small zone to the southeast corner, roughly an isosceles triangle encompassing 66 square miles, half

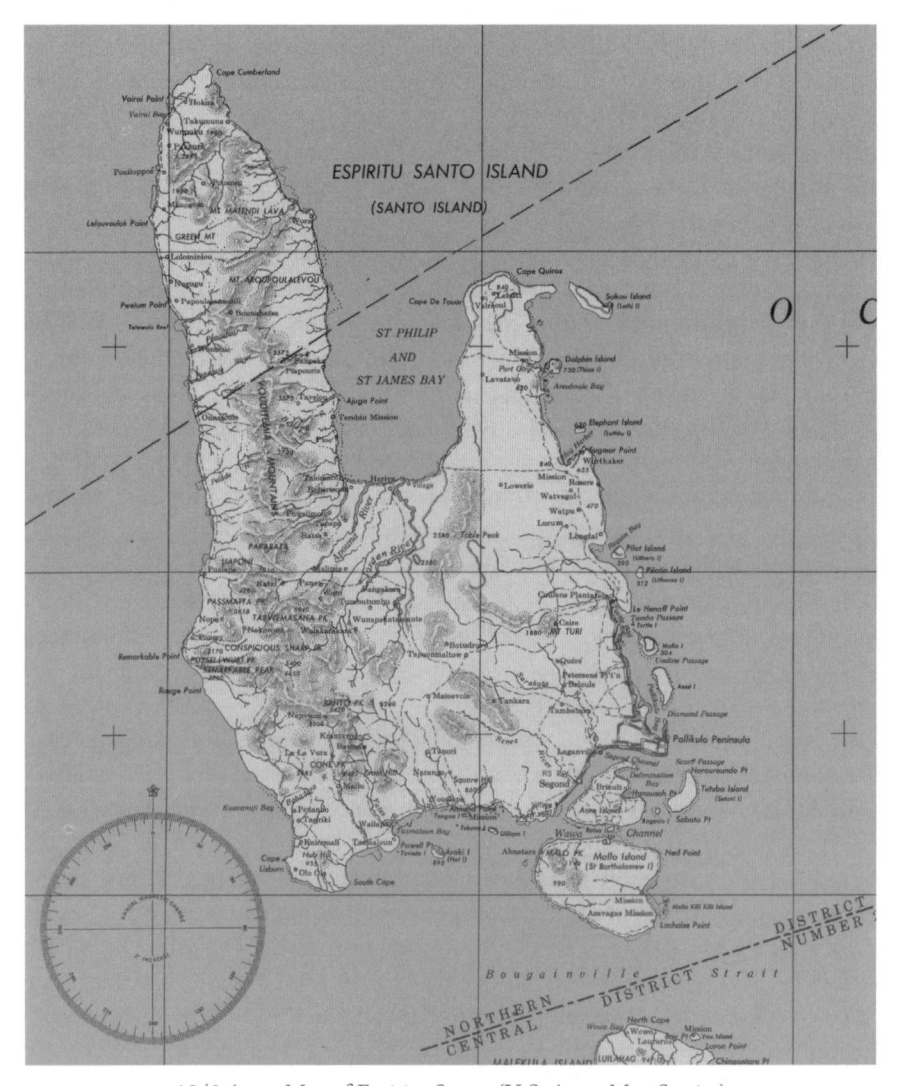

1943 Army Map of Espiritu Santo. (U.S. Army Map Service)

the size of Yellowstone National Park, about the size of Long Island, and a tad larger than the state of Rhode Island.

The base was commonly referred to as "Buttons" and, in the same day without leaving base or venturing far from his bunk, a serviceman could get a hot shower, have his laundry done, eat three hot meals, work a full shift, go for a swim, eat ice cream or drink a beer, get a haircut, post a souvenir to his family back home, go fishing, play baseball, take in a United Service Organizations (USO) show or watch a movie at one of the 54 cinemas, and get eight hours of sack time.

> There was some building or another every 100 yards in any direction, whether aircraft hangars, offices, camps, Quonset huts, tennis courts, sports grounds or workshops. Over 100,000 men were permanently stationed in Santo and over 500,000 passed through during the war. ... Every camp had electricity and running water. NCOs and officers their own refrigerators, and loudspeakers played music and relayed news daily. ... Fifty-four cinemas put on different shows every night ... [44]

Daily, the base bakery produced 12,000 loaves of bread, the servicemen ate vegetables of all types grown in Army gardens, and troops could read the base's daily newspaper, the *Santonian*, over breakfast.[45]

During 1943, logistics began catching up to combat, often in very odd ways. Author James Michener, once attached to a Navy supply depot on Espiritu Santo, would later record: "Three ships came in one week loaded mostly with paper. We built a special warehouse for it. One man did nothing but take care of brown manila envelopes! We had another man whose sole responsibility was pens, ink, paper clips, and colored pencils."[46]

The large recreation center built across the Segond on Aore and Mavea Islands offered beer bars, baseball fields, volleyball, horseshoe, tennis courts, handball, archery, soccer, badminton, and boxing arenas. Several baseball and basketball leagues operated on the island, and track, field, and boxing matches occurred regularly. And, despite the rough vegetation and occasional grazing cows, ardent golfers could maintain their handicaps on a rudimentary nine-hole golf course.

Santo became a popular stop for USO troops, and welcomed Bob Hope, Bing Crosby, Jack Benny, and dozens of other Hollywood entertainers and film stars. Tonkinese and settlers opened laundries, curio shops, and restaurants in Vila and Santo. Alcohol was rationed, so the sale of black market booze was particularly profitable. "Enterprising troops made 'jungle juice' from mangoes or pawpaw in illegal stills hidden in the bush. Some stole 'torpedo juice' (torpedo engine fuel), though a drinking bout of that usually ended with the revelers in hospital."[47]

America's arrival also marked the beginning of enormous change for the natives of Espiritu Santo. Positioned as it was on the Pacific's "Ring of Fire," the New Hebrides had experienced more than its share of earthquakes and tsunami, but nothing in their experience could have prepared them for the wave breaking over their heads as the American occupation of their island began to take hold.

The island's residents—both expat and indigenous—were astonished. Few of the planters had spent any appreciable time away from the New Hebrides, except for brief stops in New Caledonia, and were quite unaware of the evolution of agricultural machinery. The Americans' mechanized equipment—the bulldozers, drag lines, graders, and gang harrows—were new to them, and the increase in productivity they made possible were stunning. While the planters were glad of the American presence and provided whatever assistance they could, they had little conception of the magnitude of what lay ahead.[48]

The base at Espiritu Santo was hastily established to serve as a protective base for the base at Efate and to support operations during the Solomons Campaign—missions that had been ably completed. While the Navy would continue to develop Base Button, eventually spending over thirty-six million dollars at Espiritu Santo (half a billion in 2022 dollars), the fast-moving war would soon change the mission and character of the advance base.[49]

Within a year of General Rose's first steps ashore at the Segond Channel, Espiritu Santo would no longer be an advance base. Aviation remained a huge element in offensive operations out of Santo, but Allied military successes continued to move the front further to the north and west. Even as the Seabees were building Naval Advance Base (NAB) 140 (Base Button), plans were developing for creating other advance bases, bases that could be called upon to support further American advances. So while bombing and reconnaissance operations continued from Santo, Base Button had become a Supply, Service and Repair Base, a huge collection of everything needed to keep a modern military functioning—a brand new Pearl Harbor—but now well beyond any enemy threat.[50]

CHAPTER NINE

A New Garrison Force for Espiritu Santo

The practice of raising an army from within a local populace is as old as warfare itself. Particularly in foreign territories or colonies where aid from the mother country was remote in time and distance, civilians acted in their own defense, generally under the supervision of a territorial administration and with training provided by a small cadre of professional soldiers.

Commonly during America's colonial era, all able-bodied men between the ages of 16 and 60 were enrolled in their local militias; the reliance on a civilian militia only strengthened in the years leading to the American Revolution. Following independence, a sharp debate developed about the perils of maintaining a large standing army in peacetime. The State of North Carolina, in adopting its State Constitution in 1776, cautioned that "the people have a right to bear arms, for the defense of the State; and, as standing armies, in time of peace, are dangerous to liberty, they ought not to be kept up."[1]

Militias were subsequently, and frequently, raised within Illinois to deal with security threats, each continuing the heritage first established by early French and American musterings in the wilderness.[2] In 1810, shortly after completion of the Louisiana Purchase, the governor of the newly created Illinois Territory mustered a small armed force to quell the roving bands of Pottawatomi Indians that had taken to crossing the Mississippi into Louisiana Territory to raid the mostly French-speaking settlements there. That militia—the first recorded mustering of American civilians into the armed forces of Illinois—was the earliest direct progenitor of the 129th Infantry Regiment that would serve with great distinction in World War II.[3]

The 129th was mustered into service for the Black Hawk War in 1832, for the War with Mexico in 1846, for the Civil War in 1862, for the Spanish–American War in 1898, the Mexican Border conflict in 1916, and for the Allied Expeditionary Forces in 1917.[4] Continuing their history of citizen-soldiery, the 129th was mustered into federal service on March 5, 1941.[5]

Included in the muster was Morris Naudts, a man who joined the Illinois National Guard in 1937, had been commissioned as a second lieutenant in August 1940, and would one day command the 129th Infantry Regiment. Since the post-Civil War years, state militia units were organized with distinctly regional flavors in keeping with longstanding traditions. For example, the Third Regiment, created in 1876, had drawn its troops primarily from northern Illinois counties.[6] The 1941 mustering echoed the procedures established in 1876, and induction stations for the 129th opened in communities across northern Illinois. Naudts was assigned to the 1st Battalion, B Company—a unit recruited from the small town of Streater, Illinois. This pattern initially gave a distinctly local flavor to each of the infantry companies and special companies that formed the 129th Regiment.[7]

In mid-March 1941, these raw recruits were taken as a Regiment to Camp Forrest, Tennessee, 50 miles southeast of Nashville and "a few miles from the sleepy southern town of Tullahoma." It joined the 130th Infantry Regiment, together constituting the 33rd Infantry Division (the "Prairie Division").[8]

In aggregate, a full-strength regiment included 143 officers and 3,323 enlisted men—larger than the small northern Illinois towns many of the cohort called home. At the time it arrived at Camp Forrest, however, the 129th had a total strength of just 90 officers and 1,226 enlisted men—less than half its eventual strength.[9] While initially a distinctly northern Illinois assembly of troops, over the 18 months that the regiment would remain at Camp Forrest, it came to full strength largely courtesy of Selective Service. The newly arriving draftees gave the regiment a much more diverse flavor.

Training was intense, and no one in the regiment was exempt. The men underwent three training phases in the War Department's standardized 44-week-long Mobilization Training Program: Individual Training, Unit Training, and Combined Arms Training.[10]

Training continued during the spring and summer of 1941. "The one lesson that was never learned was how to keep from being miserable when dog tired and wet with sweat during the day and night."[11]

During August and September, the regiment participated in VII Corps field training exercises in Arkansas and Louisiana designed to harden and train the troops and evaluate the regiment's officer cadre. Incompetent and ineffective officers—including field grade and general officers—were quickly relieved of command. Conversely, officers showing strong leadership abilities were immediately recognized and assigned to higher levels of command. The regiment returned to Camp Forrest on October 7. The sought-after mobilization President Roosevelt desired had, at least with regard to the 129th, been attained.

***

Following the Japanese attack on Pearl Harbor, the regiment was dispersed throughout Tennessee and Arkansas to guard major cities, including Knoxville, Memphis,

Jackson, and Savannah. Other detachments were assigned to defend important industrial sites like the Alcoa aluminum plant, Norris Dam, and Chattanooga. Units also defended key military installations in the region.[12]

In June, the 129th began receiving newly commissioned ROTC and OCS second lieutenants, and other newly drafted enlisted men.[13] As it reached full regimental strength, the regiment approached full combat readiness with 48-hour field exercises, night and retrograde movements, live firing exercises, attack and defense, and combat firing exercises. "These exercises simulated combat conditions, in dense jungle, and proved to be invaluable in the months to come."[14]

By mid-July, the regiment received a movement alert to prepare for duty in the Pacific Theater of Operations: only the regiment's 2nd and 3rd Infantry Battalions were included in the embarkation: the 1st Battalion remained at Camp Forrest to form the cadre for the newly-created 123rd Infantry.[15] At the time the regiment received its movement alert, Maurice Naudts was commanding G Company, a rifle company in the 2nd Battalion.

As the regiment began making final preparations for overseas deployment, America launched its first ground offensive in the South Pacific, with Marines going ashore at Guadalcanal on August 7, 1942. This news, coming as it did with the 129th itself heading overseas, would have heightened the resolve of many in the regiment and, in more than just a few, stirred the place within where fear resided, and doubt.

During the night of August 18, after having lived and trained at Camp Forrest for 529 days, "the soldiers boarded the train at night and the trains quietly slipped through Tullahoma in the darkness. There were no bands or girls, but the men were not downhearted."[16] The regiment, if not yet battle-hardened, was battle-ready.

The regiment began arriving at Camp Stoneman, California, a central west coast military staging area, on August 21. The men received final physical exams, were immunized against tropical diseases, and settled into barracks. Company commanders ensured each man recorded correct next-of-kin, prepared a power of attorney, submitted pay allotments, and sent a postcard home to advise the family of his new Army Post Office address. Three-day passes were issued liberally and troops took advantage of the eateries and entertainment of nearby San Francisco—not knowing it would be 40 months before they would see America again.

In the South Pacific, Allied and Japanese forces desperately reinforced their ground troops on Guadalcanal. The fighting was intense, and the results were deeply uncertain, with the eventual fate of the war in the Pacific hinging very much on the outcome on that remote island in the Solomon Islands. No Army units had yet been sent to reinforce the Marines on Guadalcanal, but it was in everyone's mind—in all Army regiments in, or soon to be assigned to, the South Pacific—that they could be the Army's first commitments to the battle in the southern Solomons.

Ten days after its arrival at Camp Stoneman, the men of the regiment began to assemble in front of their barracks, with each man carrying a full pack, individual weapon, and a small bag of books, cigarettes, and sundries. They first marched to the nearby town of Pittsburg, then boarded a train for the short ride to Fort Mason.

> Emphasizing that there would be no talking or smoking during the short march to the troop train, and during the short trip from Camp Stoneman to the docks at Fort Mason in San Francisco, the general atmosphere during the march was one of somberness and realization that the regiment might soon be in combat with the Japanese. The only sound heard in the darkness was that of rifles rubbing against cartridge belts and boots striking the ground.[17]

Shortly after midnight, the regiment boarded ships that had recently been converted from grain carriers to troop transports: the 129th Regiment to the USAT *Torrens* (Norwegian) and the 130th to the USAT *Clip Fontaine* (Dutch).[18] Both ships had been built in 1939 and were equipped with five-inch guns and twin 40-mm anti-aircraft guns. Leaving San Francisco Bay on the afternoon of September 2, the regiment learned the convoy's destination shortly after passing under the Golden Gate Bridge: the island of Viti Levu in the Fiji Islands.

Eighteen days later, on September 20, in a voyage made longer by the convoy's evasive, zig-zagging anti-submarine tactics, the convoy dropped anchor in Suva Bay on the island of Viti Levu and, over the following several days, the regiment took up its assigned positions on the northwest side of the island.

Holding Fiji was critical to the Allies at this time in the war. It was one of the island strongpoints that received reinforcements shortly after Pearl Harbor to prevent Japanese forces from severing the all-important Southern Supply Line. By February, enough aircraft had arrived to offer some opposition to a Japanese attack, and the arrival of the 129th would make the island's defense all the more robust.

On arrival at Suva, the 129th Infantry Regiment was attached to the 37th Division—Ohio's "Buckeye Division," which had arrived at Suva three months earlier. Occupied as they were on Guadalcanal, a full-scale Japanese attack on Fiji was not likely but, at the time, Fiji was terrifically exposed—there were no other Allied forces between it and the Japanese military.[19]

In position on Viti Levu, the 129th included a headquarters company, a service company, an anti-tank company, two infantry battalions, a medical detachment, and three chaplains. The regiment was armed with carbines, machine guns, howitzers, rocket launchers, mortars, and pistols, all under the administration of the nine-officer headquarters staff. The motor pool included an assortment of 285 trucks, jeeps, and trailers and equipped—some would say encumbered by—with an enormous inventory of communication equipment, spare parts, tents, cots, buckets, ambulance flags, axes, sewing kits, hair clippers, snake-bite suction kits, whistles, cook pots, and all the other essential elements of a small mobile city.[20]

> The first few weeks on Fiji were spent digging beach defenses. Alternate and supplementary positions were then dug. In addition, each man had a foxhole next to his bunk in case of an air raid. There must have been some forty or fifty thousand holes dug on the northwest side of the island during the six months' occupation.[21]

The regiment's six rifle company commanders and platoon leaders developed plans for deploying machine guns, mortars, anti-tank guns, and howitzers for a variety of combat scenarios. The two battalions of the defensive forces also ran barbed wire, improved roads and bridges for better defensive lines of communication, and improved the island's airfields. Combat training expanded to include exercises in aircraft identification, jungle warfare, camouflage, night operations, and conditioning marches.[22]

The 129th's intensive jungle training continued for the next six months, and included combat problems that involved the movement of the entire regiment. The training of smaller patrols took them deep into the mountainous jungle terrain. "Small patrols were sent into the jungle to live off the land. The trips were to last four days, and just one K ration was taken to be used only in emergency."[23] One patrol from the 3rd Battalion, having no experience in mountainous, jungle terrain, completed a transit of the island, from Raki Raki in the north to Suva in the south, in just two weeks.

The men were toughened—every man, including clerks, was required to be able to march four miles, with a 40-lb pack, plus an individual weapon with ammunition, in 50 minutes. Later, the men would complete 25-mile marches, also fully loaded, in eight hours. Their morale and esprit-de-corps grew apace.

In January 1943, the 6th Field Artillery Battery was assigned to the 129th Infantry Regiment. The 6th was equipped with 105-mm Howitzers—short-barreled guns that fired shells in high trajectories, with steep angles of descent, to support infantry actions. With this new capability, the regiment was re-designated a "Combat Team," and it became clearer the 129th would soon receive a new assignment.

Japanese opposition on Guadalcanal ended on February 9, and Fiji became even less likely to see a Japanese landing. Soon after, the regiment received orders to prepare to depart Fiji. "February found the Regiment in Suva making plans for combat-loading ships for an unknown destination. With all the intensive training just completed, it looked as though a combat operation had been scheduled for the Regiment."[24] While the Japanese never came to Fiji, and the regiment was not yet battle-tested, the knowledge gained in establishing effective defensive positions would be of great value to the regiment's later combat operations.

The 129th began loading aboard USS *Hunter Ligget*, *American Legion*, and *Fuller* on March 7. By 7:00 a.m., March 11, the troopships, escorted by destroyers USS *Woodworth*, *Lardner* and *Buchanan*, sailed to the island of Espiritu Santo, northernmost of the New Hebrides islands and 400 miles south of Guadalcanal. Leaving Fiji after six months of garrison duty, the 129th was detached from the 37th Infantry Division and would again serve as a garrison force at their new station on Santo.[25] At the time, the 129th Combat Team consisted of B Company, 117th Engineer Battalion; B Company, 112th Medical Battalion; the 6th Field Artillery Battalion; and the 2nd and 3rd Battalions, and Special Units of the 129th Infantry.[26]

Army command on Espiritu Santo awaited the arrival of the 129th with keen anxiety and hoped for a better disembarkation than had occurred just five months earlier. On September 11, 1942, Commander in Chief Admiral King messaged Admiral Ghormley that an additional regimental combat team could be made available to bolster the South Pacific's defensive forces, for assignment at Ghormley's discretion.[27] In early October, the 43rd Division's 172nd Infantry Combat Team—virtually identical to the 129th Combat Team—had departed San Francisco aboard USS *President Coolidge* with its initial destination being Noumea, New Caledonia. The contingent included the complete 172nd Infantry Regiment, the 103rd Field Artillery Battalion, a detachment of the 118th Engineers, one from the 118th Medical Battalion, and the 54th Coastal Artillery—roughly forty-eight hundred officers and men with all their gear.[28]

President Coolidge arrived at Noumea on October 20, the same day Admiral Halsey replaced the somewhat embattled Ghormley as Commander South Pacific. Halsey immediately ordered the ship to Espiritu Santo, intending that the 172nd would initially serve as a defensive garrison force for Base Button while undergoing jungle combat training, and then be deployed to Guadalcanal to reinforce the hard-pressed Marines.[29] Two days later, *Coolidge* was within sight of its intended anchorage in the Segond Channel but, in making its final approach, struck one or more American mines that were part of the Navy's defensive arrangements for Base Button. The ship ran aground just long enough for all but two of the men and officers aboard to abandon ship—some walking to the nearby Santo shoreline. An hour and 20 minutes after hitting the mine, the ship heeled to port, slid off a coral ledge, and sank.[30]

"Army folklore has it that when the Commander of the 172nd Infantry Regiment, Colonel James A. Lewis, and the Island Commander, Brigadier General William I. Rose, met in waist-deep water, their exchange occurred as follows: 'Sir, Colonel Lewis, commanding, reports for duty.' Returning Colonel Lewis' salute, General Rose replied with a half-smile 'Go back and do it right.'"[31]

The 172nd, and the other units who made up the Combat Team, lost everything except the clothes on their backs. Everything that would make it an effective fighting force went down with the ship, including field-artillery pieces, the full complement of vehicles, a few light tanks, the regiment's supplies, equipment, food and ammunition, and the equipment of the 54th Coastal Artillery. Perhaps most consequential was the loss of 591 pounds of quinine—at the time, the entire stock held by the United States.[32] With more than five thousand men stranded and unarmed at Santo, the Army had to scramble to locate matériel and equipment to return the 172nd to combat readiness.[33]

To everyone's relief, the convoy carrying the 129th Infantry Regiment dropped anchor safely in the Segond Channel at Espiritu Santo just after noon on March 13. They joined dozens of cargo ships at anchor, all waiting to offload their equipment and supplies.[34]

The 129th's assistant operations officer, Captain Curtis Craver recalled his first impressions:

> The first surprise was seeing the mass of ships in Segond Channel. Santo was a large naval and air base, and from the looks of things it was growing by leaps and bounds through the efforts of the Seabees. ... The speed with which they worked was incredible; even so, only a small portion of the island had been touched by the time the Combat Team arrived.[35]

With *Hunter Ligget* at anchor, the troops climbed down cargo nets into waiting landing craft (LCVPs) and were ferried to the beach. Regimental guides met them at the beach and escorted them to assigned bivouac areas on the eastern side of the island. The regiment's equipment and stores were all offloaded by midnight.[36]

The regiment's two Battalions took positions on opposite sides of the growing base: the 2nd Battalion to the southeast, along with the regimental headquarters, the medical, engineering, and service units, and A Battery of the 6th Field Artillery. The 3rd Battalion and C Battery of the moved to the northeast. With limited shoreside transportation and poor roads, the 3rd Battalion marched the seven miles to their assigned position, just south of the new Marine fighter base at Turtle Bay. Each battalion dispersed its companies several hundred yards apart to minimize casualties in the event of an air raid.

The 129th began developing beach defenses—a task for which they had been well prepared on Vitu. Companies and squads established firing positions for machine guns and mortars and cleared communication trails between units from the dense jungle. Additionally, delaying positions were established inland, and larger supporting weapons were attached to the Combat Team.

Morris Naudts would later comment:

> Although there were some similarities between Fiji and Espiritu Santo ... the top layer of soil on Santo was very thin on a rough coral base. Which during the frequent rain squalls soon became a sea of gooey, stinking, slimy mud. The stench that emanated from the ooze in the stinking mud reminded me of a piggery—the only thing missing were the grunts of pigs.[37]

> Weather wise, Espiritu Santo was subject to frequent downpours, causing everything to remain damp, which in turn promoted rapid growth of mold, mildew and rust, causing deterioration of clothing, shoes/boots, canvas equipment, and tentage. Because of the frequent rains there were standing pockets of water which turned into breeding areas for mosquitoes. This coupled with the decaying coconuts caused the air to be filled with flies, as well. Combat engineers and Navy Seabees worked to draining the swampy areas, and over time the bivouac areas became relatively free of these pests.[38]

It was clear the 129th would soon be assigned a combat role and that their next posting would likely be to mountainous jungle terrain. Espiritu Santo was the perfect training locale.

> Groups ranging in size from a squad to a battalion sometimes spent a week living and maneuvering in the bush. These problems were excellent for physical conditioning and living in the jungle.

Stoves for heating C rations were improvised; helmets were used for washing, shaving and brewing coffee; lean-tos were made with ponchos, shelter halves, or banana leaves; hammocks were improvised out of shelter halves and vines; bamboo, coconuts, and vines furnished an emergency source of water, and although lectures were given on edible jungle plants, soldiers stuck to C rations supplemented with bananas, papayas, oranges, mangos and coconuts—when they could be found.[39]

The company hauled coral sand from the adjacent beach to create paths through the bivouac area:

Within a matter of days all units of the Regiment were connected by an infrastructure of coral surfaced roads which served several purposes, one being the ability to rapidly convoy troops from one defensive position to another, in event of an attack, and timely resupply of ammunition and supplies to all units.[40]

The troops were soon able to use surplus dunnage—rough sawn boards used in securing cargo aboard ships—to fabricate tent floors and bivouac walkways. Water heating units were built out of 55-gallon fuel drums, providing hot water for shaving and washing mess kits, kitchen utensils, and other equipment. Latrines, sumps, and garbage pits were hacked out of the underlying coral layer using pickaxes and entrenching tools.

The jungle warfare training begun in Fiji continued and intensified for the 129th on Santo. Troops underwent additional training to better coordinate the various combat units, to facilitate the movement of units on the island, and to test the plan of defense.

Men must be exposed to prolonged hardships without food, water and conveniences. Troops must learn night sounds, animal noises, not to disclose their position, where to sleep, when to sleep, the simplest of sanitary hygiene measures and water discipline, and they must learn these things in addition to a thorough knowledge of all their weapons and how to employ them.[41]

Naudts would further comment:

For those relatively untrained soldiers who had never been in the jungle they were understandably apprehensive about being in the jungle let along having to fight in such a foreign environment. However, after a few days in the bush they soon learned to identify the different night sounds, and didn't panic when a large spider fell upon them or when a giant coconut crab crawled over their legs when trying to sleep after a day's march. They also learned how to make use of "fox fire," a piece of phosphorescent wood (decayed wood) found in the jungle which jungle wise NCOs and officers used on night patrol: fastening a piece of the fox fire on the back of each man's pack or cartridge belt which made moving single file through the jungle easier to maintain contact with the man in front easier.[42]

Still, the men were not yet a match for the dense jungle of Espiritu Santo. In one notable training exercise, an infantry squad was assigned to surveil the trails and terrain in the interior of the island, beginning from near the mouth of the Sarakata River along the Segond Channel and continuing north and east to the vicinity of Turtle Bay. It was expected to be a four-day mission, but when the patrol failed to return on schedule, other patrols were dispatched to search for the missing group. A small plane was sent up daily but could find no trace of the lost party because of the interminable low-hanging clouds over the mountains. A Navy boat despatched to search the coastline finally located the troops on their ninth day in the jungle. When found, the patrol was nowhere near its intended destination at Turtle Bay, having become disoriented in the dense jungle and misjudging the distance it had covered.

Critical as this jungle training was, it exposed the men of the 129th to a force more hostile than the Japanese located just to the north. Having left the relatively benign Fiji, the troops found themselves in the pestilential New Hebrides and its resident horror, malaria.

Malarial rates on Santo had spiked just before the 129th arrived in mid-March, but decreased over the two months following its arrival due, for the most part, to locating camp sites away from mosquito-breeding areas, to the segregation of highly malarial islanders from military troops, and to effective treatment.

By June, the beginning of the dry season in Santo, the rate of new and relapse malarial cases among all Army troops dropped to an average of just 95 per thousand. But when the 129th commenced training exercises and night maneuvers beyond the base limits the incidence of malaria more than doubled, and the primary attacks and relapses among the 129th were the highest of any unit on the island.

> It was apparent that Espiritu Santo was not a tropical paradise, but a "pest hole," a far cry from our experience at Fiji, which was free of mosquito-borne disease. ... It soon became obvious that the environment on Santo would require major health control measures. ... [(Malaria)] could destroy the fighting spirit and ability of the regiment to accomplish its mission. ... What made [(malaria)] so devastating was that it was a recurring illness, requiring long periods of treatment. And malaria could be fatal.[43]

Practical, home-grown malaria discipline quickly emerged as detailed by Naudts:

> Mosquito nets [(mosquito "bars")] were used over sleeping cots, and head nets were worn over helmets while on guard or outpost duty. Particular care was taken to keep the body fully covered ... shirt sleeves rolled down and trousers tucked inside leggings or boots ... [By the time his unit arrived] Mosquito repellant was available, thought troops objected to the greasy, sticky discomfort experienced with the preparation was applied to the skin.[44]

The American military avoided native villages, and since the *Anopheles* mosquito was most active in early mornings and evenings, swimming or showering after dark was forbidden.[45]

On Santo, the Malarial Control Group's work, and that of the Navy's Seabees, began to show results by mid-1943. Road improvement was paramount; "It may safely be said that good roads have done more to control malaria mosquito breeding on this Base than perhaps any other factor." Included in the IV Island Command directive was: " ... no building, logging, road making, ditching or other projects are considered complete until all mosquito breeding hazards created by the operations are eliminated."[46]

Stagnant water sites were drained or ditched. The mosquito larvicidal program—largely based on spraying breeding sites with No. 2 Diesel using knapsack sprayers and vehicle-mounted power sprayers—began to show positive results. Ponds, creeks, and streams—even hog wallows—were treated, and vegetation was cleared from swampy shorelines.

Worldwide among Allied troops, commanders were getting the message about maintaining combat readiness. "For the first time in history a combatant officer was considered unfit to command a unit on the grounds that he had allowed his men to become ineffective through disease."[47]

Naudts was among the cognoscenti. "The greatest challenge unit commanders faced, on a daily basis, was that of 'health maintenance', repeated emphasis on personal hygiene, sanitation measures, and mosquito and fly control." He was keenly aware a commander's failure to maintain combat readiness in his unit was justifiable cause for "being sacked." After the long months of training, and with combat looming, Naudts would have been devastated to lose command so close to the action for which he had prepared for years.[48]

When the 129th arrived at Santo, the "field testing" of Atabrine on Guadalcanal was still underway, but within three months the appropriate dosage became standardized.[49] Naudts reported:

> Atabrine … was a small yellow tablet taken at meal time. Unfortunately, at the outset, it was not popular with the troops because of a rumor that it caused sterility—a bit of propaganda promoted by "Tokyo Rose." There were individuals who used every subterfuge to avoid taking the tablet. A sergeant at the head of the mess line popped the tablet into each mouth and watched him swallow it. As time passed the only side effect of atabrine was a yellowing of the skin, which coupled with a sun tan created a yellowish bronze coloration.[50]

On top of the onslaught of malaria, the regiment had to contend with the full slate of other diseases endemic to Santo—yaws, hookworm infestation, dysentery, and tuberculosis—but to make matters far worse, an epidemic of dengue fever—something not previously endemic on Santo—had erupted just a month before the regiment's arrival and would persist for nearly the entire period the 129th garrisoned the island. First reported on Tulagi in October 1942 during the Guadalcanal campaign, the dengue outbreak began in February 1943 on Santo and at about the same time at Noumea and Efate. The epidemic spread rapidly and reached a peak in the latter half of April and the first half of May.[51]

While dengue outbreaks were generally more localized than malaria, it could cause greater short-term disruption to military forces. Dengue outbreaks were abrupt: a soldier could wake up and report for duty in good health and be in hospital by lunchtime. It was referred to as "break-bone fever" because patients felt like they'd been beaten with a baseball bat; severe temperature spikes—up to 105°—with accompanying pain in the eyes, joints, and lower back, with dizziness and extreme weakness in the legs; or it may lead to loss of appetite, nausea, abdominal cramps, or waves of teeth-chattering rigors.[52]

The disease ran its course in 6–10 days, and generally troops could report for duty in two weeks. While recovering from malaria took twice as long,[53] the fatigue and muscle weakness that accompanied dengue could persist for many more weeks, leaving the soldier unfit for full duty. There was no way to either treat or prevent a severe outbreak of dengue and the only medical remedy was aspirin to treat symptoms.[54]

Dengue was caused by the *Aedes egypti* species of mosquito, a species that had an entirely different breeding preference to the *Anopheles* mosquito. The control of breeding sites—cans, bottles, pots, rain barrels, old dishes, spent tires, water pockets in tarpaulin covers, and jungle debris—was an important function for all Army units. "Signs were posted to control dumping areas, coconut fronds and husks were policed daily (which incidentally gave the Regiment the title of 129th Coconut Team)."[55]

Over the next six months the infection rate for dengue skyrocketed, reaching a peak in January and February. Twenty-five percent of Army and Navy forces on Santo were infected, causing over eighty thousand sick days. So pervasive was the disease that base hospitals set up emergency wards for the care of the sick.[56]

With the coming of the dry season and with efforts by all Army and Navy units on the island, the incidence of malaria and the dengue epidemic began to wane. By late summer suppressive Atabrine therapy was discontinued within the area encompassed by Base Button.[57]

Safe as it might have been within the base confines, for Naudt's troops operating in exposed locations outside the base treatment area, the malaria infection rate was worse than when troops first arrived. Infantry troops manned outposts and gun positions close to heavily seeded native populations, and combat troops routinely maneuvered outside the base. In October, with the main base area reporting an enviable malarial infection rate of 21 per thousand, the rate for troops in exposed locations had grown to 361 per thousand. " … Although there was adequate control within the occupied zone, the remainder of the island continued to be a malaria hazard."[58]

Just as ships were never meant to remain in port, so too an infantry regiment was never meant to loll around camp. It was into these selfsame "exposed locations" that Naudts and the men of the 129th would go.

CHAPTER TEN

Richardson Arrives in the South Pacific

As Leonard Richardson and his small cohort of embarking navigators loaded aboard USAT *Puebla,* what place in the world was untouched by war? Somewhere in landlocked South America or Africa? The cold Canadian North? What place would have no strategic importance to the Allies or the Axis? The war had become as ubiquitous as a pandemic, and potentially much more lethal. As the ship took on its passengers, others in other ports were similarly loading men and women for destinations on every continent.

By June 1943, the United States had been at war for 18 months, and most of the men aboard *Puebla* had been in one type of training or another for over a year. All were anticipating where and to which unit they would be posted, anxious about what combat they would experience and how long it would take for them to be able to return to their homes and loved ones.

On June 13, three months after the 129th Combat Team had taken up defensive stations on Espiritu Santo, *Puebla* left San Francisco harbor in a convoy that included two other troop transports—USS *Kenmore* and MS *Boschfontein*, a former Dutch cargo ship recently converted for troop transport. USAT *Puebla,* a two-stacked German passenger/cargo liner originally called SS *Orinoco,* had been seized by Mexico at Tampico in 1941 and chartered by the Army shortly after the outbreak of the Pacific War. It had undergone conversion to a troopship, outfitted with defensive guns manned by a U.S. Navy gun crew.[1]

Departing San Francisco that Sunday morning, the three troopships passed through the submarine net defenses and swept the main channel to sea. Early the next morning, the convoy shed its coastal escort and for the next week held to a southwestern course, making a steady 12 knots, with their progress slowed only by the anti-submarine zig-zagging that was standard Navy protocol.[2]

The threat of Japanese submarines was foremost in the minds of the ship's crew and passengers, and for good reason. In the two months immediately prior to *Puebla*'s departure, Japanese submarines had sunk six cargo ships and three tankers in the Pacific. Combat vessels fared little better. In April and May, five warships were sunk

United States Army Transport *Puebla*.

in the Pacific, including a destroyer, a minelayer, a Navy tanker, and two submarines. June was even more costly: the Navy lost nine ships, including a submarine, and two cargo ships were sunk near Espiritu Santo.[3] Perhaps most significantly, the troop transport USS *McCawley* was sunk in late June by Japanese torpedo bombers during the American invasion of Rendova.[4]

The transports in convoy were equipped with anti-aircraft guns and a single 5-inch anti-ship gun; each performed firing exercises during the transit. On the 21st, *Kenmore* towed a buoy as an aiming point for 30 minutes of live fire by *Boschfontein*; on the 24th, *Boschfontein* reciprocated for *Kenmore*, and the latter later streamed a towing spar as a target for *Puebla*.[5] These exercises would have meant nothing for the troops confined below decks, but would have been a welcome distraction for Richardson and his fellow officers topside on *Puebla*.

The convoy crossed the equator on June 22, 1943: Latitude 0000, Longitude 151° 46' W—smack in the mid-Pacific Ocean, midway between Hawaii and French Polynesia, and beyond the support of any land-based military resources. Those aboard making their first crossing—dubbed "Pollywogs"—were granted admission to the Domain of Neptunus Rex. In the crossing ceremony—an undisguised ruse for hazing troops—King Neptune himself boarded the ship, accompanied by his wife, Davy Jones, and their courtiers. Pollywogs entertained the royal court with dancing, songs, or skits and were then brought before the court to answer to a range of often hilarious charges brought against them by the ship's "Shellbacks." Each initiate was given a task to complete—some much more onerous than others and were served an intentionally inedible breakfast before the ceremony ended with a ritual bath in a pool of seawater.

New Shellbacks often signed each other's certificates, and Richardson appeared to have especially valued the signatures of the female officers on board—among the 32 signatures on his certificate were those of 19 women from the Army Nurse Corps. Noteworthy is "Irene J. Schnur, Lt, A.N.C," who added *all my love* (emphasis is hers), and nurse "C. Bjorklund," who added "mine too." Army Air Force signatures included friends Carl Gonder, Edward Segliwa, and Bryce Sammon.

By June 25, the unescorted convoy had been at sea for nearly two weeks and had reached a position 700 miles south of Hawaii. About to enter truly dangerous waters, the convoy was joined by the destroyer USS *Warrington*, followed two days later by the destroyer USS *Sampson* and an additional troopship, MV *Poelau Laut*.[6]

Possibly in anticipation of the coming national celebration, on July 3 the passengers in convoy were treated to a display of starshells and naval gunnery when its escorts engaged in battle practice. Further gunnery was carried out by *Warrington* on the 4th, "for training purposes," but the date may have influenced the captain to start the day off with a bang.

Evidence of the fact the passengers were aware of their destination, each serviceman was given a copy of *A Pocket Guide to New Caledonia*—a booklet describing the history, culture, and geography of the French colony, in hopes the new American troops would be better able to weather the culture shock that awaited them.[7]

The troops read that New Caledonia could be a pleasant place to spend the war—far enough south to have escaped the initial onslaught of Japanese conquest and below the longitudes where malaria raged. They learned that in the sub-tropical environment of New Caledonia, "you will not encounter the extreme heat, humidity, dangerous animals, insect pests, or fevers that make life so difficult in the real tropics." Anticipating their arrival, the men may have retained a hint of Hollywood romanticism about the South Seas, even though American newspapers had only recently given notice that the South Pacific bore little resemblance to the exotic films of Dorothy Lamour.

The men aboard ship had cause to reflect on the events of the past year—the critical naval battles fought in the south and mid-Pacific, and the costly campaign on Guadalcanal. And for them, the war had become personalized. All the strategic decisions, the mobilization, and the combat so costly in lives and equipment had conspired to bring them to that place and time; all recognized that defeating the Japanese over the vastness of the western Pacific would be a task of years.

The mental states of those on board would have ranged from deep unease to excited anticipation. All knew they would soon emerge into an environment utterly foreign to their experiences, and many knew their arrival in the South Pacific would put them one huge step closer to combat. Richardson and his fellow navigators aboard *Puebla* knew they would likely be assigned to a bomber group, and all were aware that few bomber crews at that time in the war survived a combat tour and returned home.

They would also know that the rest of the war was spinning at an increasing rate. In November, American forces had invaded North Africa in Operation *Torch*, and by May the German *Africa Korps* had surrendered. And with Guadalcanal secured in February, American bombers began attacks on airfields in the northern Solomons in preparation for MacArthur's further island-hopping ground offensives.,

Any anxiety aside, Richardson evidently enjoyed the sea voyage. He was surrounded by intelligent, committed people, and had a head ready for adventure. Some of his letters home during the voyage reflect that attitude. Writing a V-mail[8] home to his folks on June 27, still a week away from his destination:

> The trip has been smooth & little seasickness or boredom has marred even a minute of this voyage. There is so much that is different. The water is such a deep blue … the sunrises and sunsets are magnificent, and mix those in with the blue skies, a few clouds & you have some real scenery. The sun rides high in the sky—and at night thousands of stars thrill everyone (& confuse the navigator).[9]

Second Lieutenant George Bamberger, a fellow Army Air Force passenger aboard *Puebla*, would later recall:

> … in a way, it was fun. We played bridge all night, and we were out in the sun, watching the flying fish. We had 2,800 people below decks—we never saw them—and fifty-six officers above decks and some Red Cross girls and some nurses. So we all had a really nice time above deck, that is with the weather and the view.[10]

However pleasant the voyage was, some of the experiences aboard were less than agreeable. Richardson recounted: "I hung my laundry bag over the side—then imagine my dismay when the toilet just ahead of my porthole was flushed! I haven't worn the clothes yet!"[11] In a later letter to his folks, Richardson reported his wallet stolen aboard ship, and that he had borrowed $50 in poker winnings from a fellow passenger. Apparently the lucky gambler thought it safer to have Richardson owe him the money than to carry it himself in a ship's company that included at least one thief.

And despite the thus-far uneventful voyage, the convoy's poor headway across the Pacific vexed the convoy commander; the focus of his concern was *Puebla*. Within a week of leaving San Francisco the ship had begun to be a serious detriment to the convoy. The Navy might have preferred it had been left to the Germans.

On June 18, and again on the 19th, the ship dropped astern to make engine repairs, in each case rejoining the convoy 12 hours later. On the 24th, it again experienced engine problems that forced the convoy to temporarily slow to 7 knots. In each of these breakdowns, the convoy came closer to the region where Japanese submarines were more likely to be found; a slowed convoy would have been an easy target.

Puebla broke down again on the 28th, and yet again on July 5, causing the formation to slow and requiring one of the destroyers to fall astern of the convoy to screen the jinxed ship. Bamberger recalled the voyage consequently lasted longer than the provisions on board: "It took us twenty-three days and we ran out of food. We ate nothing but pork sausages and some dehydrated potatoes."[12] Finally, on July 6, *Puebla* wobbled into Noumea harbor, on the island of New Caledonia.[13]

Oriented toward the northwest and measuring 248 miles long and 20–30 miles wide, New Caledonia is roughly equal in size to the state of New Jersey. Two steep mountain ranges run the length of the island, coastal hills descended straight into the sea, and a barrier reef encircling the entire island. Ill-suited for agriculture, and with no significant resources, it was annexed by France during the global whirlwind of European imperialism in the mid-19th century more to dissuade other European governments from incursions into the region than for any intrinsic value. But a year after annexation, prospectors discovered rich deposits of metallic ore and the island gradually became, acre-for-acre, the richest source of nickel, chromite, cobalt, and iron of any country in the world.

Its rich mineral resources aside, in 1942 its value to Allied forces in the Pacific was due to its location directly astride the critical Southern Supply Line connecting the West Coast of the United States to Australia. It possessed two excellent deepwater ports to facilitate cargo movement into the South and Southwest Pacific Theaters, and had just enough flat terrain to accommodate the long landing strips needed to support Allied bomber operations. In the earliest months of the war in the Pacific, before the American success at Guadalcanal, New Caledonia was viewed as a last defensive stalwart against the rapid southern incursions by the Japanese.[14]

***

Enlisted personnel awaiting orders were commonly assigned to "casual duty," meaning they were assigned to military work teams around Noumea and the harbor—unloading ships, organizing warehouses, working at camp, and the like. The depot did not typically give casual assignments to officers awaiting orders and with trucks seemingly going in every direction, hitchhiking to town or country was never a challenge. Before enlisting, Richardson had never been far from his home in Clarkston, Washington, and was quick to take advantage of the chance to explore what could be his home for much of the war. Noumea was everyone's first stop, as recorded by the historian of the Thirteenth Air Force:

> Usually after hitch-hiking into town on trucks, the sightseers rambled through the town, searching for atmosphere. Gimcrack souvenirs, displayed in unattractive little shops, were offered to the American soldier at exorbitant prices. Yet it was a novelty to visit the shops, trying out French

phrases from Army Pocket Guides on clerks who preferred to speak English: *Je voudrai des cigarettes*, or *Comment s'appelle cet endroit?* It was likewise a novelty to visit one of the cinemas where French Westerns were shown.[15]

The new American "tourists" might have been surprised by one deeply entrenched custom in their visits to Noumea: the siesta hour is observed rigidly throughout New Caledonia, and all shops and offices are closed tight for a few hours at midday. The troops might have wondered what sort of a war they were part of.

The largest group in the population were those of European—mostly French—descent who referred to themselves as "Caledonians." The island's indigenous people, the Kanaks, of mixed Melanesian and Polynesian origin, were organized in small tribes and, in addition to their own dialects, spoke French and, recently, a smattering of English. The Tonkinese and Javanese populations totaled about twelve thousand in 1943.[16]

Nearly all the Kanak population lived in villages called "tribu," mainly in the river valleys, with fewer deep in the mountains. Reflecting French style, the residences were rectangular, with tin, bark, or thatch roofs, earthen floors, and walls made of wattle and mud, usually painted in bright colors. The old-style native huts—beehive-shaped with thatched roofs—were little seen by 1943. Kanaks slept on woven mats, and cooked on open hearths. Generally, the villages are tidy and surrounded by flowers.

Most of the Kanaks Richardson would have encountered were strongly influenced by French colonizers and were Roman Catholic in their faith. Their dress also reflected French influences, with men wearing a shirt and a cotton waistcloth, often brightly colored, called a "manou." The women mostly wore the "Mother Hubbard"—a loose cotton dress falling below the knee with elbow-length sleeves that were the hallmark of missionary influences. On festive occasions, the Kanaks wore wreaths of flowers and leaves, incorporating strings of beads, copper wire, tin bottle tops, or anything else that appealed to them.

Kanaks are fond of ornamentation and often decorate their ankles, knees, wrists, and arms with found materials and flowers. Perhaps most striking, Kanaks frequently rub lime into their scalps to dye their hair orange. The practice had once been used to kill parasites, but became a common personal adornment.[17]

Typical dress of young women on New Caledonia. (Fold 3)

***

In mid-summer 1943, air operations in and around New Caledonia was intense.

Fighter, Bomber, and reconnaissance groups all operated from the airfield at Plaine Des Gaiacs (PDG), situated on the west coast of New Caledonia, right adjacent to the Coral Sea, and 160 miles by road north of Noumea. In mid-1943, PDG was a busy airfield: it was the base for the 347th Fighter Group and its 67th Fighter Squadron, and the 4th Reconnaissance Group and its 17th Photo Reconnaissance Squadron. The 69th Bomb Squadron, 42nd Bomb Group, was based at PDG but operated from Guadalcanal. Conversely, the 75th Bomb Squadron, also of the 42nd, was based on Guadalcanal but operated from Plaine des Gaiacs.[18] PDG had become operational about a year before *Puebla* had delivered its cargo of personnel to the island, included two steel-surfaced runways suitable for bomber operations, and was considered the best airfield for military operations.[19] At the start of the Guadalcanal Campaign, PDG had been the base for heavy and medium bombers.

A second major airfield was located at Tontouta, 33 miles north by road from Noumea. In the spring of 1942, as American forces began arriving in the South Pacific, it was the only substantial airfield in the entire theater. It lay in a saddle between peaks to the north and east, bracketed by the Natire, Tamoa, and Kouembelin Rivers, and included two runways built in the months following the German conquest of France.[20]

In mid-summer 1943, the airfield at Tontouta was supporting operations of two Marine air squadrons flying the R4D transport, and a single Army Air Force

Tontouta Airfield, 1943. (U.S. Army Medical Department)

squadron—the 13th Troop Carrier Squadron (TCS)—flying the C-47. The squadrons delivered cargo and passengers to destinations throughout the South Pacific and normally returned with planeloads of sick or wounded servicemen. Their mission schedules were intense. For example, in a four-week period commencing about the time *Puebla* departed San Francisco harbor, the 13th TCS had flown 86 missions, mostly multi-day sorties. During the month, on average, each aircraft of the 13th flew supply and evacuation missions to Guadalcanal four times.[21]

By late 1943, the well-developed airfield included three large hangars, a control tower, fuel dump, and an aviation repair facility.[22]

In addition to the two primary fields on New Caledonia, Koumac Airfield, located at the northern end of New Caledonia, was considered an intermediate landing field by the U.S. Army and was unused in mid-summer 1943. Peppered across New Caledonia, wherever flat ground could be found, were other fields: Oua Tom Airfield had been used as a bomber base earlier in the war, but would soon be used as a fighter training base; Magenta Airfield—used by fighter aircraft—was the only airfield convenient to nearby Noumea, just three miles distant; and Dumbea, Bruce, Bourail, Bourake (aka *Dust Bowl*), Nepoui (*Patsy*), Thio (*Shoe Box*), and Bouloupare (*DuBois*) were grass fields useable only for light planes, or for emergency landings.[23]

Additionally, the Navy operated the well-developed Île Nou Seaplane Base, two miles west of Noumea along the southern boundary of Great Roads Harbor. The site included seven large seaplane hangars, a fuel dump, and nearly two hundred Quonset huts for enlisted and officers.

***

Since none of the newly arrived navigators had been assigned to operating units when they boarded ship at San Francisco, all reported to the 6th Replacement Depot to await orders.

At this time in the war, Army replacement depots were positioned in each theater to quickly process and assign replacements—both officers and enlisted personnel—to their respective permanent assignments. The 6th Replacement Depot had itself only recently arrived in the South Pacific, establishing a large camp at Plum Bay, roughly twenty-one miles from Noumea and accessible only via the now heavily-traveled dirt road across Mt. Dor.

New arrivals took in the sights and smells of Noumea only in passing and soon loaded aboard trucks for transport to Plum Bay, a trip taken by thousands of men over the course of the war which left a vivid recollection with many. The historian of the 42nd Bomb Group later recorded:

> We were taken across Mt. Dor on a narrow dirt road, with no guard rails, in clouds of red dust, past the nickel smelter and the Tonkinese barracks and up the tortuous and hilly road that wound to the Sixth Replacement Depot. There was little talking as eyes surfeited with

View of New Caledonia. (Howard Brodie)

battleship gray and Pacific blue drank in the lush and moist green of Caledonia in the cool of early morning. Those who could read French were pleased at their ability to translate the signs on the little groceries and estaminets along the route.[24]

Having been cooped up aboard ship, then hurriedly jostled to their first overseas camp, all the while flooded with new terrain, new people, and a new climate, the cohort of new navigators were glad to reach the depot. After marching to assigned tents, the men found the showers and the PX and began to explore the camp, the adjacent beach, and the stream that flowed out of the mountains and through the camp, a stream that would be their laundry for the duration of their stay. With their first mess, they experienced the difference between Navy and Army chow.

The unassigned navigators continued to speculate on the unit to which they would be assigned, the type of aircraft they would fly, and their first duty station. There were several possibilities. New Caledonia could be their home for the duration of the war, or a quick stop on their way to a forward assignment—it was a relatively rearward base of operations at this time. With America now on the offensive, most of the Army Air Force units were employed further to the north, beyond Guadalcanal. The only units then operating at New Caledonia that would require navigators were the aforementioned 13th TCS based at Tontouta Airfield, then assigned to the South Pacific Combat Air Transport Command, the 4th Reconnaissance Group, and the 42nd Bomb Group. They might be assigned to the Fifth Air Force, headquartered in Brisbane, Australia, and operating a huge fleet of bombers, fighters, reconnaissance, troop carriers, and cargo aircraft from myriad bases in the Southeast Pacific theater. A posting with the Fifth would involve operations to support General MacArthur's offensives, which at the time included upcoming campaigns in New Guinea and Bougainville, and elsewhere. There were also units in the newly created and somewhat smaller Thirteenth Air Force, based on Espiritu Santo, in need of navigators. The Thirteenth operated similar types of aircraft to the Fifth from bases in the New Caledonia, New Hebrides, and Solomon Islands. Military planners were also planning several campaigns for the Thirteenth to support operations moving northward out of Guadalcanal to the northern regions of the necklace of islands that made up the Solomons, including New Georgia, Vella Lavella and, most importantly, Bougainville.

Most troops passed through the 6th Replacement Depot in a week. Richardson and the other navigators waited almost three weeks for orders assigning them to an operational unit. During that time, they were granted liberal leave to visit Noumea or to explore the island, and that is just what they did.

After so many days at sea, the convoy's arrival was stunning. Army Pvt. David Dresser, making an identical arrival to New Caledonia aboard MS *Sea Witch* later in the month, would record:

> The waves breaking over the coral reefs were beautiful as they formed a dazzling white rim in the early morning sunlight. In the morning we were outside the harbor of Noumea, New Caledonia. It was a beautiful sight: bright sun, clear blue sky, red mountains, green trees, blue ocean with a long line of sparkling foam in the distance where waves broke over the coral reefs.
>
> (The ships) crept past the lighthouse in the channel, from which flew the Tricolor of Free France, and eased its way through the dense harbor traffic to anchorage at Noumea Harbor. The blue sky and crystal blue water spread before the town of Noumea, itself silhouetted against a background of lush green hills. The Stars and Stripes on the pier flagpole added one note of familiarity, but the Tricolor of the old French Republic and the Lorraine Cross of the Fighting French were a reminder that we had arrived on a foreign land, and in a theater of war.[25]

The colors of the town were stunning. The pink-colored tile roofs, a hallmark of Noumea, mixed with the yellow stucco and red tiled roofs of the French Army garrison on the slopes leading upward from the water's edge to the distant hills. The homes themselves were a jumble of geometric shapes in a vibrant palette of violet, grey, white, and cream pastels. Noumea had the appearance of a serene albeit unfamiliar town.

The men aboard *Puebla* had been impressed by the teeming ship traffic at San Francisco and would have been no less impressed by the bustle in the French harbor. Service boats, transports, freighters, destroyers, tankers, landing barges, and battleships arrived, berthed, and departed all in a single day. The busy harbor patrol boats motored incessantly among the ships at anchor and those at berth, and, all the while, aircraft droned overhead, heading to or coming from one of the three active airstrips on the island or the seaplane base near Noumea Harbor. "It was America's answer to Rabaul."[26]

The new arrivals assembled pier side and quickly became aware of how modern warfare could transform a small foreign port city. Beginning shortly after Pearl Harbor, New Caledonia had begun receiving a torrent of Allied men and *matériel*.

In the summer of 1943, the port of Noumea was offloading 10,000 tons of cargo each day—second only to San Francisco.

For the green airmen, most of whom just a year earlier had little thought beyond their hometowns, the walk down the embarkation ramp into Noumea was like stepping through the looking glass. Noumea—"one of the most humanly interesting places in the Pacific,"[27] was unlike any place they had been before. Its remarkable culture soon made itself felt among the uninitiated troops in the same way other servicemen and women in other theaters were then greeting their new environs—think Casablanca, Cairo, or Calcutta.

By the start of World War II, New Caledonia was a rich amalgam of indigenous Kanaks, European industrialists, descendants of French convicts and political dissidents, imported labor, and French administrative officials. New Caledonia is a sizeable island, but in 1943 it held only 60,000 people—the Rose Bowl in Pasadena could accommodate all, with room to spare. The capital city, Noumea, was home to 10,000.

Much of Noumea, like most cities throughout the Pacific at that time, had only a rudimentary sewage system, and troops were greeted by the sight and smell of open sewers running through the town and discharging into the sea. The men learned hookworm and intestinal parasites were endemic in New Caledonia and that skin infections were common. Commanders cautioned new arrivals about the drinking water and urged their men and women to draw water from the chlorinated lister bags hanging at camp. While there was no malaria on the island, the mosquitoes were ferocious and each man soon learned the value of their bed nets.[28]

> Noumea had been transformed from a sleepy colonial town to a noisy, over-crowded community, bustling with soldiers and sailors. Troops monopolized the sidewalks and overflowed onto the streets. Trucks rumbled from the wharf area to camps and supply dumps outside the town limits, and a steady stream of jeeps, reconnaissance and command cars made their way from Noumea to the large air bases at Tontouta and Plaine des Glace. Noumea had become the nerve center of the South Pacific war.[29]

A contemporary newspaper article in Australia cites: "Yankee hustle and the war has hit sleepy, shabby French Noumea, capital of New Caledonia, strange back-water of the South Pacific where the islanders in a queer mixture of French and Australian farewell the visitor with the phrase: 'Allez Ta-Ta.'"[30]

A streetcorner listener in Noumea was treated to a cacophony of language: French and pseudo-French, a variety of native dialects, Javanese, Tonkinese, Chinese, the broad English of the New Zealand troops, and American English spoken with a wide range in accents.

And the new population of Allied troops did nothing to make the environment more familiar. As reported in an Australian newspaper:

> Noumea's hot, dusty streets are filled with American servicemen in white, blue and khaki, mingling with dapper Fighting French troops in shirt, shorts and kepi or topee, fuzzy-headed

> native troops in boy scout hats, forage caps or black berets. New Zealanders in peaked hats with coloured [sic] puggarees, small neat Javanese women in bright sarongs. Melanesian girls, native youths with hair tinted yellow and garlanded with scarlet blooms, Tonkinese women, half-caste, quarter-castes, eighth-castes—all the strange types that throng a colonial Pacific port.
>
> Occasionally a French girl, cool and fresh in white, whose high heels might just have stepped off the Champs Elysee, appears and creates a mild sensation.[31]

Confronted with and perhaps startled by this remarkable new culture, homesick troops might have taken comfort in knowing their loved ones back home were looking up at the same moon. But their feeling of remoteness was heightened in knowing the moon would not rise for another 19 hours back home—where it was still yesterday.

Richardson, having grown up in predominantly white communities of eastern Washington state, often encountered Native American peoples of his region but had little exposure to or understanding of Asian, Pacific, or Black populations. Like many of his peers, he daily encountered a diversity of people and environments that dramatically defied his preconceptions. Preconceptions that were shaped, in large part, by Hollywood.[32]

His new experiences in New Caledonia, in which whites, Asians, and indigenous people intermixed freely, would have been fascinating. Perhaps most interesting would have been the almost complete lack of racial prejudice among the various cultures of the island.[33]

On New Caledonia, wild game was familiar and plentiful. The island was thick with deer, wild pigeon, and duck, and had no snakes. And best news for Richardson, the fishing was great. In his letters home during July, he mentions fishing frequently, which appears to have been his main diversion when he was not flying. In one letter home, he requested gear:

> Once in a while you can send me some fishhooks, & I would like some line, and if possible a few sinkers. A small package would get thru all right. You can't get fishing tackle here, and everybody wants some.

His letter would indicate that he was planning on staying on New Caledonia for a while. Richardson managed to turn fishing into a memorable multicultural experience:

> … it being Sunday I went fishing on a little stream about two miles from camp. I started with flies, but had no luck, so I switched to a hunk of liver on a plain hook. No soap. Just then a Frenchman came by, accompanied by two dogs. I laid my pole down and tried to talk to him—me with my, shall we say "limited French" and he speaking no English.
>
> We weren't doing badly, when all at once I felt a tremendous tug on my line & heard a frantic "yip," & turned to see the Frenchy's dog headed for open country—and with my fishhook in his jaw and my liver in his belly! That was the first dog I ever caught, and the only thing I caught all day! The Frenchy caught the dog, & we spent a trying half hour trying to get the hook out of the poor dog's mouth. Finally with some cutting we finally got it out—but I sure felt sorry for the pooch.[34]

His first V-mail home, written on July 7 shortly after his arrival, was prescient: "Could be that I will have lots of interesting experiences to tell about when I get back." He continued, "Laundry and cleaning is done in a small stream not far away—& bathing as well. I'm getting tired of buying new clothes—& am considering washday this very day!"[35] Later that day, he penned a more expansive letter home:

> I'm living in a tent, with no floor, & eating out of a mess kit. With the mountains around us, it reminds me a lot of some of those fishing trips we used to go on. I will probably be moving quite often, but won't be able to give you much of an idea when, where, or anything about what I'm doing. I have told you all that I can. Now it's time for me to go down to the little stream and wash my clothes and body beautiful ... [36]

He wrote again in a V-mail on July 9:

> Another letter from the new south sea islander in your family. This is written from my cot in candlelight in my corner of our tent. It is only 6:15 pm, but since it is winter here—it is already dark out. We have long nights and short days. There is an outside movie on the base, and last night I saw "Powers Girl." Also heard the news broadcast which we get from the States via short wave radio. It's getting so we know as much about how we are doing as you at home do![37]

He would have heard in those broadcasts that bombers continued to pound Japanese positions in the northern Solomon Islands, including Bougainville, Ballale, and New Georgia, all as a prelude to the ground offensives planned under MacArthur's comprehensive Operation *Cartwheel* that was designed to isolate the major Japanese base at Rabaul. Lieutenant Richardson would have imagined himself guiding one of those heavy bombers—a B-17 or B-24—to those and other targets northward of Guadalcanal.

Richardson became a fairly regular letter writer after his overseas posting. For example, from May 22 until August 24, he wrote 19 letters—one every five days or so.

But all was not leisure for Richardson and the other navigators. During this 21-day period in which they were unassigned, the navigators were nonetheless assigned to missions with units then on New Caledonia.[38] For example, on July 17, just 10 days after setting foot on New Caledonia, Richardson wrote that he had already been to Guadalcanal. His letter home of July 28 alludes to his flying time: "A letter in a somewhat busy schedule. I am not settled yet—and don't expect to be—although am about to be assigned to a permanent squadron."

The new navigators would have learned very quickly of the dangers of flying in the combat zone. Just before they arrived at New Caledonia, a Marine-operated R4D had crashed on take-off from Tontouta Airfield, killing all 24 occupants, including the six-man flight crew, and 18 Army, Navy and Marine Corps passengers, 15 of whom were from the U.S. Marine Corps torpedo bombing squadron VT-11. At the time, it was the second worst accident in the history of the aircraft.[39]

On July 25, six of the new navigators—Gonder, Selica, Sammon, Richardson, Bamburger, and Smith—along with 23 other officers, received orders releasing them from the 6th Replacement Depot and assigning them to the Thirteenth Air Force, the "Jungle Air Force," then headquartered at Espiritu Santo in the New Hebrides. Their range of service options was narrowing.[40]

***

The Thirteenth Air Force was activated on January 13, 1943, in part to provide better coordination and logistics and provide better counsel to Commander South Pacific on how best to use the B-17s at that stage in the war. But there was a catch. The Combined Chiefs of Staff were not willing to increase overall force commitments to the region, so all personnel and equipment for the new air force had to come from units already in the South Pacific. Combat units were reassigned from the Fifth and Seventh Air Forces, and included: the 11th Bomb Group (B-17) with four bomb squadrons, then based at Pekoa Airfield (Bomber 2) on Espiritu Santo in the northern New Hebrides; the 5th Bomb Group (B-17), also with four squadrons and based at Pekoa Airfield, but with squadrons operating from Espiritu Santo, Guadalcanal, and Fiji; the 69th and 70th Bomb Squadrons (B-26) of the 42nd Bomb Group; the 347th Fighter Group, with four fighter squadrons and an assortment of P-400, P-39 and P-38 aircraft; the 12th (P-39) and 44th Fighter Squadrons (P-40) of the 18th Fighter Group; plus the 482nd Ordnance Company (Av) and the 887th Chemical Company (Air Opns).[41]

The operating units now under the command of the Thirteenth Air Force had already been deeply involved in tactical and combat operations, always with fewer aircraft than were needed to complete the mission; the Thirteenth had, at inception, just 358 aircraft on hand, of which only 227 were combat ready.

Combat losses continued to mount. July 1943—the month both Richardson and the 64th Troop Carrier Squadron arrived on New Caledonia—was an especially bad month; the Thirteenth lost 60 aircraft, including 20 bombers and 34 fighters, an attrition rate of roughly twenty-six percent—far higher than was seen in other aviation combat units in any theater of the war at that time.[42]

The Thirteenth was relatively small and deeply handicapped by geography:

> It did not fight from centralized bases closely tied together. It fought from island bases, spread hundreds of miles apart. It never enjoyed the usual overland communications—telegraph, long distance telephone, and good roads or road-beds. It could communicate only by radio, ship or airplane. From its origins to V J Day, its units were spread over at least forty-five islands in the South and Southwest Pacific. They operated over an area of at least 4,000,000 square miles, which is an area approximately one and one-third times the size of the United States. Most units made many moves, and, of course, they often moved without much warning.[43]

Earlier that same month, the War Department assigned additional units to the Thirteenth Air Force, including the 6th Service Group, the 361st Base Headquarters, the 13th Air Depot Group, and a myriad of units related to communications, construction, engineering, transportation, repair, and ordnance. Significantly, the 13th TCS and 801st Medical Air Evacuation Transport Squadron were also assigned to the Thirteenth at that time.[44]

The cohort of navigators recently assigned to the Thirteenth Air Force received further orders on August 1 assigning them to the 403rd Troop Carrier Group, under the command of Col. Harry Sands. With those orders, the 64th TCS was brought to the authorized number of navigators, and the men themselves knew fairly precisely what their service in the Pacific would be. They would be flying the C-47 Skytrain and their missions would include freight hauling, troop carriage, and the evacuation of wounded, and their area of responsibility would be the entire South and Southwest Pacific theaters.[45]

CHAPTER ELEVEN

The 403rd Arrives in the South Pacific

As part of America's hurried mobilization in 1940, the Army Air Forces formed five troop carrier groups (TCG)—roughly two hundred aircraft and five thousand personnel—and all were committed to service in the U.S., Europe, or the Mediterranean—none to the Pacific.[1]

But when war came, the growth in troop carrier groups mirrored the explosive growth in all areas of the Army Air Forces. During 1942, nine new groups were activated. MacArthur's Fifth Air Force received three, and one was ordered to the Thirteenth Air Force in the South Pacific.[2]

As the war continued to evolve, the criticality of troop and cargo carrier units became more evident, especially concerning the Pacific. When the Marines first went ashore on Guadalcanal, Japan's Navy dominated the surrounding seas, making supply operations by Allied ships exceedingly dangerous. Desperate for supplies and *matériel*, the ground commanders also faced mounting battle casualties, with limits to both field hospital capacities and the types of treatment they could provide. With supply and evacuation by sea sharply limited, the only other option was by air.

In early September 1942, less than a month into the Guadalcanal Campaign, and with their fellow Marines desperately trying to gain traction on the island, the first cargo aircraft arrived on New Caledonia. Flying an R4D, Marine Air Group (MAG) 25 delivered the first planeload of supplies to Henderson Field on September 5.

The arrival of that aircraft inaugurated what was to become a comprehensive air transport service for the entire Pacific Ocean Area, and when that same aircraft returned the following day to its base on New Caledonia with a load of wounded, it also initiated the large-scale evacuation of wounded by air.[3]

At the close of the Guadalcanal Campaign, most outbound troop/cargo missions involved resupplying ground and air forces or the movement of entire air and ground units to more advanced locations in the "island hopping" campaigns of the Pacific. On the return leg, roughly half the mission included the evacuation of battle casualties.[4]

Troop carrier groups and squadrons were trained as complete units, and remained as units when they went abroad. Often, individual flight crews—pilot, copilot, navigator, radio operator, and crew chief—trained together, flew overseas together and flew combat operations together, sometimes flying the same aircraft throughout their tours.

In addition to conventional resupply missions, aircrews also trained to tow gliders for air-assault operations and to conduct air-resupply missions, making freefall or parachuted drops of supplies and equipment. These tactical missions were sometimes flown at night, over challenging terrain, and often in the face of enemy ground fire.

Troop carrier units trained at nine airfields in the continental U.S., often located on or near Army airfields or airborne division training camps. Troop carrier crew training included joint exercises between the troop carrier units and Army airborne units, starting with small-scale, company size practice drops and ultimately expanding to involve entire Army divisions, moving in concert over long distances, and using simultaneous parachute drops and infantry glider landings.[5]

The 403rd TCG was the fifteenth troop carrier group to be constituted by the Army Air Force, and was activated in December 1942 at Bowman Field in Louisville, Kentucky. The officer cadre and enlisted personnel were cobbled together from airfields in Arkansas, Texas, and Indiana. On activation, the group included four squadrons: the 63rd, 64th, 65th, and 66th Troop Carrier Squadrons.[6]

Having assembled at Bowman Field, the men of the 403rd moved almost immediately to the airfield at Alliance, Nebraska, "where they had two seasons—winter and the 4th of July." At Alliance, each squadron received aircraft they would use in training, the Douglas C-47, and a handful of gliders. But the men who had assembled at Bowman were green recruits, and the first order of business was basic training.[7]

> We were quartered in tar-paper barracks, and it was a tough winter. We were teaching pilots to fly the C-47, fly formation, tow gliders and drop paratroopers and equipment. The 82nd Airborne sent some detachments to train with us, and we had some gliders for towing practice. The plan was for each C-47 to tow 2 gliders as well as carry a full complement of paratroopers.[8]

While at Alliance, each squadron received additional officers and men and, with the exception of navigators, the unit came to full strength. Training at Alliance continued into March and concluded with aerial maneuvers that included several paratroop missions and the use of towed gliders to transport infantry units.[9]

In mid-April, the group moved to North Platte, Nebraska, for a three-day bivouac where it trained in combat tactics and were given camouflage instruction. At the end of April, as the 403rd was nearing full operational status, it was assigned to a new station at Pope Field, North Carolina, for advanced training. Pope was adjacent to Fort Bragg, and the group engaged in air maneuvers, towed gliders, transported Army infantry troops in both planes and gliders, and completed paradrops of men and supplies.

In the first week of June, the 64th Squadron suffered its first casualties of the war. Two C-47s left Pope Field in the pre-dawn hours to deliver planeloads of glider pilots to a nearby airfield for maneuvers. The lead aircraft encountered a powerful line of thunderstorms with heavy rain and lightning as it neared the base. While flying under the ceiling, about 200 feet above ground level, the pilot attempted a low-level turn to starboard. The aircraft's right wing touched the ground, and the plane cartwheeled and exploded into flames. All four crewmembers of the C-47 and all 12 glider pilots died in the crash. The second C-47, having left Pope five minutes after the first, returned to Pope after encountering the same storm front.[10]

Then-Captain Jack Roessell, commander of the 64th Squadron, who had himself just turned 24 years of age, would later recall:

> I lost the first of the 64th during this training. A young crew (all of us were) was taking some glider pilots to a field a short distance away for an early morning operation. Unfortunately, they ran into some thunderstorms—looked like they tried to go under them—were slammed into the ground killing all. It's rough working through a temporary morgue, cataloging each body and then writing a letter to each family. One grew a little faster than normal.[11]

The accident was a serious blow to the squadron. Pilots from each of the squadron's three glider units had been lost, along with the senior officer in charge of the glider unit.[12]

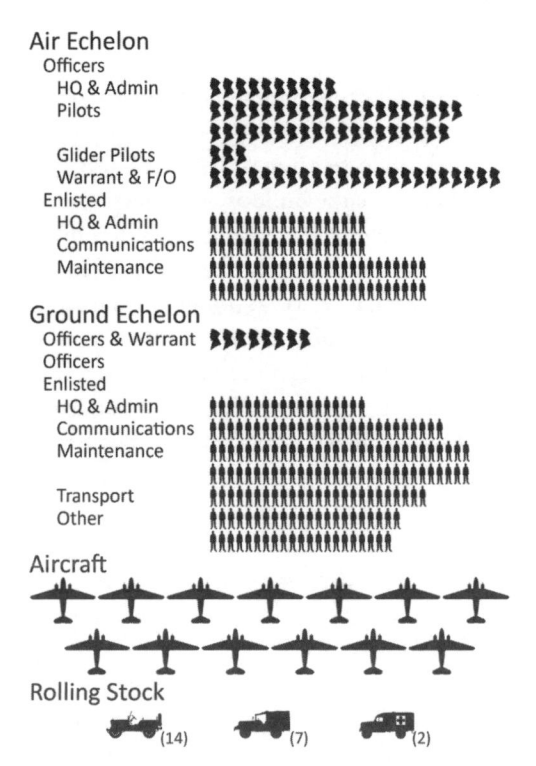

C-47 Troop Carrier Squadron Organization and Equipment. (Yosemite Productions)

In the middle of the month, the entire 403rd TCG moved to Baer Field, near Fort Wayne, Indiana, where aircraft were prepared for the overseas flight that would take them to combat. They received orientation lectures to prepare them for their overseas assignment, and drew supplies necessary for overseas duty. "We picked up 52 new airplanes there and headed for the South Pacific."[13]

The squadron was organized into air and ground echelons. the air echelon included the squadron commander and officers in charge of the engineering, communications, supply, operations, medical, and intelligence units, their assistants, and key enlisted personnel. Also included were 39 C-47 pilots and the glider cohort of three commissioned officers and 23 pilots (flight officers). In aggregate, the air echelon included 75 commissioned and flight officers, and 86 enlisted personnel.

The Ground Echelon included three officers in the headquarters unit and four additional officers for the supply, intelligence and operations units. Enlisted personnel in the administrative, technical, tactical and medical units made up the bulk of ground echelon personnel, which aggregated to seven officers, one warrant officer, and 173 enlisted personnel.

Each troop carrier squadron was allotted 13 C-47 aircraft and twenty-six 15-place gliders. The squadron's equipment included the gliders, 14 Jeeps, a 27-vehicle assortment of trucks, trailers and ambulances, and a small mountain of equipment, all of which would be transported overseas by ship, in company with the squadron's ground echelon.[14]

Dwight Eisenhower, future U.S. president and supreme Allied leader in Europe, in later relating his personal experience of the war, noted: " ... four pieces of equipment that most senior officers came to regard as among the most vital to our success in Africa and Europe were the bulldozer, the jeep, the 2½-ton truck, and the C-47 airplane. Curiously, none of these is designed for combat."[15] Military aircraft development in the late 1920s had tightly focused on bombers and fighters, but expanding air travel in the civilian sector at home and abroad created a demand for new airframes to replace the slow, low-capacity aircraft then operating, with their low ceilings and high maintenance requirements. Foremost among commercial aircraft designers was Donald Douglas, whose 1921 Cloudster biplane was the first aircraft with a payload that equaled its own weight. Beginning in the early 1930s, the Douglas Aircraft Company delivered the first of what would be a series of remarkable aircraft; the DC-1 was an aircraft that would set many American and world speed records and, for a time, was faster than many Army and Navy fighters. The DC-1 set new standards for aircraft performance, and its elegant design was a signal departure from other aircraft of the period. Within a year, Douglas would produce a follow-on design—the DC-2—described as "the supreme American achievement in transport design."[16]

The DC platform continued to evolve, and it is testament to the brilliance and nimbleness of the Douglas organization that it could design and deliver new aircraft designs so quickly during the 1930s. By 1935, it had introduced the DC-3, which soon became the preferred aircraft for American, United, TWA, Delta, and Eastern airlines. By the time the United States was embroiled in a new global war, nearly 90% of commercial airline aircraft in operation were DC-3s. The type had flown for six years, had logged over two million air hours, and had established its credentials as a well-tested and reliable aircraft.

The DC-3 easily met the military's requirements and was adopted by the then U.S. Army Air Corps as its primary troop carrier and cargo aircraft. In a windfall for the Allied mobilization effort, the DC-3 was already in production. It emerged into the war fully capable—without an exhaustive development program, without the internecine disputes that marked the development of many military aircraft, and with no confusion regarding its mission or its place in the Allies' war strategies.

The first military versions of the DC-3, designated the C-47-DL (DL for Douglas), could be outfitted for heavy cargo, as a troop carrier, or as a flying ambulance and were delivered to the Army Air Force just 16 days after Pearl Harbor. It was larger and, in most parameters, had better performance than the B-25 and B-26 medium bombers used in all theaters of the war. Further variants followed almost immediately and, during the war years, 10,368 C-47s were procured by the U.S. armed forces.[17]

The aircraft delivered to the 403rd Troop Carrier Group in the spring of 1943—the Douglas C-47 "Skytrain"—differed only slightly from the civilian DC-3. The military versions incorporated a navigator's dome (astrodome) above and just behind the cockpit; a larger "barn door" was added to the left side of the aircraft to facilitate loading; the floor was reinforced and tie-down fittings were added to accommodate heavy loads; folding bench-type seating was installed along the sides of the interior; and the landing gear was strengthened. There were subtle differences too. Six inches were added to the wing center section and the overall length was reduced by nine inches. The fuel capacity of the wing tanks was reduced from 882 gallons to 805 gallons but, for longer flights—when aircraft were delivered overseas for example—up to eight 100-gallon auxiliary tanks could be installed in the cargo hold.[18] On operational flights, the C-47 normally flew with a crew of five: pilot, copilot, navigator, radio operator, and crew chief.

The forward section of the aircraft included the cockpit, a compartment for the radio equipment and operator, the navigator's compartments, and a space for cargo behind the copilot's seat. The main cabin, lavatory, and spare-parts compartment comprised the rear section of the aircraft. In cargo configuration, the C-47 could carry up to six thousand pounds of cargo on short flights, and accommodate a fully assembled jeep or a 37-mm cannon. The aircraft could carry up to twenty-eight fully equipped soldiers as a troop transport. In its medical airlift mode, when equipped with extra fuel tanks, the C-47 could accommodate 12 stretchers.[19] To aid in camouflage while parked, the upper surfaces of the aircraft were painted a dull green. The belly was painted a light gray to make the plane less visible while in flight.

Douglas C-47 Skytrain in flight. (USAF)

The aircraft insignia in the United States Army Air Corp had remained unchanged since 1919, including "the Meatball"—a red dot centered in a white star within a large blue circular background, positioned just forward of the tail. In the spring of 1942 the red dot was removed to avoid confusion with the Japanese roundel. On June 29, 1943, white bars were added to either side of the blue circle, all encompassed within a red outline.

It was a rugged, durable airplane. "The Dakota (C-47) could lift virtually any load strapped to its back and carry it anywhere and in any weather safely." But the aircraft was not without its peculiarities. It has been widely described as a collection of parts flying in loose formation. "It groaned, it protested, it rattled, it ran hot, it ran cold, it ran rough, it staggered along on hot days and scared you half to death. Its wings flexed and twisted in a horrifying manner, it sank back to earth with a great sigh of relief. But it flew and it flew and it flew."[20]

***

After a month at Baer, the 403rd TCG began its final move toward combat. It lost half of its strength when the 65th and 66th Squadrons were divested and reassigned to the Air Transport Command.[21]

On July 14, the 403rd began moving westward in two cohorts. The air echelons of the 403rd Headquarters unit, together with the air echelons of the 63rd and 64th Squadrons, departed Baer Field for the long cross-country flight to Hamilton Field near San Francisco, which would be the jumping-off point for the South Pacific.[22] They arrived on July 15. Eleven of the 64th's aircraft were brand-new C-47A models, manufactured under the same Douglas contract and delivered to the 403rd TCG between May 18 and 24, 1943. The remaining two aircraft had been manufactured in January.[23] The ground echelon of the 403rd Headquarters and the ground echelons of the two squadrons would travel by train to the west coast and embark by ship.

On the night of July 17, the 64th Squadron's air echelon—13 aircraft, 25 enlisted men, and 27 officers—left American soil for its overseas posting—the airfield at Tontouta on the island of New Caledonia, deep in the South Pacific. It left American soil short-handed: instead of 13 navigators, it had just seven.[24]

Of these 13 aircraft, one would be condemned as irreparable following an accident shortly after commencing operations in the South Pacific and three would crash or disappear into the Pacific. Remarkably, nine would survive the war, although seven of those were condemned as unfit for flying immediately after hostilities ended. In tribute to the skill with which these aircraft were flown and maintained, two of these original aircraft would not only survive the war, but would continue in service: one was transferred to the Near East Indian Air Force in 1946; a second would be sold as surplus after the war and would continue to fly in peacetime.[25]

The formation completed the first leg of its long trans-Pacific flight on the morning of July 18, landing at Hickam Field on the Hawaiian island of Oahu. The 64th Squadron commander later recorded: "Very strict cruise control to insure that distance would go to zero before petrol. I sat in that seat for fifteen hours and fifteen minutes and finally landed the poor C-47 about twenty feet above the runway. Thank you Mister Douglas for a tough airplane that would forgive a sloppy pilot."[26]

Just as the air echelon of the 64th was touching down safely at Hawaii, the remaining ground echelons for the 403rd TCG were making their own move toward embarkation, departing Baer Field by rail for Camp Stoneman, California, on July 18. They left without their contingent of glider aircraft but retained the glider pilots.

With the train moving westward, the men were now reasonably confident their ultimate destination would be the Pacific. Camp Stoneman was known to be the staging area for units assigned to the South Pacific Theater; those men who hoped for an assignment to England or to the Mediterranean Theater would be disappointed. Those imagining palm trees, grass skirts, and warm tropical evenings were eager to get moving.[27]

At that time, each ground echelon of the 63rd and 64th Squadrons consisted of 40 officers and 236 enlisted men. These men would be sorely missed by their air echelons for the four weeks required to catch up—for a significant part of those four weeks the air echelon would be engaged in cargo and troop-transport missions, all the while without maintenance and ground support teams—no mechanics, clerks, or cooks.

The ground echelon arrived at Camp Stoneman on July 24. After two weeks, the echelons split: the group's Headquarters Detachment boarded the troopship USS *Cape San Juan* at San Francisco and sailed on the morning of August 11.[28] Four days later, the ground echelons of the 63rd and 64th Squadrons boarded MV *Noordam* at San Francisco's Pier 39, and on the morning of August 16, the ship weighed anchor and set sail for Noumea, New Caledonia.[29]

Cape San Juan arrived at Noumea on September 1, *Noordam* on the 3rd. Personnel disembarked the next morning and were attached to Service Command Casual Camp.[30] They would remain there for nine days while awaiting further ship transport to their final posting—Espiritu Santo.[31]

The men of the ground echelons were less than enthralled with their short experience on New Caledonia: "The air echelons pulled out for Buttons [Santo] while ground units later were dumped into Camp Dismal, a happy hole reminiscent of Alliance, plus SOUPAC and mosquitos. The Old Man sent planes down to rescue some of the Sad Sacks, but most of them had to languish on KP [kitchen patrol], Guard, etc. before boarding another banana boat."[32]

CHAPTER TWELVE

Air Echelon on the Move

With their "shake-down" flight from the west coast to Hickam Field in Hawaii safely completed, the aircrews of the 64th Troop Carrier Squadron paused for a day to recover from their long flight and to tend to the maintenance needs of their aircraft.

On July 20, the air echelon, together with 403rd Group Commander Lt. Col. Harry Sands and his headquarters staff, departed Hickam as a 13-plane formation and arrived safely at Christmas Island that same evening.

Next day, the squadron split up with seven aircraft leaving Christmas Island for the next intermediate stop at Canton Island and the remaining six flying to Tutuila, the main island of Samoa.

On July 23, both formations flew to their final intermediate stop at Nadi in the Fiji Islands, Four days later, 12 of the aircraft departed for Tontouta on New Caledonia, arriving late the afternoon of the same day. The remaining aircraft left Nadi the next day and flew to the islands of Penrhyn, Aitutaki, Bora Bora, and Tongatabu before arriving at Tontouta on August 1. Just short of eight months after the 403rd Troop Carrier Group (TCG) was activated, the 64th TCS had arrived in the South Pacific Theater to begin combat operations.[1]

The 403rd's second squadron, the 63rd, left Hamilton Field two weeks later but, rather than flying together as a squadron, the aircraft of the 63rd departed the U.S. on different dates and followed varying routes to a different destination —Espiritu Santo in the New Hebrides, 300 miles north of Tontouta. The first aircraft arrived at Santo on August 6 and, by the 22nd, all aircraft of the 63rd were safely assembled the island.[2]

On arrival at Tontouta, the 403rd was assigned to XIII Air Force Service Command (AFSC) and operated under the direction of the AFSC's 13th Air Depot.[3] The AAF's Table of Organization and Equipment (TO&E) for a Troop Carrier Squadron authorized thirteen navigators, but having left the United States with just seven, the commander of the 64th Squadron, recently promoted Maj. Jack Roessell wasted no time securing the additional navigators he would need to complete his aircrew personnel. On the very day of his arrival at Tontouta, Roessell rounded up six navigators: Gonder, Selica, Sammon, Richardson, Bamberger, and Smith.[4]

Neither did the 13th Air Depot waste any time in assigning cargo and troop missions for the group's two squadrons. Records for the 63rd are illustrative: the day after arriving at Espiritu Santo, aircrews went to work flying freight and passengers to and from Guadalcanal, Tontouta, Auckland, Nadi and Suva in Fiji, Efate, Samoa, Tongatabu Island, Aitutaki in the Cook Islands, the Russel Islands, New Georgia, and elsewhere. "A total of 1541 hours were flown between the 6th and the 31st of August—each of the squadron's 12 aircraft averaging 5 flying hours *per day* without rest, and with additional hours spent in mission planning and briefings."[5]

> I saw Jack Roessell here yesterday [July 27], & am now with his outfit. I like the bunch very well—they are good eggs—mostly pilots, and hope to stay with them permanently ... Jack Roessell is from Lewiston—about my age. He is the skipper of the outfit—and a good one ... Geography down here is confusing—and navigation needs to be fairly good ... Jungles and swamp and rain & mud—boy what a mess ... I am well—and think I have as good a job as there is over here. It isn't too dangerous, is interesting, and should be a real education for me. I'm looking forward as usual to telling you all about it. We have some good times when we all get together and swap yarns, and get to have a lot in common. Some guy tells how he first met his wife. Another about a close call in a plane. Some other has to brag about his home state, and then has an argument on his hands. We always talk over the progress of the war & speculate on the future. Rumors are thick, but we've learned how to handle them.[6]

Despite his earlier rough landing at Hickam, Jack Roessell was evidently a good pilot and a capable leader. At the time he arrived New Caledonia, he was just 25 years of age, had been a commissioned officer and pilot for just two years, and had been promoted three times.

It was evident he was also a pragmatic commander. In his preflight briefings with aircrews, he often included this mantra:

(1) fuel on the ground does you no good
(2) runway behind you does you no good
(3) altitude above you does you no good.[7]

Second Lieutenant Leonard Richardson's "Short Snorter," a nearly universal item in each airman's wallet at that time in the war. It was a banknote, almost always a $1 bill, inscribed by people encountered during aviation operations. Alaskan bush pilots started the practice in the 1920s: if someone had signed a short snorter and the owner couldn't later produce it upon request, he was obliged to buy drinks—a short snort. Note that the first signature on Richardson's Short Snorter was Jack Roessell.

The work was intensive, and stayed that way. Writing to his folks on August 5, shortly after joining the 403rd, Richardson wrote:

> We're working hard every day now—and can't even see a promise of less than 7 days a week. We get up at 4:30, and get to bed between 9 & 10 pm. Flying is tiresome anyway—so we can sure use the sleep. Needless to say we are seeing a lot of country and live under a variety of conditions.[8]
>
> I have been to all the islands of any size down here and have lots to tell you when I get home ... We rarely miss a day flying, and are really getting in flying time. I'm getting better as a navigator all the time, and can hit those "oh-so-small" islands every time.[9]

In the South Pacific, with most of their flying over open water, pilotage—the navigation practice that relies on ground features to determine position—was of little value, and navigators relied on dead reckoning, a straightforward process but one that required careful observations and records:

> By means of the drift meter the navigator is able to determine drift, the angle between the heading of the airplane and its track over the ground. The true heading of the airplane is obtained by application of compass error to the compass reading. The true heading plus or minus the drift (as read on the drift meter) gives the track of the airplane. At a constant airspeed, drift on 2 or more headings will give then navigator information necessary to obtain the wind by use of his computer. Groundspeed is computed easily once the wind, heading, and airspeed are known. So, by constant recording of true heading, true airspeed, drift, and groundspeed, the navigator is able to determine accurately the position of the airplane at any given time. For greatest accuracy, the pilot must maintain constant courses and airspeeds. If course or airspeed is changed, notify the navigator so he can record these changes.[10]

By the time Richardson penned his note of the 5th, he had already flown six missions since reporting to the squadron just nine days earlier. The squadron's other navigators also flew with the same frequency. The pace of flight operations started fast, and never slowed.

The XIII Service Command was already a huge organization by the time the 403rd TCG joined it. Its subordinate units included air service groups, air depot groups, aviation engineering battalions, communications groups, and units responsible for ordnance, transportation, base security, and quartermaster units. Significantly, it also included the 13th TCS and the 801st Medical Air Evacuation Squadron (MAES).[11]

After less than two weeks at Tontouta, the 403rd and its two squadrons were ordered to the "Bomber 2" airfield located on the southeast corner of the island of Espiritu Santo, APO 708. Within a couple of months, the airfield would be redesignated as "Pekoa Airfield", "Pekoa" being the indigenous word meaning "second."[12]

The islands of the New Hebrides form an elongated "Y" shape, orientated southeasterly over an extent of roughly five hundred and fifty miles, centered between Fiji, the Solomon Islands, and New Caledonia. The principal islands in the archipelago are Espiritu Santo, Malo, Malekula, Aoba, Maewo, Pentecost, Ambrym, Epi, Efate, Erromango, Tanna, and Aneityum.

The combined land area of the islands is 4,700 square miles, about the size of the state of Connecticut, but the "footprint" of the archipelago—its archipelagic claim—is the size of Connecticut, New Hampshire, Vermont, and Rhode Island combined.[13]

Espiritu Santo is the largest of the islands, measuring 73 miles north to south and 36 miles east to west. Intense volcanism has shaped the island's western half, with peaks of over six thousand feet rising nearly vertically out of the sea for nearly the entire length of the island. Big Bay (Bay of St. Philip and St. James), the location of Quiros's first visit, is formed by two large peninsulas that extend northward, enclosing an embayment 10 miles wide and 18 miles in length.

The island's eastern half consists mainly of uplifted coral and limestone terraces and plateaus rising 300–600 feet above sea level. Mt. Turi is the only mountain of any significance in that area; at 1,837 feet, it is more of a hummock compared to the other mountains to the west.[14]

Espiritu Santo's Apuna and Ora Rivers are the two largest in the archipelago, each flowing northward to drain in to Big Bay.

Felix Speiser described the western coastline of Santo in 1913:

> High mountains came close to the shore, falling in almost perpendicular walls straight down into the sea. Deep narrow valleys led inland into the very heart of the island. Several times, when we were passing the openings of these valleys, a squall caught us, and rain poured down; then, again, everything lay in bright sunshine and the coast was picturesque indeed with its violet shadows and reddish rocks. The only level ground to be seen was at the mouths of the valleys in the shape of little river deltas.[15]

The 64th flew into Santo as a complete squadron on August 7.[16] For the men of the 64th, making this move required little preparation—they were operating with only what they had brought with them from the U.S. little more than a week earlier. With the ground echelon for both squadrons still en route, all that was required was to file a flight plan, check the weather, preflight the aircraft, load, and go.

The men on the C-47s might have thought that Noumea Harbor was bustling, but they would have been unprepared for the scale of operations at Santo. They were about to witness the result of industrialized warfare on a scale seen nowhere else.

As the pilots began their final approaches to Pekoa, they would have brought their aircraft down the length of the Segond Channel, the busiest harbor in the Pacific Theater. On this day, August 7, sixty-six vessels were either anchored or operating in the waters of the Segond Channel, including two of America's older battleships (USS *Colorado* and *Maryland*), plus three escort carriers, an Australian heavy cruiser, and three light cruisers. Among the smaller craft reported were 18 destroyers, eight cargo vessels, five oiler/tankers, four troopships, and a sizeable contingent of tenders, minesweepers, patrol vessels, repair ships, subchasers, and yard patrol craft. There was also a single submarine, *S-38*.[17]

And this was not an exceptionally busy time for the harbor. The month prior had seen the arrival of 63 cargo vessels alone—two ships a day![18]

When their flight schedules permitted a quick perusal of the base and the surrounding waters, the aircrews would have seen an endless queue of cargo ships waiting to unload at the newly built docks; ships at anchor, ships arriving, ships departing, Sometimes singly, sometimes as part of a larger task force; and ships being repaired at anchor, as well as larger ships undergoing more extensive repairs in the huge floating dry dock.

Segond Channel, August 1943.

All along the roads leading away from the busy harbor were mountains of supplies waiting to be sorted and stored in the blocks of warehouses—acres of combat vehicles, heavy weapons carriers, artillery shells, and bombs. During daylight hours, Army engineers and Navy Seabees continued to build and improve the roads that laced the southeastern part of Santo, bulldozing more coconut trees to make room for more warehousing and storage, more administrative buildings, and more barracks.[19]

The entire landscape of aviation bases in the South Pacific had reached a point of maturity by the time the 403rd was assigned to Santo. Beginning with a single airfield on New Caledonia, the Army and Naval air forces had, in little over a year, developed four airfields on New Caledonia, three at Espiritu Santo, four on Guadalcanal, and two further north in the Russell Islands and on New Georgia. If, in the summer of 1943, the air and naval operations at Santo were beginning to shift from an advance base—one which supported tactical operations against relatively close Japanese forces—to a rear base more oriented toward staging, supply, training, and shipping, that change merely served to increase the demand for the type of missions flown by the 403rd TCG.[20]

On landing, the headquarters of the 403rd and both squadrons set up permanent quarters adjacent to the Pekoa Airfield and saw first-hand that the southeastern corner of Espiritu Santo was a hotbed of both naval and aviation activities.

Pekoa was home to the 5th Bombardment Group and its four squadrons flying B-17s on reconnaissance and strike missions in the northern Solomons. In August, the group began transitioning to new aircraft—the larger, better performing, and longer-range B-24 Liberator heavy bombers, a change that added many more planes to the airfield and required more training flights for current and replacement crews.[21] Also based at Pekoa was the 18th Photographic Squadron, equipped with three reconnaissance versions of the B-25 bomber, flying a heavy schedule of mapping missions.[22] The 822nd Engineer Aviation Battalion and several other aviation-related service and operational units were also based at Pekoa, including: a combat camera unit, a statistical control unit, an airways communication squadron, a weather squadron, an airdrome squadron, and the 321st Air Service Group, with eight sub-units for signals, ordnance, and quartermaster units.

Ground traffic was intense. Bombers were being towed to hard stands and parking areas, while fueling, ordnance, and maintenance trucks, and personnel vehicles, plied the airfield and the adjacent roadways.

Missions flown by the 403rd's squadrons added further to the congestion on the airfield. Up to twelve times a day, often in predawn hours, aircraft of the 64th were preflighted and refueled, supply trucks brought cargo for delivery to Guadalcanal and elsewhere. Inbound, repair vehicles met arriving aircraft to offload spent engines for delivery to the repair facilities on the island, and Army ambulances arrived to treat and offload wounded soldiers returning from the front.[23]

And just a mile away, Bomber 1, now called Palikulo Field, was operating with the same intensity as Pekoa. The 307th Bomb Group and its four bomb squadrons, also recently re-equipped with B-24D bombers, operated from Palikulo, and was coming off what had been a terrible month. Its forward squadrons had flown 16 bombing missions, targeting strongly held Japanese positions in the northern Solomons. Eight

Aerial view of the Pekoa Airfield. (The Engineer Board, U.S. Army)

planes and 68 crewmen were lost in those missions—it was the worst month the group would experience in the war.[24]

Historian D. W. Kralovec noted the intense flight operations at Palikulo Field:

> ... for the month of November 1943, a total of two thousand five hundred fifty two [2552] planes of twenty different types landed. About one-half of these were C-47s, indicating the great number of passengers and air cargo carried. Also high in the figures were the nine hundred fifteen [915] B-24 landings.[25]

Marine Air Group 11 (MAG-11) also ran an extensive shore-based aviation operation at the Turtle Bay Airfield just eight miles north of Pekoa. At Turtle Bay, returned combat pilots were rehabilitated, new replacement pilots were trained and new Grumman Avenger torpedo bombers and F4F Wildcat carrier-based fighters, brought into the theater by Navy CVE "jeep carriers," were received and qualified before forwarding them to carriers or airfields to the north. Other aircraft operating from this busy Navy field included Douglas Dauntless dive bombers, Duck amphibians, Vought Corsair fighters, and Lockheed Ventura, Consolidated Liberator, and Consolidated PBY Catalina patrol aircraft.[26]

The airfield could accommodate up to three hundred carrier aircraft; flight operations at Turtle Bay were non-stop during daylight hours.

The Naval Air Transport Service (NATS) also contributed to the air traffic over Santo. Operating both seaplanes from its shoreside base on the Segond Channel, and R4D/C-47s from Pekoa, NATS was flying just over half a million miles a month in the summer of 1943. Carrying priority passengers, critical freight, and all-important mail for naval forces, the monthly miles flown would double by the end of the year and the unit would begin to resemble a commercial airline in operating practice.[27]

As the 403rd arrived at Santo to commence operations, a third bomber field on the island was also coming online. Designated "Bomber 3," or "Luganville" due to its proximity to the town of the same name, the airfield was completed in mid-July and commenced operations on August 1. It was home to a carrier aircraft service unit and a field overhaul unit that serviced, repaired, and prepped every type of aircraft that could fly off carriers, including fighters and torpedo bombers. Additionally, land-based Army, Navy, and Marine squadrons came to Bomber 3 for repairs, testing, and training, and in August, six Navy squadrons were based there, flying PV-1 Venturas, PB4Y-1 Liberators (equivalent to the Army's B-24), and PBY-5A Catalina search and patrol aircraft. Within a year of opening, the base would reach a capacity of 650 airplanes, with a ground staff of some thirty-five hundred officers and men.[28]

Operating units at Palikulo included a Navy photo unit, fighter and medium bomber units from the Royal New Zealand Air Force, and Navy reconnaissance aircraft. Significantly, Palikulo also served as the base for the South Pacific Combat Air Transport Command (SCAT).

***

Ambulance meeting a C-47 troop transport and offloading wounded. (64th T.C. Sq, 13th Jungle Air Force Sydney: Waite & Bull, Sydney, undated)

MAG-25's initial resupply and evacuation mission to Guadalcanal in 1942 marked the beginning of a critically important new logistics capability for the South, Southwest, and Western Pacific theaters. MAG-25's capacity doubled in late October when a second Marine squadron, VMJ-152, also operating R4D transports, arrived at Tontouta. The resupply and evacuation capability of the region was further bolstered with the arrival of the Army Air Force's 13th TCS, operating C-47s, on October 10.[29]

These three squadrons transported personnel and cargo from New Caledonia to Fiji, the New Hebrides, New Zealand, and, most importantly, Guadalcanal. For a critical 10-day period in October, every plane operating from Henderson Field on Guadalcanal depended on the gasoline flown there—12 barrels per planeload—by MAG-25 and the 13th TCS.[30]

By mid-December, in order to better coordinate the critical resupply and evacuation missions to remote regions of the vast South Pacific Theater, these three units had been combined within the newly constituted South Pacific Combat Air Transport Command, SCAT. In short order, SCAT became responsible for airlifting key personnel, matériel, and mail for all branches of the American military in the South Pacific.[31]

A true amalgam, SCAT operated under a Marine commander, an Army Air Force executive officer, and with the Navy providing maintenance and support for the aircraft. Its assets included 36 aircraft: 12 C-47s of the 13th TCS and 24 R4Ds from the two squadrons of MAG-25. It was a complicated arrangement and one of critical importance, but it worked.[32]

When the 403rd TCG arrived, the 13th TCS had already been operating on a relatively independent basis for almost a year from its base at Tontouta. On August 22, the 13th was assigned as the third squadron of the 403rd, bringing with it the 801st MAES.[33] The 13th TCS remained attached to SCAT for operational purposes, despite its assignment to the 403rd.

SCAT's headquarters had been at Tontouta, but moved to Pekoa shortly after the 403rd arrived, with the 13th TCS and the 801st MAES continuing operation from Tontouta. On October 10, 1943, the 403rd TCG's 63rd Squadron was also attached to SCAT for operational purposes and flew its first mission under SCAT on the 13th.[34] The 403rd's remaining squadron, the 64th, was not attached to SCAT but occasionally aircrews from the 64th were assigned Detached Service (DS) to SCAT for short-term flight assignments. For example, during November 1943, seven aircrews were assigned DS to SCAT, some for as little as two days and some for as long as two weeks.[35]

On flights, for example from Tontouta to Santo or from Santo to Guadalcanal, the average load carried was 4,000 lbs, but there was an element of "winging it" in cargo loading. "Loading of freight on the Skytrains was usually by volume: the Skytrains were stuffed with everything that could fit, regardless of total tonnage. The supply depot transported priority items to the airfield and left them under the shade of a tree near the runway. No equipment was available for weighing, storing or carting matériel."[36]

A certain cowboy attitude permeated SCAT. "The outstanding feature of the SCAT operation traffic-wise, and of New Caledonia in general, was the lack of adequate planning and proper traffic coordination and control."[37] Record keeping was also a bit cavalier and later critiques observed that "Figures on the movement of traffic by SCAT are very limited and unsatisfactory," and referenced the "lack of necessary statistics," the "indifferent staff procedures and ... patchy record keeping" and found "no figures are available" ... "Due to lack of necessary statistics."[38]

But even with these deficiencies, by April 1943, SCAT was operating five trips a day to Guadalcanal from Tontouta, plus three daily flights to Australia, occasional flights to Fiji, and many additional local flights to other airfields on the island. In the words of Army Air Force Col. Harry Sands, SCAT's Operations Officer: " ... SCAT came to be a sort of regular airline running up and down the islands, from New Caledonia to the New Hebrides, up to the Russells, to Munda, and beyond,"[39] and the number of scheduled SCAT flights were not far off those seen at Chicago or La Guardia airport.[40]

In early operations, Marine hospital corpsmen flew medical evacuation missions on MAG-25 and 13th TCS transports and, during 1942, provided care to nearly forty-five hundred sick and wounded evacuees.[41] But in early 1943, SCAT's medical capabilities received a tremendous boost with the arrival of the flight surgeons and Army nurses of the 801st MAES.[42]

The 801st MAES had been activated to "furnish rapid, efficient, and comfortable medical care and evacuation by Air Transport to as near the battle as possible."[43]

The advanced echelon of the 801st arrived on New Caledonia on January 3, 1943, and included just five medical officers and a small cohort of enlisted men. They were immediately attached to the 13th TCS, with rather more responsibilities than supplies or equipment.[44]

With only the minimum camp established, just six days after arriving at Tontouta, a MAES flight surgeon flew the first evacuation mission with the 13th to Guadalcanal, returning the following day with 16 patients.[45] When nurses began flying evacuation missions on March 1, the rate of evacuation picked up markedly: over fifteen hundred patients that month and, in July, the teams set a record with 189 evacuees in a single day.[46]

Until July 1, 1943, with the United States heavily committed to combat operations in the northern Solomons, "almost no patients were evacuated from north of Espiritu Santos (by boat), all evacuations being done adequately by air." SCAT was one of the few organizations in the United States armed forces to successfully combine Army, Navy, and Marine Corps personnel into one smoothly operating union.[47]

By September, it was the opinion of the commander of the 801st that it was possible to evacuate as many as five thousand patients per month.[48]

By the end of the summer of 1943, Base Button had been developed into an enormous war-fighting infrastructure. Beyond the Army Air Force's potent combat capabilities, other Army units on the island possibly surpassed even the Naval units. Three forces assured the island's defense: the 129th Combat Team, which itself included the 129th Infantry Regiment, a full field artillery battalion, and two attached engineering and medical companies; two battalions of coastal artillery; and an anti-aircraft command that included one regiment and an attached coastal artillery battalion.[49] Also operating at Base Button were the 822nd Engineer Aviation Battalion, two air service groups, and many additional squadron and company size units for maintenance, quartermaster, signal, and service support. Serving those aviation units was XIII Service Command, which included an engineering regiment, the 25th Evacuation Hospital, the 122nd Station Hospital, and many smaller units for ordnance, ammunition, maintenance, and malarial control.

At the time, the U.S. Army, Navy and Marines had 39,000 men and women on the island, and the Royal New Zealand Air Force added another 1,000; it was a force that equaled the entire population of the New Hebrides at the time and was equal to that of many American cities, including Albuquerque, New Mexico, Raleigh, North Carolina, Steubenville, Ohio, or Laredo, Texas.[50]

As the two squadrons of the 403rd settled into their new quarters adjacent to Pekoa Airfield, amid the drone of single, twin, and four-engine aircraft warming up, taking off, landing, and taxiing, from the pre-dawn darkness to after sunset, it was as if the 64th had landed at the Brooklyn Navy Yard with Fort Bragg and Pensacola Naval Air Station next door. Fuel of all classes, food and provisions of all sorts, spare parts, mail, trash disposal, and even a regular bus service were there for the asking.

CHAPTER THIRTEEN

Flight Operations from Santo

Espiritu Santo was home to an interesting mix of units in the summer of 1943. Many of the units—those whose mission was supply or maintenance or training of combat units—would never see combat. Others, like the surface vessels then in the Segond Channel for retrofitting, repair, or provisioning, or the 129th Infantry Regiment, would eventually see intense combat. Some units, like the bomber groups, saw combat daily.

But despite the massive military complex all around them, for a newly arrived troop carrier squadron, especially one operating without its ground echelon, it was "hunt and peck" for everything.[1]

In his report to Thirteenth Air Force Service Command, the Group's Adjutant, Capt. T. H. Taylor reflected on the difficulties encountered by the 403rd Troop Carrier Group (TCG) and its squadrons without its ground echelon personnel:

> It might be remarked here that the air echelon had been operating since early in August with none of the personnel, records or equipment needed for administrative functions as well as maintenance on the airplanes. Such service units and facilities as were available were used for this purpose, but this arrangement was not entirely satisfactory ... [2]

In other words, the air echelon of both the 63rd and 64th Troop Carrier Squadrons had to scrounge whatever it could from other operating units in the area—a situation many newly arriving units had faced in the formative months of Base Button. The aircrews were being fed by other units, and medical care was provided at Army or Navy units. Whatever they needed that they had not brought with them on the flight from the U.S. had to be secured locally. Unlikely as it may seem, particularly having been based in the middle of a teeming military complex, life for the men of the 64th TCS meant washing clothes in a nearby stream, eating out of a mess kit, sleeping in a tent with a dirt floor, and flying every day.

The 64th was designed to be self-sufficient in many respects, but without its ground echelon the aircrews were hard pressed: "Everyone who could pound a typewriter was drafted, and personnel were borrowed to assist in administrative details. Supplies and equipment were chiseled and we learned that a 'moonlight requisition' was the best medium of acquiring supply."[3]

A typical mission for the 64th was described in detail in a 1945 retrospective:[4]

"Come on, let's go! You won't go back to sleep will you?" Thus starts a day of flying with the familiar words of the CQ[5] at about 0400. After a little breakfast, which isn't particularly desired at this early hour, you drop by your tent and pick up your bag with enough clothes for about a week's trip. Next stop is Operations, and immediately following is the "Floating Ride" in the Weapon's Carrier to the Line.

After the Crew Chief checks everything thoroughly during his pre-flight, he assures you that all is OK.

"Sadie Tower, this is 6305, take-off instructions please?" This is what you'll hear the co-pilot ask the tower over the radio. "6305 from Sadie, from East to West take-off," the tower will reply. Everything is all set now and you'll soon be rolling on the first flight of this trip.

Life during a flight is pretty much routine. Pilots spend their time keeping on course, watching weather, reading, and maybe nap a little. The navigator will be found checking his course or with his eye glued to the drift meter. You might find him reading a little too. If numerous clicks are heard in the crew's compartment, you'll find the radio operator "beating it out," finding the weather or maybe sending in an ETA. The engineer will probably be checking the instruments to make sure his engines are performing all right, or he might be in the rear answering questions of the passengers: "What time will we land? Where are we now? Can I go up front?" You might possibly find him resting a little too.

After the landing, which might possibly be a "grease job," or the other extreme, "A ride 'em cowboy number," the plane is taxied to a parking ramp.

An hour's wait is to be expected here because first, the load has to be removed. Next, a new load has to be put on and tied properly, and last, the gasoline and oil trucks, which are always difficult to stop, must fuel the plane for the next flight.

Some missions were out-an-back from Santo to Guadalcanal and return. Others involved two or more destinations, and required the aircrews to remain overnight ("RON") at various airfields for up to a week.

"RONING" is probably the most interesting part of the entire trip. This involves eating, sleeping, and living in the plane for the duration of the fifty hours of flying time. The eating during flights is very little, just coffee and possibly some cheese and crackers from the ten-in-one ration boxes. The evening meal is prepared over the gas stove and consists of the contents of the ration boxes. Sometimes different items are borrowed from the Mess Hall or anyone who is willing to be borrowed from. A loaf of bread is acquired from the Red Cross or nearest mess, and perhaps some eggs or steak can be found on one of the neighboring planes. Of course every meal is topped off with a good hot cup of coffee. After eating a search is made for a shower. Sometimes one is located, usually at the other end of the strip, but more often, none can be found, so the showers are postponed until the next day. The bedding-down process is always an extremely important episode. Litters, air mattresses, and blankets are gotten out and a suitable "sack" is assembled. Mosquito nets are tied to different places on the bottom of the plane and the less ambitious individual rely on "Scat" to keep the mosquitoes away ... Sleeping under the plane is fine unless a rain happens along, which often occurs, then there is a mass movement for the interior of the plane.

Finally the point of destination is the Home Base, and every member of the crew is looking forward to getting his mail, a good shower, some clean clothes, and complete bed.

Thus goes the life during a week's flying aboard one of our planes.

Airfield control towers managed air traffic on Espiritu Santo. At Palikulo (Bomber 1), the tower was named "Blondie," after Major "Blondy" Saunders who commanded the 11th Bomber Group. At Pekoa (Bomber 2), the tower was designated "Dagwood";

at Luganville (Bomber 3), "Lugan"; at the fighter airstrip at Turtle Bay, the tower was "Tripoli Base"; and at the Sarakata seaplane base, it was "Hazel."[6]

Navigation aids on Santo were rudimentary. There was no instrument landing system in place, but a four-course radio range apparatus had been established about a mile north of the Dagwood at Pekoa to help pilots locate themselves above southeast Santo in the event of low clouds and visibility. The system was limited. It did not lead the pilot to his intended airfield. Rather, it was a set of procedures that brought the pilot to the vicinity of his airfields, to an altitude (750 feet) where the weather conditions would permit a visual sighting of his base. Following these procedures, if a pilot descended to 750 feet and lost the tower signal, it meant he was directly over the radio beacon. If at that point he could still not see his airfield, he would have to either find another field or return to altitude to hold until the weather improved. "It is on the worst case side of a non-precision approach."[7]

***

Also at Pekoa was the 25th Evacuation Hospital, ready to provide major medical and surgical treatment of casualties and to assemble cohorts of casualties to facilitate evacuation. It had been constituted in mid-1942 with a medical staff drawn from Chicago's West Suburban Hospital. After completing basic training in Missouri, the 32 doctors and 46 nurses embarked for Espiritu Santo in late October, and their ship dropped anchor in the Segond Channel on November 29.[8] At the time of its arrival, and until at least early 1945, the 25th would be the sole evacuation hospital in the South Pacific.

The site selected for the hospital was in a grove of coconut palms at the southeast end of Pekoa Airfield. The rainy season was well underway when the 25th disembarked, and the personnel arrived at their campsite to find a sea of mud, daily rainstorms, and relentless flies and mosquitoes.

"And then we started getting sick. And I mean we really got sick—diarrhea, malaria, fatigue, depression." Their commanding officer came down with malaria on December 16, right on cue given the incubation period for the disease, and had to be evacuated back to the U.S. with cerebral malaria.[9]

"They were waylaid with the same tropical diseases that we were battling. We did the best we could for them, housing them in makeshift medical tents while we continued to build a proper hospital, while trying to gather as much information as we could about these diseases." But the pervasive diseases of Santo continued to take a toll on the men and women of the 25th. By March 3, 1944, 38% of the officers who had first departed San Francisco in October 1942 had been returned to hospitals in the States because of illness of one kind or another.[10]

The Seabees of the 15th Construction Battalion came to the aid of the 25th. By February, in cooperation with the 822nd and 350th Army Engineers, the 15th had constructed Quonset huts for staff quarters, wards, laboratories, and messing facilities. "The first two huts were erected end to end, providing … three operating rooms and a scrub room."[11]

"By March 7, 1943, our wards were filled with more than five hundred patients with illnesses like hepatitis, dengue fever, malaria, and various skin diseases. On March 15, 1943, we opened our operating rooms, about seven months after we'd left Oak Park. Surgical teams were formed, and the battle casualties began arriving."[12]

Navy casualties went to the Navy's hospitals, and the adage that "the Navy got the Gravy" held true for a time on Santo. Army hospitals on both Efate and Espiritu Santo remained "vastly inferior to the naval hospitals, which were housed in prefabricated buildings, with connecting corridors and linoleum covered floors, and were equipped with white enameled hospital beds, white blankets, adequate supplies of linen, and unit laundries."[13]

***

From Pekoa, the troop carrier squadrons would cover an expanse from Sydney, Australia, in the west to the Cook Islands to the east—a straight-line distance of over thirty-five hundred miles—and from New Zealand in the south to Vella Lavella to the north—nearly twenty-five hundred miles. This equated to a total land area of over seven million square miles, over twice the size of the United States west of the Mississippi. Within that huge stretch of salt water, the island area was just 31,000 square miles, less than half a percent of the total expanse, and much of that mountainous.[14]

In his letter of August 10, Leonard Richardson mentioned his crew assignment for the first time: "My pilot is from Rhode Island, and my co-pilot from Rochester, N.Y. The radio man is from N.Y.N.Y. and the crew chief from a small town in Ohio."[15] The aircrew had been assigned C-47 [serial number] 42-23711, an aircraft built at the Douglas Aircraft factory in Long Beach, California, and delivered to the Army Air Force on May 20, 1943. It was one of 1,948 C-47s supplied by the Long Beach plant in 1943 under contract AC-20669 at a cost per plane of $92,417.[16]

By August 20, Richardson could report that his living conditions had improved at Pekoa:

> We are living in wooden "Quonset" huts now & I have electric lights. It looks as though it may be permanent, and isn't bad—but doesn't approach the splendor of navy quarters. The Navy puts out money for their boys.
>
> You also asked about tropical diseases. Yes—there are some, and we have to take caution at night. We sleep under a net, called a "mosquito bar" & wear our shirts with sleeves rolled down. They provide us with atabrine and quinine. Malaria and Dengue Fever are the most common, but those who get it are well take care of.
>
> This is (Friday) morning, and I am stealing a moment—high in the sky—9 miles from land. It could be made to sound fascinating—but I have 40 hours this week already and am a little tired.[17]

There had been no honeymoon for the air crews of the 64th and Richardson's earlier prediction of daily flights proved to be true. The squadron came immediately to full operational tempo in August and never a day passed without multiple missions flown. On an average day, eight of the squadron's 13 C-47s would complete missions, but it was not unusual for as many as 10 or 11 aircraft to be assigned missions. With the squadron's ground echelon and its full contingent of mechanics and technicians still at sea, it was testament to the aircraft's durability that the squadron could maintain a 96% aircraft availability during the month.[18]

Some missions were quite short—as little as 90 minutes. The longest was Richardson's flight of August 26 at 11½ hours duration and roughly 1,850 miles, which included landings at Tontouta and Norfolk en route to Auckland, New Zealand.[19]

Most missions were flown to Guadalcanal (629 miles, R/T 8 hours), Tontouta (427 miles, R/T 5½ hours), or Efate (167 miles, R/T 2 hours).

The squadron's aircrews proved to be equally durable, at least for the first month of operations. During the month of August each navigator flew an average of twenty missions. Flying time for each was variable—one navigator flew just 75 hours, while another 137 hours. Richardson logged 135 flying hours in 22 flights, two more than the rest of his aircrew because he was seconded to another aircraft for two missions.

On August 30, Richardson wrote that he had been to Auckland, New Zealand:

> It was just swell. In the first place, girls were easy to date, and we made the best of it. I had one date the first night, then wandered about town the next day. Then in the middle of the afternoon I met a WREN [Women's Royal Naval Service], who invited me to her home for tea and then for dinner in the evening ... I went to a dance and met a nice little Irish girl there. We had to leave the next morning and sure hated to leave. I can honestly say it was the nicest experience I've had since I left home. Am back on the job now—with flying to do, a sackfull of laundry staring me in the face, and still looking forward to your letters.[20]

His "rest leave" was more of an extended stopover and consisted of a day-and-a-half of recreation sandwiched between an 11½ hour outbound flight on the 26th and a seven-hour return flight on the 28th.

Still, even a short break from the rigors of daily flights was rejuvenating. This brief hiatus brought the chance to glimpse the normal life he had left behind:

> ... [the airman is] impressed with the sight of streets and sidewalks; he is impressed with the sight of women in dresses, and of children, their voices and their laughter. He finds a brightness in the life about him to which he has not been accustomed. He notices colors he had almost forgotten. He is impressed too with the paraphernalia of civilization; the tools, the fabrics, the roofs and walls that keep out the heat and rain, and the hot and cold running water. All these recreate interest that for some time had been little more than a memory.[21]

As Richardson alluded to in his letters home, the Navy knew how to take care of its own, and its care included an extensive welfare and recreation program, much of which was available to Army personnel.

Had they the time, which they most assuredly did not, the flight crews of the 64th could have swum at the Sarakata beach, joined one of 140 teams to compete in the station-wide horseshoe tournament, played tennis, softball, baseball, or volleyball, and viewed or participated in station-wide softball and hardball tournaments.

Or they might have trained for the upcoming Christmas Day South Pacific Area Boxing Championship at Guadalcanal. The elimination round on Santo for that competition drew over one hundred entrants, most of whom were Golden Glove or had professional experience.

The 2,500-seat NAB Theater was formally commissioned on August 8, and in its first 23 days offered 21 feature films, two United Service Organizations Stage Shows, and band performances from the bands aboard the destroyer tender USS *Dixie* and from the 129th Infantry. "The handsomest and the most complimented (by visiting performers) movie palace in the South Pacific."[22]

The Navy was well set; so many services and facilities were available on Santo and along the Segond Channel, that it issued a series of bulletins to acquaint arriving ships and personnel with the facilities available at Espiritu Santo. From trash to torpedoes, bombs to bacon, or gas to gyros, the Navy had it, and a warehouse to store it.

The pace of operations remained high in September. Pilots in the three squadrons flew an average of 96½ hours in September; navigators averaged 115 hours for the month. Richardson's friend and fellow navigator, Lt. Bryce Sammon, flew 24 missions in 30 days, logging over one hundred sixty-three flight hours.[23]

By the end of the month, the 64th TCS would fly 169,606 mission miles, over twelve hundred eighty flying hours, and carry 727,588 lbs of freight, 1,432 passengers, and 52 wounded.

While the 64th was operating with the approved number of navigators and pilots, it soon became evident the aircrews available for combat and forward assignments needed to be increased to meet the demand. In a November report, the 403rd TCG's Adjutant, Capt. T. H. Taylor, noted " ... sufficient navigators were not available to meet scheduled trips and operations were limited to the number of navigators available.[24]

He further commented that:

> ... the 87 pilots and 39 navigators authorized by the T/O [table of organization] for three Troop Carrier Squadrons are inadequate for operations of this type. Further, the type of operations performed by this Group during the period under review was similar to Airline operation in that regular runs were being made daily which fact added the problem of providing sufficient crews to operate the airplanes assigned.

As early as April 1943 flight surgeons detected a growing "aeroneuroses" among their aircrews: "The need was urgent. The strain of constant overwater flying rested particularly heavily upon the navigators, but it was severe for all air personnel; and so long as there was no definite goal short of physical collapse, there followed a general reduction of morale and combat efficiency."[25]

The heavy flying schedule placed tremendous strain on flight crews. Writing in April 1943, the Intelligence Officer of one troop carrier unit in the Pacific reported on the condition of aircrews and offered a litany of reasons for aircrew fatigue. Specifically cited were the lengthy missions on overloaded aircraft over long water distances, deplorable weather and poor weather reports, the increased landing and take-off hazards associated with operating from hurriedly improvised airfields, the lack of fighter protection when flying in combat areas, the prevalence of malaria and dengue in forward areas, and much more.[26]

In a report submitted to Troop Carrier Command shortly after his arrival on New Caledonia in early 1943, the 801st MAES' commander provided commentary on the intensity of South Pacific Combat Air Transport Command flight operations and its effect on the flight crews, and specifically referred to the aircrews of the 13th TCS who had been flying in theater for just three months. He did not mince words:

> The pilots and crews of the 13th Troop Carrier are subjected to grave mental strain, caused by the nature of their flights here in the Southwest Pacific. Many individuals do not realize the type of flying and strain which a transport pilot operates under. Living conditions in this area are far from ideal. The mess is extremely poor and certainly does not contain adequate nourishment and vitamins. Several of the pilots have developed types of neuroses and ... one individual will never be qualified to fly again. If the men continue to go on as they are they will pass the point of rejuvenation.

The commander recommended that all transport pilots be rotated Stateside after no more than nine months of operations, and that "some form of citation should be given to the Squadron for its meritorious service."[27]

Throughout the course of the war, the only trouble that arose between the commander of the 403rd, Col. Harry Sands, and the squadron commander of the 64th TCS, Maj. Jack Roessell, had to do with flying hours for the squadron's navigators. Roessell had met with Maj. Gen. Hubert Harmon, then commanding the Thirteenth Air Force, and, when asked, informed the general that his navigators and some other crew members were flying 125 hours or more per month.

The general later upbraided Sands for not monitoring the flying time of his troops better, a reprimand Sands did not enjoy. He confronted Roessell, asking how he dared to complain to the general about flying hours, effectively circumventing normal channels. After an acrimonious meeting, during which Sands threatened to send the major home. Roessell replied: "I'm ready to go home as soon as you sign the orders, but you have to admit we are your best Squadron." Roessell remained as commander of the squadron and, in 1944, headquarters reduced the flying hours so 100 a month became the norm.[28]

So intense was the flying schedule that even the glider pilots were put to work. "The fifty-four glider pilots in the 63rd and 64th TCS are being used in the ground echelon work of each squadron, and also in connection with our combined operations with SCAT."[29] Qualified glider pilots began to fly the C-47s on submarine patrol missions.[30]

Every flying hour with a glider pilot at the controls meant one more hour of cargo or medivac missions by a "regular" pilot, or, less likely, an extra hour of sack time.

The flight crews of the 63rd and 64th—and most especially the crew chiefs—were elated at the impending arrival of the ground echelon. It arrived at Noumea Harbor aboard the MS *Noordam* just before noon on September 3, and left the next morning for the casual camp outside of Noumea. On the 5th, as most of the ground echelon began receiving unwelcome casual duties, a small advance group of three officers and seven enlisted men from each of the squadrons left by air to join the 403rd at Santo—the lucky "Sad Sacks" mentioned earlier who thereby escaped the unpleasant work details at Casual Camp near Noumea.

Five days later the slightly diminished ground echelons boarded the Cape San Juan for the short voyage to Espiritu Santo, expected to arrive on September 15.[31]

***

The 64th began flight operations from Santo at a time when the previous malaria outbreak had abated. Rainfall for the year was below normal and August was exceptionally dry—only 1¼ inch of rain fell in the month, compared to an average monthly total of just over five inches. Less rain meant less mosquito breeding and less malaria.

Within the base limits, from the fighter strip at Turtle Bay to the Renee River, malaria was well controlled. The vicious outbreak of dengue fever had also abated. By August, concurrent with the arrival of the 403rd, the rate of dengue had fallen 50-fold from its March peak.[32]

But just as the men of the 129th Infantry routinely ventured away from the healthy confines of Base Button to conduct combat patrols in the deep bush, or to maintain outposts and gun positions beyond the base perimeter, so too did the aircrews on Santo travel to other, less healthy islands.

As late as mid-July 1943, well after the issue on Guadalcanal had ended and with the 403rd preparing to advance to Espiritu Santo, General Marshall cabled Army commanders in malarious areas, advising: "Malaria portends to be one of the greatest dangers to military operations in this war ... The most important measures are careful screening at bases ... and servicing of forward units with antimalarial supplies [including Atabrine]."[33]

Among the infantry, malaria continued to rage. "The fall of 1943 in the Pacific saw ten hospital admissions for malaria for every one battle casualty, and a majority of the Allied divisions were incapable of effective military duty." An Army circular in late October 1943 noted the equivalent of six divisions—ninety thousand officers and men—had been incapacitated in one theater alone. In another, the equivalent of one battalion a month was being evacuated with malaria.[34]

From their earliest cargo and troop carrier missions, the aircrews of the 403rd entered some of the most virulent regions of the world, but by following good hygiene practices, using bed nets, and limiting time spent outside after dark, the health risks could be managed. There was one operational factor, however, that was completely beyond the ability of anyone to control, a factor that would invariably terrorize anyone venturing into the skies of the South Pacific. Weather. If malaria ranked as one of the worst enemies for ground troops in the South Pacific Theater, weather was surely among the worst for aircrews.

The New Hebrides are just south of "The Doldrums"—a belt around the Earth where, in earlier eras, sailing ships commonly experienced windless conditions. Today, the region is less colorfully referred to as the Inter-Tropical Convergence Zone (ITCZ, or "itch"). In this zone, extending roughly five degrees north and south of the equator, the prevailing trade winds of the northern hemisphere blow southwesterly and collide with the southern hemisphere's northeasterly trade winds. This convergence results in a rising mass of warm, moist air which, on reaching higher altitudes, results in intense thunderstorms, vigorous turbulence, and even hurricanes; persistent bands of squalls and thunderstorms can merge, spreading to hundreds of miles in breadth and depth. With most of the severe weather generated at altitude, the sparse islands of the South Pacific had little attenuating effect and, paradoxically, because the air circulates in an upward direction, there is often little wind at the surface.[35]

Weather often dominated land, air, and sea operations in the Pacific. One war correspondent reported, "This is how important weather is in the Pacific war: weather ranks with guns and ammunition. Weather is the first step in planning, and the final determination in execution."[36]

Weather had been a determinant from the very inception of hostilities. Japan chose to approach the Hawaiian Islands from the north in early December 1941 because the severe weather and tortuous seas at northern latitudes normally precluded ship traffic, making an undetected approach possible.[37]

> To the boys flying the Solomons circuit, weather was the worst foe of all. Massive fronts, turbulent and unpredictable, would roll across the Coral Sea without warning, blotting out sky and water. These huge, black tumbleweeds of the air sometimes blacked out whole island chains. You were crazy if you tried to fly into them and you couldn't always fly around or over them. We tried every dodge possible, but sometimes it was no go.
>
> You'd try to climb over a front and maybe you'd get up to 20,000 feet and still the clouds would be piling up around you. Or you'd go down to sea level and try to hop the waves. But after you'd pushed in under the overcast for a little way your plane would start bobbing and twisting and you'd better damned well get out while you were able![38]

Even for the C-47, nearly the size of the B-17 heavy bomber, turbulence could be deadly. A sudden downdraft could cause a large plane to lose 10–15 thousand feet of elevation in seconds, and turbulence could easily flip low-flying aircraft into the sea.

Flying around these storms was a good option if the storm's size and the onboard fuel permitted. But the risks of skirting a storm were brought clearly into focus in late January 1943 when a B-17 carrying the commander of the Thirteenth Air Force, Maj. Gen. Nathan Twining, ran into severe weather on a routine flight from Guadalcanal to the New Hebrides. The pilot ran out of fuel in trying to circumvent the storm and was forced to ditch at sea. Adrift in small rubber boats for six days, the general and his team were rescued by a Navy PBY off the coast of Malekula Island.[39]

Even for the Army's largest aircraft, the B-17 and B-24, the weather had an extraordinary effect on operations. Many missions were canceled or aborted when weather obscured the target. Often, however, the consequences of severe weather were more devastating, as the events of "Black Sunday" would show.

After a successful bombing mission against Japanese forces on New Guinea in April 1944, the returning formation of B-24 heavy bombers, B-25 medium bombers, and A-20 light bombers found itself blocked from reaching home airfields by low clouds and fog that had moved inland. Desperate pilots looked in vain for breaks in the weather, frantic to save their plane and crews. Of the mission's 170 strike aircraft, 31 were lost—effectively an entire bomb group.

The commander of MacArthur's air forces in the Southwest Pacific, Gen. George Kenney, would later record, "We took a beating. It was not administered by the Jap. The weather did us wrong. It was the worst blow I took in the whole war."[40]

Other units reported similarly. In commenting on the Japanese fighters, the unit historian of the 11th Bomb Group noted that "Despite their increased efficiency we continued to lose more airplanes because of weather and navigation than in combat."[41]

But conditions that would force the cancellation of fighter or bomber missions would not impede C-47 operations. Normally, C-47 flights took place regardless of weather. Flying the slow but stable transports, pilots of the 403rd TCG took pride in their ability to complete missions under the worst of conditions, but later memoirs documented the drama that could develop even on routine routes.

Radioman Arthur Driedger recalled that the weather was often described in "Savannah" units: "Savannah 1 indicated clear weather with unlimited visibility, Savannah 2 was almost as good, and so it went to Savannah 5, which was flying through water with fish on the outside."[42]

Pilot Richard Jenkins described a heavy weather mission:

> Our navigator could not see the sky and he could not see the water. We were flying on instruments. I dropped the plane down low to where I thought we might be able to see the water. Suddenly a mountain rose up from the clouds. I veered off and we missed it, but 15 more seconds and we would have exploded against the side of that mountain.[43]

If caught in a severe thunderstorm, pilots were taught to get through them by reducing air speed and aiming for the darkest cloud where the rain was strongest and the turbulence least. Then, if cold rain caused the engines to cool and cut out, pilots increased drag on the aircraft by lowering landing gear and flaps, then ramped up the engine RPM to keep the engines hot.

The 64th Squadron received a lesson in heavy weather flying on its first mission to Guadalcanal. Its commander, Jack Roessell, recalled: "Don't think I have ever been in heavier rain than on the first flight. I ended up running the Pratt & Whitneys at military power just to stay at a constant altitude! I didn't know that much water could come down in one place!"[44]

The 403rd prided itself in always getting into the air, regardless of weather conditions. With one notable exception:

> The lone demerit of our entire operational record during two years flying came in early February (1944) when a tropical hurricane swept the entire SOPAC area. In spite of our efforts, we were forced to cancel all missions during one day of the storm ... the first time that the Sandmen failed to take to the air.[45]

CHAPTER FOURTEEN

September 5, 1943

In the spring and summer of 1943, Allied operations showed very encouraging results in all theaters. However much they might have been "on the back foot," though, Japanese forces in the South Pacific during the summer of 1943 were still as dangerous as a cobra and, as a result, American combat operations in the South Pacific during the months of July and August were both carefully planned and occasionally quite frenzied.

In the Pacific, Operation *Cartwheel* was launched with the ultimate goal of neutralizing the large Japanese bastions at Rabaul, Kavieng, and Kolombangara. *Cartwheel* included 13 subordinate operations targeting specific strategic points in the Southwest Pacific Theater.

The first of these operations, *Chronicle*, began on June 30, 1943, to capture Woodlark and Kiriwina Islands—two islands in the middle of the Solomon Sea, midway between Guadalcanal and New Guinea. The Allied occupation was unopposed, and by the end of June the two islands, and the islets surrounding them, were under solid American control.

Next up was Operation *Toenails*, targeting the islands of the New Georgia archipelago. These were situated to the north and west of Guadalcanal and included the islands of Vella Lavella, Kolombangara, Rendova, and the island of New Georgia itself. The geographical location of the New Georgia group made it the next logical step in America's move out of the southern Solomons. The campaign included a series of land and naval battles that began on June 30, with American forces landing at Rendova and several adjacent islands.

By early August, the key Japanese airfield at Munda on the island of New Georgia had been secured and, within a week, the badly damaged airfield was repaired and ready for use by Army Air Force units. Munda provided a base 150 miles north of Guadalcanal from which bombing missions could be launched deeper into the northern Solomons; an entirely new phase of air operations in the New Georgia Campaign could now begin.

Throughout the New Georgia campaign, the Thirteenth Air Force was especially busy, mounting daily fighter and bomber missions from Henderson Field. With each ground advance, American Army engineers quickly built or improved new airfields from which further airstrikes could be mounted. Airfields on the Russell Islands and at Munda and Vella Lavella, which had themselves been the targets of massive bombing raids just weeks earlier, were used to launch bomber strikes deeper into the northern Solomons. By the end of the New Georgia campaign, with four new airfields in operation, all of Bougainville now fell within bomber range; significantly, those bombing missions could also receive fighter cover.[1]

Bougainville, the northernmost island of the Solomons chain, was located just 231 air miles from Rabaul. Securing Bougainville would place New Britain, including Rabaul and Kavieng, and much more of New Guinea within easy striking distance by Allied bombers.

The Allied strategy was to strike fast and hard into the northern Solomons and, for the men of the 403rd Troop Carrier Group, the writing was on the wall. In the five weeks that the 63rd and 64th Troop Carrier Squadrons were based on Espiritu Santo, the Allies had already made substantial gains in the northern Solomons, in the small islands west of New Guinea, and along the northern coastline of New Guinea itself. As combat continued deeper in the northern Solomons, and new Allied initiatives developed on New Guinea, the attacking forces would need to be advanced and resupplied, and their wounded would need evacuation.

Continuing to launch troop and cargo missions from Santo to the newly secured northern airfields was not an option. The distance was now simply too great, even with a refueling stop at Henderson Field, and the most remote airstrips could provide no maintenance support to the C-47s. A more advanced position for the 63rd and 64th TCS was essential, and the most logical point for that was on Guadalcanal itself.

By early September, the chow-line chatter was less about whether the troop transport squadrons would move and more about when.

***

Except for the vagaries of weather, the supply and evacuation missions from Santo to Guadalcanal and beyond had, by this time, become somewhat routine. The squadron's aircraft flew missions every day. Typical of these missions was one laid on for Sunday morning on September 5, 1943, for 1st Lt. "Red" Healy and his crew in C-47 42-23711.

Robert H. Healy hailed from Tiverton, Rhode Island, and was the only married man on his flight crew. Also aboard were 2nd Lt. Augustus Miller (copilot), 23, from Avon, New York, 2nd Lt. Leonard Richardson (navigator) from Clarkston, Washington, and the eldest of the crew at age 26, M/Sgt Harry Wlodarsky (crew chief), 25 from Burghill, Ohio, and Cpl. Joseph O'Connell (radioman), 19 years

Mission crew, September 5, 1942. Left to right: O'Connell, Miller, Healy, and Wlodarsky.

of age, from New York. Except for Richardson, the crew had been together since the squadron's training days at Alliance and Pope airfields and had flown their aircraft across the Pacific in early July.

The day's mission was to deliver materials to the Fighter 2 airfield at Kukum, a few miles west of Henderson Field, and return spent aircraft engines for refurbishing at Base Button.

Guadalcanal is a paramecium-shaped island measuring 84 x 30 miles creased from one end to the other with ridgelines and steep wooded valleys. Thirty-eight named peaks reach to 7,600 feet, but rising abruptly from sea level seem much higher. And nowhere is there terrain suitable for airfields other than the relatively flat land on the Lunga Plain on the northwest corner of the island.

Both Henderson Field and Fighter 2 had become a very active airfield, and was the home base for three AAF fighter squadrons, the 12th, 68th, and 339th, each of which operated the game-changing P-38 Lightning fighter. Also at Fighter 2 was Marine Corps VMF-124, flying the new F4U Corsair, and the Royal New Zealand Air Forces' 15 Squadron equipped with P-40s.

Anti-submarine and anti-ship reconnaissance missions were also being flown from Pekoa and Palikulo that Sunday morning: a B-17 from the 23rd Bomb Squadron (5th Bomb Group) took off at 5:30; a B-24 from its sister squadron, the 72nd, took off at 5:45, and a B-24 from the 370th Bomb Squadron (307th Bomb Group) took off at 5:51.

With an early departure, Healy's C-47 would likely have been loaded the evening before.

> In the States there were strict loading requirements. I remember seeing an engineer with a special slide rule trying to place each piece of cargo in the correct place to balance the load and distribute the weight. I never saw this done overseas. We would just tell the loaders to put the cargo about here or there and used our judgment to balance the cargo. We didn't want a nose- or tail-heavy plane. On the floor there were special tie down holders to pass rope through to tie down the cargo. We carried 5000 pounds, which may seem small now, but then it was large. We also carried about 12 litters on board for the wounded, and we had special straps so that they could be placed two high on the side of the plane. We used them to sleep on while out on flight over night.[2]

Sunrise on this day came at 5:55 a.m.; the sun would set almost exactly 12 hours later. Flights normally departed Santo early to reduce the possibility of being located by enemy fighters and to ensure the outbound and return legs could be completed before dark.

With an assumed "wheels up" at 6:00 a.m., the C-47 crew were awakened around 4:30 am to eat, receive flight briefings and weather reports, and to conduct preflight checks on the aircraft. Their sleep the night before was interrupted when a "Condition Red" was called at 10:30 p.m. on the evening before the mission. After taking the usual precautions against bombing and gas attack, "Condition Green" was called just over an hour later. Small comfort to those who were suddenly wide awake.[3]

The flight distance to Fighter 2 on Guadalcanal is 644 miles.[4] At a normal cruising speed of 150 mph, the outbound flight to Guadalcanal would take just under 4½ hours on a course 131° True, entirely over open ocean. On a direct course, there were no landfalls or landmarks between islands.

During the prior week, the weather in the region had been fairly uniform. Winds were steady out of the southeast, averaging 8 miles per hour, with occasional gusts to 18.

Ceilings were an entirely different matter. While not especially turbulent, the skies over Santo were everchanging at this time of the year. On the 1st and 2nd, ceilings had been unlimited for most daylight hours. On the 3rd and 4th, they became highly variable; some periods of the day had unlimited visibility, while ceilings would then drop for part of each day to as low as 1,500 feet.

As Healy, Miller, and Richardson reported for their weather briefing, the ceiling was 3,500 feet, with wind predictably out of the southeast at a negligible 10 mph. A blue-gray scrim of broken altostratus clouds covered half the sky, a cloud type that often presaged an approaching storm front. Like most recent days, the temperature on the island did not go much below 72°, nor exceed 83°, day or night. They learned that, the day before, a reconnaissance patrol aircraft from the 424th Bomb Squadron had reported two weather fronts slightly north of Guadalcanal and extending in an east–west direction, and that the cloud deck over the Lunga Plain region had persisted at under 3,000 feet. It was likely any flights to Guadalcanal on this day would encounter these fronts.[5]

For the flight crew, it was just another mission on another day. Their aircraft was flying well, all systems were functioning as required, and it would be unlikely they would encounter any unfriendly aircraft during the day. While the men of the 64th were still quite new to the South Pacific and were still learning what constituted "normal" weather for that time of the year at Santo, there was nothing exceptional about this day's mission—it was one they had flown several times before under similar weather conditions.

With Pekoa Airfield subject to nearly constant trade winds from the southeast, most take-offs to any destination were in that direction. Pilots headed for Guadalcanal banked to the left after take-off and skirted Santo's eastern shoreline in a northerly direction to Cape Quiros on the northeastern tip of the island. From there, another left turn would take them to Cape Cumberland on Santo's northwest tip, and then a direct course to Guadalcanal. Less experienced or more cautious pilots sometimes preferred to fly a course from Cape Cumberland to San Cristobal, an island on the southern end of the Solomons, using it as a way-point on the route to Guadalcanal, a diversion that added a few additional miles to the crossing. From that landfall, a left turn could be made for the final leg to Guadalcanal.

On this route, the aircraft would quickly leave behind the vast military base on the southeast corner of Santo, and the view of central Santo would be essentially unobstructed. Glancing to the left after take-off, the crew could see the fighter airfield at Turtle Bay, and the only elevated terrain mentioned in any of Button's airfield alerts—Mt. Turi (Tiouri) at just under 2000 feet.

Other pilots, knowing that the heading to Guadalcanal lined up precisely with Pekoa's orientation, took off to the northwest. On this heading the pilots would almost directly overfly Mt. Turi, glimpsing Turtle Bay off their right wingtip as they climbed briskly to the altitude needed to clear the island's western mountains—roughly 4500 feet.

Regardless of their take-off vector, the view of Santo was of a solid blanket of tropical forest—even the Sarakata River would often be obscured by vegetation.[6]

Flying at 5,000 feet, within 30 minutes even the tallest mountains on Santo would have been out of sight. The aircrew could scan the ocean from horizon to horizon and not see land; during their flight to Guadalcanal they would overfly an area the size of Arizona and see only water.

Healy's course is unknown, but it is known that by the time he lifted the C-47 off Pekoa the prevailing clouds had settled somewhat, and as he eased his aircraft onto a Guadalcanal heading the cloud cover was mostly beneath him. And with Santo just coming to the end of its relatively dry season, it would not rain that day. Healy's squadron commander, Maj. Jack Roessell, would later comment on the dry conditions, warm temperature, light wind, and limited cloud cover that day, noting it was "a beautiful day" for flying.[7]

The mission would include two other C-47s, one piloted by 1st Lt. James Smith (2nd Lt. Phillip Anders as co-pilot), the other by 1st Lt. Victor Morton (co-pilot 2nd Lt. Max Maeder), all three aircraft flying in loose formation to Fighter 2.[8] The outbound aircraft encountered the storm front mentioned by the 424th Bomb Squadron, with the weather ceiling over 15,000 feet. While the C-47 was capable of operating at over 24,000 feet, the aircraft of the 64th TCS were not equipped with oxygen, making it necessary for the pilots to fly either through or under the weather. "We flew on the deck, getting an occasional glimpse of the ocean below."[9]

The pilots in the 64th relied on their copilots to take a turn at the controls on long flights. Captain Healy was no exception and showed a high degree of confidence in his young copilot, 2nd Lt. Augustus Miller; he had turned the controls over to him in over half the missions they flew during the month of August, providing Miller with valuable experience. It is also true that Healy often flew the aircraft for the entirety of the mission, probably on flights involving severe weather.

Just as take-offs from Pekoa varied, so too did approaches to Henderson Field and Fighter 2, depending on weather and the pilot's preferences. Both airfields were on the northwestern coastline of Guadalcanal. High mountains, reaching 8,000 feet, lined the southern coastline and required inbound flights to either skirt the eastern and northern shores or gain altitude just prior to reaching the island to overfly the mountain range. When flying under conditions of reduced visibility, the pilots ran the risk of missing the field and continuing into the northern Solomons, territory still held by the Japanese and patrolled by their fighters.

On this day, fortune favored the men of the 64th. Earlier in the day, the skies over Fighter 2 had been completely obscured, with a weather ceiling of 3,400 feet and occasional clouds much lower. But between 10:00 and 11:00 a.m., the skies cleared rapidly and the ceiling was unlimited. The three C-47s spiraled down to an estimated 10:00 a.m. landing.[10]

> We reported into weather while our plane was being unloaded and then re loaded for our trip back to Espiritu.

At that time in the Pacific, Japanese bombers were still making occasional raids on Guadalcanal, including one attack just two weeks earlier that sank the attack transport USS *John Penn*. On this very day, Japanese fighters reportedly attempted to shoot down South Pacific Combat Air Transport Command C-47s.[11] The 64th TCS Historian would later relate: "Jap Bettys were still making raids on Guadalcanal,

Kukum Airfield (Fighter 2) on the Lunga Plain adjacent to Henderson Field. (USMC)

and occasionally the squadron pilots would reach the 'canal after a night flight from Santos and arrive about dawn to be guided by the smoke and flames left by successful Jap raiders."[12]

> We wanted to get away because the Japanese bombed at night. Our source of weather information came from pilots who flew in from other areas. Since we were retracing our steps, we knew the front was over 15,000, and didn't know how far around it was to get around it. Our three pilots decided to try three different routes. One would try to fly over it, one would try to fly around it, and we were going to try to fly under it.[13]

Their C-47s was loaded with spent aircraft engines, most likely the 1,500-hp Allison engines used on aircraft of the three P-38 squadrons then based at Fighter 2. Each engine was roughly the size of two oil drums laid end to end and weighted 1,400 lbs each. Each C-47 would have carried three.

The freshly-loaded C-47s departed just before noon and calculated an arrival back at Santo around 4:00 p.m. that afternoon. Flying under the weather meant just over the waves—very hazardous under any conditions, but especially dangerous in severe weather.

At 1:30 p.m., an hour and three quarters out of Henderson, Richardson confirmed their course and position, and the radioman, Corporal O'Connell, reported their position to air traffic control on Santo: they were at Lat 11° 50'S Long 162° 55'E. They had covered 260 miles, with 384 miles yet to fly. The weather had improved; they were flying in scattered-to-broken clouds, with seven miles visibility. They could expect another 2½ hours in the air before being safely down at Pekoa.[14]

"We flew just over the waves, and in about four hours came to the northern tip of our island of Espiritu Santo." Richardson's navigation was spot-on, and Healy had piloted the aircraft to Cape Cumberland, the tip of Santo's Northwest Peninsula, at about 3:00 pm. "We flew fairly low over a radar site there, and then I gave the pilot directions to veer slightly left so as to avoid a mountain range ahead and to our right. This way we could skirt the island and then just set down at our air base."

Santo's northwest peninsula is deeply corrugated, with many peaks reaching 3,000 feet. On reaching Cape Cumberland, Richardson's direction to "veer slightly left" to a more easterly course would bring the aircraft to Cape Quiros on the northern tip of the Sakau Peninsula, a very flat region nowhere more than 600 feet in elevation. Having reached Cape Quiros, the pilots could set a southerly course to reach the airfields on the southeastern corner of Santo.

By this time, the pilots had been at the controls for 8–9 hours of arduous flying, and were doubtless looking forward to a shower, a nap, and dinner. Official weather reports would later record that nimbostratus clouds blanketed the island at 7,000 feet, with intermittent clouds and rain squalls at lower altitudes. Wind was from the southeast, almost in their face, at 13 mph.[15]

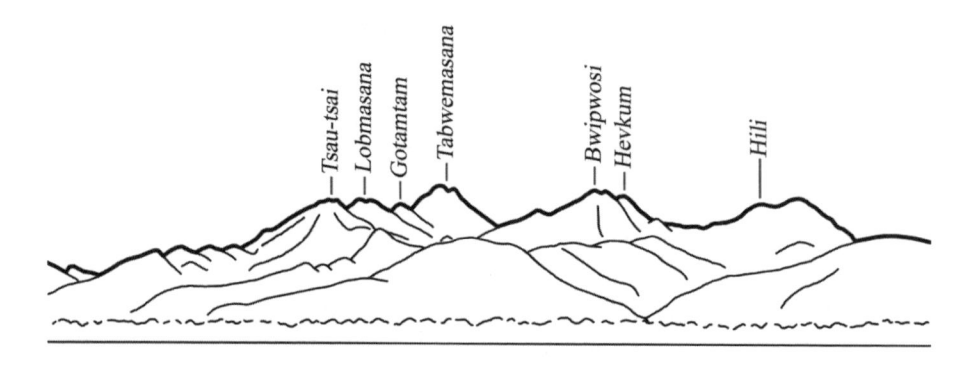

Panoramic view of St. Philip & St. James Bay (Big Bay), vertical scale exaggerated 1.5 times. After passing Cumberland Point, the inner bay opened in front of the pilot, and in the near distance loomed the high mountains of western and southern Espiritu Santo. (*The Geographical Journal*, John R. Baker, March 1935)

> Pilots are apt to take over directional control of the plane as soon as they are sure they are on course and near the destination. Red took a straight route from where we were to the base, not realizing that we were letting down, not climbing, and that a small mountain peak was right on our course. I wasn't aware of a change in course.
>
> I finished writing up my log of the trip, and went forward to stand between the pilot and copilot, to watch as we neared our destination. The copilot was taking it in.

Healy had already logged a handful of flights to Guadalcanal, and had overflown the northern coastline of Espiritu Santo several times previously. He knew precisely where he was in relation to Pekoa airfield, and it is unremarkable that he would take over the directional control, with their home airfield just a few minutes away.

Healy was much more experienced than his copilot. Considering the difficult flight conditions encountered all day, it can be assumed the majority of flying up to this point was done by Healy. At this time in the war the C-47s were not equipped with the Sperry 3-A automatic pilot, requiring aircrews to hand fly the aircraft at all times. Healy and Miller had flown nine missions in the prior 12 days, and after eight-plus hours of very challenging flying, it might be expected that both were fatigued.

The available narratives—some official, some anecdotal—indicate weather in the immediate vicinity of the base had changed by the late afternoon of August 5. Roussell, who in his memoir had earlier mentioned it was a good day for flying, later amended his thoughts: " ... we had a spell of pretty foul weather (rain etc.) and the clouds were pretty low, and visibility not very good.[16] Official reports indicate Healy was approaching Pekoa "on instruments" because of a severe rainstorm in the immediate vicinity of the airfield, and was relying on the established and highly reliable four-course radio range that was used by every pilot in similar weather conditions. He was essentially "flying the beam" to the radio station located just north of Pekoa, and from there he would enter the landing pattern to the airfield.[17]

From Cape Cumberland, Pekoa lies just 45 miles ahead on a southeasterly course. Flying this route on instruments was not unsafe, but care was required to avoid the only obstruction noted in the official Army Air Force airfield instructions for Santo—Mt. Turi, located on a direct line between Cape Cumberland and Pekoa, rising to 1,837 feet.

While it is clear that Healy did not follow Richardson's suggestion to take the coastal route to the airfields on southeastern Santo, his precise course is not known. Neither is it known when the co-pilot assumed control of the aircraft, when he began to descend toward the airfield or from what altitude.

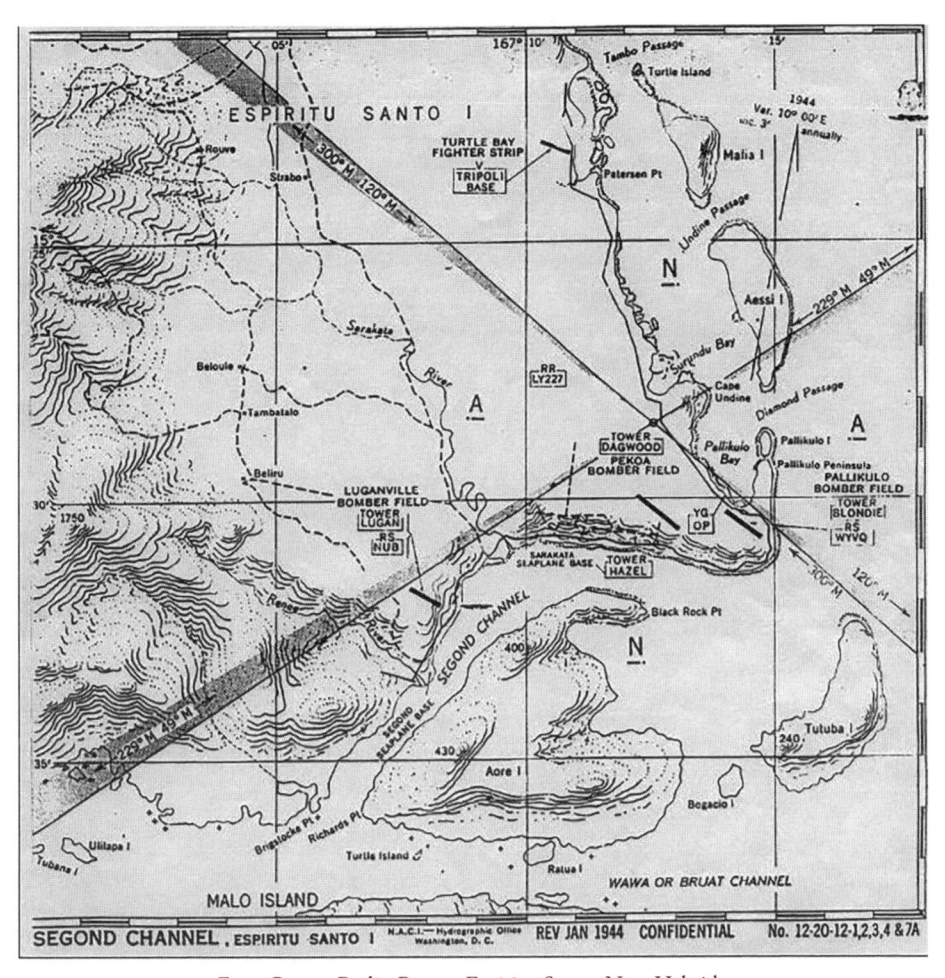

Four-Course Radio Range, Espiritu Santo, New Hebrides.

For whatever reason, the aircraft was flying directly at Mt. Turi, the only significant high ground on the island's east side. It was misaligned with the 300 degree azimuth for the radio range beam, and was at too low an altitude.

Normally on final approach to landing the crew chief stands between the pilot and copilot, and the fact that Richardson took that position may indicate that he was aware the pilots were having difficulty with their approach.

> Suddenly trees loomed up before us in a split second, and I threw my hands up before my face in an involuntary gesture of protection. Then blackness ...

CHAPTER FIFTEEN

Survival

The aircraft crashed around 4:00 in the afternoon atop Mt. Turi. In the regional dialect, "Turi" means "stands up," alluding to the mountain's abrupt rise from the surrounding jungle plain. To refer to it as a mountain, in the context of the overall geography of the island, is misleading. Mt. Turi is essentially a hummock—rising to just 1,837 feet above sea level, only 650 feet above the flat jungle plain drained by the Sarakata River on southeastern Santo, and just 30 air miles from the end of the runway at Pekoa.[1]

Mt. Turi is, admittedly, inconsequential in comparison to nearby Mt. Tabwemasana, just 20 miles to the east and rising steeply to 6,165 feet. That mountain, part of a chain of peaks along the western coastline, is impossible to miss. It would be easy for pilots not to give Mt. Turi a second thought.

The winds at Santo are almost always from the east-southeast; most aircraft leaving any of the land bases would therefore have taken off in that direction. So, while most aircraft would not have overflown Mt. Turi on take-off, nearly all would have on landing, and it would have appeared slightly to the right on approach vectors for both Pekoa and Palikulo.

Mt. Turi would have been well known, if perhaps dismissed as inconsequential, by any but the most inexperienced replacement pilots for the aviation units then on Espiritu Santo. Only the Airfield Data for Turtle Bay mentioned Mt. Turi as an obstruction. Pilot alerts for other airfields on Santo noted only "Hills to the N and NW."[2]

It was later recorded that, in crashing, the aircraft had essentially "skimmed" the apex of the mountain, coming to rest just 15 feet vertical feet from the domed crest. To the untrained eye, it might appear as if the pilot had been attempting a landing on the small mountaintop. Just 30 feet of additional altitude would have prevented the accident from happening.

As Leonard Richardson later wrote, the airplane's course from Big Bay to Pekoa was decided by Lt. Healy. It had initially been recorded that the aircraft was making its approach to Pekoa "on the beam," although later evidence would indicate the aircraft's course was too far to the south. In following the northwesterly-oriented

Mt. Turi, south central Espiritu Santo, New Hebrides. (Richardson Family Archives)

radio signal emanating from just north of Dagwood Tower, the tone of the radio signal would have informed the pilots that the aircraft was off course. The pilot at the controls of the aircraft at the time of the crash, Lieutenant Miller, may have attempted to correct his approach, or he may have continued on the same course, knowing that he was just five minutes from landing at the airfield more or less directly ahead, and not realizing Mt. Turi lurked in the surrounding clouds.

The aircraft was at an unusually low altitude, even for a pilot beginning his landing approach. Mt. Turi is just under 2,000 feet in elevation; Pekoa was fully 12 miles distant.

> I realized what had happened, and the words "Thank God" came from my lips. I guess I knew I was alive and had a chance. I called out, and a faint answer came back: "Get me out of here." I crawled up to the plane which was tilted over so that the door was pointed up about 45 degrees. With all the wreckage I was able to get in the plane, but could find no one alive. I called out several times but never was answered.[3]
>
> Since the plane was still burning I crawled back out and then lay down near the plane so as to get its heat and avoid shock. Besides, bullets from our sidearms and a Tommy Gun we had been carrying kept going off from the heat of the plane.

Sunset on the 5th came at 6:14 p.m., and characteristic of the tropics, nightfall was quickly followed by full darkness. There was little or no moon for most of the days following the crash. Despite the fact the temperature rarely dips below 68° on

Santo, and that it had not rained on the 5th, the persistent rainfall in prior days and a moon not quite in the first quarter would have made for a damp, dark and cold night for Richardson.

The wings had sheared off on impact, and the fuselage had ruptured just forward of the main cargo door. The front part of the plane, including the cockpit, had broken away from the main fuselage. It was originally assumed Richardson had been thrown out of the aircraft through its front windscreen, but it now seems more likely he was ejected from the cockpit when the plane fractured on impact.

At the moment of impact, the cargo of aircraft engines broke free from their tie-downs, tumbled forward with nearly a million pounds of momentum, and destroyed everything ahead of them. It is quite likely the crashing cargo swept up Lieutenant Miller, Master Sergeant Wlodarsky, and Corporal O'Connell.

On Santo, with the air echelon working alone and without support from the ground echelon, a particular "esprit" would have quickly developed. There were only 138 men in the air echelon at Santo, and all shared the realization they were essentially on their own despite their position amid a teeming military complex. The aircrews relied on each other, trusted each other, and supported each other.

"Red" Healy had become a notable figure within the squadron—a red-headed Irishman with a ready grin and a lot of air miles under his wings. The other crewmen had also served with the 64th long enough to have made many good friends. So, as the late afternoon began turning to dusk, with Healy's aircraft overdue, the commander and the rest of the squadron became alarmed. By the time evening settled over the airfield, it had become clear something had happened to the airplane. The possibilities were not encouraging.

Richardson lay atop Mt. Turi in shock and a fair degree of pain. Having started the day already somewhat fatigued from his extensive flight schedule, Richardson slept, lying on the open ground, seeing the stars overhead. The same stars he had used for navigation. Alongside the plane that had carried him safely through many missions. Accompanied only by the bodies of his crewmates he had come to like and respect.

Day 2, September 6

It didn't rain overnight, but low clouds shrouded the mountain during the hours of darkness. Except for a two-hour period after dawn, the crash site remained in dense clouds all day. No rain would fall that day, but the jungle dripped with condensation and accumulated moisture, and the ground was soaked.[4]

> Somehow the night passed, and the next morning I assessed the situation. I was the only survivor. I thought that both my legs were broken—the right one the worst, and I had burns on my lower right leg. I had some deep cuts or gouges on my upper right leg, just above and behind my knee. All bleeding had stopped.

> I examined my injuries and discovered huge blisters in the burned area filled with blood and pus. Some lizards were around, and one accidentally punctured a blister and then I had to keep him and his friend away. I also realized I had a fracture in my right hand near the joint of my thumb.
>
> My right leg fracture lost all bone support for my leg, so my toes just pointed down. The burns dictated that I must crawl on my back, and as I crawled, my broken hand bone kept popping out, not through the skin, but it became a nuisance.
>
> My first thought was to salvage what I could from the plane, so, although it was still smoldering, and there was a lot of hot metal, I was able to get back in the door. I found some clothing.
>
> I fixed a piece of rope I found so that it went over a piece of the overhead frame, and down to where I could tie my leg to it like a pulley. Then I could pull my leg up and while it was hanging, I could move about in a circle from where my leg was. I found some clothes—pants, etc., and from a smashed medicine kit I rescued a syrette of morphine and some rock candy.
>
> I stayed in the plane most of the day, and then in the afternoon crawled out and made a resting place under the plane. The inside was too rough with sharp metal from the wreckage. I decided to keep the morphine until my situation demanded it, and decided to have a couple of pieces of candy each day so that it would last three or four days.
>
> The day turned clear and warm, and among the things I saw were Air Force planes flying north towards Guadalcanal and south to our base. We were almost exactly under their flight path![5]

Richardson would have been briefed as to the basic unhealthiness of Santo. "Minute scratches usually produced a suppurating sore in Santo. There seemed to be something in the very atmosphere which defied antiseptics. There is no place for weaklings in a primeval tropic jungle."[6]

Apart from his experience in the woods of Idaho, Richardson may have recollected the survival advice given in an Army publication—the *Castaway's Baedeker to the South Seas*.[7] Much of the information in that and other survival publications issued by the Army were written for lost airmen who were uninjured and equipped with minimal survival material: emergency rations, water, a knife, parachute, mirror, signal flares, etc.

A later report by the Navy noted that "A signal mirror, small compass, blood chits, and medicinal packets will readily fit into the pockets of a flight suit, and they should be so carried."[8] A signaling mirror would have greatly increased Richardson's chances of discovery and rescue. He had none of these items. Having been ejected as the crashing aircraft broke asunder, Richardson carried nothing to aid in his own survival.

And as for getting around in the bush, the Baedeker's urged "Easy swinging steps are the best." But those techniques were only of value to ambulatory personnel, and of no use at all to one crawling on his back. But the guide did contain some helpful advice:

> Once you find a trail or track, stick to it. The tracks are always single file and some of them are almost invisible. Where no trails are available the best rule is to follow streams, wading in them until they become rivers, then taking time to build a raft. There is also a good chance of finding a native village on the banks of the stream or along ridges.

The guide also gave advice about meeting with natives: " … the natives are quite likely to be more timid than curious and may wait for you to approach them. In most islands of Melanesia, generosity is a cardinal virtue." And this: "There need be no fear of headhunters and cannibals. In remote areas a castaway is more apt to be regarded as a super-natural being than a man."

The guide was less sanguine about food: "Despite the lushness of jungle vegetation, there is even less food to be had in the jungles than on all but the most desert atolls." One exception noted in the guide was insects. Particularly endorsed were termites which, it noted, tasted like roasted chestnuts. Grasshoppers and grubs were also recommended for survival rations, and Richardson knew where to look for them.

The guide also gave a glossary of pidgin terms that could be potentially useful on any number of Melanesian islands, including Santo. On first meeting a native in the jungle, ask "*Nambleeyuo?*" [name belong you]. "Bring me food" was "*Bring em Kai Kai.*" "Guide me to the coast" was "*One fellow boy bring em me long nambis.*" For good water to drink, ask, "*Good fella water?*" "Did you see the plane crash?" was "*You lookim balus e fall down?*"

Maybe the best advice, and the hardest to act upon in Richardson's desperate circumstance, was "Don't worry":

> The greatest of all obstacles for a castaway to overcome is psychological—the fear of the unknown. If the bogies of the imagination which completely distort the true picture of the areas in the Pacific in which this war is being fought can be dispelled, a return to base will not only be a possibility but a high probability.

Sound advice. But in an utterly alien environment, hard to follow.

> Deep among the Jungles there, by tracks of moonless gloom,
> The nightmare creatures crawl and creep, like Messengers of Doom,
> Dark forms among the shadow ways, ugly and undefined,
> And dark as are the thoughts, the Jungles of their minds.[9]

COMAIRSOPAC's (Commander, Aircraft, South Pacific) Lost Plane Procedure (LPP) had been substantially revised just 11 days before the crash occurred.[10] It directed the aircraft's unit commander to contact COMAIRSOPAC Operations Office whenever an aircraft operating in the Espiritu Santo area became 30 minutes overdue and request that the Lost Plane Procedure be put into effect.

With Richardson's aircraft due to arrive around 4:00 p.m., squadron commander Jack Roussell would have made that call just about dusk on the afternoon of the 5th. In that call, he would have provided the plane type and number, the unit to which it was assigned, the originating base, radio frequencies being used, the pilot's name, the aircraft's last known position, and the estimated hours of gas remaining aboard.

COMAIRSOPAC Operations would then put the lost plane procedure in effect, which would trigger several actions: Santo's Interceptor Command would alert all radars on the island to monitor IFF (Identification, Friend or Foe) distress signals and to report any contacts to Operations; Army and Navy direction finders on the island would be similarly alerted, with instructions to report the time, bearing, and plane identification for any aircraft detected; Operations offices at Bomber Fields 1, 2, and 3, and the Fighter Strip at Turtle Island, would also be alerted; The COMAIRSOPAC Communications Office would be instructed to attempt to contact the aircraft; Operations (COMAIRSOPAC Operations Watch Officer) would contact the originating airfield, Fighter 2 on Guadalcanal in this case, to determine if they were in contact with the missing aircraft. Their message, plain and uncoded, would have been: "SINGING FOR C47 23711 X IS HE YOURS," meaning "C-47 23711 is lost. Is he at your station? We are trying to home him. Help as practicable, and give complete information"; and Interceptor command would illuminate searchlights.

Roussell would have been aware of all these actions and by the end of the day on September 5 would have known no contact had been made with the missing aircraft. Nor could they have—by the time the LPP had been put in effect, the C-47 was already down.

By 8:00 p.m. that evening, when it became clear the aircraft could no longer be in the air, COMAIRSOPAC Operations would have messaged all stations "LOST PLANE PROCEDURE COMPLETED," and again in plain language to Fighter 2 on Guadalcanal, "STOP SINGING."

The morning of September 6, as Richardson began to stir at the crash site, Roussell began questioning the crews of the other two aircraft that had left Henderson Field at the same time and on the same heading as the missing aircraft. But the most useful information available to him was the routine radio call made by the crew at 1:30 in the afternoon which gave the aircraft's location—roughly 400 miles north and west of Espiritu Santo. The pilot did not report any problems with the aircraft or with navigation.

Had the pilot become lost and run low on fuel, perhaps due to having been thrown off course by weather, or as a result of a navigational error, the radio operator would have reported their situation to base. Absent better information, the most likely cause of the loss would have been a sudden weather event or equipment malfunction that prevented the crew from making a distress call, making it most likely the aircraft had gone into the water.[11]

Roussell was advised by air control at Fighter 2 on Guadalcanal that the missing aircraft had departed around noon, had not returned, and that flying a standard course to Santo would not have overflown any islands. Had a mechanical problem arisen that prevented a return to Guadalcanal, the pilot may have attempted to reach San Cristobal Island, east of his course. While a landing would have been impossible on that rugged island, a water landing near shore might have been feasible. But after two hours of flying, there would have been no further landfall possibilities.

Major Roussell dispatched four of the squadron's C-47s to search for the missing aircraft. Each plane was assigned a specific search sector, encompassing all immediate islands and the ocean areas around Espiritu Santo. As Roussell would later report, "Weather during the morning of the search was variable with ceilings from 1,000 feet down to 400 feet with light to heavy rain showers. It was impossible to cover the island of Espiritu Santo other than the shore lines."[12]

Even had weather permitted, by the time those search planes were airborne the smoke and flames from the crash site would have dissipated, and the now-still plane would have been very hard to spot.

Writer James Michener, reflecting in 1947 on a flight he once took on the identical course as Richardson's commented on the foreboding jungle:

> We hurried past the great bay at the northern end of Santo, the eastern side of the island, well clear of its gaunt, still unexplored mountains. The morning sun was low when we passed the central part of Santo ... A hard, forbidding green mat hid every feature of the island ... Planes had crashed into this green sea of Espiritu and had never been seen again. Ten minutes after the smoke cleared, a burnt plane was invisible.[13]

In early September, four bomb squadrons were operating from bases on Santo. As "rear" elements, these squadrons had been rotated from combat operations at Guadalcanal and were assigned regular daily search missions, seeking enemy shipping and submarines in the waters adjacent to Santo. On a typical day, two or three aircraft were involved, and each plane was assigned a specific sector, usually an arc of nine degrees extending north from Santo a distance of 800 miles and covering roughly 50,000 square miles. In the days following the crash, 20 such regular missions were flown by these bomber units, some by B-17s, others by B-24s.

On these regular search patrols, none of the aircrews were looking specifically for the missing C-47, but all would have been briefed on the lost aircraft and would have kept watch for a downed airplane. But the take-off directions for these aircraft would likely have been to the southeast, away from the crash site. On returning, they might have flown near Mt. Turi on their landing approaches, but even so the dense jungle would have obscured the crash site. None of these search aircraft reported any sighting.[14]

In addition to these routine reconnaissance missions, special search missions were often laid on when aircraft were reported downed or failed to return on schedule. On this day, a B-24 from the 72nd Bomb Squadron (BS), one from the 424th BS, and a B-17 from the 23rd BS were tapped for search missions, covering an arc from 347° to 014°—precisely the region Richardson's aircraft overflew on the return from Guadalcanal. Lying near his plane, Richardson would have heard the distant throbbing drone of these heavy bombers warming up at both Palikulo and Pekoa for the early search missions.

Local air traffic to and from the fighter field at Turtle Bay and a variety of aircraft operating out of Luganville would have contributed many more aircraft in the skies in the vicinity of Mt. Turi, all of which would have been alerted for the lost aircraft, and some of which would have directly overflown Mt. Turi. Still, no sightings were reported.

Flight operations for the bomber and troop carrier units on Santo continued unabated for the most part. But for bomber anti-sub and anti-ship search missions in the days following the take-off and landing directions for these missions would have been to the southeast and would not have overflown Mt. Turi. Again, none reported any sighting.[15]

The effort by the units of the Thirteenth Air Force and Navy aviation units at Base Button was testament to the value placed on aircrews by their commanders. All planes scheduled to fly to Guadalcanal on the 6th—bombers, fighters, seaplanes, and transports—were ordered to fly line-abreast courses, each covering an area of approximately thirty-five miles in width up to Henderson Field and return. Two additional B-24 bombers and three Navy PBY aircraft from "Button" joined in searching the immediate area, and two other PBY aircraft flying from Button to *Cactus* also joined in the search.

All searches were negative.

Two SCR-270 long-range aircraft warning radar units had been installed on Espiritu Santo shortly after the American invasion of Guadalcanal. The first was located in the northernmost reaches of the island, at the tip of Cape Cumberland along the western shore of Big Bay, in order to provide early warning of any impending Japanese raids. The second radar set was located on the east coast of Santo, just south of the fighter airfield at Turtle Bay to provide close-in direction for the busy fighter airfield. By the early fall of 1943, the prospect of a Japanese air raid on Santo was becoming remote, but the system could easily monitor friendly traffic inbound and outbound from the airfields in the southern part of the island.[16]

The ground-based radar included an RC-150 interrogator system (IFF) that "pinged" incoming aircraft to ascertain its IFF status. Allied aircraft carried a corresponding transponder—the SCR-595 combination radio receiver and transmitter—that operated in a listening condition while in flight. When it detected an incoming IFF query it automatically sent a radio signal identifying it as "friend."[17]

The Cape Cumberland radar site was about six miles south of Cape Cumberland and about 900 feet above sea level. Originally installed by the Navy, by September 1943 both radar systems had been turned over to the Army.[18]

The SCR-270 was intended to establish a radar warning screen to identify approaching aircraft as early as possible. In these early radar systems, their detection performance was largely determined by the incoming aircraft's size and altitude: the larger the aircraft, and the greater its altitude, the further away it could be detected. As an example of its capability, a radar located at sea level could detect a single bomber flying at 1,000 feet when it was 20 miles away. For aircraft at higher altitudes, and radar systems located on more elevated locations, the operating range of the system was up to 140 miles.[19]

Conversely, the systems were not good at detecting low-flying aircraft; their performance was also affected by atmospheric conditions and by the proficiency and attentiveness of the operators. In a report issued just a month before Healy's C-47 went missing, the Navy found that early radars, like the SCR-270, "were still a new weapon, rushed through production and into field use in so short a time that frequent instances of faulty operation and breakdown are encountered."[20]

COMAIRSOPAC'S Chief of Staff, Capt. M. B. Gardner, would later comment on the radar system at Cumberland: "The radar at Cumberland worked very well, but the communications from Cumberland, which had to be by voice telephone to the interceptor control room, were not satisfactory."[21]

As Healy flew the length of Big Bay at the head of the island, the inbound C-47 would have passed within 15 miles of the northern radar unit and could have been heard and seen by ground personnel. But if it was still maintaining a very low altitude, it may have been undetectable to the radar operators; or possibly the aircraft had been detected but telephone problems prevented the operators from reporting the contact. For whatever reason, the operators of the northern radar unit had nothing to say; this lack of critical information was to have a significant effect on subsequent search efforts. IV Island Command would have been flummoxed that Healy's slow-moving C-47, entering Santo airspace at a low altitude, could pass undetected or unreported so close to the Cumberland radar station.

Search efforts intensified throughout the day of September 6 and, seeing and hearing the aircraft overhead, Richardson would have been increasingly frustrated: "But no one saw us this day or the next four days either."[22]

Richardson's dilemma had been foreseen in another survival monogram issued by the Airlines War Training Institute (AWTI) just five months earlier: "A plane forced down in the jungle is completely hidden by heavy green leaves which close over it just as waves close over a sinking ship."[23]

Beyond this less-than-sanguine observation, the AWTI document had as little relevance for Richardson as did the Baedeker mentioned above. For example, it cautioned "Never sleep on bare ground," "be sure to cover yourself with mosquito netting," "don't rely on your instincts ... consult your compass frequently," "all water must be boiled for five minutes ... before you drink it," and "paint every little scratch and cut with whatever antiseptic you have." Lucky was the downed pilot who survived his crash and had the gear that would have permitted these precautions.

Day 3, September 7

> The quiet of the jungle was broken by a particular sound like that of a gasoline motor, throbbing continually, and making me think that where ever it was I would find civilization. The sound seemed then to come from the east, and down the mountain, possibly on the coast.
> On the third day I crawled up the mountain looking for it.[24]

In its impact, the aircraft had created a small clearing, but in crawling up to the crest of Mt. Turi, Richardson would have entered the deep bush. The crawl up to the top of the mountain would have been not much more than 100 yards—the plane had crashed almost exactly at the mountain's summit, and just slightly to the west. The crawl from the crash site to the mountain top would have been quite steep initially and then fairly flat as the apex of the mountain was approached.

The faint noise he hoped to identify might be coming from a nearby settlement or Army post. In any case, it would have represented a touch of familiarity, and a reason for hope of rescue.

This would have been Richardson's first exposure to the true Santo bush. He'd spent a lot of time in the northwest woods of Washington, and would not have been intimidated by the wildness around him, but the nearly impenetrable bush of Santo was something he had not been prepared for. Lying on his back, a machete—if he had one—would have been useless to him. He could only reach overhead, grasp whatever vegetation came to hand and pull himself upward. Or he could have made some progress by rising on his elbows and dragging his torso.

Alternately crawling and resting on his back, staring up through the canopy of trees, listening to the birdcall and the buzz of insects, Richardson would have found the bush an untidy affair. Trees of every size, thick scrub at ground level, fallen and rotting trunks, and everywhere trailing lianas—some as big as an arm, others finger sized. By now hungry, he would have cast his eye around him, hoping to find some fruit or berry, a nut tree, or even a grub.

Adding to his difficulties, it rained hard on Santo this day. Back at base, the nighttime temperatures were 70 degrees. At his elevation—roughly 1,900 feet—the temperatures could have been as much as 15 degrees cooler at night, and the ceilings on Santo were tending lower in the first half of September; it was likely he lay in the mist much of the time.

Reaching the summit, Richardson lay quietly, hoping to get a fix on the sound he had been hearing:

> But the sound was getting no closer. In fact seemed to come from another direction. So I crawled back to the plane. This took all of that day.[25]

Day 4, September 8

Roessell, perhaps approaching resignation that the aircraft and its crew would not be found, but still holding on to a faint hope of its discovery, requested additional search support from other aviation units on the island. On this day, two bombers from the 23rd Bomb Squadron, 5th Bomb Group, conducted special searches for the lost plane, each of six hours' duration, and each assigned specific search sectors. One bomber took a westerly heading for a distance of 140 miles, then turning to the northwest for 300 miles, then turning again toward the northeast for 10 miles, then making a last turn to the southeast for the return to base. The second plane left Pekoa on a similar search patten but shifted toward the east. Their courses took them out into the Coral Sea and to the waters north of Espiritu Santo. Their search would have covered the region from Pekoa to the point where Corporal O'Connell had last reported the lost aircraft's position: Lat 11° 50'S Long 162° 55'E—roughly 400 miles to the north of Santo.

It is evident from the assigned searches that the aircraft were seeking crewmen who may have survived a water landing. Each covered just under 22,000 square miles, most clear of cloud cover. "No trace found of survivors of lost C-47 Transport Plane."[26]

The effort expended by the aircraft of the Thirteenth Air Force was not unusual. An indication of how vital each crew was to the squadron is contained in Missing Air Crew Report 10455, involving the loss of an aircraft and crew from the 13th Troop Carrier Squadron (TCS) on November 11, 1944: "A search was conducted as soon as it was determined that the airplane was lost. From 25 to 30 C-47's [*sic*] and one A-20 continued to search for two days. They followed predetermined plan and flew at 500 feet."

Considering the vast ocean expanses, such searches seem doomed to fail, but that was sometimes not the case. The 13th TCS had earlier lost an airplane while based at Plaine des Gaiacs. It was discovered after eight days, resting atop a small coral reef. And on September 11, just three days after the bombers from the 23rd BS had failed to find Healy's missing aircraft, a sole B-17 from that same squadron had conducted an eight-hour search for a lost B-25 bomber. In that instance, the crew was located in life rafts and recovered.

But unbeknown to all at the time, the searchers were looking in the wrong place. While there was some chance local air traffic could have incidentally spotted the C-47 wreckage, the chances of that happening would have been remote.

> As it turned out, the radar station we passed over didn't hear us or pick us up on their radar. So the search that started the day after the crash did not include our own island. Incidentally, I found out later that the other two planes made it to our base safely.

Day 5, September 9

> After another day, with the planes still passing me by, I decided to try to crawl down the mountain, find a stream, and then float down to the coast where I was sure I would find people.[27]

He might have been onto something. Many times as a young man he had been carried downstream by the Snake River, and he reasoned that the moving water could buoy his injured leg. The idea may have arisen from his experiences in the Pacific Northwest woods, or from reading survival manuals:

Plot a course to the nearest or most accessible river. Plan to go downstream. Somewhere on the shore you will almost always find a native village. The natives will bring you help, load you to a white settlement, or carry messages for you.[28]

It was unlikely that Richardson knew anything about the local hydrology, but it was reasonable for him to expect that streams would course through the deeply corrugated landscape. And he was right: to the west of the ridgeline that leads up to Mt. Turi are two streams, the Meno and the Melelo. Both streams flow in a northerly direction before making a clockwise arc on the north end of Turi, then merge with the Sarakata River which drains into the Segond Channel not far from Pekoa Airfield.

Richardson was not to know that there then were no significant permanent settlements along the Sarakata, or that in the last few weeks of Santo's dry season the local streams and rivers might hold too little water for Richardson's plan to work.[29]

Still, it was a plan, and Richardson believed that doing something, anything, was better than lying in the bush, waiting for the death that would inevitably come.

Sarakata River, Espiritu Santo, New Hebrides. (Fergus Young / Young Wiki)

Day 6, September 10

> On the sixth day I left the plane, crawling on my back, and heading down the mountain. I soon discovered the mountain was made of dead coral which cut my hands and exposed flesh.

Coral, mud and dense bush. Very challenging to walk through, even with a machete. Unimaginably difficult to crawl through, especially with serious injuries.

> I had tried to get some container from the plane to catch water when it rained, but everything I tried had the bitter taste of hydraulic fluid or oil, so I caught water using a large leaf when it rained. The jungle was mostly dense undergrowth, and huge Banyan trees whose roots spread out so that the tree was about 30 feet across around those roots. There were fallen trees all through the floor of the jungle, just like in the north woods in the Pacific Northwest.[30]

As he crawled, and apart from the drone of passing aircraft, Richardson would have found the jungle a very quiet place. Santo is home to just one species of frog and only 50 species of terrestrial birds. Thankfully, only one type of terrestrial snake lives on the island, and it was non-venomous. The fauna of Espiritu Santo is much less remarkable than its flora. Sea levels have never been low enough for a land bridge to develop connecting Asia with Oceania, and no land vertebrates were able to cross the open waters of the eastern Pacific. For that reason, and also because the islands in the archipelago emerged above the sea surface relatively recently, none of the large Asian mammals have become established in the New Hebrides. Only two land mammals are widespread: the Polynesian rat arrived before human settlement, to be joined later by the larger black and brown rats that came with the Europeans; and feral pigs.[31]

***

Espiritu Santo, at this time in the war, was garrisoned by the 129th Combat Team, and every troop in the 129th knew they would see action and that the combat would likely occur in the deep bush. Continuing the practice first begun while the unit was garrisoning Fiji, the commanders of the 129th conducted regular and occasionally quite challenging field exercises in the mountainous terrain to the north and west of the secured base on Santo.

One of the prerequisites of a garrison force was the ability to quickly occupy defensive positions, night or day, on short notice—tasks that initially were challenging for the newly arrived troops. As Capt. Morris Naudts, regimental intelligence officer would later note: "The night time movement and occupation of defensive positions under strict blackout conditions, manhandling heavy machine guns, mortars and ammunition was … tricky. The troops suffered unavoidable cuts, strains and bruises enroute to the defensive sector."[32]

The men of the 129th had learned on Fiji how to move silently, at night, through the jungle with complete confidence. On Santo the night maneuvers continued, emphasizing night patrolling, setting up ambushes, and attacking simulated enemy positions. The men became fully at home in the jungle environment, and learned to identify night noises as animal, insect, or manmade. But while the training was familiar, the troops learned of a further difference between Fiji and the New Hebrides—the challenge of the Santo bush.[33]

The Army garrison on Espiritu Santo had been ordered to establish an Outpost Line of Resistance (OPLR) against the possibility of an enemy attack. A Field Order Map was developed to give a general trace of the required defensive line, but the particulars of the OPLR could only be confirmed by an on-the-ground combat survey, and that was the job of the 129th Infantry.

The OPLR would span the waist of the island, extending from the Segond Channel west of the main Button base, arcing northward and eastward well above the island's fighter and bomber bases and other critical assets, and ending north of the fighter base at Turtle Bay. It would establish a course that would later be improved to facilitate troop movement along the trail and would be wide enough to accommodate jeep travel. The OPLR would identify useful observation points or defensive positions and would confirm the location and direction of smaller communication trails that would connect the OPLR to the base's Main Line of Resistance.

When complete, the OPLR would incorporate considerations of fields of fire, observation, cover and concealment, obstacles, and key terrain features. It would be placed outward of the base beyond the range of likely enemy artillery fire and would provide an initial—if limited—defense against enemy attack.[34]

The 129th Infantry Regiment organized a patrol in early June 1943 to follow the trace provided by the Field Order Map and to provide the details needed to establish a fully-capable OPLR. The unit consisted of 13 officers and enlisted men, and a team of 22 natives hired to carry equipment, personal baggage, rations, and water, and to take turns cutting through the dense bush. In command was Morris Naudts, recently assigned regimental intelligence officer.

The patrol jumped off in line with the OPLR near its southwestern terminus on June 3 on a heading of 12 degrees. Their course would require crossing both the Renee and Sarakata Rivers, would skirt the steep terrain adjacent to Mt. Turi, the highest point in the southern half of the island, and would pass through several abandoned native settlements whose positions were known only from an old French map, as well as some still occupied settlements. The patrol expected to reach the head of Turtle Bay five days later.

As was noted in the report later submitted:

> The jungle was dense and required cutting almost continuously. The leading cutter cleared a path only wide enough to permit passage by one individual. Five other cutters followed,

widening the trail to about three feet. In rear of all cutters an axe detail blazed trees and cut heavy growth along the trail.[35]

The patrol, aided by their native bushmen cutting the way, covered two miles the first day. As if to reaffirm the advice contained in the Castaway's Baedeker mentioned above, Naudts noted:

> Whenever we looked at the natives they were eating something, such as tender roots, bamboo shoots, wild finger bananas, and large plump white grubs dug out of decaying vegetation. Other than the bamboo shoots none of the patrol members were inclined to partake of the native fare, particularly the grubs which were considered to be a delicacy and a form of protein.[36]

The terrain was rugged and uneven, requiring the patrol to cross many steep ravines and ascend many sharp ridgelines. Two more miles were covered on the second day, and just one on the third:

> This was the roughest piece of ground covered so far. Not only rugged but covered with a type of low tree of heavy density with a mass of entangled thick branches from the ground to the tree tops. It was necessary to tunnel through this mess almost every foot of the way.[37]

After covering a total of roughly 18 miles—two-thirds of which required cutting through the dense jungle to permit passage—and after having seen the sun for only about three hours in five days due to the dense overhead forest cover, the patrol emerged at Turtle Bay as expected on the evening of the fifth day, its progress having improved considerably after encountering well-defined trails leading in their direction of travel. The patrol also recorded over a dozen clear trails that extended northward in the direction of Big Bay.

Such was the experience of fully fit and jungle-hardened troops, aided by two dozen indigenous bearers and cutters. How much more challenging would crawling through the jungle have been for an individual with the serious injuries Richardson had sustained and with no medical care, equipment, help, or food?

Day 7, September 11

> The second day of crawling I came to a cliff, about 20 feet to the bottom, although I couldn't see the bottom. It was overgrown with vines and vegetation, and loose rock made the going unsure. As I was crawling along looking for a place to get down, I suddenly started sliding, and so with my head down, and legs above me, I decided to continue on down. I used vines to lower myself with one hand, and protecting my leg with the other. I made it to the bottom without hurting myself, and then resumed my travels down the mountain, only to come to another cliff much like the first. I was now experienced so made it down fine.
> My mind was clear during the day(s), but I had nightmares at night. In one I thought that if I died I would come back in another body and serve in the European theatre of war. I awoke cursing because I couldn't find my knife to help that possibility come true.

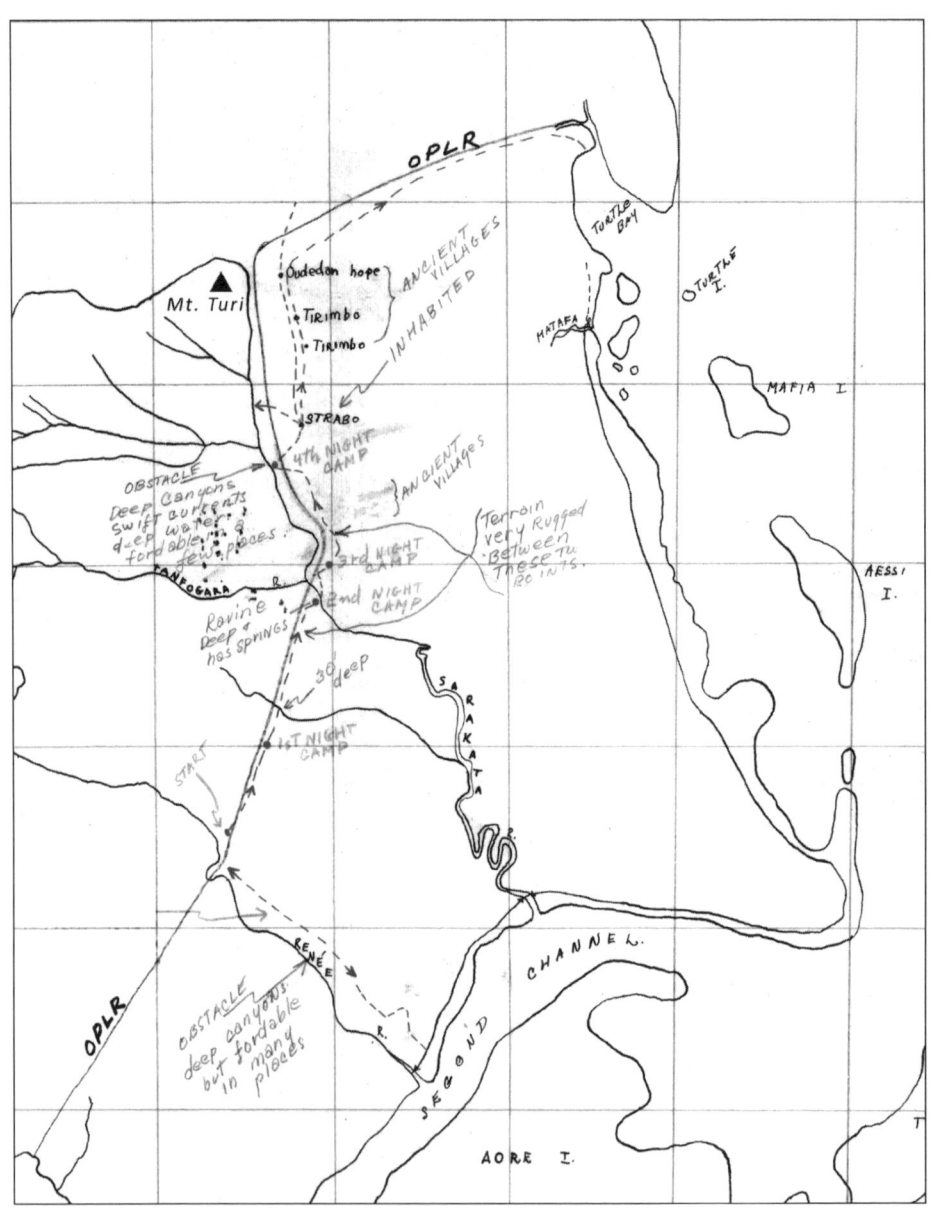

Outpost Line of Resistance Track, Capt. Morris Naudts, commander. (Report of OPLR to CO Naval Advance Base, Lt. Col. Carl Westlund, 129th Infantry Regiment, June 12, 1943)

> One day I was thrilled to see a small airplane come by and circle not far from where I was. I tried to find a clearing so I could wave to him. I tried shaking small trees. Shouting was no answer because he couldn't hear me. Finally he just flew away.[38]

Richardson had long hours to think about what had occurred, and why. Inching through the bush, he might have wondered what he could have done to prevent the crash, or what the pilots might have done. Certainly M/Sgt Wlodarsky and Cpl. O'Connell would have been unaware of the plane's location, and it would never have occurred to them to question how the aircraft was being flown. Only the three officers aboard could have taken the necessary action. Had Lt. Healy checked the aircraft's altitude and directed a correction to his co-pilot, the aircraft would have sailed over Mt. Turi. Or if either pilot had quickly adjusted the aircraft's course to more exactly align with the radio signal coming from near Dagwood Tower, Mt. Turi would have safely passed to the side of the right wingtip. Had Richardson double-checked to confirm that the pilots had moved enough to left as it transited the island, the plane would not have plowed into Mt. Turi.

What is known is that there was never any assignment of fault in the official squadron reports, or in the unofficial memoires of the event. The crash on Mt. Turi was one of many aircraft accidents that occurred on that September 5. Time and resources did not permit an analysis of the accident: the war simply moved along, and it was left to the AAF and Navy leadership to take the necessary action to prevent a recurrence of the accident.

Unbeknown to Richardson, and against all odds, that small aircraft had spotted the crash site on Mt. Turi. Exactly who made the discovery and on what date is unclear. Lt. Al McCreight, a pilot in the 64th TCS, reported this sighting was made five days after the crash. Roussell would later note: "One day about a week (after the plane went missing) one of the boys saw the plane on a jungle mountain. Just about 12 miles from our home field." A postwar document from the 64th TCS indicates the wreckage was spotted on September 8, just three days after the crash. The fact that Richardson identified the aircraft as a "small plane" would indicate it was not from his squadron, which was only equipped with C-47s, though one of the squadron's pilots may have borrowed an aircraft from another operating unit. Morris Naudts would later recall the sighting came five days after the crash. With the wreckage located, the 64th Squadron took upon itself the responsibility for mounting a rescue effort. Since the squadron's ground echelon had still not arrived, it fell to the air echelon to assemble a rescue team using the available personnel and equipment.

The effort, however laudatory, would soon fail. Captain Naudts later reported: "Although the Air Corps had attempted to investigate the crash site, their personnel were not experienced in land navigation through dense jungle and had failed to reach the crash site." It is also likely the overall physical conditioning of the Air Corps personnel, and their equipment, were equally not up to the rigors of jungle trekking.[39]

Though encouraged by the circling aircraft, and hopeful that the wreckage of his C-47 had finally been spotted, Richardson would have realized the discovery of his crash site would not hasten his rescue. Now a week after the crash, he had evacuated himself from the crash site, and the pilot of the aircraft who spotted the wreckage likely would not realize he had survived or that he had begun to effect his own rescue. Lying in the bush, Richardson's presence would not have been observed, and he was left with little choice but to continue crawling.

> The rains came and went, some days were sunny and warm and some were cool and wet. I discovered a more sure source of water. The down trunks of old and rotten trees in the floor of the jungle were water soaked. I'd grab a handful of the wood pulp, squeeze it so that the water came down my thumb and into my mouth. This kept me going.
> As I crawled I noticed some large birds circling overhead like the vultures we used to read about in the Old West. They didn't worry me because I fully expected to make it.[40]

One week post-crash. Seven days into a desperate but determined attempt to survive the plane crash. Richardson was stockily built and had commented in an earlier letter to his folks that he had gained a bit of weight since commencing his combat tour. It would be reasonable to reckon that an otherwise healthy adult male of Richardson's size and conformation could survive well, if not comfortably, for seven days without food. But he was badly injured and had lost blood. Despite his confidence that he would survive, there would come a day when his strength would no longer permit him to continue his crawl. While the daily rainfall would provide sufficient drinking water, when his strength finally left him he would be able to make no further progress across the jungle ground.

Further, Richardson had open wounds. His broken right leg was not a compound fracture in the conventional sense—the lower leg bones had not broken the skin. But both legs and his torso had received at least second-degree burns, with widespread blistering of the skin. Those blisters had already burst and he was at great risk of developing infection.

He was a remarkably self-confident man; his senior picture in his college yearbook carried the caption "One side, Professor, let me show you how." He was strong, durable, and confident. And he was a man of deep faith. All of these elements, in combination, gave him the unshakable confidence he would survive his predicament; an estimate that flew in the face of reality. At this point in his self-extraction, his wounds were untreated, he had not eaten, no one knew his whereabouts, and he was many miles from the nearest settlement. Any objective observer would be much more likely to predict Richardson would soon die, alone and undiscovered, in the dense Santo bush.

For the time being, he could crawl. On his back, dragging his legs behind him.

Day 9, September 13

Eight days after the crash, Richardson came close to being killed.

> I believe it was the ninth day of my jungle experience—five days at the plane and four days in the jungle. It was evening, and I was lying in a spot I had chosen for the night, when suddenly an old sow with some little pigs showed up, grunting and foraging for food. She was about

10 feet away and still hadn't seen me. I waited until she was even closer and then gave a wild Comanche yell. Wild mother pigs are dangerous, but this pig was terrified by my yell and crashed off through the jungles.

Richardson understates the danger of these feral pigs. Having been established on the island thousands of years earlier, the pigs were countless generations wild and, in the hinterlands, pigs had little fear of humans. The reverse was true. In trekking through the bush, locals kept a watchful eye for wallows that would indicate the presence of pigs and would occasionally shout to be sure they did not surprise any of the dangerous animals. Sows with litters were especially dangerous, and being omnivorous, would likely take advantage of any meal that presented itself.

***

Back at Pekoa, Major Roessell, having received no good results from the admirable but ineffectual rescue effort his squadron personnel had attempted, submitted a request through 403rd Group Headquarters and Air Force Command for help from the commander of the 129th Combat Team, Col. J. D. Frederick. Captain Curtis Craver, the assistant operations officer for the 129th later recalled: "They wanted to know if we could help, and of course, our answer was yes."[41]

Colonel Frederick directed Captain Naudts to develop a mission plan and to organize and lead a search patrol. At the time of this new assignment, Naudts was in the process of establishing 11 coastwatching stations around the island. Given his familiarity with the island and his extensive jungle training, Naudts was a natural choice for the assignment.

For his second in command, Naudts selected Craver, an officer whom he had come to know during his recent orientation as regimental intelligence officer.

Naudts, reckoning there would be casualties at the crash site, included the regimental chaplain in the team, but in case they located survivors, he also included a technical sergeant from the regimental medical detachment and the flight surgeon from the 64th TCS. He hand-picked 19 other enlisted personnel from a range of units within the regiment, all men who "had demonstrated their ability to function in jungle terrain." As for the chaplain and flight surgeon, "both had actively participated in jungle training exercises."[42]

The chaplain, Casimir Andruskevitch, had previously volunteered for a rescue patrol into the island's interior. On May 3, a team was dispatched to find an Army patrol that had become lost in the jungle. "The three day trip took the rescue patrol over little used native jungle trails, through swift rivers and into rugged mountainous territory where the going was hazardous as well as difficult."[43]

Like the chaplain, the 64th's flight surgeon, Capt. Alfred Richwine had also previously ventured into the bush. A naturally inquisitive man, Richwine and pilot Lt. James Moyle had hired a guide to take them into the bush shortly after their arrival at Santo—a wholly unauthorized foray into malaria country. Richwine would have been somewhat aware of what the tribesmen looked like in the deep bush and would have seen some of the dense jungle that lay ahead.[44]

Fourteen of the search team came from the Regimental Headquarters Company, and included Sergeants Carl Hagen and Clifford Gothard, Corporals Ralph Salley and Ramon Powel, T/5 Herman Barnett, Privates First Class Delbert Bullen, Arnold Byers, Paul Kelly, Clifford Key, and Henry Tremont, and Privates Rufus Enlow, Joseph Gabriel, Joseph Hershey and Walter Likes.

Hagen, Byers, and Gabriel had all been part of the OPLR trek undertaken by the 129th just three months earlier.

Also selected were Sgt. Guy Carter of Naudt's former command, M Company, Sgt Harry Bulfer, T/5 Henry Searcy from the regimental medical detachment, Pvt. Tony Secar from I Company, and Pvt Guel Salbrack from K Company.[45]

Two other men from the 64th TCS also joined the rescue team:: pilot Lt. Al McCreight, and Cpl. Raymond Buchheit, an operations clerk assigned to the air echelon.[46]

In total, the patrol numbered 26 officers and men. No native guides, porters or cutters were included.

Naudts selected what he considered the most direct route to Mt. Turi using a recently completed air reconnaissance map of that sector of the island, and the Army Air Force provided a small aircraft to fly Naudts along the proposed route. From the air, he observed no major obstacles, such as large rivers or steep cliffs along the base of the mountain. Naudts also observed, wrongly in this case, that "there were no native trails near Mt. Turi." Significantly, he did not spot the downed aircraft during the flight.[47]

Back at the 129th's base camp, in the late afternoon of the 13th—the same day that Roussell's request had been made to Colonel Frederick, the search team moved by weapons carrier as far northward as the roads would permit. Each man on the patrol carried a light pack with two days of rations, a poncho and shelter half, extra socks, and a first-aid pack. Each was armed with a pistol and carried two canteens and a machete.

At the point where he expected to exit the jungle on the completion of the mission, Naudts established a base camp that included a radio operator team through which he could communicate with regimental headquarters. His plan also included an airdrop to resupply the search team.

The rescue team would start early the next day.

Day 10, September 14

> The next morning I made a terrific discovery. I discovered a trail![48]

A trail in that remote jungle could only have been made by indigenous villagers. With a bit of luck, and provided his stamina held out, there was every possibility someone would come along. But who? If he were discovered by a native, what would be the native's disposition?

Richardson had almost no experience relating to any person of color. The communities of the inland Pacific Northwest had minimal racial diversity in the 1940s, and Spokane's population of one hundred sixty-five thousand included only 644 black people. Throughout his school years, including high school and college, he never had a classmate of Asian, Black, or Native American ancestry, and in the northern suburb of Spokane where Whitworth College was located, the populace included just 24 Blacks, living in nine households.[49]

He had begun to glimpse a much larger world when he joined the Army Air Corps in 1942, spending time in Arizona, Utah, and California, but the armed services were segregated, and his experience with people of color would have primarily been limited to service personnel at the various bases where his training occurred.

His first significant exposure to indigenous people came during his month-long posting on New Caledonia. He'd spent much of his free time exploring the island and would have been interested, possibly fascinated, and perhaps occasionally astonished at the people he encountered and their customs.

But, notwithstanding their occasionally alarming taste for personal adornment, the indigenous peoples of New Caledonia would have shared some points of commonality with Richardson. They were Christian. They had been significantly influenced by European cultures—most notably French. Many spoke French, and some a bit of English. They had a civilized social structure as evidenced by their villages. And they were clothed: male Kanaks normally wore shirts and waistcloth and females had adopted the loose-fitting cotton dresses that marked the influence of European missionaries.

The indigenous peoples of Santo were much less influenced by the West. A medical doctor with the 25th Evac Hospital would later record:

> The natives who inhabited Espiritu Santo ... were mostly small in stature, with hair that was dyed an odd red color and teeth that were discolored a bloody red using "betel juice," a local plant that was chewed like tobacco. They had all the devastating effects of longstanding malarial infection, even the children, [including] huge bellies, the result of distended spleens and livers.[50]

Richardson's introduction to the peoples of the New Hebrides would have been slight. The urgency of flight operations left little time for any exploration around Pekoa, and much of the little free time the aircrews had was consumed with getting their laundry done, sleeping, and possibly catching a film. Much more likely, he and his squadron mates would have been cautioned to strictly avoid indigenous people to minimize their risk of contracting malaria. Back at Pekoa, few native Santonians would have been within five miles of Richardson's squadron camp.

Mess hall conversations would have invariably included someone introducing the salacious topic of cannibalism, a practice that had only recently ended on Espiritu

Santo. Fertile imaginations would have no doubt speculated that cannibalism was still practiced somewhere on the island, and, in 1943, in the more remote regions of the island, far from the civilizing influences of missionaries and colonial governments, they might have been right.

Lying on the jungle floor, Richardson may have entertained some anxiety over the possibility that any villager he encountered might have been less interested in giving him a meal than in having him for a meal. It was also possible the native's own fear would overtake them, and they would flee, leaving him lying right where he was.

About the time that Richardson discovered the trail, the men of the 129th began their rescue attempt, jumping off at 7:00 a.m. into the dense bush north of Base Button.

Little is recorded about the first day of their trek into the deep bush.

> Because of the possibility of finding injured men at the wreck, speed was essential and this increased the hazards of the trip. The party was forced to travel over little used native trails which frequently were found to be overgrown with dense jungle vegetation, making it necessary for the men to cut new trails through the tropical growth. The trip was a hard one, leading up and down steep hills, across streams and through mud and swampy jungle terrain. The patrol travelled all day, not stopping until dusk.[51]

Unlike Naudts's prior foray into the bush in June to establish the OPLR across the island, in this case the men of the 129th did not have native guides to aid in carrying supplies or cutting trail. They did it all themselves.

CHAPTER SIXTEEN

Tan Pants

The village of Butmas (Boutmas) is located just three miles northwest of Mt. Turi, and was home to the families of six local clans, speaking the Butmas–Tur Communalect. As was typical of many communities on the island, the people of Butmas were nomadic farmers, moving between gardens at lower elevations and the village located about 2,000 feet above sea level. Of the roughly one hundred individuals in Butmas, some lived in the village and others lived in garden houses.[1]

According to the villager's oral history:

> Se long naet oli harem plen i fly over long haos I go afta I no long taem oli luk bigfala faea I kamaot long hil. Afta oli save wantaem se plen I crash antap long hil.
> [They saw a plane flying over their houses at night. And immediately after that they saw huge flames of fire on the hills. They knew that the plane had crashed on the hill.][2]

At the time, villagers had made no attempt to investigate the crash. It was something that had come from the white men and belonged to them.

> I stayed on (the trail) all morning and just after noon I heard voices (coming) from down the trail ahead of me. Soon I saw some natives walking single file up the trail. I believe there were three men and two or three women, plus some children. They were Negroid in appearance, and Melanesian. They were dressed only with leaves hanging from a G string. I called out, and after getting over being startled, they came to me.[3]

From a Western perspective, the villagers were among the least civilized peoples in the Pacific and surely among the most superstitious. They might have thought Richardson a specter. Near dead, caked in clay, his clothes torn, he was quite possibly the first white person the villagers had seen up close. At that moment, two worlds collided, and it would soon be known if humanity and empathy could overcome centuries of antagonism and anxiety.

The men who now purposely approached Richardson were not the first to encounter him that morning. Earlier that morning, nine days after the villagers noticed the plane crash, two women left Butmas, walking the quiet jungle trail to the village of Fanafo. As the crow flies, the distance is just 7½ miles but, with the meandering path, the trek would take most of the day. The women had just stopped for a midday meal when they caught sight of Richardson lying across the trail. Alarmed, the women watched unseen:

> *Afta long moning taem ol mama oli wokabaot long rod blong go long narafala vilij oli faenem hemia we leg blong hem i brobrok i stap long saed blong rod I stap kakae ol wud we I roten. Afta oli ron I go long haos oli go talemaot long ol man blong olgeta se mifala I faenem man we I foldaon antap long hil long plen.*
>
> [The village women on their way to the nearby village found the one with broken legs sitting on the side of the road trying out rotten wood in search for food. So they ran home and told their husbands about this man.][4]

A villager named Tome, with his two brothers and two women, immediately set out to investigate.

Since first being seen, Richardson had not moved; when the villagers returned, Tome approached with great caution:

The villagers approaching Richardson would have differed very little in appearance from this photo. Men and women wore nearly nothing. The tiny leaf strip over their genitals brought attention to, rather than concealment of, their private places. (Martin Johnson)

> *Yu karekil? Nem blong mi Tome, mo hemia famle blong mi. Bambae mifala i save helpem yu. Long wea ples nao bodi blong yu i so long hem? Hao nao yu kam long ples ya? Blong kam long Turi hem i longwe tumas blong yu wokabaot fo leg.*[5]
>
> [Are you hurt? I am Tome from Butmas, and these are my family. We can help you. Where are your injuries? How did you get here? Turi is a long way to crawl.]

Richardson:

> They carried poles between two native men and from the pole were hanging woven bags and pouches. They carried short sections of bamboo in which they carried water. From one of the bags they brought out a white pulpy "fruit" for food. After they had given me water they gave me some food, and did it taste good![6]

Tome said to Richardson:

> "*Yu tekem wota ya. Yu drinkim. Yu mas kakae. Yu tekem kakae ya yu kakae. Bae i mekem yu strong bakegen.*"
>
> [You need water. Drink this. You need food. Eat this, it will help you get strong again.]

Like many servicemen at the time, Richardson was a smoker, and his preferred brand was Lucky Strike.

> I saw a native pipe sticking in the g string of one of the men, so I tried to bum a smoke. They jabbered some, and then went to a bag and brought out a package of molded Lucky Strike cigarettes! Boy, did one of those taste good! I don't remember how they lit it.

It turned out that one of the young men had worked for the Air Force so he knew a few words of English. He would say "Me Kelly" and grin.[7]

The older man was slight in build, grey hair, and the husband of one of the women. He had a piece of paper he was very proud of. He was the chief, and the paper made him "Chief Guide and Jungle Watcher," and was signed by an Air Force official.

They were trying to decide how to move me to their village. I showed them the hand cradle carry, but they vetoed that idea. Finally they made a litter by using two saplings, and wrapping vines around them until it would carry me. Then the two young men put me on the litter and they put their shoulders under each end, and away we went.

> *Bae i soa smol be bambae yu oraet. Sori tumas. Bae yumi mekem wan hip toti wetem ol smol tri mo ol rop ya. I gat ol ami oli stap olbaot ya. Ating oli stap lukaot yu. Bambae mifala i tekem yu i go long Matevulu. Bae yumi wokabaot tu dei blong kasem ples ya. I gat wan hospitel blong ol ami long Matevulu we oli save helpem yu. Lukaot long leg blong hem.*
>
> [We will try not to hurt you too much. I am so sorry that you are hurt. We will make a litter using these small trees and some vines. Some Army troops are in the area. I think they are looking for you. We are going to take you to Matevulu. It will take two days to get there. There is an Army hospital at Matevulu and they will help you.]

It would later become evident that "Kelly" was well-travelled for a Santo islander:

> When reconnaissance parties first came down from Vila to Santo, General Rose made contact with Mr. Harris, Burns Philp local manager, who got the chiefs from this and neighbouring [sic] islands to come in and make the Americans' acquaintance. They arrived, many of them, "as naked as jay birds"—to use the American expression—with all sorts of queer ornaments thrust through ears and noses. Harris told them should American fliers come down on their islands they were to take good care of them and bring them in. They should give them kai kai and safe guidance, for Americans were their friends.
>
> Some who arrived were the real "wild men" of South Seas literature, at least to look at. But in reality they were easy to get along with, and a mutual liking developed between them and the happy-go-lucky troops.
>
> What they liked most of all were safety pins which they stuck through their ear-lobes and noses, thinking them much finer than ordinary ear-rings. The soldiers found nicknames for them; one, for example, became Chief Safety Pin, and another Chief Kelly.[8]

Tome turned to his family:

> *Wan leg blong hem i brok mo bodi blong hem i bon nogud long faea. Mi no save se bae hem i laef no nogat. Lukaot long leg blong hem.*
>
> [His leg is broken and his body is badly burned. I don't know if he will live. Be careful with his leg.]

While the men were building the litter, the women were taking care of me. They whimpered out of sympathy when they saw what kind of shape I was in. They held a large elephant leaf over me to keep the rain off, and gave me water from the bamboo sections.[9]

> *Be yumi gat meresin long Santo blong givim long yu. Mo ol mama ya bae oli helpem yu.*
>
> [We have Santo medicine to help you. The women will help you.]

Writing in 1936, British polymath Harrisson noted, "Among the bushmen anti-white feeling is generally strong but passive; for here there is little concern with the small world outside."[10] But these villagers, who had rarely seen white men, had come upon an injured person and their natural tendencies toward kindness came to the fore.

The tribespeople of the New Hebrides were constantly warring cannibals until around 1910, but, by the war years, much of the population had become devout

Christians. So despite their startling appearance, it can be reasonably assumed the villagers who saved Richardson were Christians or were in the process of converting to Christianity, or they might have subsumed some of the principles of Christianity in their own way of life.

Matevulu is a coastal village adjacent to the Army fighter airfield at Turtle Bay, nine air miles to the east but much further on the winding jungle paths. By the early evening of that day, September 14, the three brothers from the village had carried Richardson as far as the village of Fanafo, about halfway to Matevulu. They settled in for the night before completing their evacuation the following day.

> It wasn't long before we arrived at their village. I think there were three or four huts made of bamboo walls and roofs thatched with jungle vegetation. I was taken inside one of the huts and laid on a woven mat.
>
> By now it was evening, so they prepared a meal by digging a hole in the floor of the hut, lining it with rocks, and building a fire. The smoke went out a hole in the roof. As soon as there were coals, they lined the pit with leaves, put in some food like taro roots, and covered that with more leaves, and the food was baked. When it was done one of the women served me a portion on a big leaf. It didn't have much taste, but I'm sure it was nourishing. It was the first food I had had in 10 days, not counting the leaves I ate occasionally in the jungle.[11]
>
> It was time for bed, and these natives had an unusual procedure. Each native had his own woven mat, and beside it he had a little fire that he fed occasionally during the night, blowing on it to keep it alive. There must have been seven or eight natives in the hut, plus my mat and my fire that they fixed for me and which the native next to me kept going during the night. I went to sleep, and then sometime during the night I had another nightmare. I awoke partially and saw all the fires and thought I was back in the plane. I reacted, and my native came to me and calmed me down.[12]

Richardson and his rescuers, both the natives in the village and the U.S. Army still in the bush, might have been aware of intense activity to the south just before midnight. A Japanese bomber obligingly celebrated Richardson's recovery in a nighttime raid over Palikulo Bay and Bomber 1. The aircraft had first been detected by Army early warning radar 50 miles northeast of Cape Quiros—the same type of radar that had apparently not detected Richardson's aircraft a few days earlier.

Three minutes later, after three more radar plots, "Condition Red" went into effect: searchlights were released, a P-40 search plane was dispatched to Hog Island, just north of the Turtle Bay fighter base, a PBY was sent to Cape Quiros to search that area, and the antiaircraft (AA) batteries were "released" and were poised to fire.

The "bogie" continued to be tracked as it flew south on a course parallel with the east coast of Santo, 15 miles offshore. AA batteries commenced firing 16 minutes after midnight, filling the air with aerial bursts of 3.5-inch shells.

The bogie, not hit by AA fire, continued on a southerly course, then turned north and headed straight for Palikulo Airfield. It dropped two flares over the airfield and then released 14 bombs of several types. The P-40 interceptor briefly spotted the Japanese bomber, but despite unlimited visibility and a brightly moonlit night, it could not maintain contact. The bomber exited the island airspace on a northern track, headed towards the Banks Group of Islands. Forty-eight minutes after the initial spotting, "Condition Red" was off, and "Condition Green" was in place.

The next day's reports confirmed all bombs had struck roughly 1½miles northwest of Palikulo, most landing in the jungle area adjacent to the 350th Engineering Regiment and not far from the Army's 25th Evacuation Hospital. Craters up to 14 feet in diameter and evidence of air bursts were found. The bombs did no damage; the only casualty was a cow killed in a bomb burst. The island defense force surmised the aircraft was a four-engine, bomb-equipped flying boat, probably operating from a Japanese seaplane base in the Gilbert Islands.[13]

***

Squadron commanders were required to report missing aircraft to the Headquarters of the Army Air Forces within two days so, back at Pekoa, Captain Roessell duly filed Missing Air Crew Report (MACR) No. 466 on September 7. His report summarized the aerial search efforts made by several Army and Navy units and provided details pertaining to the aircraft, the points of departure and intended destination, course, weather, and the type of mission. It also provided the names of all men aboard the missing aircraft.

The MACR triggered action by the War Department, including issuing a telegram message to the next-of-kin of the missing airmen. Family members Stateside dreaded

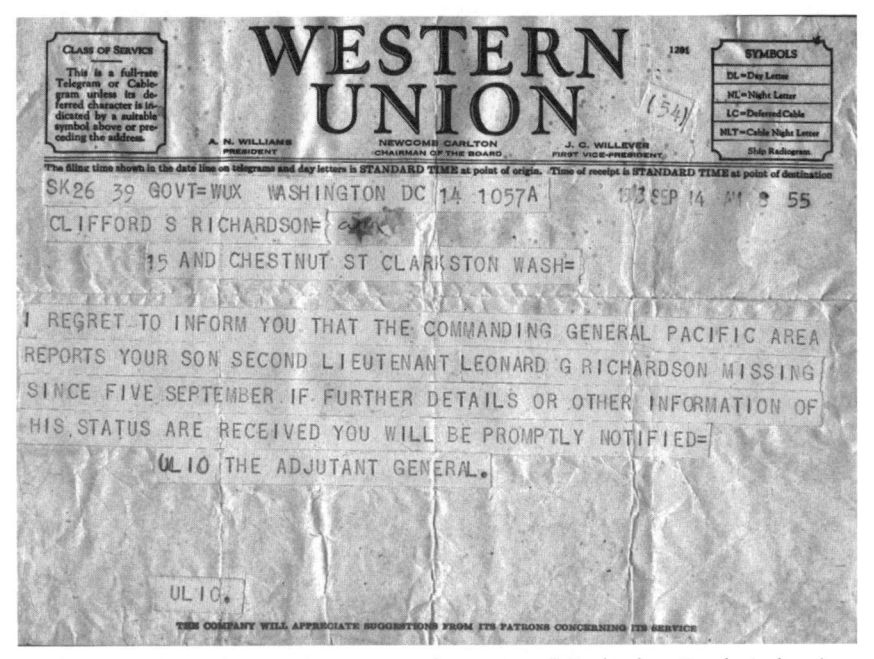

War Department telegram—"I regret to inform you … " (Richardson Family Archives)

the arrival of telegrams from the Army; they came to mean only one thing: that their loved one in service had been killed, injured, or was missing. Clifford and Lillian Richardson received their telegram on the very day their son was found lying on the jungle floor.

> I regret to inform you that the commanding general Pacific reports your son Second Lieutenant Leonard G. Richardson missing since five September. If further details or other information of his status are received you will be promptly notified.

Even before the arrival of the telegram, Richardson's parents might have had reason to worry. He had been a regular letter writer after his overseas posting and on average had written once every five days, but after his letter dated September 1, his letters had stopped.

Their first call was to their son Norman, then living with his wife and their new daughter in Chicago. They realized their son had been missing for nine days. For those nine days, they had all carried on with their lives, knowing Leonard was in harm's way, but also comforted by his letters telling them now to worry and that he was not in too much danger.

Norm wrote a heartfelt letter to his parents, hoping to raise their spirits in the face of this awful news. His letter was, in many ways, prescient:

> Your phone call a few minutes ago came as quite a shock to Jan and I. Well, the first thing to think of is that it could be a lot worse. I have the feeling that Len is alive & safe somewhere. He's a pretty good man, you know, and wherever he is, I know he'll be able to take care of himself.
> The Army & Navy don't just let men like that stay missing – they go out & find them. They probably have an idea of about where he is, & they'll have ships & planes out looking for him & the rest of the boys in the crew.
> Keep those chins up. I know everything is going to turn out all right. Our Heavenly Father is watching over Len for us, and I know He's going to bring him back to us, safe and sound.[14]

Despite their deep faith and abiding hope for his safety, they knew he was serving in the South Pacific and that duties included long overwater flights. They dreaded that his plane had gone down in the ocean, that he was lost and would not be found.

On this tenth day post-crash, the same day Tome and his family found Richardson astride that faint path and the same day his family was notified of his missing status, Captain Naudts's search team was still seven miles distant in the deep bush. They were making slow but steady progress in their determined trek to their mission's objective—the crash site atop Mt. Turi. Writing in 1943, Maurice Naudts described a boots-on-the-ground ordeal his patrol encountered in 1943 while following a trail through the dense bush:

> Because it was a narrow trail it had to be widened. The jungle floor was slick and covered with a tangle of roots and vines. One type of vine was covered with one- and one-half inch long spikes that frequently penetrated our clothing and flesh, causing minor cuts. This vine was named the "Wait a Minute Vine" because it abruptly halted any forward movement until cut loose from our web equipment or clothing. In addition, there were vines as thick as a man's wrist that hung from the trees that further impeded movement. Even though each member of the patrol was in top physical condition the oppressive jungle heat taxed each man's strength.[15]

By the evening of their first day in the bush, Naudts's team came to a village and decided to remain for the night, expecting to reach the wreckage the following day. The villagers were a revelation to the patrol's second-in-command, Curtis Craver: "The chief wore a belt with a loin cloth which was tucked between his legs and tucked into the belt on the backside as well as the front. The girls were absolutely nude except for a belt and a blade of grass about two inches wide tucked between their legs."[16]

Day 11, September 15

The following morning, the chief of Fanafo made it known to Richardson that he was aware of Army patrols in the area and he would leave to find them and return with help. The Army patrols he referred to were undoubtedly the men of the 129th Combat Team, who were then making their final approach to Mt. Turi, not following any indigenous trails, but hacking their way through the jungle. They were not far from Fanafo.

Mid-morning, the patrol came to another small settlement. Through Pidgin and gestures, the headman made it clear he had knowledge of the crashed aircraft. Pilot McCreight later provided a narration of the final outbound leg:

> About 10 o'clock we came to a native village and through a lot of jestures [sic] and pidgin English we finally got the chief to give us 2 men to lead us to the plane.[17]

Naudts had scheduled the resupply airdrop for that morning. He decided to split the search team. Captain Craver would remain at the village, recover the food drop, and await further instruction. Naudts would continue to the crash site, taking some of his men, the Catholic priest, and the three men from the 64th Squadron (Richwine, McCreight, and Buchheit).

The rescue team had fought the jungle for two days, hacking through the dense underbrush and struggling against clinging vines and downed trees. Until now, the trek had been arduous but relatively flat. As they came to the end of their search, Santo had a nasty surprise in store. Naudts's aerial survey of his intended course to the mountain had missed the native trails in the region, and his assessment of "no steep cliffs along the base of the mountain" was also somewhat off the mark. The ascent from the jungle floor to the top of Mt. Turi was as steep as any point on the island, with the final climb at a nearly 45-degree angle.

After a tough final climb, by midday of the 15th Naudts's party reached the summit of Mt. Turi and the crash site. Richwine, older and perhaps less fit than the other men, struggled to stay with the group and eventually fell behind. Naudts would later report: "In spite of the dense jungle, heat, high humidity, frequent rain and precarious footing caused by exposed roots and slimy mud on the jungle floor, the patrol hacked its way to the crash site in a matter of 40 hours, locating the C-47 200 feet from the mountain's peak."[18] McCreight's narrative continues:

Sgt (Raymond Buchheit) and I were dripping with sweat when we finally got to it. The first thing we discovered was that someone was still alive, but to our dismay we couldn't find him. We sent the native guides out to see if they could find which way the man had gone. While they were gone I identified one body and counted 3 pelvic bones and picked up a set of dog tags and an identification bracelet and some change laying in the middle of the fire where the ship had burned.

The dead crewmen—Healy, Miller, Wlodarsky, and O'Connell—were buried near the fuselage, with Chaplain Andruskevitch conducting the interment.

> By late afternoon the patrol completed its search of the entire area, finding evidence that the injured crew member had crawled down the southeast slope of the mountain. In following his trail we met a lone native clothed only in a G string, who handed us an identification tag taken from the lieutenant's leather jacket. He motioned for the patrol to follow him, and in doing so we found the lieutenant at the native's hut, suffering from a broken leg.[19]

This was undoubtedly the headman of Fanafo, who had earlier made known to Richardson his intention to leave the village to seek help.[20]

> The rescue party reached the plane and found three bodies inside, and one under a wing nearby. He must have been the one who answered when I first called out. While they were looking about, the native chief stepped out of the jungle, showed them his piece of paper and told them "Me got sick boy." They buried my crewmates, and followed the chief. They told me I must have covered about five miles.[21]

Craver's party had awaited the resupply airdrop at their makeshift base camp. The drop was on schedule but not on target: " ... the drop overshot the village and cases of 'C-rations' fell to the valley." Craver was able to make the chief understand the situation, and the chief ordered some of the village's young women to descend to the drop site, recover the rations, and return to the village.

Captain Naudts sent word for Craver to collect the airdrop and join the advance team at the crash site. Craver recalled:

> The chief wanted the food because they liked our "C-rations." I told him that his girls should bring all of the food with them to the airplane wreck and we would determine what we should do at that time. The girls put the cases on top of their heads and took off and when we stopped to take a ten-minute breather, they remained standing with the cases on their heads smoking a cigarette.[22]

Richardson:

> I was lying in the hut when I heard voices in the English language, and between the bamboo poles of the hut I saw suntan pants. Then into the hut came the medics and later the rescue party. They were happy because I was the first crash victim they had ever hauled out alive! They weren't half as happy as I was.[23]

The oral history of the villagers recalls the moment:

> *Afta ol man America oli kam, wan family blong hem I krae long hem gogo finis I talem long ol native se yufala I karem hem I go daon long Matevulu.*
>
> [Then they (Americans) came; one of them was a relative who wept when he saw his injured relative. They asked the natives if they could take the man to Matevulu. So they lifted him up on a bag and carried him to Matevulu.][24]

This coming together held great significance for everyone involved. It was the villager's first encounter with the Americans, and one that ended encouragingly; after years of training and preparation, it was the first positive outcome for the men of the 129th, saving Lieutenant Richardson's life.

Which of the rescue team wept at the sight of Richardson? It is unknown but it was most likely one of his crewmates from the 64th Squadron—McCreight, Richwine, or Buchheit. Their tears may have been of joy at locating their friend or grief at knowing their other good friends, perhaps best friends, were dead. Naudts:

> While the doctor and chaplain cared for the airman, the patrol set up camp for the night, clearing space in the jungle and building a fire to heat water for coffee. While this activity was going on I contacted the patrol's base camp reporting that we had found the survivor, and requesting that an ambulance be at the base camp when we arrived.[25]

Richwine examined Richardson and found his wounds included a severely broken leg, broken hand, and ribs, and found that his body was covered with cuts and bruises. Richwine gave him morphine to ease his pain. The morphine Richardson had carried with him on his crawl, the morphine he had decided to keep until he absolutely needed it, was still in his pocket.

Richardson had suffered deep lacerations to his upper thigh in the crash.

> When they went to dress my wounds they discovered that most of my cuts were healed. They bandaged one coral cut. "Kelly" saw their safety pins and wanted one to stick in his ear!

McCreight wrote, "When I got to the village I found Richardson in one of the huts and was surprised at how well he looked after crawling around in the jungle for 7 days with a broken leg and a broken hand."

Naudts and Richardson talked about the crash:

> Richardson related that "as the plane approached the mountain it became covered with clouds, blocking out all visibility, and moments later it plowed into the juggle covered mountain" ... I informed him that in inspecting the fuselage it appeared that the cargo of replacement aircraft engines, was hurled through the cockpit upon crashing, killing the crew.[26]

Richardson recorded:

> As it turned out, a pilot on a regular patrol had seen a flash of reflected light, and upon investigation saw the wreckage of our plane. A rescue party had been formed from a platoon of infantry that was getting ready to invade Bougainville, and some pilots from my outfit. Two chaplains were in the party: one Catholic and one Protestant. The Protestant minister got sick on the trek inland towards the mountain so he returned to the base.[27]

Day 12, September 16

At daylight the following day, September 16, the search patrol—now truly a rescue party—began the 18-mile trek to base camp on the east coast of the island. It was at this point that Richardson said goodbye to his native rescuers. They had saved his life.

Ale tata. Mi hop se bae yu kambak bakegen blong luk mifala long vilij blong mifala. Bambae mi tokabaot yu long olgeta pikinini.

[Goodbye. I hope you will come back to visit our village one day. I will tell the children about you.]

Had it not been for the intervention of Tome and his party, Richardson would likely not have survived. In another three days or so, his strength might have left him. Or he might have caught fever or been stricken with an infection in his injuries. His endurance and his confidence could only have gotten him so far. He would likely have died on the jungle floor, never to be found. Like so many others at that time in the war, his family would never know what had become of him. For the rest of their lives, they would remember him with a sense of loss and pain that would diminish over time, but only slightly. Most aggrieved would be his identical twin brother, Norman.

But dying in the bush was not Leonard's fate, and it was to the villagers in the central bush of remote and primitive Espiritu Santo to whom Richardson owed his life.

Naudts gave the headman all the excess food and two machetes in appreciation for caring for the injured airman.

The patrol jury rigged carrying straps for a stretcher salvaged from the crashed plane. "In that there was no native trail to the coast the patrol had to hack its way through the jungle, which was physically exhausting work. Fortunately we were all in excellent physical condition and after taking a short break every thirty minutes we made good progress through the heavy jungle growth."

> Although it was tiring work, it was worse for the (stretcher) bearers because the jungle floor was slick and covered with a tangle of roots and vines … All of these hazards made it extremely difficult to maintain footing, so as not to drop the litter, which could have added to the injured man's discomfort.[28]

The contrast was astounding. Just a few miles away—within earshot—was the throbbing military complex operating at full speed; aircraft capable of operating near the speed of sound and warships able to fire one-ton shells at twice the speed of sound; radar systems and medical capabilities at the forefront of science. But here, on the jungle floor, it was one step at a time, progress repeatedly halted by the sharp spines of a prickly vine. War at its slowest.

The patrol divided into two four-man teams, each taking a 30-minute turn in carrying the litter, with McCreight and Buchheit each taking a turn.[29]

> I was proud that my pilot buddies could keep up with those infantrymen. They were all toughened to jungle life, and were real men. They were great to me.[30]

After about four hours of hacking through the jungle the patrol reached a narrow native trail that led in the direction of the 129th's base camp, allowing the patrol to make better progress.

> Even though each member of the patrol was in top physical condition, the oppressive jungle heat taxed each man's strength. Consequently by midday everyone welcomed the opportunity to rest for an hour and eat a meal of dry K-rations and enjoy a cup of hot coffee over a small fire which was possible because the K-ration boxes were, by design, heavily impregnated with wax and ... generated enough heat (when burned) to boil a canteen cup of water for coffee or cocoa.

Fearing the severe burns on Richardson's leg could become infected, Richwine had decided not to splint Richardson's leg for the trek out. So, left unset and unsplinted, the leg had a tendency to "shrink" up to a couple of inches. From time to time, the surgeon would have to stop the team and pull the leg down a bit, just to be sure the shrinkage did not allow the bones to break through the skin. Sergeant Buchheit would later comment: "I reckoned that he was a pretty tough guy to be able to withstand that treatment."[31]

By the end of the day, the patrol had managed about ten miles. Naudts:

> Just before darkness on our fourth day we stopped for the night and ate another meal of K-rations. In order to create a dry place to sleep we cut enough leafy jungle growth to construct rude pallets. Thick enough to get above the muck and damp of the jungle floor. Then placing shelter half on the pallet and using our ponchos as a top cover we were able to get a night's rest. Although it was an exercise in futility to build a blazing fire, from the wet jungle growth, there was enough heat to create smoke, which helped to keep the insects away. As a security measure each patrol member stood a two-hour watch and also maintained the smoldering camp fire. In spite of our uniforms being soaked with sweat and being bone tired, everyone ... quickly went to sleep. Our surviving airman, in spite of his injuries, also enjoyed a night of rest.[32]

Richardson explained in his account that:

> I had told them about my nightmares, and the natives had told them about my nightmare with the native fires, so the first night on the trail they were alert for what I might do. After a tough and long day on the trail they made camp and prepared their meal. For me they had some powdered onion soup, and one of those great infantrymen gave me an onion from his precious supply. I still love onion soup!
>
> Late that night I awoke, and after laying quietly for a while I sensed that a pilot next to me (Al McCreight) was awake too. He was ready to pounce on me when I quietly asked him for a cigarette!
>
> The next day (Sept. 17th) we had to ford a stream (the Sarakata) about 30 feet across and about waist deep. They had a rough time getting down the banks with my 190 pounds going over wet and slippery terrain. In fact they dropped me off the litter. When we got into the water they had men all around the litter, and we made it safely. There were about 30 men, so they traded off carrying and cutting trail.[33]

Day 13, September 17

Naudts had sent Flight Surgeon Richwine ahead to alert the base camp to the patrol's location and the survivor's condition. By noon, with five miles still remaining, the patrol was relieved by other troops from the 129th who had been dispatched as a result of the doctor's alert. Late in the afternoon of the second evacuation day, the patrol emerged from the jungle into a coconut plantation, where trucks and an ambulance waited. Richardson and Richwine were quickly loaded onto the ambulance for the 40-mile trip to the 25th Evacuation Hospital.

> At the hospital I was taken right to x ray where the medical technicians had me handle my own legs and point out to them where I thought the fractures were. I thought my left leg was broken too, because it was swollen badly. It wasn't broken, but they found that the right leg was shattered. I thought they insulted me when they called my fractures compound. I had taken care that no bones broke through the skin. They said the cuts and burns made the fractures compound.
>
> Next I was taken to a ward full of combat casualties mostly, and two nurses were assigned to clean me up. First I was given a bath and thirteen days of jungle mud was removed. They also had orders to remove the burn scabs down to the pink skin. The only visible infection they found was where the Medics had put a Band-Aid over a small coral cut!
>
> I had a few days in which they built my strength back up so I could take surgery. In surgery the doctor told me later he had a rough time with the shattered leg, but finally with pins in my knee joint, and a "Roger Anderson" splint to keep my leg from shortening, he turned his attention to my hand. A pin thru the thumb and a rubber attachment to the cast to keep my thumb under traction took care of that.
>
> The nurses, doctors, and ward men were terrific. One guy even came on his day off and played his guitar for me. The nurses sneaked me in some bourbon when they were off duty. The doctors would come in on their free time, sit on my bed and shoot the bull.
>
> Then came a momentous day. Eleanor Roosevelt was coming to visit. Those of us with bloody bandages, or soaked thru with sweat had fresh bandages wound over the old.
>
> Eleanor came, brought us a message from "Franklin," and then stopped by each patient to say hello. Her aide was with her, and she was a nice lady.

A kid from Clarkston heard from his mom that I was hospitalized somewhere in the Pacific, so he looked in all the hospitals on our island, and walked in to see me!

Jack Roessell, my commanding officer, and all my squadron buddies came to visit me, and finally I received some mail from home.[34]

Roussell recalled this sequence of events vividly in later years:

> Upon returning from the Canal, the pilot had called the tower several miles out for a straight in approach—was granted and as the pilot moved a little to the left for a proper line up with the runway he went through a small afternoon shower (a beautiful day). Of course the shower had a hill in it and the aircraft hit about twenty feet from the top.[35]

Members of the rescue team would later provide their own commentary on the rescue mission from Mt. Turi. Craver reported:

> We went by foot from the coast, 40 hours up to the mountain. I didn't figure it was tough, we just did it. We were young.[36]

McCreight reported on his return to base:

> I didn't have much trouble sleeping that night and the next day turned the dog tags and my report over to the group intelligence officer. Later, a letter from the commanding general of the 13th Air Force was posted on the bulletin board which commended the doc and myself for the good work we had done.[37]

Naudts reported:

> The patrol climbed aboard a weapons carrier and a jeep for the trip to regimental headquarters where a well-deserved hot meal, shower, change of uniform and a dry bed were enjoyed. My first responsibility upon arrival was to report to the regimental commander to brief him on the patrol's successful mission, along with a detailed briefing on the terrain that we traveled over in crossing the island from west to east.
>
> Within a few days the Army Air Force Troop Carrier Command, as a gesture of appreciation, offered to fly the members of the patrol to the Island Command's Rest and Rehabilitation Center in Brisbane, Australia, for a week. Because of a priority mission I was unable to make the trip, but all of the other patrol members were able to enjoy a well-earned rest in Australia. So I asked the Chaplain—a good friend—to do some shopping for me while in Brisbane. One of the items I asked for was a small stuffed Koala Bear to send to Morine, and two sets of fine woolen Australian blankets for Margaret, which they received several weeks later.[38]

Naudts would later receive a commendation from Colonel Frederick, Commander of the 129th, citing, in part:

> Your ability to organize your patrol quickly and to reach your destination in the shortest possible time and still have your men in good condition upon their arrival is an indication of your superior qualities of leadership. It was indeed a job well done and ... your action (is) a model of resourcefulness and competent leadership. They are a credit to yourself, your organization and the Armed Forces of the United States.[39]

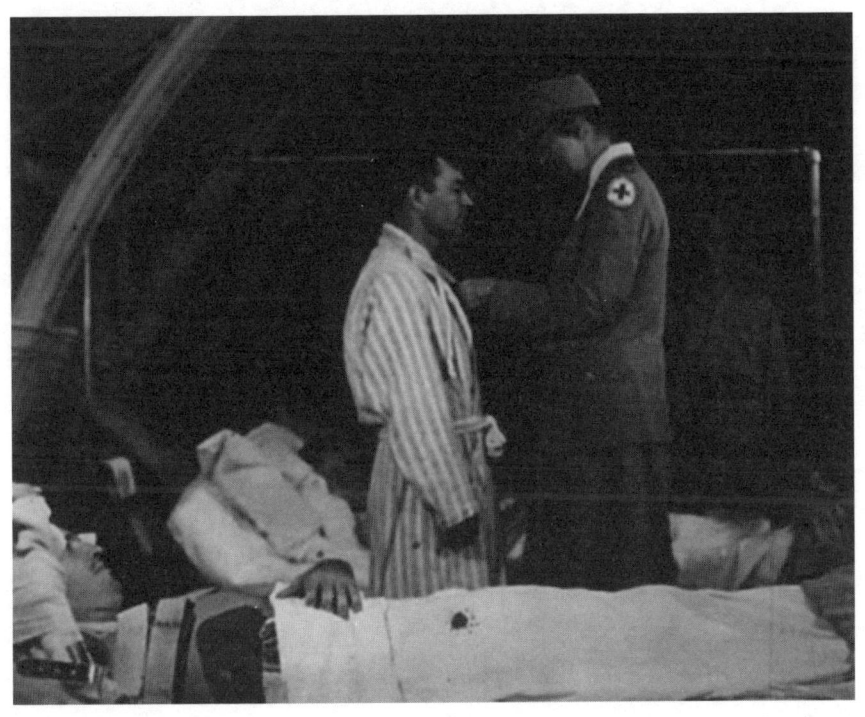

Eleanor Roosevelt's Visit to the 25th Evacuation Hospital and its patients. (National Archives)

On the day of Richardson's arrival at the 25th Evacuation Hospital, still believing he was missing in action, the Clarkston newspaper speculated that his plane had been lost during MacArthur's landing at Lae on September 4. But his safe return prompted a second message from his commanding officer to Army Air Force headquarters in Washington; that message would have generated a second telegram to Richardson's family in Clarkston, Washington state:

> Report received from Pacific Area states your son Second Lieutenant Leonard G. Richardson who was previously reported missing since Five September was found Sixteen September and hospitalized diagnosis fracture right leg you will be advised as reports of condition are received.[40]

That message was delivered on September 24. For the past 10 days, their lives had been suspended, and they were sustained only by prayer, their strong faith, the support and encouragement of their friends, and by a desperate hope. It was with incalculable joy that they received the good news.

Len's parents received the telegram at 11:30 and Clifford contacted KRLC, the local radio station, with the news. By 12:15 the station had announced his rescue. "Boy did you raise a rumpus when you were reported found! [Dad said] It was all over both towns in an hour. I understand it was broadcast 2 or 3 times. You've got a lot of friends."[41]

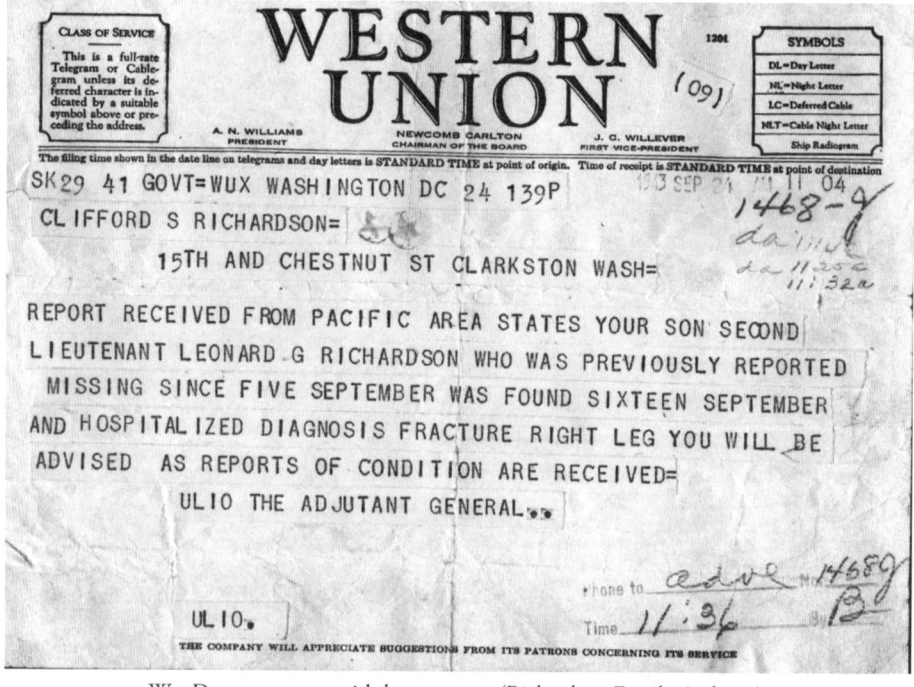

War Department ... with better news. (Richardson Family Archives)

His brother Norm, beyond elated with the news, reached out to Leonard in the only way he could, by V-mail:

> Brother—I take my hat off to you—you are a real man, & I do mean real!! Yessir, never before would I admit that you were a better man than I—but now if anyone considers me even half the man you are—I'll be very proud of myself. Needless to say we are all very very proud of you—I can hardly contain myself—& of course Jan had to shed some tears! And signing, Your proud twin, Norm.[42]

***

The squadron's losses in 1943 continued. About the time that the 64th Troop Carrier Squadron arrived at Noumea in July, a Marine aviation unit of an entirely different sort also arrived there to begin its combat assignment in the South Pacific. Marine Torpedo Bombing Squadron 232 (VMTB-232) stopped briefly in New Caledonia en route to its assigned station at Turtle Bay on Espiritu Santo.

The squadron already had a long combat history. In late 1941, it was operating as a scout bomber squadron (VTSB-232) based at Ewa Airfield in Hawaii, flying the two-man Douglas Dauntless dive bomber. Nearly all its aircraft were destroyed or heavily damaged in the Japanese attack on Hawaii. Later, a detachment of enlisted men from the squadron were assigned to help defend Wake Island, where twenty-five men were killed or captured. The squadron became part of the Cactus Air Force at Guadalcanal in August 1942, and was the first Marine dive bomber squadron to fly against the Japanese. Returning Stateside in late October of that year, the squadron was redesignated as Marine Torpedo Squadron 232 (VMTB-232) and was equipped with the new Grumman Avenger aircraft, which operated with a crew of three: pilot, rear gunner, and radio/bombardier.

The air echelon of VTMB-232 set down on Santo on July 24 and 25 and immediately began familiarization hops in their new aircraft before being assigned combat missions in the Northern Solomons Campaign. Included in the move to the squadron's new station was Capt. Vernon G. Rubincam, an experienced pilot and one of the squadron's three Flight Leaders.[43]

The squadron's training at Turtle Bay included glide bombing and mission tactics for large and small aircraft formations. It became part of Marine Air Group 11 (MAG-11) on August 9th preparatory to commencing combat operations and flew its first combat assignment—a search mission—on August 10. Training continued in torpedo drops and glide bombing, and the squadron flew search missions throughout the month of August.[44] Somewhat remarkably, during this intense training the squadron suffered no operational losses, and reported no casualties among the flight personnel.

The squadron began flying strike missions on October 1 and, by the 22nd, began daily strike missions to targets in the Northern Solomons, all in support of MacArthur's landings at Empress Bay on the island of Bougainville. And mid-month, the flight echelon of the squadron moved to the airfield at Munda, relieving its sister squadron—VMTB-233—and placing it closer to Japanese targets.

In accordance with standard Navy protocol, the squadron was relieved from combat after its month-long series of strike and search missions and replaced by the now-rested VMTB-233.[45] During -232's period of recovery, the 106-man air echelon was flown to Sydney for 7 days of R&R. Included were Capt. Rubincam and his flight crew, Radio/Gunner S/Sgt Don Barker and Turret Gunner Sgt. Bob Nichols. These three men had trained together and had completed six strike missions in the latter part of October. They doubtless relished their time away from the grind of training and strike missions.

At the end of their week in Sydney, the air echelon began returning to Santo and expected to return to combat operations in December. Rubincam, his flight crew, and other officers and men of the -232 left Sydney for an intermediate stop at Tontouta Airfield on New Caledonia before completing the flight to Santo. For that final leg, the men of VMTB-232 boarded a C-47 piloted by 2nd Lt. Philip C. Anders of the 64th Troop Carrier Squadron. The same Lt. Anders who had co-piloted Lt. Smith's aircraft on the fateful mission of September 5, flying alongside Lt. Healy's plane.[46]

Anders took off from Tontouta just before 8 am on November 23 in formation with one other C-47, headed for Santo, and was never seen or heard from again. Presumably forced down by severe weather, the casualties numbered 25 officers and men: the five-man C-47 crew, sixteen men of VMTB-232, three men from the Royal New Zealand Air Force, and a Navy medical corpsman.[47] And in strange irony, the C-47's navigator aboard the missing aircraft was 2nd Lt. George S. Richardson, one of two replacement navigators who had joined the 64th TCS on Sept. 19 in the wake of Healy's crash and navigator Leonard Richardson's incapacitation.

George Bamberger was the navigator on the C-47 that survived this dangerous mission, and the following passage, taken from his memoir, explains:

> We … went over to operations to check on the weather before we took off. The Marines were running the weather station, but they really weren't very good at it. They didn't have much contact with what went on around. They said, "Well, looks fine to us as far as we know." So, we took off.
>
> [On take-off from Tontouta] you go off over a mountain, and then you come down over the ocean. You have, maybe four or five hours, over the ocean between New Caledonia and Guadalcanal. Oh my god, right after we left the island, the weather was so fierce. I was measuring wind speed. I had seventy-eight knots, and it ran off the computer. The wind was so bad that the waves were like sixty feet high. The ceiling was like 100, 150 feet above the water, above that was all this terrific hurricane or typhoon in that area. We were desperately trying to stay above the waves and below the ceiling. The wind was so bad, we didn't have any idea where we

were ... we didn't know what kind of course we were on. We were flying wing to wing with the other plane [and] you could see right across 'cause we are real close, and he [the other navigator] pointed upward, [indicating that] they are going up. I pointed down, said, "No. We are going to stay down." I mean, it was just obvious to me. So, they went up. I was more worried about them because of terrific wind shear you encounter in those storm clouds.

They sent out search planes for a couple of days, never found even a piece of their plane, never seen again. And, here we are, all friends of ours.[48]

HQ of the -232 squadron received a report of the lost aircraft on the morning of 24 November, and twenty aircraft were immediately dispatched on a search mission. A further twenty aircraft continued the search that afternoon. On the following day, another 24 pilots flew search missions, and still more searches were conducted on the 26th. All results were negative.[49]

The loss of so many men was a great blow to the squadron. In prior action, the unit had lost just one aircraft and its three-man crew during a strike at the Kahili Airstrip in October.

The squadron remained at Santo until early December. Air crews replacing the men lost in the Tontouta incident trained in glide bombing, and the squadron undertook search missions in the waters of the Northern New Hebrides. On December 9 and 10, with the fighting at Bougainville still intense, the air echelon again transferred to Munda Airfield to relieve VMTB-233 and return to combat as part of the regular unit rotation.[50]

***

The news of an accidental plane crash occurring so close to its base would have reverberated through the aviation units on Santo. The eyes of every pilot taking off or landing from any of the island's five airfields would have been drawn to the small hummock that was Mt. Turi, straining to see the wrecked airplane at its crest. And while the aircrews may have wondered how the accident could have happened or why it had taken so long to locate it, for the military leadership the loss called for more than idle speculation.

The long delay in locating the downed C-47 on Santo had made it apparent that the Lost Plane Procedure—only promulgated two weeks before the crash[51]—was ineffective, and COMAIRSOPAC called for a thorough review and revamping.[52]

A month after Richardson's deliverance to the 25th Evacuation Hospital, and in what he might have considered "closing the barn door", a new Standing Operating Procedures was issued by the Air Commander on Espiritu Santo that included specific, and quite expanded directions related to Lost Plane Procedures.[53] A week later, the Command Staff of the South Pacific Force issued an important memorandum to *all* island bases in the SoPac on the subject of aircraft movements, and in Lost Plane Procedures.[54]

In particular, it noted: "Numerous occasions of aircraft being unreported while proceeding from one island base to another have demonstrated a lack of proper control of inter-island air traffic in this theater," and went on to note several specific deficiencies. Among them, "Failure of airdrome operations officers to appreciate their full responsibility in regard to the follow-up on aircraft which clear their airdrome."

In the plainest English, the Command Staff was stipulating that base Operations Officers at every airfield were responsible for initiating tracer action in cases where aircraft were overdue:

> In other words, an airplane which departs field "A" for field "B" must invariably (sic) be carried on the operations board at field "A" until a positive report of its arrival at field "B" is received. Follow up action will always be initiated when an aircraft is unreported after the estimated time enroute plus normal transmission time of arrival message has elapsed.

The memorandum went on to note that the Lost Plane Procedures adopted a week earlier by IV Island Air Command at Espiritu Santo and Guadalcanal—the LPP specifically developed following the loss of aircraft 42-23711 on Sept. 5th—were laudable, and should be considered as guides for the other 8 island bases in the SoPac.

On October 25, the Air Center Command on Espiritu Santo issued detailed instructions governing inbound aircraft making their landing approach to any of Santo's airfields and seaplane bases under instrument flight conditions. Under these new regulations, a detailed radio range let-down procedure was established, including approach altitudes.[55]

Still later, on November 1, the Air Center Command on Espiritu Santo issued detailed regulations pertaining to landing and takeoffs from all of Santo's airfields and seaplane bases. These new flight rules required aircraft approaching from the north to alert their intended airfield upon reaching the northeastern shoulder of the island. Further, the new rules required the approaching aircraft to fly a southerly course offshore of Santo's eastern coastline until nearly abreast Pallikula Bay before making a right turn to enter the landing circle for the Bomber 1 or 2 airfields. And finally, Air Center Command specified the ceilings and visibility levels below which pilots would be required to operate under instrument flight rules.

Just as the infamous crash of VMJ-253 near Tontouta a year earlier had become part of the aviator's lore on New Caledonia, so too did the loss of the 64th's C-47 on Mount Turi sharpen the senses of all the aircrews and become part of every new pilot's orientation to the island. No more would pilots independently assume directional control of their aircraft, or make their approach to the bomber airfields overland once reaching the head of the island.

Mount Turi would claim no more aircraft.[56]

CHAPTER SEVENTEEN

Lieutenant Richardson's Private War

The war was not yet done with Leonard Richardson. He had been rescued, and his medical treatment had begun, but his adventure was not yet over. On October 14, in the last overflight Japanese forces would make of Espiritu Santo, a Japanese reconnaissance plane appeared over Bombers 1 and 2, dropping flares over the former and Palikulo Bay. No bombs were dropped.[1]

> About once a month a lone Jap bomber came over and dropped bombs on our airfield. Our hospital was just off the end of the runway, so precautions had to be taken. I was put under my bed, with a mattress over me.[2]

At the 25th Evacuation Hospital, the treatment of injuries followed a strict protocol: "Wound treatment began with debridement and meticulous removal of all foreign bodies. We would then irrigate and put sulfa powder in the wounds, then put a cast on ... the only antibiotic we had was sulfa powder. We put it on ... like a saltshaker."[3]

Sulfonamide drugs were the first broadly effective drugs for treating bacterial infections but, unlike penicillin, which is bactericidal, sulfa drugs were bacteriostatic; they inhibited the growth of bacteria but did not kill them. This difference would have a profound effect on Leonard's treatment and recovery.

His most severe injuries were fractures of both bones in his lower right leg and a fracture at the base of his right femur, injuries that were easily managed by the 25th Evacuation Hospital.[4] The medical team at Santo operated on September 21, 1943, and set the fractures in his lower leg. The broken fragments of his femur were pinned in place using a Roger Anderson fixation.[5]

With his treatment underway, Leonard may have thought his injuries were not terribly serious—certainly not life-threatening. His broken hand and ribs were knitting, his cuts and bruises were already healing, there was no sign of gangrene, and although his leg was badly broken, he might have expected to return to duty after six weeks of recuperation at a rear-echelon recovery area and return to flying with his unit, and his friends.

And so it would have been with both relief and dismay to learn in early October that he would not remain in the South Pacific to recuperate but instead would be returned stateside. His leg injuries would take longer to heal than a simple fracture; Army policy at the time stipulated the evacuation of patients home if their expected convalescence exceeded 90 days.[6]

On October 2, he received medical evacuation orders "by first available Government water transportation," assigning him to a general hospital stateside for further treatment. Later orders directed him to Letterman General Hospital at the Presidio in San Francisco.[7]

His friend and fellow navigator Phil Gonder helped Leonard return his kit, everything issued by the Army, down to his socks: helmet, gloves, trousers, and jacket, plus the tin of Impregnite used to waterproof his shoes.[8]

On October 22, Leonard was released from service with the 64th Troop Carrier Squadron and assigned to the General Hospital Detachment of Patients. On the 25th, Army medics carried him aboard MS *Tabinta*, along with 11 other injured men, all ambulatory, including a young corporal in D company of the 129th Infantry. *Tabinta* would have also loaded patients from other hospitals on Santo, which at the time included the Naval Advance Base Hospital, the US Naval Hospital No. 3, and the 122nd Station Hospital.[9]

Tabinta had previously plied the Pacific before being acquired by the War Shipping Administration shortly after Pearl Harbor and converted to a combined troop/cargo/medical evac ship. It could accommodate just over one thousand passengers, nearly three hundred thousand cubic feet of cargo, and could make 15 knots.[10]

The Navy limited the amount and content of accompanying baggage the returning troops could bring for security purposes. Officers were permitted 25 lbs of baggage in addition to what they had brought when they first left the U.S. They were required to inventory all baggage: how many shoes, blankets, socks, etc.[11] Captured war souvenirs were permitted, with the individual's commanding officer's approval.

Not permitted were undeveloped film, opium and absinthe, fresh fruits and vegetables, or the skins of wild birds or fruit bats, among other things. Also prohibited were documents or photographs unless passed by a military censor.

On the day Leonard was carried aboard, *Tabinta* was one of 36 vessels, plus various naval district and small craft, at anchor in the Segond Channel.[12] *Tabinta* stood out from Segond Harbor at 10:02 a.m. on the 26th, accompanied by a single escort, *SC-1047*, a small sub-chaser.[13]

The war in the northern Solomons raged on as *Tabinta* eased down the Segond Channel, with the Allies deeply committed to the coming invasion of Bougainville. At 9:00 a.m., a formation of 176 aircraft—very large for the South Pacific at that point in the war—struck the airfield at Kahili on the southern tip of Bougainville. Included were Navy dive bombers, torpedo bombers, and fighters, and 22 Army

MS *Tabinta*. (Naval History and Heritage Command, NH 89842)

B-25 medium bombers. Ninety minutes later, a formation of 27 B-24 heavy bombers made a second strike against Kahili. P-38 fighter-bombers and B-25 medium bombers also hit the airfield at Buka, northernmost of the Solomon islands and located just northwest of Bougainville. By the end of the day, all Japanese airfields in southern Bougainville were unserviceable.

Tabinta's first port call on the homeward leg was Noumea, where it arrived to load additional cargo, personnel, and evacuees in the late evening of October 28.[14] Leonard's service in the war was beginning to come full circle. It was at Noumea's harbor that he had first reported for duty in the South Pacific, just 114 days before. After a two-day stay, *Tabinta*, again escorted by *SC-1047*, stood out from Noumea harbor in the late afternoon, with its next destination Suva, in the Fiji Islands.[15] *Tabinta* arrived at Suva on November 2 to take on more patients and casuals for the return voyage to the U.S.[16]

> We stopped by the Fiji Island. I had a porthole so I could look out and see the natives on the dock. Some young people were singing in their sing-song way. I thought it was a native tribal song, but it had a familiar ring to it. Then I realized they were singing "You Are My Sunshine"![17]

Remaining at Suva for just one day, on the 3rd *Tabinta* departed just after noon for its next port of call, Pago Pago in Samoa, still escorted by *SC-1047*.[18]

> (One night) a general alarm sounded, and guys running back and forth past my room door said there were ships on fire on the horizon. They came to me—the only litter patient on the ship and brought one of those wire basket litters, put some blankets and stuff in, and made ready in case those Jap submarines got us too. We steamed to pick up survivors, when after an eternity,

the running around stopped, and it was reported that what was seen were not ships on fire, but an entire island way beyond the horizon had blown up like a volcano.[19]

The volcanic eruption they encountered was on the small island of Niuafo'ou, located in the Tonga group of islands about halfway between Fiji and Samoa. The ships came within twelve miles of the eruption, which was captured on film by a Marine cameraman on air patrol.[20]

At 01:30 a.m., just offshore Pago Pago, *SC-1047* left *Tabinta*, which then proceeded unescorted to San Francisco under an arcing display of shooting stars from the Leonid meteor shower. *Tabinta* arrived at San Francisco on November 18 and was given the usual air coverage by a Navy ZNP—a K-class blimp used for patrol and anti-submarine warfare.[21]

Leonard was immediately taken to Letterman General Hospital:

> I was unloaded first and put in a Cadillac Air Force Ambulance, and taken to Letterman General Hospital, on Fort Mason. I was given a bed in a ward, and then as soon as they could they got me a wheel chair and I found a telephone to call the folks.[22]

Within a week, he was transferred to Hammond General Hospital in Modesto, California, via ambulance convoy. "Upon arriving there I was assigned to an officer's ward and had a cast change. In changing the cast, they discovered I had a case of osteomyelitis—a bone infection in my leg." The infection was evident from the drainage emanating from his injured tibia. Today, treating such a condition would involve antibiotics and the infection would normally be quickly resolved. But this was November 1943: "(Hammond) had just received their first supply of penicillin, and decided that since I would be sent to the State of Washington, they wouldn't use any penicillin on me."[23]

Soon after his initial examination at Hammond, he underwent a sequestrectomy—a surgical procedure to remove dead bone and tissue from the site of the infection. As his wounds were assessed, Leonard's care-givers would not know his injuries would not respond well to their treatments and that further sequestrectomies would be required, and Leonard had no way of knowing he would spend the next four years in hospital, undergoing thirty-plus surgeries, and that he would never fully recover from his wounds.

His stay at Hammond was brief and, on December 3, 1943, he was ordered to report to McCaw General Hospital in Walla Walla, Washington.[24] Also transferring from Hammond to McCaw was infantry Capt. Ronald Husk, who was soon to figure briefly but significantly in Leonard's future.

> On Dec. 9 1943 I was shipped by train to McCaw General Hospital in Walla Walla, Washington, where I was taken out of the train window on a frosty snowy December morning to officer's ward 17.[25]

At Walla Walla, he was just 100 miles from his hometown.

> I had been sent to McCaw General Hospital in Walla Walla, for treatment at the nearest hospital to my home. This was to be my home for two years, and countless different kinds of surgeries. I started getting penicillin in February. And I was in ward 17, which is the officer's ward there at Walla Walla. And when the nurses had their assignments, sometimes they lost and were given the job of working on ward 17. All the other wards were enlisted men's wards.[26]

As he settled into his new surroundings, Leonard gradually met and made friends with his fellow patients and the people on his care team. While visiting with two fellow patients, Captains Hart and the aforementioned Husk, he first met one of new nurses, 1st Lt. Evelyn Dickelman. "They were good friends, and they knew Lt. Dickelman before I did. When she came in one morning they said 'Hi Evie,' and she blew up and said 'My name is Lt. Dickelman—you will please address me as such.' Well, that was my introduction, and finally later on I got acquainted with her."[27]

They did a lot more than get acquainted. A whirlwind courtship ensued—or at least as much courtship as can be managed with the suitor confined to a hospital bed and the object of his affection busy caring for a ward full of injured servicemen.

> I started "dating" Mom, and by dating, I mean we'd go up to the officers club, 'cause I was in a wheel chair. Sometimes at night she'd stop by my room, and she'd get a sandwich from the

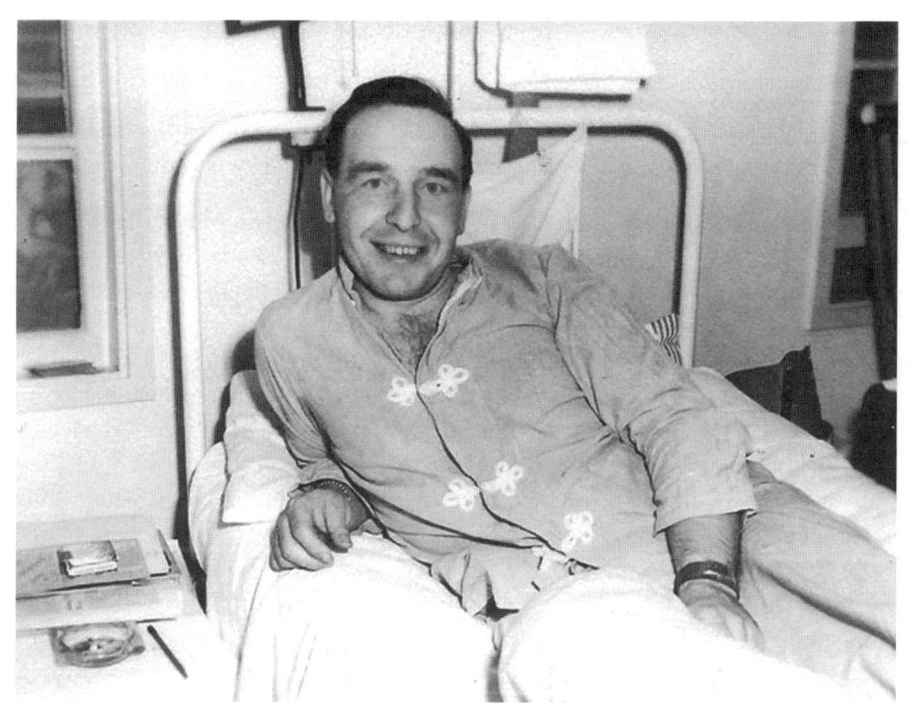

Lt. Leonard G. Richardson, Corp of Patients, McCaw General Hospital, Walla Walla, Washington. (Richardson Family Archives)

kitchen which was next door, and a cup of coffee and we'd just talk and get acquainted. And once in a while when I was able to walk and get out, we'd go into town to go to a movie. Or go out with some other friends to the officer's club at Walla Walla Air Force Base … we'd go up in the wheelchairs—a big long line of guys and we'd go up and meet the nurses up there and just have a good time.[28]

Their courtship included much correspondence—love notes sent back and forth, sharing thoughts and feelings. All are safely archived and unread by anyone except the recipient—except for one.

Just a month before their wedding, Leonard slipped Evelyn an envelope bearing the note: "To be read not sooner than midnight."

My dearest Evelyn
This is written a little past midnight … the ward is quiet. Somewhere a fan is going, and someone down the hall is talking in low tones. The lights are off—all except my bed lamp—and the radios are still. I can hear a truck out on the highway, and wonder what the driver is thinking at this time of night.

I thought about how peaceful everything was, like old times at home, and how often I have lain here like this before. Only this time it is different. Then I wished things. I thought about how nice it would be to have a girl to care for & who cared for me. Now I have you, and I think how wonderful it is, and how much more wonderful it will be.

Probably somewhere else people are dancing, or at a party, or maybe driving thru the night. Some kid is parked somewhere with his girl, and a man is sleeping with his wife. Some are happy & some are not. You're on Ward 1, and you're probably thinking too—maybe a little bit of me.

I'm happy & I think when a guy is happy he has all he can ask for. You caused me to be this way.

All my love.
Richie

Leonard and Evelyn were married nine months after meeting in Walla Walla, on September 3, 1944. They were wed at the small chapel on the hospital grounds. Sergeant Howard Warrick was Leonard's best man, and Lt. Marguerite Hanlon was Evelyn's maid of honor.

Their daughter, Madonna Lee, was born a scant nine months later in June 1945.

On November 6, 1945, Leonard was sent to the Army Air Force Regional Station Hospital at Fort George Wright, Spokane, for observation and convalescence.[29] "After two years at Walla Walla, I was sent to Fort George Wright in Spokane to see if they could cure my osteo by resting me. I was there for a year, with a house off base, and only reporting to the hospital occasionally."[30]

On September 9, 1946, he was transferred again, this time to Madigan General Hospital in Tacoma for further observation and treatment. After just two months at Madigan, he was sent to McCornack General Hospital in Pasadena; his orders this time were different: he was sent there for observation, treatment, and disposition.[31] The Army was trying to decide what to do with him. Among their options: continue to treat his wounds in the expectation he could return to full service in the Army

The wedding of Lts. Evelyn and Leonard Richardson. (Richardson Family Archives)

Air Force; discharge from the service with a full bill of health; or discharge from the service under a medical retirement.

At McCornack, Leonard began a series of surgeries in a final bid to resolve his bone infection, the last of which was performed on May 21, 1947. The procedures once again failed to heal his now long-standing bone infection. "The wound continued to drain and the patient had a rather stormy course."[32]

On August, his medical condition was reviewed by the Disposition Board for Officers at McCornack. Leonard, who until then had remained classified as qualified for full military duty, was ordered to appear before the Army Retiring Board.[33]

On August 28, a Medical Board was convened to determine his fate. It was their task to judge whether it was likely that he would recover from his injuries sufficiently to return to active duty or whether he would be retired from the Army.

At the time the Board convened, Leonard was in complete health save for his continuing osteomyelitis and its resultant drainage from his bone. X-rays taken at the time revealed his leg had lost a large amount of bone due to infection, and that the remaining bone was corrupt, displaying a "pin moth-eaten appearance." While drainage from his leg had stopped in mid-1947, two physicians from the medical staff at McCornack ominously testified:

We all realize that, to give this man benefit of the doubt, he will never do general duty. He isn't capable of that. Our question is will we be doing him an injustice by giving him general duty and not retiring him. (I feel) that we would be doing him an injustice not retiring him because of the possibility of future difficulty. Any individual who has had osteomyelitis from 1943 to 1947, it stands to reason that he may have recurrent osteomyelitis for a long long time.[34]

During his own testimony, the Board asked, "Do you desire to be relieved from active duty?" "No, Sir" was Leonard's reply.[35]

Seeing the medical evidence and hearing the expert testimony of his doctors, the Board reached its decision in less than 45 minutes. "1st Lt. Leonard G. Richardson is permanently incapacitated for active service. Unfit for any type of duty."[36]

On September 23, he was notified that "having been found physically disqualified for all flying duty, [his] suspension from flying status is confirmed." On October 2, he was advised he would revert to inactive status effective October 3 by reason of physical disability. At that time, he was promoted to the rank of captain, and at last was no longer outranked by his wife Evelyn.[37]

Leonard was left with a large lump of flesh at the site of injury—a pedicle mass. In normal cases, the surgeons would have "refined" the pedicle, removing fat tissue and smoothing the skin through plastic surgery. This was not done in Leonard's case because his osteomyelitis was never permanently healed. He suffered from recurrent outbreaks for the rest of his life, with occasional troubling discharge from a sinus tract in the pedicle tissue. Having spent 46 months in various hospitals and enduring innumerable operations, Leonard was medically discharged on October 3, 1947:

> Capt. Leonard G. Richardson, O744866, AC, AUS (component) having been found permanently incapacitated for active duty by the ARB (Army Retirement Board) of this General Hospital and recommended no type of service is relieved from further observation and treatment and ... (will) revert to inactive status 3 Oct 1947 by reason of physical disability.[38]

He retired as a captain, and settled at Lompoc, near Pasadena. In later years, he would be appointed to the Air Force Honorary Reserve and was assigned to the Ground Observer Corps of the United States Air Force in 1953.

His first civilian job after being released from the Army was teaching industrial arts and physical education at Lompoc High School. While coaching football, however, he reinjured his leg and had to quit his job. He and Evelyn decided to move to Spokane, where Evelyn could find nursing work, and Leonard could work on his master's degree while recuperating. They used his discharge money—about $3,000—as a down payment on a house at 2528 N. Normandie. He completed his graduate degree in about a year and was hired soon after as principal at the Rosalia High School.[39]

Further children arrived: Patrick (1946), Robert (1949), Ronald (1951), Thomas (1952), and Denis (1954).

Leonard took a teaching job at Shadle Park High School in 1956 and Evelyn continued her nursing career at Sacred Heart Hospital. After a couple of years at Shadle, Leonard was named vice-principal in the Spokane junior high school system,

Leonard and Evelyn Richardson and family. (Richardson Family Archives)

was subsequently named principal at Libby Junior High, and would end his career as principal at Chief Spokane Gary.

Over the years, Leonard had the appearance of a man of character. His face was leathery and deeply etched, partially from his predilection for the outdoors but almost certainly also due to the pain he had suffered during his endless rehabilitation.

Leonard and Evelyn enjoyed the family life that comes with a passel of kids, mostly boys. Someone was always in trouble, hurt, or sad, but, mostly, the family was happy, healthy, and full of life.

Their son Pat died of Hodgkin's disease in January 1975, Evelyn died of breast cancer in December 1978, and his beloved daughter Madonna died in 2018.

Leonard retired from his career in education in 1977 and continued to struggle with health issues. He developed chronic lymphatic leukemia, possibly due to his lifelong bone infection. He contracted skin cancer and, finally, lung cancer. When told by his physician of the lung cancer diagnosis, he commented: "I hope you're wrong doc, 'cause I got all the cancer I can handle already." A bit later, as he dealt with radiation and chemotherapy, Leonard gave a glimpse into his philosophy of life—a philosophy that had kept him in good stead through all his years of adversity. He confided to one of his sons: "I don't have to like it; I just have to do it."

He might have had that in mind when he lay prone on the jungle floor in 1943. Or during his innumerable surgeries or painful recoveries. Or when he had the hardest job of all—burying his first son, and his wife.

Leonard Gordon Richardson. (Richardson Family Archives)

Leonard Richardson died on July 28, 1980. Strong to the end. An enduring example to his children.

EPILOGUE

Back to Espiritu Santo

The silence would have been deafening. Throughout the war trucks had run unceasingly on the newly built roads on the southeastern tip of Espiritu Santo. But now, with the roll-up of Santo nearly complete, the only movement was vehicles moving to their new owners—the wealthy plantation operators on the island or the French or British bureaucrats. Where formerly scores of ships and small craft beat the waters in the Segond Channel, now only a few ships could be seen. The vast aerodromes were still, warehouses empty, and everywhere the detritus of a vast army lay about, gaining rust and entrapping pools of rainwater that would spawn clouds of malarial mosquitoes in due course.

On Santo, what remained after the departure of the Americans was a greatly improved infrastructure, including roads, permanent buildings, water systems, airfields, new communication systems, piers, and docks. Also remaining was the utterly ineffectual French-British Condominium, which became the primary beneficiary of these many improvements.[1]

While some roads and communication improvements reached into the remoter regions of the island, most of the development work done by the Americans was concentrated on the southeastern corner. Most indigenous Santonians lived elsewhere on the island, connected only by faint paths often so overgrown with vegetation they were evident only to locals. Most never interacted in any way with the Americans. They were not directly affected by the arrival of the Americans and were less so on their departure. The people of Santo largely continued the subsistence agriculture that had served them well for 5,000 years. Their social structure, still largely based on clans and villages, and their traditional culture, remained superficially unchanged.

But with the Americans gone or going, one persistent, familiar, and heartbreaking element on the island remained almost unchanged—malaria. During the war years, the American-led mosquito eradication program had been geared primarily to protecting Allied forces on a relatively small part of the island and had, thus, largely been discontinued. Post-war, in all malarial regions of the South Pacific, residual DDT spraying by local health agencies served as the primary malaria control activity, and the drug chloroquine was the standard pharmaceutical treatment. While these protocols were effective in the more developed south and east coastal plans of Santo, they were infeasible in the remote hinterlands. Outside of the developed region of Santo, malaria among the indigenes continued to be widespread—i.e., having "high mesoendemicity"—and its incidence was seven times higher than in the developed region of the island.[2] The fight against malaria would not get a major boost until 1988 with the introduction of insecticide-treated bed nets.[3] After 2003, the sharp upward trend in malaria infections began to decrease rapidly. Rapid diagnostic tests and effective antimalarial medications became available from 2009 and Vanuatu reported its last malarial death in 2012, and by 2018 the incident rate in the northern New Hebrides had dropped to just four per thousand people, roughly equivalent to the malaria rates reported in much more economically developed countries like Ecuador, Brazil, and India.[4]

Perhaps the most enduring legacies of the American occupation were metaphysical: among them, many of the New Hebrideans felt an enduring admiration and regard for their former occupying force, sentiments that would persist into the present day.

The regard with which Ni-Vanuatu viewed America and Americans was due in part to how America treated them during the period of occupation, but also because of how Americans treated each other, and of the often hard-to-see similarities in character between the two peoples.

Prewar, the colonial powers in the New Hebrides maintained a rigid apartheid with the islanders, what sociologist Lamont Lindstrom has described as "rigid sumptuary codes."[5] This code extended to what clothes were worn, what food was eaten, and with whom. Most Americans—former colonists themselves—were uninterested in further enabling these colonial mores, and troops often dined and smoked with the locals. The American access to "cargo"—the trappings of an industrial society beyond the grasp of the islanders—and their willingness to share their wealth in gifts of clothing, food, candy, and more also distinguished them from the less-generous French and British condominium administration.

The presence of Black American troops in the South Pacific was of great significance. On Efate, Santo, and other islands in the New Hebrides, military personnel of African–American heritage—men who in some ways resembled some of the islanders—often displayed the same skills, confidence, clothing, and equipment as White troops. The obvious segregation of troops on the basis of race seems not to have impressed the islanders to the same extent as their otherwise apparent equality.

The individualism perceived in the Americans also resonated with the islanders, as did the concepts of personal honor and dignity. In America, a man could succeed based on his own integrity, perseverance, and work ethic. Similarly, in Vanuatu, a man could prosper in his clan or village on the merits of his own abilities and in his capacity to create a network of supporters.

But of greatest importance for the people of the archipelago, some indigenous visionaries perceived the economic opportunities and cultural interactions that attended the American presence could result in an entirely different future for the islands and their people, incorporating a fundamental change in their relationships with foreign governments and expatriates:

> Postwar changes in the Islander identity and sociopolitical aspirations are as much relics of the war as are the infrastructural contributions, roads, airfields, crashed planes, abandoned Quonset huts, and other debris left behind when Truman brought home his troops ... the war also engendered more mundane and more routinized cross-cultural relations between Islanders and outsiders on an unprecedented scale. Encounters with Americans, their allies, and the Japanese stimulated the social imaginations of all parties and led many war workers to rethink their relations with Europeans and colonial regimes.[6]

And where else would those fresh imaginings turn but on the most glaring inequity on the islands—the bizarre arrangement officially designated the "British–French Condominium," but widely referred to as the "Pandemonium." Brought about by the unwillingness of both France and Great Britain to claim dominion over the archipelago, under this arrangement each power administered its citizens, but neither country exercised sovereignty. Within this "region of joint influence," Britain and France each established separate "Residencies," each identically structured and staffed, and enacting precisely parallel laws and regulations for their citizens. Two mirror-image bureaucracies developed: two postage systems, currencies, police forces, prison systems, education and health systems, and taxing structures.[7] The islanders had no access to commercial and administrative services within the Condominium. They could not form companies, register their fishing boats, or execute contracts, and up to 1967, they could not register their births, deaths, and marriages.

By the early 1960s, the long-simmering resentment among the people of Santo over the loss of clan property to foreign interests reached boiling point, coalescing into a grassroots movement that came to be called "Nagriamel." The movement established itself in a few huts on a former French-operated plantation along the Sarakata River, naming the location Vanafo (variously rendered as Fanafo, Fanefo, or Tanafo)—the same village to which Leonard had been carried after his trailside discovery, and where the men of the 129th Infantry had first come to his aid.

Concurrent with the emergence of the Nagriamel movement, the New Hebrides Cultural Association formed and quickly morphed into an organization that was manifestly a political party—the New Hebrides National Party (NHNP). The NHNP was both Anglophile and non-Catholic, a "self-consciously anti-colonial and somewhat socialistic national liberation movement, [that] concentrated on Kastom and land issues."[8] Twelve years of mostly non-violent chaos ensued, and, by 1977, Britain and France convened in Paris to draft the terms and conditions for full independence for the new nation of Vanuatu—an indigenous word meaning, depending on dialect, "Our Land," "Abiding Land," "The Land Remains," or "Land that Stands Up."

A new constitution was written in 1979, and the new country's first general election was held in November. The new republic would join the Commonwealth of Nations, a voluntary association of 53 independent sovereign states, all but one of which were former British colonies.⁹ The anglophone Vanua'aku Party maintained political control of parliament and the executive for 11 uninterrupted years but, in 1991, owing to a growing disunity within the party, control of the government went to a francophone-led coalition government and, for the next four years, politics within the country became increasingly divisive, the government more decentralized, and political parties more diverse. The coalition governments that have become the norm in Vanuatu tend to be weak.[10] Political instability is as endemic in Vanuatu today as malaria was before the arrival of the Americans.

Along with other struggling countries that emerged in the postwar years, Vanuatu has undergone the scrutiny of the United Nations, non-government organizations, and non-profits focusing on development, equity, and the environment.

In 1971, Vanuatu was identified by the UN General Assembly as one of 54 Least Developed Countries (LDCs) to "generate international attention and action to reverse the continuing deterioration of the socio-economic condition of these most vulnerable countries."[11] Despite the enormous setback that resulted from Cyclone *Pam* in 2015, in 2020, Vanuatu "graduated" from the roster of Least Developed Countries. In what might seem to be trivially bureaucratic, but is of huge import to its people, Vanuatu is now officially classified as a "Developing Country."[12]

While Vanuatu may be seen as improving according to the UN's LDC index, it is on a discouraging trend based on the factors measured by the Human Development Index.[13] In fact, relative to all other countries in the world, the human condition in Vanuatu has degraded every year since the HDI was instituted. Vanuatu currently ranks below Bangladesh, North Korea, and El Salvador in terms of life expectancy; below Bhutan, Djibouti, and Palestine in terms of per capita Gross National Income; and while adult literacy in Vanuatu is high—85%—the country ranks below Zimbabwe, Tajikistan, and Dominica in education.[14]

Other indicators are equally disquieting for Vanuatu; the World Risk Index postulates a country's vulnerability to natural disasters, its capacity to cope with those disruptions, and its citizens' susceptibility to environmental calamities. Under those criteria, in five separate assessments made between 2011 and 2021, Vanuatu was ranked as the most hazardous country in the world.[15] Cyclone *Pam* made landfall in 2015 as if to justify Vanuatu's ranking in the World Risk Index, "(ripping) through Vanuatu with winds of up to 155 mph, killing eleven people and inflicted severe damage to the country's southern and central provinces. The cyclone affected two-thirds of the population, damaged or destroyed much of the housing stock, disrupted food and water supply, cut off electricity and communication, and forced many schools and medical facilities to close."[16]

Foreign aid has become an important supporting element for Vanuatu's economy. In brief, the country is doing poorly and, more worrisome still, it is failing at a slightly but still measurably increasing rate. However, in 2006, the country was rated highest among 178 countries by the Happy Planet Index, a measure of human wellbeing and environmental impact introduced by the New Economics Foundation (NEF). In 2024, Vanuatu again attained the highest rating in the Happy Planet Index, narrowly beating Sweden for the honor.[17]

From its postwar population of forty thousand, Vanuatu has experienced a steady increase, reaching three hundred and seven thousand in 2020.[18] Three-quarters of the population is rural, living either in coastal settlements or inland villages ranging in size from a few families to several hundred people. Contrary to expected trends, the rural population is increasing and, unsurprisingly, given its rapid population growth, the country is young—over half the population is under the age of 24.

Vanuatu is unique in so many ways that estimates of its future prospects have to be carefully parsed. Certainly the predictions for the nation of Vanuatu are very different than those of the Ni-Vanuatu society.

There is no reason to expect a turnaround in Vanuatu's economy. With no resource base, little manufacturing, an imbalance in trade, and a heavy reliance on tourism, Vanuatu will likely continue on its current track. For many reasons—islandism, language, and religion among them—it is also unlikely a widespread sense of national unity will emerge in the foreseeable future. With a low population and lacking any strategic value to developed nations, it carries little weight within the international community.

Vanuatu's contribution to the accumulation of global greenhouse gases is vanishingly small, but already beset by frequent cyclones, the Ni-Vanuatu will be among the first to experience the depredations resulting from climate change. It is projected wet season rainfall will increase and dry season rainfall will decrease, though not to the point where drought is anticipated. The days of extreme heat and rainfall will increase. Ocean acidification will increase, as will surface air temperatures and sea-surface temperatures.[19]

One school would hold that Vanuatu will be what it has always been and that the status quo suits it best. Author William Miles has written: "They are a very special people, and the country is the way the world should be: a myriad of interconnecting indigenous languages and cultures with intense respect for the material, physical and spiritual world."[20]

Forty years ago MacClancy wrote, with a sense of fatalism, that:

> Only one thing is certain among the collection of extrapolated possibilities that we call the future: whatever changes do actually occur, the result will not be a mere imitation of elsewhere, but a dynamic, unique conjunction of the past and present. Whether that amalgam is satisfactory to the people of the islands is a question to which they alone will create the answer. One's future is one's own responsibility.[21]

***

Luganville is a very simple airport—no loading ramp, limited security, and not much to separate arriving passengers from people there to greet them. As I've experienced many times in similar situations, just outside customs clearance awaits a swarm of taxi drivers eager to get a fare. In this case, it was a smaller throng, politer, and more reserved than I was accustomed to, but still large enough to be familiar.[22]

Two or three drivers approached me, all reaching for my bag and asking if I needed a taxi. I declined them all and, having had a lot of experience with gypsy drivers, kept a grip on my suitcase and continued walking toward the "official" taxi queue. A bit farther on, a young man approached me and asked if I needed a taxi. I don't know why—I must have liked his slight reserve or the way he handled himself. I accepted his offer and loaded my gear into his small Chevy.

I happened to have run into Mr. Douglas Dick. I had no way of knowing it, but my luck had taken a sharp turn in a good direction.

Douglas was young, but with broad experiences, a good bit of technical training, and a solid work ethic. He spoke English very well, as well as Bislama and other local dialects. And he seems to know or be related to everyone on Santo.

He asked me what I was doing in Santo, and I gave him the answer I would give many times in the coming days. He was familiar with people coming to Santo to explore some of the artifacts surviving from World War II, so he seemed not overly impressed by my endeavor. He knew of some historical sites in the vicinity, and we left immediately on a short driving tour of southeast Santo.

Late that afternoon, having developed a keen interest in the project, Douglas called friends and acquaintances in the Butmas–Fanafo region, in particular, his friend and former classmate Pascal Tome. He learned that the people in the village of Fanafo–Kona had quite a lot of information about the crash.

The next morning, Thursday, July 14, 2011 Douglas related the results of his telephone calls from the evening before. It was decided to drive to the village of Fanafo–Kona, about ninety minutes north of Luganville, on what was the primary north–south route on the island. The village had moved to its current location many years before: the small settlement to which Leonard Richardson had first been taken was now abandoned.

We left Luganville immediately. I had spent a lot of time driving on very primitive roads in my prior travels, and was anticipating bad roads in the interior of Santo, but I was still surprised at what we encountered. Douglas told me taxi tires last just three months on Santo because of the rough road conditions.

In brief, this section of Santo is characterized by thick jungle, poor villages, bad roads, and villagers who are initially guarded but soon warm to strangers. The area is intensely Christian, and though it is not difficult even today to believe this culture could have been hostile and aggressive to outsiders, it was challenging to imagine that just a couple of generations ago, the islanders were in a constant state of warfare, and were cannibals.[23]

The road to Fanafo–Kona. (Author's collection)

On arrival at Fanafo–Kona, Douglas and I approached the nakamal where a few men were gathered. They looked at me with a great deal of interest and surprise, and were initially reserved, perhaps wary. Despite Douglas's phone call, these men were not expecting us, and I was undoubtedly the first foreigner to visit their small village in a long time. I was also a bit guarded. The village men all walked around with two-foot machetes and untrusting attitudes.[24]

The villagers spoke almost no English, and even Bislama was spoken only on a limited basis. It was good luck Douglas could understand their regional dialect—little would have been accomplished without Douglas to interpret.

Douglas and I took a seat on the wooden bench of the nakamal and, after a brief conversation between the villagers and Douglas, in their dialect, he turned to me and asked me to explain why I was there.

I began to speak and had not gotten very far when the villagers became animated. It soon became evident from their gestures that they knew all about the story of my father's crash and rescue. They knew that the front half of the aircraft, just aft of the navigator and radio operator station, had broken away from the main fuselage. They knew about the dead men and that one survivor had suffered a broken leg. They knew that the painted "Star" of the U.S. Army Air Force was still clearly visible.

It became evident the story of the crash, and my father's survival, had been part of their village narrative since 1943 and, most importantly for me, they knew precisely where the plane was located.

I was introduced to Harry Job, the village chief, and to Thomas Tavuli, a young man whose father had been a chief in that region for many years and who had developed a wide reputation among the villagers.

No women were seen in the village except for one young woman who appeared to be tending to the many small children there. Douglas told me that the men would clear small patches of jungle and, when cleared, the women would leave the village early each morning and go out to the fields to plant and tend crops. The women returned in the evening just in time to cook supper and turn in for the night.[25]

The village lived on subsistence agriculture. Other than chickens, no protein source was evident. The village appeared not wealthy enough to raise their own pigs, though the villagers have a strong tradition of hunting the wild pigs that thrive on the island.

I later asked Douglas if the villagers were ever hungry. He looked at me as though my question was absurd and maybe a bit offensive. "No," he said, and then he gave me a primer on subsistence farming on Santo. If you want bananas, just dig a small banana tree sapling from the ground and plant it where you want the bananas to grow. In three months, you will have an abundance of bananas.

Fruits of every sort grew on the island, almost none of which were familiar to Westerners. In addition to banana, villagers eat taro, yams, papayas, pineapples, mangoes, plantains, and sweet potatoes. And coconut and coconut milk. Most of the cooking is done using hot stones, or through boiling and steaming.

Fanafo–Kona's nakamal.

The children of Fanafo–Kona.

The village children were mostly shy, but I won them over with lollipops. "Lollies," as they are called. I also brought bars of perfumed soap for the women of the village. I gave the soap to the assistant chief, and asked him to please present them to the ladies with my compliments.

In preparation for my travel to Santo, I had a bronze plaque cast. I planned to affix this plaque to the side of the aircraft if I ever found it. I had the plaque in my backpack on the morning of my visit to Fanafo–Kona.

During our initial conversation in the nakamal, I mentioned the plaque and drew it from my backpack. This also caused a bit of a stir among them, and it quickly became evident they thought placing the plaque at the crash site was not a good idea. No one would ever go there after me. They said the place for the plaque was right there in the village; I quickly agreed.

Chief Job personally began digging the hole to accept the plaque and mounting pipes. Everyone helped out with the digging while the other village men mixed the cement. The work was completed in 30 minutes.

I recalled that Dad's journal included this: "It turned out that one of the young men had worked for the Air Force so he knew a few words of English. He would say 'Me Kelley' and grin." So after the plaque was installed, I asked if anyone remembered someone by the name of "Kelly."

This question led to more animated discussion in the group, and it became clear the name "Kelly" was not quite accurate. The villagers refer to him as "Kalif" or

230 • SURVIVAL IN THE SOUTH PACIFIC

Plaque installed at the site of the new provincial building at Fanafo–Kona. Including Harry Job, assistant chief (left), Douglas Dick (holding framework, Simione Selier (rear), and Thomas Tavuli, chief (right).

"Kalliv," and one of the older men in the group, Simione Selier, told me in his dialect that Kelly was his father-in-law. More astonishingly, Simione related that his mother was one of the two women who first discovered Leonard lying on the jungle trail.

Simione went on to relate all he knew about the incident. His recollection exactly matched that heard from Harry Job and others earlier in the day. He knew how many casualties there were, where they were found (inside or outside the plane), the fact that the front half of the aircraft had broken and burned, and that there was one survivor who crawled several days through the bush.

After reconvening at the nakamal, and without my asking and with almost no discussion, it was agreed the villagers would guide me to the crash site. They were ready to leave immediately and spend the night at the crash site, but I demurred, having brought no food or water, or rain cover. The villagers said it was about a 15-minute drive to the trailhead and a five-hour walk to the crash site. Progress would be slow because a narrow path through the jungle would have to be cleared by machete every step of the way.

We decided to leave at first light the following day, July 15. Three men from the village would lead me. Douglas said if there was to be a hike to the crash site, he definitely wanted to go. His participation would prove to be of immense help.

We arrived at Fanafo–Kona about a half-hour before dawn on July 15 and the trekking team assembled fairly quickly: Pascal Tome, Thomas Tavuli, and Mark Tome. All wore shorts and plastic flip-flops, and T-shirts I had given them the day before.

BACK TO ESPIRITU SANTO • 231

Walking to the jumping-off point for the trek to the crash site. (Author's collection)

Mark Tome cutting trail. (Author's collection)

We piled into a car for the short drive to the jumping-off point. I was surprised to learn there was no "trailhead" or trail. We got out of the car, I put on my raincoat, shouldered a backpack in which I had loaded water and a bit of food, looped my camera around my neck, and together we set off into the bush. The bush was immediately thick, and the road where we had left the car disappeared in a minute or less.

The Fanafo team cut trail continuously from the start of the climb to the end of the day. Using their two-foot bush knives, Pascal, Mark, and Thomas hacked and cut through the dense bush, taking turns in the lead position. The bush was nearly impenetrable with incredibly dense vegetation—vines lying on the ground, vines hanging down from the trees, ferns and dense vegetation, copses of heavy bamboo growth. Higher up, a canopy of trees, and above that, another canopy.

With neither trail nor map, the hike started with a steep descent leading to a dry riverbed that, when running full in the wet season, would have been 20 feet across and two feet deep. After a short pause, the team started up the very steep climb to the top of Mount Turi.

At that time in Vanuatu, malaria was still prevalent and I had begun taking daily doses of malarone, an anti-malarial medicine, at the start of my visit to Vanuatu. As we were climbing, I spoke with Pascal Tome about malaria. He was very matter-of-fact: he said yes, he'd had it before, and that the "bishops" (missionaries) frequently died from malaria.

It was up steeply for the next three hours, and I was carrying 40 lbs of food, water, and supplies in what became a tough climb, always in the semi-light of the deep bush, rarely coming to any openings where the sky showed. The ground was odd: coral everywhere, but covered with a clay that became extremely slippery and slimy with the continuing rain. And steep. The villagers had no trouble at all, but for me it was less a hike and more a tough climb. I grabbed at every tree root, vine, or rock to get up the steeper sections and fell several times. Just as I got over a particularly slippery piece of steep trail, I would feel my foot caught in a ground vine, and down I'd go again. I was climbing slower than the rest of the team, and Pascal stayed with me while the other three continued forward to hack out a rough path.

The villagers quickly discarded their footwear, preferring to climb the slippery ground barefoot. Trailing them, I grew accustomed to seeing their toeprints where they had gained purchase in the muddy jungle soil. These were tough men, accustomed to swinging their bush knives for hours on end, clearing fields in the jungle for their fruit and vegetable gardens.

My father had recorded that, after five days of crawling, he came across a trail and stayed there, hoping someone would pass by. That trail still exists; our trek into the crash site intersected it, though it was nearly imperceptible to me. Mark Tome's father was one of the villagers who carried my father to the village and, with pride, Mark showed me just where my father had been found. The trail connects the village of Butmas to the north of Turi to the village of Fanafo to the southeast.

BACK TO ESPIRITU SANTO • 233

Mark Tome and Douglas Dick. (Author's collection)

Along the dry riverbed. Thomas Tavuli, Mark Tome, Pascal Tome. (Author's collection)

Pascal Tome with author. (Author's collection)

From time to time, the villagers would hoot and call out to ensure they did not come upon wild pigs in the bush. All the men were knowledgeable about the wild pigs in the region, and all had a great respect for them. Later, coming upon a fresh pig wallow, the team grew watchful: feral pigs were not to be taken lightly.

The bush was incredibly dense, and I found myself thinking, "Dad, how could you ever do such a thing. How was it possible that you could make that effort." I always knew him to be tough, but I never realized until this day just how tough he was, how determined he could be, or how strong was his faith.

His confidence and his faith served him well; it was unimaginable that he could think it possible that he could crawl to safety, with his injuries, through this dense jungle. He must have felt there was no other choice—that if he remained with the plane any longer, he would not be discovered and would die there. As he told me years later when he was struggling with so many physical problems, "I don't have to like it; I just have to do it." He must have said those very words when he started his crawl down the mountain.

Soon, the sound of metal banging on metal was heard. I knew it could only be the villagers banging their bush knives on the side of the aircraft. I hurried as best I could with what little energy I had left, pulling myself hand-over-hand up the steep slippery bush. And then, looking up, I saw ahead of me, just within arm's reach, a propeller lying upright in the bush, laced with vines, blades bent, but in remarkably good condition. Seeing it, knowing what it was, I froze. The moment haunts me to this day. The realization that, after 50 years, I had come to my father's plane.

The propeller. (Author's collection)

Looking a bit further up the slope, the rear portion of the fuselage came into view. Similarly laced with vines and vegetation, it was lying tail to my left, upright but rotated to the right. The vertical stabilizer—the "tail fin"—was broken off, as were the elevators, but these empennage components were lying nearby.

It was stunning to see the plane. This was a bad crash, with the plane under full power at the point of impact. The wings had sheared off: the right wing was fairly easily identified; the left wing was obscured partially under the fuselage and covered in vegetation. The fuselage was broken in half just forward from where the wings attached.

I could not locate the front end—the nose, windscreen area and cockpit. It may have tumbled down the mountain after breaking away from the main fuselage, or it may have burned, or possibly both. I located both propellers and was impressed by how large they were and in what good condition. Each propeller exhibited the type of damage that would indicate they were still operating at power when they hit the ground.

The fixed, non-retractable rear wheel was located in roughly its original position, the rubber tire still in good condition. Since the main landing gear would have been retracted at impact, the wheels would have been underneath the wings and were not found. The C-47 had been carrying a cargo of large airplane engines, two of which were found adjacent to the crash site. These engines were somewhat corroded, but some engine markings were still evident. In some places, stainless steel bands or wire was used, and these components were still in like-new condition.

Most of the C-47's components were aluminum and so were likewise in good condition. Just as Leonard had written in his journal, the fuselage of the plane was rotated about forty-five degrees to the right and the main loading doors were pointed skyward.

Rear tire crumpled, but still in its original position. (Author's collection)

Army Air Force insignia with scratched-in names from prior visitors. All three of the Kona villagers who were with me on this date had been to the crash site previously.

At the crash site. Ni-Van Chief Thomas Tavuli of Fanafo–Kona village standing at the tail section of the aircraft.

Douglas Dick and Thomas Tavuli atop the main fuselage. There was no place else to rest in the dense bush. The left side main loading door is still attached with working hinges.

BACK TO ESPIRITU SANTO • 237

The main cargo doors were in good condition. The right-side door was off its hinges, but the left-side door was in position and closed. It swung open easily. Inside, the airframe was also in good condition. There was no rust, and much of the framework still bore the original olive-green paint. There was no sign of cargo within the fuselage.

Just aft of the main cargo doors, the large red, white-and-blue "star and bars" was still quite clear. Leonard had been told that some villagers had previously visited the crash site, but I was still surprised and a bit amused to see names scratched into the paint—"Abraham," and others.

I could make a few conjectures about the crash from what I saw. The wreckage is located at the very apex of the mountain, and the debris field was compact—the wreckage was not spread out over an extended area. I assume the plane crashed and stopped abruptly due to its approach angle and the massive trees that would have been in the area at that time. Also, seeing the rear wheel in its original position leads me to believe the plane did not skid or slide very much. It must have come to a stop almost instantly.

The crash site was fairly level. Despite this, and even though this part of the fuselage was in good condition, it was clear this had been a particularly violent crash—the wings had sheared away, and the forward cabin, the navigator and radioman's station, and the cockpit, was not to be found. The portion of the aircraft I found and investigated was basically the aft portion, from wings to tail.

The copilot came very close to missing the mountain. Another 30 feet of elevation would have prevented the crash, or 150 yards to the right or left. The C-47 appeared to "pancake" onto the very summit of the small mountain.

We explored the wreckage for about 1½ hours. Not having planned to spend the night, our time was limited because we had to complete the hike out before dark. Before leaving, I found a five-foot section of aluminum bracing from inside the aircraft. I took it, thinking it would help with the hike out. In retrospect, I realize I should have asked my friends for their permission before taking this relic. Only later would I comprehend I had no ownership of this relic—it and the remnants of the crash belonged to the island and the islanders. They should have been consulted.[26]

The hike out was punishing. The first stretch, leading from the crash site back down to the riverbed, was steep and slippery. All the water was gone by the time the team started back, except for one swallow the Ni-Vans insisted I drink when the party again reached the riverbed. My legs started to cramp, and I was afraid I was going to cramp so badly that I could not continue. The cramps did continue and worsened, and I was careful to stretch whenever I paused.

By the time we reached the riverbed, I was cooked, with a steep two-hour climb still ahead. I would climb 20 feet, take 20 breaths, climb another 20 feet, take 20 breaths. My cardio was maxed out the whole day. In this last climb, I stopped every 200 feet or so for what I called a "one minute"—mostly a standing rest for a short recovery. Towards the end, I would have to drop to one knee or sit on a tree root,

Right side main loading door with USAAF decal.

Pascal Tome with an engine.

The author within the C-47 fuselage. (Author's collection)

and I was cramping badly by now and had to stop every 50 feet or so to catch my breath and stretch out my legs. Pascal was with me for most of this section, and he looked at me carefully, many times, to see if I would to be able to continue.

We reached the car about 4:00 in the afternoon, with about an hour of daylight left. I recovered well enough after a short rest. I told the guys I thought I could have climbed for one more hour, but after that I would have been done. I said if we had to continue climbing, they would have had another Richardson to rescue. They were all slightly built guys and in very good physical condition, weighing maybe 140–150 lbs. They were blunt but kind; they told me I was too big and too old for this kind of climbing. I could only agree.

Later, with intense cramps making sleep impossible, I reflected on the indelible impressions left by the climb:

> Dense dense foliage everywhere, and slick dark brown mud: when I was the tiredest I would slip back the most. The nasty ferns with the serious spikes. Not a hike—more a hands and feet scramble up a continually steep slope. Lizards all over. Dried bamboo makes a lousy hand hold. Being amazed that my pulse could be so high for so long. Two deep breaths for each step up. My friends watching but not speaking, and with no judgement. The terrain never flat—either up, steep up, down or steep down, but not flat. My Ni-vans friends are amazing with bush knives; gentle people—no cursing, no talk about women, wanting to know if I was Christian and then wanting to know more. Ants, but no mosquitos. My new brothers.

Bob Richardson with Mt. Turi in the distance. Big Bay and the north side of the island is to the right, the airfield is to the left. The crash site is just below the brow of Mt. Turi. (Author's collection)

On the short drive back to Fanafo–Kona, I spoke further with Thomas about pigs. For villages like Fanafo–Kona, eating pig means killing wild pigs and that is a dangerous game. Mark and Pascal related that Thomas Tavuli had developed a reputation for being a skilled pig hunter, sometimes hunting with dogs, and other times hunting with just a knife. In addition to paying them for their work, I had brought a few gifts: to Mark, a good flashlight; to Pascal, a raincoat; to Douglas, a Leatherman tool. I gave a good folding knife to Thomas and told him I wanted him to kill a pig with it. He seemed pleased.

Two days later, I made arrangements for a short charter flight in order to conduct an aerial survey of Mt. Turi, and to spot the crash site from the air. I had a better chart than the pilot, Alex, and I used it to show him where the mountain was, and explained how I wanted the fly-by to be done. Basically, we flew to Mt. Turi and then made a series of clockwise rotations at varying altitudes. It was Douglas's first time in an aircraft, and he was very apprehensive. When I asked for his thoughts, he show little excitement, only concern. When he mentioned this flight to his family, his father told him to be sure to tell the pilot to be very careful about the mountains in the area.

The flight to Mt. Turi from the airport was brief—not more than 15 minutes. Upon reaching it, the local weather was a bit unsettled with cloud cover that occasionally obscured view of the mountain. We spent 30 minutes orbiting, looking down at the unrelieved dense tree cover. There was no sign of the crash site, no indication of any clearing, and no visible trails. The aircraft had been swallowed by the enduring bush.

During the flight, Douglas was both intimidated and fascinated by the experience and what he saw. After landing, he was all smiles and was pleased he had been invited to go on the trip.

After my experiences on the island, the *Crash of '43* came to also encompass the narrative of the Ni-Vanuatu on Espiritu Santo, and their role in my father's recovery. My father's survival had become very much a part of the village culture as well, and the story began to increase even more as I began to consider individuals who were on the rescue team itself, and to include their stories, not just during this rescue, but during the ferocious 2½ years of fighting they endured following the rescue of my father.

Writing in 1990, noted island anthropologists and historians Lamont Lindstrom and Geoffrey White recorded: "The Pacific theater survives only as long as its stories. The war exists now in Pacific communities as story, and 'warriors' as storytellers. The active, continued retelling maintains, and also reworks, the script and the meanings of the war."[27]

They also posed this question: "Will these war narratives and songs survive, particularly given the passing of the generation for whom they record personal experience?"

Judging from my own experience at one small village, the answer is a resounding, irrefutable, YES.

APPENDIX I

The 64th's Rescue Team and their Casualties

Lt. Albert Noble McCreight

Richardson never attended any postwar reunions organized by the 403rd Troop Carrier Group (TCG) or the 64th Troop Carrier Squadron (TCS). Had he done so, he would likely have had an opportunity to reunite with his former friends in the squadron and the men who had so much to do with his rescue: McCreight, Buchheit, Rosewine, and Roussell.

He reunited just once with one of the heroes who had mustered long ago on a small mountaintop on Espiritu Santo. Being medically retired from the Army, Richardson retained access to United States Air Force facilities and services and occasionally used the Post Exchange at Fairchild Air Force Base near his home in Spokane. On one visit, while waiting in line, he glanced back and noticed Al McCreight standing behind him.

It was the warmest of welcomes. Despite all the water under their bridges since the war, neither party had the least difficulty transporting themselves back to that time and place. In an instant, they would have recollected the most vivid details of their last meeting, and each would have recalled the difficulty of the days that led to their first meeting—Richardson inching along the jungle floor on his back and McCreight fighting through the dense jungle with his fellow rescuers, the men of the 64th TCS and the 129th Combat Team.

They never met again, even though they lived in the same town. Perhaps the memories were too strong to be considered more. It is less likely, but still possible, that when viewed through the long filter of their postwar lives, the events of 1943 seemed somehow less important than those of the present day.

McCreight was born into a military family on January 10, 1921. Referred to by his middle name by his family, he had attended two years of college before enlisting in the Army Air Corps as an aviation cadet on January, 1941.

McCreight served with the 64th TCS from its inception in December 1942 to the end of the war in the Pacific and, during the three years his unit was abroad, he would come to know every man in the squadron and many in the group.

When the 64th was preparing for embarkation to the South Pacific in mid-summer 1943, McCreight, then a first lieutenant, was designated as A Flight commander.[1] Nine months after arriving in the South Pacific, McCreight was promoted to the rank of captain and was the squadron's operations officer. He was placed in command of the 64th Squadron in November 1944, and was reassigned as operations officer of the 403rd TCG in March 1945.

McCreight was 22 when he, Richwine, and Buchheit joined the 129th Combat Team's search mission in September 1943. At the time, his father, then Col. William McCreight, was serving under General MacArthur in Hollandia (New Guinea).

McCreight returned home with the rest of the 64th Squadron at the end

Albert Noble McCreight. (Richard McCreight Collection)

of the war at the age of 25 and holding the rank of major. He accepted a commission in the Air Force Reserve and was assigned to the Spokane Air Technical Service Command.

He was called back to active duty for the Korean War, again flying cargo aircraft.[2]

After Korea, McCreight remained an active-duty pilot in the Air Force, and retired at the rank of colonel on January 7, 1963.

After 22 years in the Air Force, he returned to complete his college degree and began teaching math at a high school in Spokane. On September 5, 1971, McCreight died in a pickup truck accident in northern Idaho. His death came in the remote wilderness along the Little Coeur d'Alene River, 28 years to the day that Richardson's C-47 from the 64th TCS went missing.

Albert Noble McCreight and his wife Virginia had three sons, Michael Noble, Richard Douglas ("Doug"), and Alan Scott. At the time of his death, Al McCreight was married to Elaine Kessler, and was stepfather to her two daughters, Chya and Kerry, and son Quin.

Captain Alfred Henry Richwine

Alfred Richwine was born March 23, 1910, in Lancaster County, Pennsylvania. His father and uncle were both physicians and, as a boy, Richwine accompanied his father on visits to patients in their buggy.

Alfred graduated from the George Washington University School of Medicine in 1933, began his practice in Chevy Chase, Maryland, and married Martha Myers, also a George Washington graduate, on March 15, 1940. Their daughter, Linda Ann, was born just over a year later.[3]

Like all men his age, Alfred registered for the Draft, but did not wait to be inducted. In late September 1942, at the age of 32, with his medical practice becoming well established in the affluent suburb of Chevy Chase, Alfred joined up, the only member of his medical school graduating class to volunteer for duty with the Army.

His daughter reported that his wife was not pleased with this decision, an attitude that any young wife might understand.[4]

He received his commission as first lieutenant on April 22, 1943, and was assigned as flight surgeon to the 64th TCS shortly before the squadron left for overseas duty.[5]

Alfred Henry Richwine. (Linda Richwine Horton Family Archive)

In the Pacific, Alfred and his medical team repeatedly moved as the 64th was reassigned to ever more northerly bases. At each of his stations, he created a vegetable garden, a pastime that would endure.[6]

His daughter recalled, "He apparently developed a strong liking for life in the South Pacific. After the war, he had a strong interest in moving his family to the South Pacific to continue his medical career and to spend the rest of their lives. His wife was not supportive of that, and he never went."[7]

He was released from the service on March 26, 1946, returned to Maryland to restart his private medical practice, and lived and worked in Chevy Chase. He died on November 6, 1982.

Corporal Raymond N. Buchheit

Raymond Buchheit was born in 1923 in Queens, New York, and before the war worked as a clerk for the B&O Railroad. He enlisted in the Army on December 4, 1942, Serial No. 12193085, and six months later found himself in the far South Pacific.[8]

He was assigned as a clerk to the Operations Office of the 64th TCS, and was part of the ground echelon that traveled by ship to Noumea aboard *Noordam*, sailing from San Francisco on August 16, 1943. Immediately on arrival, the mess sergeant and a handful of squadron staff—the "Sad Sacks" mentioned in the 403rd TCG History—were flown to Espiritu Santo where the air echelon was already established and conducting troop and cargo missions. This small cohort, which included Ray Buchheit, would serve as the advance party to prepare for the arrival of the ground echelon, scheduled to come by ship from Noumea two weeks later.

Raymond N. Buchheit. (Raymond N. Buchheit)

Raymond had barely set foot on Espiritu Santo when Richardson went missing. He did not know him but was familiar with Healy, O'Connell, Wlodarsky, and Miller. When he was called upon to join the rescue team, he was just 19 years of age and a newly promoted corporal.[9]

Raymond later commented that he came to know Richardson fairly well by the time they got back to base since he took his turns carrying the stretcher. Richardson would later reflect on the men from the 64th who had participated in his rescue:

> I must have weighed 190 pounds, so the going was tough. It was to be a two-day trek. I was proud that my pilot buddies could keep up with those infantrymen. They were all toughened to jungle life, and were real men. They were great to me.[10]

Buchheit recalled, "The ambulance was waiting at the foothills of the mountain & that's the last time I saw him (Richardson). I always thought of him & wondered if he survived the ordeal."[11]

Corporal Raymond Buchheit was promoted to sergeant on November 1, 1943, and would later write that he and McCreight became good friends over the course of the war. McCreight, in a letter to his mother dated May 9, 1944, wrote, "Sgt. Buchheit ... is my ranking noncom and is a pretty efficient and logical guy even though he can't write a military letter in the proper form."[12]

Raymond served with the 64th for the duration of the war in the Pacific. He returned home to New York in February 1946; the B&O Railroad had kept a job for him, and he quickly transitioned back to civilian life.

He and Marjorie married in 1949, a union that would last for over sixty-eight years. They raised six children, and the Buchheit clan would later grow to 15 grandchildren and 12 great grandchildren. Raymond introduced his family in a letter, saying, "I'm not bragging." But maybe he was, just a little.

Ray Buchheit died at his home on Staten Island on February 28, 2017, at the age of 93.

Major Jack Roessell

Jack was born on March 4, 1918, at Greensburg, Kansas, and moved with his family to Lewiston, Idaho, in 1927.

He attended Lewiston High, the archenemy of Clarkston High across the Snake River. He competed against Leonard Richardson often in both football and basketball and, at that time, these high school athletic events were huge events for both towns. Jack showed leadership qualities in many aspects of life: in May 1936 he received an award from the Lewiston–Clarkston Kiwanis Club "In recognition of outstanding qualities of citizenship."[13]

In November 1940, Jack applied for and was admitted to the Army Air Corps pilot training program. He earned his wings and was commissioned a second lieutenant in July 1941.

Many of his fellow flight trainees were instinctively good at handling an aircraft. Not so Jack Roessell. In his memoir, he noted, "I found out very early that I was not a pilot's pilot … I had to work at it."[14]

He married Jean Margaret Erb six months after Pearl Harbor, a union that would last for 65 years.

Promotions came quickly for competent young officers in the first year of war. In mid-1942, Jack was promoted to first lieutenant and, by the end of the year, was promoted to captain and was put in command of the 64th TCS, 403rd TCG.[15]

The squadron was based at Pope Field—part of what is now known as Fort Bragg in North Carolina—in early May 1943; he was in command in July 1943 when the squadron suffered its first casualties in a training flight.

Jack was promoted to major on July 15, 1943—just two years after earning his wings as a second lieutenant. At the time of the events recorded here, Jack had just been promoted to major, was just 25 years of age, and was commander of 13 aircraft and 341 enlisted men and officers.[16]

Jack Roessell in World War II. (Gig Sheet, Yearbook of Kelly Airfield training class 41-E)

In a letter to his mother, Jack gave details about the aircraft lost on Mt. Turi, and added: "I lost 4 very good men and friends there, mother. A little later I will ask you to write each parent or wife, for they are the first casualties for us." He continued:

> I believe the Chaplin was right about Rich, and that was that God desired larger things for him to obtain, thus he was spared. You may assure his family that he is getting along fine—they set his leg yesterday and I took him up some beer today—all shock has left. The boy is to be commended for his presence of mind under adverse conditions and harboring a strong will and desire to live. I'm more than proud to have him a member of my organization.[17]

In his memoir, Jack wrote objectively about his time with the 64th Squadron, and later the 403rd Group: "I do not know if I was a good Commander. I can look back on just about as many minuses as pluses. So be it—I did my best and helped somewhat in the eventual victory."

As the war progressed, the 64th frequently moved to more forward bases and in these moves, Jack demonstrated an important ability utterly unrelated to aviation:—he was good at wrangling deals with local construction battalions. In November, 1943, "for a few cases of rot gut from our monthly ration of liquor," Roessell talked the Navy into building camp facilities for his squadron at Henderson Field, including "the only brick baking oven on the Canal. No one put out bread and pastry like our bakers." In September 1944, the squadron moved to Biak, a small island northwest of New Guinea. Back in tents, Roessell again sought out a Seabee chief who, for a delivery of "firewater," built a nice set of quarters for Colonel Sands and Roussell. And in the summer of 1945, when the squadron moved again to Dulag on the eastern shore of Leyte in the Philippines, he was able to replicate the deal he made with the Seabees on Guadalcanal: "For a few cases of firewater, we got enough 2×4s and 4×8s and plywood and screening so that we could build a frame with a wooden floor and top over our 16-foot tents. Lovely quarters ... "[18]

Jack continued as commanding officer of the 64th for much of the war—New Caledonia, New Hebrides, Biak, Leyte, and innumerable flights and stops in between. His last post was at Leyte in the Philippines.

During the war years, he learned many important lessons, not least: "Wartime is not unique in providing tense moments. Never be in a hurry to do anything! I've made several 180' [sic] turns in an aircraft during my time and was never sorry I did it—the same theory applies to life. Don't be afraid to play safe and go again another time."[19]

Jack remained in the Air Force following the war, commanded the 37th Airlift Squadron, and served with the Air Defense Command. His last posting was as base commander at Selfridge Air Force Base in Mount Clemens, Michigan. He retired after 27 years of service, having been awarded the Air Medal with one Oak Leaf Cluster for his service in the Pacific.[20]

Jack and Jean had two sons, David and Jack Douglas. They retired to Sunnyvale, California, and later moved to Indio. They both passed away in April 2007, Jean at age 87, Jack at 89.

***

The families of the other men in Richardson's aircraft would have received the same telegram message delivered to his family on September 14, notifying them their sons or husband had gone missing.

A week or so later, they would have received the second message from the War Department, a much different message than received by the family of Lieutenant Richardson. As with the letter to Lieutenant Healy's family, their messages all read:

> Report received from Commanding General Pacific Area states that your husband First Lieutenant Robert H. Healy who was previously reported missing since Five September died Five September. The Secretary of War Extends his deep sympathy. Letter follows.[21]

First Lieutenant Robert Harding Healy

The flight from Santo to Henderson Field on Guadalcanal was commanded by 1st Lt. Robert Harding Healy, age 22, from Tiverton, Rhode Island Known to all as "Red" Healy, he was born August 27, 1921, in Lewiston, Maine.[22] Joining the Air Corps as an aviation cadet, he completed all phases of his flight school at Texas airfields, earned his wings and commission with ID No. O-667514. After completing his flight training, Healy joined the 64th Squadron at Alliance, Nebraska, in 1942.[23]

At the time the 64th departed the west coast of the United States for the South Pacific, now 1st Lt. Robert Healy was at the controls of C-47 42-23714. Also on this aircraft was the crew that would join Healy on most of his future missions: 2nd Lt. Augustus Miller as copilot, M/Sgt Harry Wlodarsky as crew chief, and Cpl. Joe O'Connell as radio operator.[24]

"Red" Healy was the only married man on the crew, and his wife, Irene, lived with his mother on Main Road in Tiverton, Rhode Island, while he was overseas. Irene was four months pregnant when she bade goodbye to Robert in the summer of 1943.

Eight days after the crash occurred on Mt. Turi, with the wreckage not yet located, Irene received the missing-in-action message from the War Department. On September 22, she received the second Casualty Message advising that her husband had died on September 5.[25] Three months later, Irene gave birth to their daughter, whom she named for her husband: Roberta Harding Healy.

Lieutenant Healy was promoted posthumously to captain. He was initially buried at the crash site, but later reinterred at the Espiritu Santo Military Cemetery. In 1945, he was again reinterred at the Army Navy Marine Cemetery on Guadalcanal. He was repatriated to the U.S. in 1948, and is buried in the Healy Family lot at Oak Grove Cemetery, Fall River, Massachusetts.

Irene Healy later remarried and she and her second husband, William Valentine Halligan, had a daughter Jane. Irene and Roberta changed their names back to Healy (from Halligan) in the 1990s. At the time of her death in 2011, Mrs. Irene Healy had three grandchildren and two great-grandchildren.[26]

Second Lieutenant Augustus W. Miller

Lieutenant Healy's copilot was 2nd Lt. Augustus W. Miller from Avon, New York. He was born on October 23, 1920, and was 23 at the time of the crash.

Miller's parents, Augustus Sr. and Katherine, were immigrants to America: Augustus Sr. from Germany, Katherine from the Irish Free State. They settled in the Avon area, just west of the Finger Lakes region of New York. Augustus was tall and slim, with blue eyes and brown hair. He graduated from Avon Central School in 1938, a school that his father, a local contractor, had built in 1907. Following graduation, he attended Rochester Business Institute. He was Catholic.[27]

Miller joined the Army as an enlisted man, serial number 20242062 in October 1940, over a year before Pearl Harbor and America's entry into World War II.[28] "Gus" received his appointment as an air cadet in February 1942, and earned his wings and his second lieutenant commission on March 20, 1943, serial number O-675266.

He joined the 64th TCS in mid-May 1943 at Pope Field and flew with Healy with the air echelon from Hamilton Field, near San Francisco, when it made the long trip to New Caledonia on July 17, 1943.[29]

By the time he reached the South Pacific, he had been a commissioned pilot for just four months and had trained with the C-47 for just three. Gus wrote to his father on September 4, the day before his death, including a $100 money order, saying, "Keep fifty or so for yourself to buy beer with, but be sure to have some in the icebox for me when I get home ... Things are going OK here, food and everything is OK. We have a devil of a time keeping track of the days. I'll write you soon."[30]

Master Sergeant Harry Wlodarsky

Harry Wlodarsky was born on March 2, 1918, and was 25 years old at the time of the crash. From Burghill, Ohio, Harry lived on the 90-acre family farm with his parents, Mary and Stefan, brothers Joseph, Theofil, John, and Henry, and sisters Elisabeth, Agatha and Barbara.

Like his older brothers Theofil, John and Henry, Harry enlisted in the Army on August 19, 1940, 16 months before Pearl Harbor.[31] Following two years of training as an airplane mechanic and flight engineer, he joined the 64th TCS at Pope Field in December 1942. He was part of the air echelon that made the move from San Francisco to New Caledonia in July 1943, and was crew chief on the aircraft flown across the Pacific by Robert Healy.[32]

At that time in the war, aircrews were assigned to a specific aircraft and Wlodarsky was essentially "wedded" to C-47, 42-23711. He preflighted the aircraft for every mission, flew on every mission, and did whatever maintenance was required after each flight, regardless of how remote and unsupported the location.

Corporal Joseph E. O'Connell

Radioman Corporal Joseph E. O'Connell was 20 years of age at the time of the crash. Born September 16, 1923, to Irish immigrant parents, he enlisted in the Army Air Force on November 5, 1942.[33] By March 1943, he was with the 64th TCS at Alliance Field in Nebraska. By the time he boarded the C-47 at Hamilton Field to fly across the Pacific to New Caledonia, he had been promoted to corporal.[34]

Joe had attended Iona College prior to his enlistment, which would later run a brief biography, noting:

> Joseph E. O'Connell was the first Iona College student to give his life in the service of his country and the first outstanding student-athlete in Iona's history. Every year since 1947 Iona has awarded the Joseph E. O'Connell plaque to the finest athlete or athletes among its graduating seniors. The O'Connell Award and the Sullivan Award (for the senior who has done the most for Iona) are the two oldest prizes given by the College.[35]

Iona would later dedicate its new field house as the Joseph E. O'Connell Memorial Gymnasium.

***

Augustus, Harry, and Joe were also all initially buried at the crash site and relocated to a common grave at Espiritu Santo Military Cemetery on December 8, 1943. The Army advised the men's families that "It is regretted to inform you that … due to the nature of the accident, their remains could not be individually identified." Their remains were relocated to the Army Navy Marine Cemetery on Guadalcanal and later to the Schofield Barracks Mausoleum in Hawaii. They were co-interred at their final resting place, the Winchester National Cemetery, in June 1951.

Winchester National Cemetery.

APPENDIX 2

The 129th Combat Team

> I suddenly realized that from the farms, and towns, and cities all over America an unbroken line ran straight to the few who storm the blockhouses. No matter where along that line you stood, if you were not the man at the end of it, the ultimate man with his sweating hands upon the blockhouse, you didn't know what war was. You had only an intimation, as of a bugle blown far in the distance. You might have flashing insights, but you did not know. By the grace of God you would never know.
>
> —JAMES MICHENER, *TALES OF THE SOUTH PACIFIC*

In World War II, as in any armed conflict, there were military units that exemplified organizational effectiveness, combat readiness, military results, and bravery. The 129th Infantry Regiment deserves special commendation in all those categories.

Captain Morris J. Naudts

Morris Naudts was born in Gurnee, Illinois, in 1914, and was 29 years of age at the time the events described took place. His pathway to the Army began in the junior Reserve Officers' Training Corps program at his high school. He married Margaret Miller in 1936 and in 1937 enlisted in the Illinois National Guard. By August 1940, with the war in Europe raging, he was commissioned as a second lieutenant in the 129th Infantry Regiment. In February 1942, he was promoted to first lieutenant and appointed commander of G Company, a rifle company of the 2nd Battalion. His promotion to captain came in December 1942 while the 129th was garrisoning Viti Levu (Fiji).

Naudts became an effective commander for heavy weapons units and during the war would be called to command the heavy weapons companies in all three of the regiment's battalions.[1] His competence in other command assignments also became evident, and he would serve as regimental intelligence officer, battalion operations officer, and as executive officer for each of the regiment's battalions. In May 1945, as the U.S. Army began the last ground campaign in the Philippines, Naudts was given overall command of the regiment's 2nd Battalion, an assignment that led to his promotion to lieutenant colonel. At war's end, Colonel Naudts was given overall command of the 129th Infantry Regiment, an assignment he likely never imagined when he first joined the regiment just four years earlier.

He remained on active duty in the postwar years, and served with the 19th Infantry Regiment during the Korean conflict. Postwar, he served as post commander at Fort Kobbe in the Canal Zone and, after being promoted to full colonel in 1957, served as attaché chief of the military mission at the American Embassy in Rangoon, Burma.

Naudts was involved in all campaigns and actions of the 129th throughout the war, and over the course of his career was decorated with three Silver Stars for gallantry in action, four Bronze Stars for bravery in action, and two Purple Hearts, four Legions of Merit, and many other decorations and commendations. His service with the 129th is well documented in his comprehensive memoir.

Colonel Naudts retired in 1969 and with his wife of 33 years took up residence in Inverness, Florida.

Morris Naudts died on December 28, 2009, and is buried at Arlington National Cemetery.

Morris J. Naudts, pictured with his brother-in-law Les Miller, when they met on Espiritu Santo in 1943. (John Averett Family Archives)

Captain Curtis R. Craver

Craver was born in North Carolina on September 17, 1917. In May 1939, while a student at North Carolina State, he was commissioned as second lieutenant in the Army Reserve.

He first joined the 129th Infantry in mid-1942 and, as the 129th made final preparations to embark for overseas assignment, Craver was promoted to first lieutenant and was named assistant operations officer for the battalion.

When the 129th arrived in Fiji to serve as the garrison force, the commander of the 129th, Col. John Frederick, assigned Craver to G Company for him to gain more experience as a platoon leader. His company commander was 1st Lt. Morris Naudts.

Craver was a crack shot. His college rifle team was champion for two years running, and at Fort Benning he had scored first among his infantry company. When a shooting competition was held on Espiritu Santo, he scored highest among the 5,000 troops who participated.

"Naudts was the intelligence officer—S2—(at Santo) and he was familiar with a lot of things there, the rivers and the mountains and all that sort of thing."[2] Naudts knew Curtis, trusted him, and believed he would contribute well to the rescue party assembled to recover the men of the 64th Troop Carrier Squadron. Craver was 26 years old when the rescue on Mt. Turi was made.

The left sleeve of Craver's dress uniform holds seven service bars, representing his wartime service with the 129th Regiment for three years and four months, from Fiji, through Santo, to the heavy fighting in Bougainville, and the awful combat in the Philippines.

Curtis R. Craver. (State College News, North Carolina State College, October 1944, and Robert Richardson)

Craver returned stateside with a ship load of other regimental officers and enlisted men on the vessel *President Hayes*. Also aboard the ship was regimental commander Morris Naudts, who asked Craver to write a history of the regiment's service during the war. But his direction was clear—he was to mention no names in the narrative. "You just put in there the story of what the regiment did. We all did it." Craver did just that.

He delivered the resulting manuscript to Naudts, who later arranged for its publication. Neither Naudts's name, nor Craver's, nor any of the commanders, officers or enlisted men is mentioned by name, save one—"a BAR man who got (a medal) on Bougainville. His name is in there, and it was not supposed to be in there."[3] The book was published as *The 129th Infantry in World War II* by the Infantry Journal Press. Authorship is credited to "the Regimental Staff." A recounting of the rescue on Mt. Turi is included in the book.

The regiment arrived home on December 12, 1945, and was officially deactivated the next day.

Curtis Craver returned to his wife, Sarah, who he had married in 1940 before going overseas. Back home in North Carolina, he began a thirty-plus year career with the U.S. Postal Service, eventually retiring as Director of Employee and Labor Relations for 134 offices in eastern North Carolina.

Curtis Craver died on October 13, 2013, at the age of 96.

Captain Casmir Andruskevitch

Andruskevitch was born of Lithuanian heritage on February 19, 1911, in South Wilmington, Illinois, and was 32 when the rescue party began its search for Richardson.

Casmir had attempted to join the Navy in early 1940, but was rejected twice because his physical examination showed evidence of tachycardia. Instead, he joined the Illinois National Guard in March 1941, was assigned to the 129th at Camp Forrest in November, and was promoted to captain in February 1942, seven months before the 129th sailed for Fiji.

His commander wrote of him: "An excellent and enthusiastic Chaplain. Conscientious, beloved, and admired by men of all faiths. A born leader [with] a fine sense of humor and is loyal and unselfish. He has a keen mind and is well read."

Over the course of his service with the 129th, including facing enemy fire, Chaplain Andruskevitch was awarded the Bronze Star " ... for meritorious achievement in connection with military operations against the enemy at Luzon, Philippine Islands, from 9 Jan to 10 May, 1945." He also received the Legion of Merit:

> During combat, he distinguished himself in many undertakings which increased the morale among the troops. Capt. Andruskevitch risked his life on many occasions at the front-lines tending the wounded and conducting burial rites ... His presence, in the rear or forward areas, was always a source of inspiration. Capt. Andruskevitch was highly valued by the 129th HQ.[4]

He served with the 129th Infantry overseas for three years, three months and 11 days. On returning to civilian life, Casmir served most of his career as pastor of the Catholic Children's Home, 1400 State Street, Alton, Illinois.

Casmir Andruskevitch died on September 19, 1965.

Capt. Casmir "Andy" Andruskevitch.

The Enlisted Personnel

From the 129th Regimental Headquarters Company

Sgt. Clifford Gothard	Hampshire, Illinois
Sgt Carl L. Hagen	Chicago, Illinois
Cpl. Ralph W. Salley	Kewanee, Illinois
Cpl. Ramon A. Powell	Buncombe, Illinois
Pfc. Arnold R. Byers (Byars)	Edinburg, North Dakota
Pfc. Paul J. Kelly	Philadelphia, Pennsylvania
Pfc. Clifford G. Key	Huntsville, Missouri
Pvt. Rufus W. Enlow	Zion, Illinois
Sgt. Harry M. Bulfer, 3rd Battalion	Sublette, Illinois
Pfc. Joseph Paul Gabriel	Chicago, Illinois

Patrol members from other units

Sgt. Guy L. Carter Company M
 Marion, Illinois
Pvt. Walter E. Likes
 Company A
 Galesburg, Illinois
T/5 Herman Barnett
Pfc. Delbert J. Bullen
Pfc. Henry P. Tremont
Pvt. Joseph J. Hershey, Medic
T/5 Henry Searcy, Medical Tech
Pvt. Tony Secar
Pvt. Guel H. Salbrack

Harry Bulfer

Harry was born in 1918 and worked on a family farm prior to his enlistment. He had four years of high school and enlisted March 5, 1941 in Dixon, Illinois.

He saw a lot of combat in the war, including some very hard fighting in the Philippines when he and his patrol became separated from their main unit. He was wounded and received a Purple Heart.

He returned to Illinois after the war, lived with his brother Pat and his family, and was known to be a hard worker.

Harry's life postwar was representative of countless other combat veterans and illustrates that all wounds cannot be seen and that many heal only very slowly. He suffered from combat-related stress—now known as post-traumatic stress disorder. Back in his Illinois home, as evenings approached, he began to fear the nightmares that beset him. His brother would hear his screaming in the night and would come to calm him, but Harry increasingly turned to drinking.

Harry eventually married, and after his marriage his health improved. He and his wife settled in East St. Louis, and had no children.[5]

Joseph Gabriel

Somewhat remarkably, especially considering the horrific combat they experienced, of all the men of the 129th's rescue team, Joe Gabriel was the only man to die during the war.

He was born December 9, 1913, in Aurora, Illinois, and grew up on Superior Street with his mother and father, Elizabeth and John, older brother John Charles, and younger brother Stephen Robert, in a plain, two-story, wood-frame home just across from St. Nicholas Catholic Church, and not more than ½ mile from the Fox River. In Joe's youth, Aurora was mostly white European in heritage. It called itself the "City of Lights" because it was one of the first cities in the U.S. to install an all-electric lighting system. Aurora was a broad-shouldered city back then; the Burlington Northern Railroad started there.

Joe's parents were both born in Hungary, and his father John (Johann) worked as a streetcar repairman for the CB & O Rail Line. When the Japanese attacked Pearl Harbor, Joe was managing a shoe store in the Chicago area, making $27.50 a week, coming home occasionally to visit his parents and his friends. He was single and Catholic.[6]

The Selective Training and Service Act—the Draft—had passed in 1940 and, just as their father had done 22 years earlier as part of America's mobilization for World War I, John, Joe, and Steven all registered for the draft on October 16. His local draft board assigned him Serial No. 3716. Both John and Joe worked for the Bata Shoe Company—in Chicago and Melrose Park respectively. Steven worked for Campana, a leading cosmetics company.

Joe received his induction orders on April 10. A week later, following a standard physical and mental examination, he was inducted into the Army at his local draft board and immediately sent to nearby Fort Sheridan.

At the time, he was 27 years of age, stood 5′10″, weighed 136 lbs, had brown hair, blue eyes, a fair complexion, and wore glasses. His induction papers listed his mother as a dependent.

He was promptly immunized for smallpox, typhoid, tetanus, and yellow fever, and assigned Army Serial Number 36 026 783.

Joe was first sent to D Company of the 37th Infantry Training Battalion at Camp Croft, South Carolina. He earned $21 a month—less than he had been earning in the shoe store. Right after arriving at Camp Croft, Joe took out a $1,000 life insurance policy, costing him 69 cents each month.

Joe was a good shot and earned the marksmanship badge at Camp Croft but, otherwise, he was a less-than-model soldier in basic training. After about eight weeks, he apparently felt he'd earned a break and gave himself a week's holiday. He was "placed in arrest in quarters" on July 8. Military charges were that he "did, without proper leave, absent himself from his duty at Camp Croft." He was found guilty on July 10, was confined to hard labor for 24 days, and forfeited $11 in pay.

Joe was posted to the Headquarters Company of the 129th Infantry following basic training. His first job was as ammunition carrier, and then later scout and observer.

At Santo, he continued to be less than rigid in his adherence to military disciple. A year after being convicted of having gone AWOL from Camp Croft, he again awarded himself a brief holiday when he went AWOL for a day from his station on Espiritu Santo.

Gabriel evidently earned the regard of Captain Naudts, despite his apparent disdain for the Army's regimentation. He was handpicked in June 1943 to be part of the team surveying the Outpost Line of Resistance across the island of Espiritu Santo. In the process, he become familiar with arduous trekking in the deep bush of Santo.

Three months later, in September, Naudts again handpicked all 23 rescue team members that struggled through the jungle for four days to reach Richardson's crash site. He would have only taken jungle-hardened men, and we can assume that, by the time of the rescue attempt, Joe was a tough man in good condition.

Joe had been a buck private for nearly three years but, in February 1944 was promoted to private first class. In September, perhaps sensing intensified combat ahead, Joe increased his life insurance to $10,000.

He fought with the 129th through the Bougainville campaign and the Battle of Luzon and was awarded the Philippine Liberation Ribbon with Star on February 5, 1945. He also earned the Combat Infantry Badge in February 1944 and the Bronze Battle Star.

During the Luzon Campaign, the fighting was often intense and sometimes horrific. Joe's regiment was deeply engaged in the brutal combat in the Battle of Manila, suffering extensive losses in killed and wounded. In the subsequent Battle of Baguio, which raged from March until early May 1945, the 129th lost three officers and 49 enlisted men, with 25 officers and 339 enlisted men wounded. It was the kind of combat that left all men scarred.

At that time, Joe was serving as a scout and observer with the regimental HQ's Intelligence and Reconnaissance Platoon. The 129th was scheduled to be relieved from combat on May 5 and moved to Lupao for a rest, but Private First Class Joe Gabriel died the day before, just five months before the war in the Pacific ended with the Japanese surrender.

Two days earlier, Joe had fallen ill after getting hold of what turned out to be methyl alcohol, sold by the locals as ordinary liquor. He and other similarly afflicted men coming in from combat reported to the regimental aid station at Baguio at 8:00 pm on May 3. He was held for observation due to nausea and vomiting. He expired at 5:00 pm on May 4, 1945.

U.S. Army troops shielded by a tank secure an area on the island of Bougainville in the Solomons in March 1944. (U.S. Army)

At the time of his death, Joe was 31 years of age, old for an infantryman. Among his possessions at the time of his death were his wallet with photos, a ring, a wristwatch, and a rosary.

His commanding officer, Col. J. D. Frederick, wrote a letter of condolence to his mother on May 21, 1945, in which he said: "There is little I can say to alleviate your sorrow except that Joseph was a good soldier and that I was proud to have him as a member of my unit."

His captain, John A. Binder, also wrote to say: "He, as you undoubtedly are aware, had been a member of the Regimental Intelligence and Reconnaissance Platoon and only several days before had entered Baguio with his platoon among the advance elements that liberated the city ... the men of his platoon, as well as others from his company, attended his funeral."

Elizabeth, his mother, was issued a Gold Star Lapel Pin—identifying all parents of members of the armed forces who lost their lives in the U.S. armed services in World War II.

Joe was buried at the United States Armed Forces Cemetery No. 1, Santa Barbara, Pangasinan Province, Luzon, Philippines. His brother Steven was drafted into the Army six months after Joe at the age of 27. He survived the war and died in 1980.[7]

APPENDIX 3

The 64th Troop Carrier Squadron

Of necessity, beyond the special search missions ordered by Roessell the morning after the crash atop Turi, operations for the 64th Troop Carrier Squadron (TCS) continued as before. The squadron was finally fully assembled when its ground echelon arrived in the Segond Channel at Espiritu Santo just after noon on September 15 aboard USS *Cape San Juan*. Squadron operations became more measured, more ordered.[1]

Group commander Col. Harry Sands created the standard: " … the Old Man made it clear that living in the jungle was no excuse for falling apart at the seams, and it was a lesson we never forgot, and one that eventually gave us the reputation of always having the finest and most livable areas, regardless of our location."[2]

The 403rd Troop Carrier Group (TCG) and its squadrons settled into an operational routine that fulfilled the mission for air transport during the war: "For all of the dash and importance of airborne operations, the main contribution of Troop Carrier Aviation to American victory turned out to be logistics, the simple transport of materiel and personnel from airfield to airfield."[3]

Aftermath for the 64th TCS

The Air Command of the Solomon Islands (COMAIRSOLS) was established in February 1943 at Guadalcanal to better coordinate air operations, and its commander assumed operational control of all U.S. Army Air Force, Marine Corps and Navy aircraft in the South Pacific, along with those of the Royal New Zealand Air Force.[4] COMAIRSOLS would direct combat operations of all land-based air forces in the Solomons during the initial phases of Operation *Cartwheel*.

The campaign to defeat Japanese forces in the Solomon Islands intensified following the Allied victory on Guadalcanal. By August 1943, Allied forces had occupied the island of Vella Lavella, midway up the Solomons chain. Kolombangara and the Treasury Islands fell to the Allies in October and, on November 1, Allied forces landed at Empress Bay on the island of Bougainville.[5]

With Army, Navy, and Marine ground forces rapidly advancing northward, support units like the 64th TCS were required to keep pace. After just a month at Santo, the 64th received orders to relocate to Henderson Field on Guadalcanal. The move began on October 22 with the squadron's aircrews transporting their aircraft and some ground echelon personnel to their new station; other ground echelon personnel traveled by ship. By November 1, the squadron had reassembled at their new encampment at Lunga Beach, ready to continue flight operations.[6]

And, just as had occurred when the air echelon had first departed New Caledonia for Pekoa, personnel assigned to the air echelon movement included Cpl. Ray Buchheit.[7] He arrived just in time to be promoted to sergeant.

He was also in time to get sick. Three weeks after arriving at Henderson Field, illness overtook the squadron, the nature of which is unrecorded in the unit's War History. The first cases reported to hospital on November 11, and the number of fresh cases continued for nearly two weeks. Buchheit fell ill on November 16 and was confined to quarters by the squadron medical officer. He worsened overnight and was sent to the 20th Station Hospital, where he remained until the 21st. Before the illness abated, 75 officers and enlisted men—nearly a third of the squadron—had come down with the ailment.

The 64th was under the operational control of COMAIRSOLS and, much as the 63rd TCS had been operating for the Navy-led South Pacific Combat Air Transport Command (SCAT), now too the 64th found itself operating under the command of the Navy. Temporary reassignments were common: Lieutenant McCreight and two other aircraft and their flight crews were given detached service (DS) with SCAT on November 13. Four additional aircrews were similarly assigned to SCAT on the 24th. These DS assignments were short-lived: some were for as little as two days. Others for as many as fourteen.[8]

On Guadalcanal, the 64th camp was located right adjacent to Lunga Beach and a short distance to the north of Henderson Field and the "Lunga" Fighter 1 airfield. Fighter 2, "Kukum", the airfield to which Lieutenant Healy had flown on December 5, was a short distance to the west.

From Henderson, cargo and personnel missions then included more northern destinations, including Vella Lavella, Munda, the Russell Islands, the Treasurys, and Segi, as well as occasional flights to Efate and Tontouta.[9]

> We literally followed the war up the Solomon chain and working for the Commander Comairsols was a distinct pleasure. He was a Rear Admiral and my Operations Officer and I would go up to his quarters every week to meet with him and his Operations Officer. You should have seen what the Navy could do with a Quonset hut for an Admiral! As soon as we were in the doors—he would say "Help yourselves"—his refrig (only one I saw on the Canal) had every liquid in it you could want. He liked the way we responded to his directives. Sometime later when HQ. (of the) 13 A.F. came to the Canal and we reverted to their command, he wrote us a very nice letter thanking us for our efforts. A great gentleman.[10]

The squadron remained on Guadalcanal for 10 months—its longest residency at any airfield during the war. Its next move would be to Munda, further up the Solomon chain of islands, where it operated under the control of Admiral Kendall, Commander of Air Munda (ComAirMunda), for two months.

MacArthur's return to the Philippines required clearing Japanese forces from New Guinea. His classic stepping-stone strategy led to a landing by Allied forces on New Britain, the island group just to the north of the Solomons, in December. The Admiralty Islands further to the north and west of New Britain were invaded in February 1944 and, by April, Allied forces had occupied Hollandia on the north-central coast of New Guinea. From May to August, control of Noemfoor, Sansapor, and Biak Islands off northwest New Guinea was being wrested from the Japanese.

During those offensives, the 64th remained on station at Guadalcanal. "Squadron ships were then making flights from their base on the 'Canal to the Admiralties, nearly a thousand miles away, many times making it necessary for the crews to stay out as long as two weeks."[11]

Apart from its exceptional aircraft, the greatest attribute of the troop carrier squadrons of World War II was their mobility. That ability to move quickly and self-sustain was demonstrated frequently by the 64th TCS and its sister units in the 403rd TCG.

Having moved to Guadalcanal, the 64th Squadron was replaced at Pekoa in late October by its sister squadron, the 13th, which moved up from Tontouta on New Caledonia and occupied the quarters formerly used by the 64th. In October, the 801st Medical Air Evacuation Squadron (MAES) had also been attached to the 403rd TCG and would operate with both the 13th and the 63rd Squadrons.[12]

After relocating to Guadalcanal, the 64th was the subject of a medical experiment to test the efficacy of the malaria suppression drug Atabrine.

> The Malarial Control Officer of the Thirteenth Air Force (decided) to use this squadron in an experiment to test the effectiveness of mosquito control in this area. Therefore, the atabrine was discontinued (by the squadron) on the first of February (1944) and no atabrine was used during the entire month by the members of this organization. There have been no malaria cases as yet.[13]

Squadron records do not mention any outbreak of malaria in March, but a single case was reported in April. It was thought the airman had contracted malaria while sleeping in the plane during an overnight stay at Munda and that the malarial discipline at the 64th's base on Guadalcanal was effective, perhaps even exemplary.[14]

It should be expected that the flight surgeon for the 64th—the same Captain Richwine who had helped rescue Richardson from Mt. Turi—was less than thrilled with this experiment. When that single case was reported, "Captain Richwine spoke to all the flying personnel, impressing them again with the importance of using mosquito nets, repellant, and spray when sleeping in the airplanes." In May, it was reported that, except for one case of malaria reported in April, there had been no cases of tropical disease other than fungus infection of the skin and ears.[15]

A later commentary by the 403rd TCG would note: "None of our fatalities have been due to malaria or other tropical diseases, indicating our medics have done their job well." This is a remarkable statement, considering the many inherently malarious regions the various squadrons of the 403rd had visited.

Captain Richwine was relieved from his assignment as flight surgeon to the 64th TCS in May 1944 and assigned to the 70th Bomb Squadron, then based on the Treasury Islands.

64th TCS Operations

The 64th had a run of bad luck in its first six months of operations. It had lost one aircraft during a stateside training exercise and three more after commencing operations in the South Pacific. In addition, one aircrew of the 64th TCS was lost while operating an aircraft assigned to the 13th TCS. Three of these five aircraft losses included deaths or crews going missing:

> June 7, 1943, aircraft '23512. Crash during training mission. Four crewmen and twelve glider pilots killed.[16]
> September 5, 1943, aircraft '23711. Crash on Mt. Turi. Four deaths.[17]
> November 24, 1943, aircraft '18675. Missing. Five crewmen from 64th TCS presumed killed while flying an aircraft assigned to the 13th TCS.[18]
> November 28, 1943, '38742. Take-off accident due to engine failure. No casualties.[19]
> January 26, 1944, aircraft '23722. Ditched due to engine failure off northwest tip of San Cristobal Island. No casualties.[20]

Having gotten through this costly half-year of operations, the squadron would lose just two more aircraft during the balance of the war, regrettably in the war's final days.[21]

In addition to the 13 crewmen lost in the abovementioned events, the 64th lost another crewman in the spring of 1945. Lieutenant Carl Copeland, a squadron navigator, had been placed on detached service with the 57th TCS while awaiting orders to return stateside. An aircraft to which he was assigned crashed shortly after take-off from Biak in yet another incident arising from turbulent weather. During the war, five squadrons of the 403rd TCG would lose a total of 18 aircraft in crashes of one type or another. Of those, just one was the result of enemy action. Five were weather related, three could be attributed to pilot error, six were mechanical problems, and three were unattributed losses.[22]

Operations of the individual squadrons were independent of where the headquarters of the 403rd were located. In August 1944, for example, the 403rd HQ and 63rd Squadron were based at Los Negros, an island just north of New Guinea. At the same time, the 13th operated from Espiritu Santo, the 64th was at Guadalcanal, and the 65th and 66th were still operating under the Fifth Air Force command in New Guinea. The C-47 units arced over a northwesterly span of more than two thousand miles, doing resupply and evacuation missions to a myriad of bases, large and small.

While based at Henderson, the 64th Squadron began what would become a standard element of its service—airdropping supplies and equipment to ground forces.

The postwar history of the Thirteenth Air Force, *From Fiji to the Philippines*, described the operation:

> Drop missions were for the most part free-fall, necessitating low level flying midst the high mountains, rugged foothills, canyons, gorges and ravines. Drop areas were usually small and extremely hard to hit accurately. Panels of white cloth were used by the ground forces to assist the Skytrains in locating the drop area.
>
> The Skytrains flew across mountain ranges, cut their power, and glided down over the contours of the mountains to the drop areas, then flew a trusting course to gain altitude and get out. As many as eight passes per mission were made in this manner."

Other drop missions involved using "parapacks" in which different colored nylon parachutes indicted different classes of supplies, for example red for ammunition, and blue for food These parapack missions involved essentially the same hazards as the free-fall drops, although a somewhat higher altitude was possible.[23]

Paradrop mission, 64th Troop Carrier Squadron. (64th T.C. Sq., Jungle Air Force, Waite & Bull, Sydney, Australia, undated)

The 64th Squadron made its first paradrop on 2 November in support of the 2nd Marine Parachute Battalion fighting on Choiseul Island. In late November and early December, with the fighting on Bougainville intense, 20 paradrop sorties were flown to deliver critically needed stores and equipment to isolated ground forces.[24]

With the mounting Allied victories, the 64th TCS was again refocused: effective March 8, 1944, the 64th was instructed that it would be used only on flights forward of Guadalcanal, except on specific orders from ComAirSols or at the request of the commanding officer. No more Santo, Efate, Fiji, Samoa, or Tontouta for regular mission assignments. Concurrently, other XIII Air Force assets continued moving closer to the battlefront, and the Air Force presence on Santo began to wane:

"It become evident … that the function of Pekoa Airfield, and the Service Center at Espiritu Santo is being curtailed. Its use as a base for the operation of tactical aircraft has … ceased." [25]

On September 1, the 403rd shook off control by XIII Service Command and, likewise, the 13th and 63rd Squadrons were relieved from assignment to SCAT and the 64th from ComAirMunda. All were reassigned directly to Headquarters, Thirteenth Air Force.[26]

MacArthur's step-wise advances meant combat units of all kinds were continually moved forward, to the north and northwest. Many complete units were relocated to their new stations by the 403rd's C-47s.

The entire group was occupied in support of these large-scale shifts to the north. "From July to September we moved, in whole or in part, 24 combat units. This required 414 plane loads, aggregating more than a million pounds of cargo and 1442 passengers."[27] On September 16, in the midst of moving numerous combat units further forward, the 64th itself received orders to relocate from Henderson Field to Biak, off the northwestern coast of New Guinea.

Air operations on Biak were controlled by MacArthur's Fifth Air Force, and the 64th's orders to relocate there came perhaps a bit sooner than circumstances would favor. The squadron commander, then Major Jack Roessell would later recall: "It was (at Biak) where we met up with McArthur's 5th Air Force; the meeting was not pleasant."[28]

> Col. Sands flew in with us, and when we landed, we had no place to park our aircraft, so we parked on the side of the runway. Sands and I were called into the tent of the Operations Officer of the 5th, a full Colonel and seasoned—probably 40–50 years old. He told us to remove our aircraft. Sands said 13th Air Force ordered us to Biak—Operations Officer said the 13th Air Force had no authority in that area. Sands said we would stay until the 13th settled the matter.
>
> 5th Operations Officer said—You are off this island by mid-morning or I will have every one of your aircraft bulldozed into the ocean!
>
> So the next morning I took the 14 aircraft to Wadke [150 miles to the east]—a tiny speck of an island off the North central coast of New Guinea.[29]

The miniscule island had been hammered so thoroughly from the air and sea that it was "only a pile of rubble"; it was so small the airstrip ran from one end of the island to the other. The 403rd's historian would later relate: "Wadke was ... the nearest thing to a Pacific Devil's Island. It was about the size of Ebbets Field and you could stand in the center of it and spit into the ocean on all four sides."[30]

Roessell:

> By this time the ground echelons had arrived by ship at Biak and we started building our Biak home. I would commute between Wadke and Biak to oversee the building on Biak and the flying out of Wadke—hectic living! We had to take a few of our cooks, field stoves, supplies—etc, for there were no quarters for transients on Wadke.[31]

The air echelon of the 64th would operate from Wadke for just 19 days and then be posted to yet another temporary field at Noemfoor while work on its semi-permanent base at Biak continued. The men of the 64th groused: "We were hitting a new low (at Wadke), but soon we were back at Biak again. A week later, however, we were shoved out once more, this time to Noemfoor, which was Wadke all over again—poor chow, crowded living conditions and no nothing."[32]

The 64th left Wadke just two days after its sister squadron, the 63rd, had arrived there to take its miserable turn on the minute, primitive, and barely habitable airfield. The 64th would operate from Noemfoor for just over two months and, on January 1, 1945, the air echelon would rejoin the ground echelon at Biak.[33] In July, the 64th would recognize, if not celebrate, its second year in the Pacific while based at Biak.

Squadron area, Biak, New Guinea. (64th T.C. Sq., Jungle Air Force, Waite & Bull, Sydney, Australia, undated)

The camp at Biak was well developed and carefully laid out. It included uniform rows of tents for enlisted and officers, a chapel, a movie location, and eventually officer and enlisted men clubs. But it was evident at Biak that the 64th little resembled the unit that had sailed from San Francisco two years earlier. By the time the squadron settled in Biak, fewer than half the original men remained.[34]

While in the combat theaters, the personnel of the group and squadron were in a relatively constant state of controlled flux. Men and officers, both ground personnel and flight crews, rotated back to the United States, or to other combat units. Some returned home for medical reasons. Not a few were reassigned because of job performance issues. Some died. The 64th's standard personnel allotment was 342 officers and men. Over its two years of overseas service, as many as a thousand men would serve with the 64th TCS, in one capacity or another, for one duration or another, and some men, like Sgt. Raymond Buchheit and Captain McCreight, would serve with the unit for the entire duration of the war.[35]

MacArthur's Sixth Army and units of the Fifth Air Force and the Seventh Fleet returned to the Philippines in mid-October 1944, landing on the island of Leyte. In the coming months, the C-47s of all squadrons of the 403rd ranged far and wide over the Philippines: " ... landing on strips as fast as they were opened up, and sometimes a bit sooner. In addition we were going into crude grass strips and guerrilla-controlled 'dromes ... including Mindanao, Panay, Negros, and Palawan islands, still in Jap hands."[36]

Officers from the 64th began to be assigned to command positions within the 403rd Group Headquarters. About the time the 64th was coping with station life at Noemfoor, Roessell was reassigned as group executive officer, working directly for Colonel Sands. Captain Al McCreight, operations officer for the 64th, became its new commanding officer. In March, he would assume new duties as group operations officer—working again with Roessell—and, in July, Roessell was made deputy commander of the group and would be promoted to lieutenant colonel in November 1944.

Aircrew fatigue, first mentioned in a report by the 801st MAES in early 1943 never abated. For pilots, fatigue can come from many sources. In some cases, unrelenting combat missions against a prepared and tenacious enemy can cause a man to lose confidence, competence, or even hope. In other cases, physical breakdown from disease or poor living conditions can result in a man reaching a point of diminished capacity, and, for others, the sheer amount the flying hours, the constant adverse weather, and the responsibility for crewmates and wounded passengers can lead to debilitating fatigue.

The commander of the 403rd would later comment: "You know, combat fatigue even among pilots is an interesting thing. I never witnessed much combat fatigue. Perhaps because my flight surgeons would alert me when they thought some of our people ought to be rotated. I seldom saw the late signs of combat fatigue."

But fatigue finally caught up with one of his men, a pilot who had been in the air echelon when the squadrons first entered combat operations:

> We had been in the Pacific for a couple of years … the flight surgeon mentioned that we should put him on the roster to rotate back to the States. I said "sakes, [he] came over here with me, and we've only been here two years. He should be good for another year or so." So I went by the squadron and sat down with the Chief for a beer, and he could hardly hold the bottle. His hands were shaking so badly … it was the first time I'd seen serious combat fatigue.[37]

With still later advances, the 64th would move further to the north and west in a huge arc that would end at Japan.

The unit moved to Dulag on the island of Leyte on July 16, 1945. At that time, the 403rd TCG included the Headquarters Detachment, the 13th, 63rd, and 64th Squadron, the 65th and 66th Squadrons, each with a newly-acquired glider echelon, the 801st MAES, and the 8th Combat Cargo Squadron (CCS). The 8th CCS had joined the group on arrival at the Philippines in June 1945 and was the first unit of its type to see action in the Pacific Theater. It represented something of a milestone: it was a squadron of Black personnel trained explicitly for the type of resupply work that was the group's primary mission.[38]

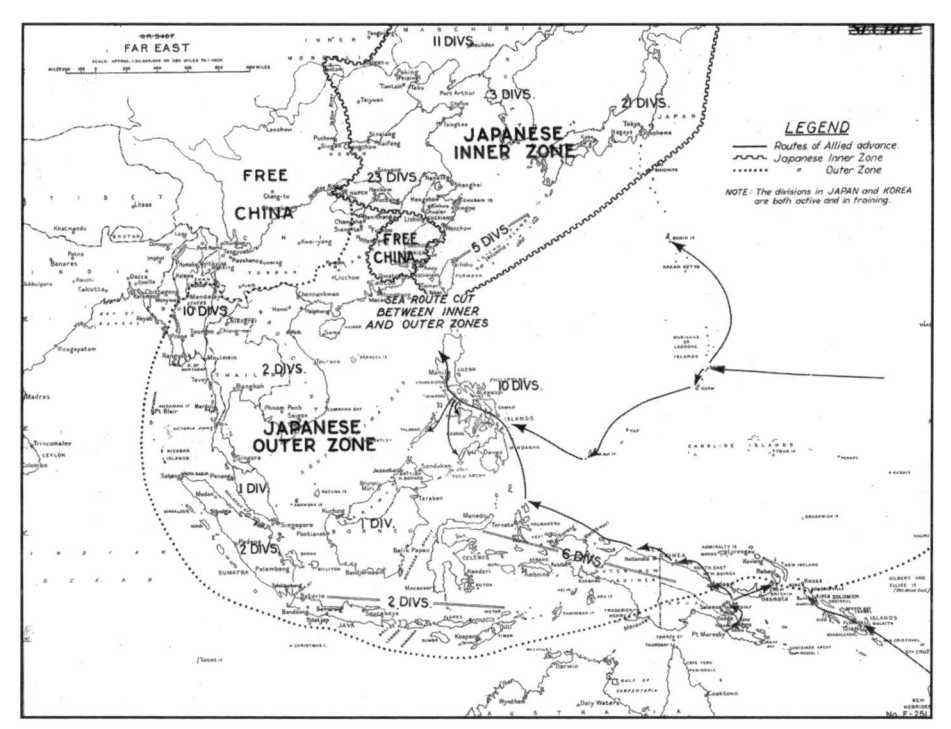

Map of Allied Advance in Pacific Theater, 1942. (Records of Allied Operational and Occupation Headquarters, World War II, Record Group 331; National Archives at College Park, College Park, MD)

During its wartime period of service, the squadrons of the 403rd TCG were often posted at different airfields to provide supply and medivac coverage over an increasingly wide geographical spectrum. It wasn't until its 15th month overseas that the three squadrons of the 403rd, and the headquarters unit, were all based at the same location—Biak. The units remained together at the group's next station—Dulag on Leyte, to which it was posted on July 1945. The squadrons would similarly remain intact when the 403rd moved to Clark Field on Luzon in January 1946. The 64th was inactivated on May 15, 1946.

The 64th Troop Carrier Squadron would serve in the Pacific War for two years, nine months, and 28 days. During that period of service, it was fated to move—lock, stock, and barrel—six times. Every bolt, loaf of bread, cot, jeep, and spare engine was crated, loaded, and either flown or shipped to the next base. Each of its moves had this in common—always in a northwesterly direction and always deeper into the Western Pacific.

Some departures were with reluctance. In other cases, the men couldn't leave fast enough. Santo, surprisingly, was an example of the latter: " ... we were so glad to get out of the New Hebrides we didn't even pause to say goodbye."[39]

The man who had commanded the 403rd TCG for the entirety of the war in the Pacific, Col. Harry Sands, would later reflect:

> My pilots were pretty experienced. Some were with me for two years. In the European theater they measured tours by the number of missions—25 or 50; in the Pacific we measured tours by the number of years.[40]

In the spring of 1945, the war's end was in sight, but there was no easing of combat operations. With an Allied invasion of Japan likely to be required to end the conflict, it was clear all combat and supply units would not be coasting their way to the final victory. The 64th Squadron history reported:

> In May (1945) the squadron again broke all its previous records by making landings on 48 different strips, carrying 1,040 medical evacuees and 3,509 other passengers, and well over three million pounds of freight, during 3,667 operational hours covering 447,771 nautical miles. Squadron planes were flyable 98 per cent of the time for the second consecutive month. Twelve of the planes were flown over two hundred hours each.[41]

The 64th had arrived in the South Pacific in the late summer of 1943. By June 1945, with the war's end just two months ahead, the squadron had hauled nearly 37 million pounds of freight, flown roughly 6½ million miles, evacuated 3,165 sick and wounded patients, and carried in the vicinity of fifty thousand passengers. The 64th's sister squadrons all posted similar numbers.

August 13, 1945, was long-awaited by every man and woman in the armed services in the Pacific. On that day, the Thirteenth Air Force forwarded the following message:

> Offensive operations against enemy cities, land communications, and other land targets except direct support for Allied ground forces in contact with enemy will cease until further order ... [42]

From that moment, a different timeline came into being, a timeline that would end with the men of the 64th stepping foot back in America.

At war's end, the unit was based at Clark Field on the island of Luzon. In late August 1945, it participated in the U.S. occupation of Japan when it airlifted a portion of the 11th Airborne Division from Okinawa to Atsugi Airfield outside of Yokohama. Sands would later note: "The Japanese had prepared tents and food for the men, and they provided gasoline if we needed it. We didn't need any gas, and we didn't trust the Japanese, so we didn't eat the food."[43]

In a testament to the durability of these C-47 aircraft and the effectiveness of the squadron's maintenance team, of the aircraft flown originally to the South Pacific by the 64th TCS in July 1943, nine would fly for the duration of the war, including the planes first flown from Hamilton Field by (now) Colonel Sands, Lieutenant Colonel Roessell, and Major McCreight. At the end of hostilities, seven of those surviving aircraft were condemned as unsuitable for further flight; one was sold to the Netherlands East Indies Air Force; and aircraft # 38751, first flown across the Pacific by Stoneburner, would return to the United States after the war. Its fame grew when, in 1946 it was featured in the Marx Brothers film *A Night in Casablanca*.[44]

Aircraft No.	Piloted to New Caledonia by	Fate
41-38737	Roessell	Written Off—Spare Parts, October 1945
42-23690	Sands	Written Off—Salvage, December 1946
42-23718	McCreight	Written Off—Salvage, June 1945
42-23724	Wood	Written Off—Salvage, July 1945
42-23725	Atwell	Written Off—Salvage, October 1945
42-23689	Morton	Survived and transferred to Netherlands East Indies Air Force, June 1946. Preserved at Halim Perdanakusuma Airport, Jakarta, from 1985.
42-23712	Carson	Survived—Withdrawn from use, June 1946
41-38751	Stoneburner	Survived—Sent to Reconstruction Finance Corp for disposal of surplus aircraft, March 1946
42-23714	Healy	Written Off—Salvage, Dec. 31, 1945
42-23711	Myers	Crash, September 5, 1943
42-23696	Foster	Written Off—Salvage, Dec. 31, 1945
42-23707	Couvillion	Written Off—Salvage, Dec. 31, 1945
42-23722	Smith	Crash, Jan. 26, 1944

The 64th was reactivated for the Korean War and the Vietnam War. In subsequent years, it bounced between inactive and active duty. In its present incarnation, it operates as the 64th Air Refueling Squadron, a component of the 22nd Operations Group. It is based at Pease Air National Guard Base in New Hampshire flying KC-46A Pegasus military aerial refueling and military transport aircraft. The 64th received a Distinguished Unit Citation and was credited with having participated in seven campaigns over the course of the war: New Guinea; Northern Solomons; Bismarck Archipelago; Western Pacific; Leyte; Luzon; and the Southern Philippines.[45]

In testimony to the commitment of the 403rd and its squadrons to the mission, in a later memoir, its commander, Colonel Sands, would write:

> I take great pride in noting that our aircraft were grounded only ONE DAY during this entire period, and this was due to a tropical storm which had blanketed the whole South Pacific area.[46]

Endnotes

Prologue
1   Tome was likely speaking in the Butmas–Tur Communalect.

Preface
1   IDPF for M/Sgt Wlodarsky: "Mount Terrin." IDPF for Lt. Healy: "Mt. Touri." IDPF for Lt. Miller: "Mount Tourin." IDPF for Cpl. O'Connell: "Mount Turin."

Introduction
1   "New Hebrides" is the term used to describe the archipelago around which this narration is based. Its modern designation, "Vanuatu," will be used in narration following the date of the country's independence, July 30, 1980.

Chapter 1
1   John E. Rees, *Idaho Chronology, Nomenclature, Bibliography* (Chicago: W. B. Conkey Company, 1918). The naming of the town was the subject of debate for nearly fifty years. Known initially as "Jawbone Flats," the name "Lewiston, WA." was suggested in 1896 but was quashed by the Post Office in order to eliminate confusion with Lewiston, Idaho, just across the river. The name Clarkston was finally selected when the town was incorporated in 1902. "100 years, Clarkston, Washington," *Lewiston Morning Tribune*, August 4, 2002.
2   Leonard G. Richardson, *The Crash of '43*, unpublished autobiography, Winter, 1980.
3   Hadley Cantril, Editor, *Public Opinion, 1935–1946* (Princeton University Press, 1951).
4   *Spokane Spokesman-Review*, May 23, 1939, 5.
5   "Enroll Students for Air Course," *Lewiston Morning Tribune* (December 2, 1940). Jane Gardner Birch, *They Flew Proud* (United States), 2007. See also: "Putt Putt Air Force: The Story of the Civilian Pilot Training Program and the War Training Service, 1939–1944," Department of Transportation, Federal Aviation Administration, Aviation Education Staff, GA-20-84; *Training to Fly: Military Flight Training, 1907–1945* (CreateSpace, 2012); and the Virginia Aeronautical Historical Society (vahsonline.publishpath.com/).
6   *Lewiston Morning Tribune*, December 2, 1940, February 22 and 28, 1941. The program initially offered only the Preliminary course, but by mid-summer 1941 the Lewiston program had also been approved for the Secondary course.
7   "World War II: Japanese Military Aviation Training," *Children in History*, March 23, 2024, https://www.histclo.com/essay/war/ww2/cou/jap/force/air/w2jfai-trainc.html.
8   Roster of student pilots is included in the *Lewiston Morning Tribune*, March 22, 1941, 12. The Lewiston Normal CPT consortium was authorized in October 1939 and began with an initial cohort of 10 flight

students. By the end of 1943, it had trained over fifteen hundred pilots, more than any other program in the country.
9   Richard R. Roth, *Empire in the Sky: The Bert Zimmerly Story* (Orting, WA: Heritage Quest Press, 2018).
10 These aircraft were included in a purchase of 19 Piper Cubs by Zimmerly in September 1940 to replace the previous fleet of 35-hp Cubs. *Lewiston Tribune*, August 1, 1940.
11 Now the most important wheat- and lentil-growing region in the country, the Palouse was named by early French-Canadian fur traders who adapted the name of the local indigenous peoples, the Palus, to a more familiar French word which translated to "land with short and thick grass." The Palouse encompasses the southeast corner of Washington state and is bordered by Blue Mountains in Oregon to the south, the state of Idaho and the Camas Prairie to the east, and by the Columbia River on the west. The Palouse had been rapidly settled in the late 19th century when it was found that the region was superbly suited for dry land farming of wheat and legumes.
12 License awards were described in the *Lewiston Morning Tribune* of June 14, 1941. License details per Letter, Leonard G. Richardson to Administrator, Civil Aeronautics Authority (CAA), Sept. 29, 1941.
13 Letter, Civilian Aeronautics Administration (CAA), July 9, 1941.
14 Roth, *Empire in the Sky*.
15 Richardson family archives.
16 Letter, July 9, 1941.
17 Ibid.
18 The Victory Program of 1941, prepared just prior to America's entry into World War II, was remarkably accurate regarding the total manpower requirements. The estimated total manpower requirements were 8.8 million. The actual peak strength as reported in May 1945 was 8.2 million. It should be added that the actual composition of the 1945 Army (number of divisions, type of divisions, etc.) differed significantly from the 1941 projections. CMH Pub. 1-1. See also: Joint Board Estimates of United States Over-all Production Requirements, September 11, 1941, Joint Board No. 355 (Serial 707), NARA RG 225.
19 Richard W. Stewart, General Editor, *American Military History, Vol II, the United States Army in a Global Era, 1917–2003* (U.S. Army Center of Military History, CMH Pub 30-22, 2005).
20 Mark Watson, *The United States Army in World War II, Chief of Staff: Prewar Plans and Preparations*, Chapter XI, the Victory Program (CMH Publication 1-1, 1991); and Charles E. Kirkpatrick, *Writing the Victory Plan of 1941* (Washington, D.C.: Center of Military History, 1992).
21 Joe Baugher, "Joe Baugher's Encyclopedia of American military aircraft," March 23, 2024, http://www.joebaugher.com/uscombataircraft.html; and John T. Correll, "The Air Force on the Eve of World War II," *Air Force Magazine*, October 1, 2007.
22 "The Victory Program, September 11, 1941," in *US War Plans: 1938–1945*, ed. Steven Ross, Appendix I: Decision on Production Requirements for Major Categories of Materials Recommended by the Navy.
23 Army and Navy Estimate of United States Over-all Production Requirements, September 11, 1941, Joint Board No. 355 (Serial 707). As recorded in www.navsource.org/Naval/usf.htm, the total number of U.S. Navy combat vessels on December 7, 1941, was 902.
24 *Administration of the Navy Department in World War II*, Chapter XIV, the United States Marine Corps, Julius Furer, U.S. Government Printing Office, OCLC 1103231458; and Joint Board No. 355.
25 Joint Board No. 355.
26 "Induction Statistics," Selective Service System, March 23, 2024, https://www.sss.gov/history-and-records/induction-statistics/.
27 Asotin County Local Selective Service Board, December 29, 1941.

Chapter 2

1   Due to the international dateline, December 8 for places like Wake Island, Guam, Singapore and Hong Kong.
2   Vern Haugland, *The AAF Against Japan* (New York: Harper & Brothers Publishers, 1948). Japan's devastating attack on the Philippines was by aircraft based in Formosa (now Taiwan), the island that

ENDNOTES • 273

Japan first acquired in 1895 following its victory in the First Sino-Japanese War, an acquisition that was the start of Japan's advance to Empire.

3   The Army Air Force's 19th Bomb Group began evacuations from the Philippines for Australia in mid-December. General MacArthur evacuated by PT boat on March 11, and the balance of American and Filipino forces on Bataan surrendered on April 9. A small force occupying the small island of Corregidor held out until May 6.
4   Proceedings of the American–British Joint Chiefs of Staff Conferences (*Arcadia*), Dec. 24, 1941–January 14, 1942, Parts I and II (U.S.) Joint History Office, Government Printing Office (GPO): 2017.
5   Wesley F. Craven and James Lea Cate, eds, *The Army Air Forces in World War II, Volume Four, The Pacific: Guadalcanal to Saipan, August 1942 to July 1944* (Office of Air Force History, 1983).
6   Ibid.
7   Report of the U.S.–British Joint Planning Committee, Defense of Island Bases Between Hawaii and Australia (U.S. British Chiefs of Staff, Jan. 13, 1942, U.S. Serial ABC-4/8). Department of State, Office of the Historian, accessed March 23, 2024.
8   *Arcadia*, Annex 1, Memorandum of Proposed Shipping Adjustments.
9   As Admiral Leahy had no command responsibility, and General Arnold was technically subordinate to General Marshall, the dominant members of the Joint Chiefs (JCS) throughout the war were Marshall and Admiral King. See: Lt. Col. Henry G. Morgan, *Planning the Defeat of Japan: A Study of Total War Strategy* (Office of the Chief of Military History, 3 Feb. 1980).
10 Richard B. Frank, *Guadalcanal: The Definitive Account of the Landmark Battle* (New York: Random House, 1990).
11 Ernest J. King and Walter Muir Whitehill, *Fleet Admiral King, A Naval Record* (New York: W. W. Norton & Co., 1952).
12 Cited in Vern Haugland, *The AAF Against Japan* (New York: Harper & Brothers Publishers, 1948).
13 The toponym New Hebrides is used to describe the archipelago around which this narration is based in accordance with usage during the war years. Later in the narrative, when the current conditions and prospects for the country are discussed, the current country name—Vanuatu—is used.
14 King and Whitehill, *Fleet Admiral King*.
15 COMINCH, letters, FF1/A16-3/F-1, Ser 00105 of 18 Feb 1942, quoted in Samuel E. Morison, *Coral Sea, Midway and Submarine Actions, May 1942–Aug 1942, Vol. IV of History Of United States Naval Operations In World War II* (Boston: Little, Brown & Co., 1943), 246; and King and Whitehill, *Fleet Admiral King*.
16 COMINCH to C/S USA, letter, FF1/A16/c/F1, Ser 00105 of 18 Feb. 1942 and 00149 of 2 March 1942; and Memo, Admiral King for JCS, 2 Mar 42, sub: Occupation for Def of Tonga Tabu and Efate, ABC 381 (3-2-42). (2) Min, 6th mtg JCS, 16 Mar 42.
17 Personal and Official Diary of Lieut. General Dwight D. Eisenhower, February 17, 1942.
18 United States Army in World War II, Strategic Planning for Coalition Warfare, 1941–1942, Chapter VII, Army Deployments in the Pacific and Grand Strategy, January–March 1942, Maurice Matloff and Edwin M. Snell, Center of Military History, 1999.
19 Memo, CofS for Admiral King, 24 Feb 42, sub: Est of U.S. Garrison in Efate, New Hebrides Islands.
20 Directive to the Supreme Commander, ABDA Area, Joint Chiefs of Staff, January 3, 1942 (ABC-4/5).
21 Robert Cressman, *Official Chronology of the US Navy in World War II* (Annapolis, MD: Naval Institute Press, 2000).
22 Louis Morton, *The United States Army in World War II, The War in the Pacific, Strategy and Command: The First Two Years* (Washington, D.C.: Center of Military History, CMH Pub 1–5, 1962).
23 "Battle of Makassar Strait, Battle of Bandung Strait, Battle of Java Sea, and the Battle of Sunda Strait," *Pacific Naval Surface Battles*, Center for Military History, CMH Vol. I Ch. 1, Naval History and Heritage Command.
24 Leonid Kondratiuk, *History of the National Lancers, 1836–2018* (Concord, MA: Historical Services, The Adjutant General's Office, 2019); *Armor on Luzon, A Research Report* (Fort Knox, KY: Armored School, 1949); Francis D. Cronin, *Under the Southern Cross, the Saga of the Americal Division* (Washington, D.C.: Combat Forces Press, 1951); and Ritchie Garrison, *Task Force 9156 and III Island Command: A*

Story of a South Pacific Advanced Base During World War II, Efate, New Hebrides (Waban, MA: 1983). The Combined Chiefs approved this plan on January 12. 5. JCCSS-10, January 12, 1942.

25 Narrative History of Task Force 6814 and Americal Division, January 23, 1942 to June 30, 1943, World War II Operational Documents (Fort Leavenworth, KS:Ike Skelton Combined Arms Research Library).

26 The USAT vessels were *Argentina, Thomas H. Barry, Cristobal, J. W. McAndrew, John Ericsson, Santa Elena*, and *Santa Rosa*. "… practically all the vessels available along the East Coast in those hectic early days of the war." Narrative History of Task Force 6814 and Americal Division. The sailing date for the task force is reported variably. Reference to histories of units included in TF 6814 confirms units began loading aboard ships on January 20, and sailed from New York Harbor on the 23rd. History of the 182nd Infantry, 16 January 1941 to 12 November 1942, HQ 182nd Infantry, 21 October 1943, Eisenhower Library, Project 735035, Box 1420; and, History of the 811 Engineer Aviation Bn, in XIII Air Force Service Command Historical Monographs, Number 17: The Operations of Aviation Engineers in the South Pacific, Battalion History (811th EAB), AFHRA Iris Ref A7711, Iris No. 00262040. After the task force arrived in New Caledonia, additional units were attached. During April, the 164th Infantry Regiment, the 97th Field Artillery Battalion (pack), the 72nd Field Artillery Regiment, and the 700th Signal Air Warning Company arrived at New Caledonia. On 24 May 1942, the Americal Division was constituted and organized from units of TF 6814.

27 Memorandum, Somerville to the Army Chief of Staff, February 18, 1942, NA/RG 165 [OCS, 21381–1).

28 Op. cit *Strategic Planning for Coalition Warfare*.

29 Memo, Admiral King for JCS, 2 Mar 42, sub: Occupation for Def of Tonga Tabu and Efate, ABC 381 (3-2-42); and Min, 6th mtg JCS, 16 Mar 42.

30 Memorandum for the President, Headquarters of the Commander in Chief, United States Fleet, March 5, 1942.

31 *United States Administration in World War II, The Logistics of Advance Bases, Base Maintenance Division* (Office of Naval Operations), Chapter V, Bases in the South Pacific Area.

32 Secret letter, CNO to Bureaus and Directors of Divisions of Operations, ser 014612, 6 Mar 1942. Cited in *The Logistics of Advance Bases, United States Naval Administration in World War II* (Office of Naval Operations), Vol. XXI, Chapter V.

33 Joint Basic Plan for Occupation and Defense of Efate, New Hebrides, 20 Mar 1942, OPD 381 Efate, New Hebrides, 8.

34 Letter, Navy Department, Bureau of Navigation, Randall Jacobs, Chief of Bureau. January 30, 1942.

35 United States Air Force Historical Studies (AAFHS), No. 2, "Initial Selection of Candidates for Pilot, Bombardier, and Navigator Training." Some text in this chapter is taken from Robert Richardson, *The Jagged Edge of Duty: a fighter pilot's World War II* (Guilford, Connecticut: Stackpole Books, 2017), and is used by permission.

36 Report of Physical Examination, Lt. E. I. Mulmed, Medical Corps, February 9, 1942.

37 The Aviation Cadet Qualifying Examination (ACQE), 1942–1943, See AFHRA Historical Studies: No. 2, Initial Selection of Candidates for Pilot, Bombardier and Navigator Training, Chapter IV, Assistant Chief for Air Staff, Intelligence, Historical Division, November, 1943.

38 *Aviation Cadet Manual, 1942* (Governors Island, NY: War Department, Recruiting Publicity Bureau, US Army, 1942).

39 Rebecca Hancock Cameron, *Training to Fly: Military Fight Training, 1907–1945* (Air Force History and Museums Program, 1999).

40 Dr. Bruce Ashcroft, *We Wanted Wings: A History of the Aviation Cadet Program* (Randolph Air Force Base, TX: HQ AETC Office of History and Research, 2005).

41 Letter, Air Base Headquarters, Aviation Cadet Examining Board, Geiger Field, WA., March 12, 1942, Lt. J.C. Rollins, Air Corps.

42 Enlistment Record, Army of the United States, March 19, 1942, Lt. J. C. Rollins, Air Corps.

43 Patty's brother, Harlan, was killed on June 11, 1944, five days after the landings at Normandy, near Colleville, France, in action that earned him the Bronze Star.

Chapter 3

1. From 1938 to 1939, Admiral Ghormley had served as head of the War Plans Division in the Office of the Chief of Naval Operations, and was the Navy's direct counterpart to General Eisenhower in the War Department.
2. Directive to the Supreme Commander in the Southwest Pacific Area (CCS 57/1), 30 March 1942.
3. JCS Directive to CINCPOA, 30 Mar 42, ABC 323.31 (1-29-42 sec. 1 B) POA). See also: Louis Morton, *The United States Army in World War II, The War in the Pacific, Strategy and Command: The First Two Years* (Washington, D.C.: Center of Military History, CMH Pub 1-5, 1962). See also Op. cit. Craven and Cate, *The Pacific*.
4. Early dates associated with Task Force 6814 vary. Narrative History of Task Force 6814 and Americal Division, Jan. 23, 1942 to June 30, 1943, World War II Operational Documents (Fort Leavenworth, KS: Ike Skelton Combined Arms Research Library) is used as the authoritative source, unless otherwise indicated.
5. Cited in Francis D. Cronin, *Under the Southern Cross, the Saga of the Americal Division* (Washington, D.C.: Combat Forces Press, 1951).
6. Narrative History of Task Force 6814. Two months after the Task Force's arrival at Noumea, many of its component units would be re-designated as the "Americal Division," a portmanteau of America and Caledonia. The date of the constitution of the Americal Division was May 27, 1943.
7. Advanced Bases South Pacific, Inspection Report of, prepared by "Senior Member, South Pacific Advanced Base Inspection Board," August 15, 1942. NARA Micro Serial NO. 53305, Reel A475, Catalog ID 4697018. Fold3 image 269712796. The author of the report was Admiral Richard E. Byrd, Jr.
8. Command Summary of Fleet Admiral Chester W. Nimitz, USN, Nimitz "Graybook," Vol. 1, March 8, 1942, 282.
9. Rose served as commanding general of Santo from October 14, 1942, to February 16, 1943, when Guadalcanal was secured.
10. Cronin, *Under the Southern Cross*; and Stanley C. Jersey, *Military Postal History of the United States Forces 1942—1946, New Hebrides Islands*, Collectors' Club of Chicago; and AONH; Order of Battle of the United States Army Ground Forces in World War II, Pacific Theater of Operations (Fort Leavenworth, KS: Ike Skelton Combined Arms Research Library, 1959), call no. 940.5426 U5650 c.1.
11. Geoffrey Mason, *Service Histories of Royal Navy Warships in World War 2*, Naval History Net, 2004; Order of Battle of the United States Army Ground Forces in World War II, Pacific Theater of Operations, Administrative and Logistical Commands, Armies, Corps, and Divisions, Office of the Chief of Military History, Department of the Army, Wa. DC, 1959.
12. Max Brand, *Fighter Squadron at Guadalcanal*, Naval Institute; and War Diary of the USS *Crescent City*, 1 Apr 1942–30 Apr 1942, NARA RG 38, Catalog ID 4697018, Micro Serial No. 40313.
13. Op. cit.
14. At the time MAG-24 consisted of HQ&SS-24 (the "Forward Echelon" of MAG-24) plus VMF-211 and -212. Muster Roll of Officers and Enlisted Men, Marine Fighting Squadron Two-Twelve, 1 July–31 July, 1942.
15. Stanley Coleman Jersey, *Hell's Islands: The Untold Story of Guadalcanal* (Texas A&M University Press; Illustrated edition, 2007).
16. Cited in *Hell's Island* and *Naval History of Espiritu Santo*.
17. Allen Longe, *The defense of New Zealand: Internal problems and diplomatic relations, 1935–1943* (Omaha: University of Nebraska, 1968). Representatives of the United Kingdom, Australia and New Zealand convened in Wellington, New Zealand, in April 1939 to discuss the defense of the South Pacific, the need for increased defense cooperation between Australia and New Zealand, and the clarification of defense procedures between these two Pacific Dominions and the UK.
18. R.A.A.F. Advanced Operational Base, Vila, New Hebrides, Air Board, Agenda No. 3190/1941, National Archives of Australia, NAA: A14487, 17/AB/3180.
19. No. 2 Section, A Platoon, 1 Dependent Company, Vila Detachment, New Hebrides. Australian War Memorial Item No. 25/3/1/4.

20 AWM52 Unit War Diaries, Item No. 25/3/1/4, December 1941 to February 1942.
21 Order S.M. 7102, Department of the Army, Military Board, Army HQ, Victoria Barracks, Melbourne, 20 June 1941; and AWM52 Unit War Diaries, Item No. 25/3/12, June to August 1941, see S.M.12901 of 11 October.
22 William Osler, *The Evolution of Modern Medicine*, A Series of Lectures Delivered at Yale University, April 1913.
23 New Hebrides, Great Britain Foreign Office, Historical Section, London, 1920.
24 Field-Marshal Viscount William Slim, *Defeat Into Victory, Battling Japan in Burma and India, 1942–1945* (New York: Cooper Square Press, 2000).
25 Reported in Monica Ann Hoffman, "Malaria, Mosquitoes, and Maps: Practices and Articulations of Malaria Control in British India and WWII" (San Diego: University of California, 2016).
26 John Boyd Coates, Editor in Chief, *Preventive Medicine in World War II, Vol. VI, Communicable Diseases, Malaria*, Chapter I (Washington, D.C.: Office of the Surgeon General, 1963).
27 Herbert Merillat, *Guadalcanal Remembered* (New York: Dodd, Mead and Co., 1982).
28 Personal Diary, Harold Simmons Tate, University of South Carolina archives, file reference 14863.
29 Malaria rates on Efate reached 2,678 per thousand in April. Coates, *Preventive Medicine in World War II, Vol. VI*; and Dr. David Line, Program Director, Public Health, Eastern Washington University, personal correspondence, June 2020.
30 Op. cit., *Fighter Squadron at Guadalcanal*.
31 Coates, *Preventive Medicine in World War II, Vol. VI*.
32 Beatrice Grimshaw, *From Fiji to the Cannibal Islands* (London: Eveleigh Nash, 1907).
33 W. G. Beasley, "Operation Magic," in *Encyclopedia of Espionage, Intelligence and Security*, Adrienne Wilmonth Lerner; and Geoffrey Sinclair, "Magic, the Intellegence War", JN-25 fact sheet, *Hyperwar, Pacific Theater of War*.
34 Command Summary of Fleet Admiral Chester W. Nimitz, USN, Nimitz "Graybook," Vol. 1, May 14, 1942, 432.
35 Milan Vego, "The Moresby–Solomons Operation and the Allied Reaction, 27 April–11 May 1942," *Naval War College Review*, Volume 65, Number 1, Winter 2012; and Vern Haugland, *The AAF Against Japan* (New York: Harper & Brothers Publishers, 1948).
36 General Outline of Policy of Future War Guidance, adopted by Liaison Conference, 7 March 1942, and Report of Prime Minister and Chiefs of Staff to Emperor 13 March 1942.
37 Vego, "The Moresby–Solomons Operation and the Allied Reaction."
38 Aircraft losses are cited in Vego, "The Moresby–Solomons Operation and the Allied Reaction."
39 Joint Basic Plan for Occupation and Defense of Efate, New Hebrides, 20 Mar 1942, OPD 381 Efate, New Hebrides.
40 Lamont Lindstrom, "The American Occupation of the New Hebrides (Vanuatu)," Macmillan Brown Working Paper Series No. 5, Macmillan Brown Centre for Pacific Studies, 1996. The 24th Infantry Regiment was responsible for a large part of the perimeter defense of Efate. With the later American success on Guadalcanal, the danger of Japanese attack had passed and the 24th remained on the island continuing its training and field duties, and taking on additional responsibilities for loading and unloading ships, guarding air bases, building roads, spraying and draining as part of mosquito control, installing and maintaining wire communications for a large part of the base. See: Ulysses Lee, *United States Army in World War II: Special Studies: Employment of Negro Troops* (Washington: Office of the Chief of Military History, U.S. Army, 1966); and Kenneth Jones, *The Last Black Regulars*Strategy Research Project, U.S. Army War College, Carlisle Barracks, PA., 2000.
41 *Building the Navy's Bases in World War II: History of the Bureau of Yards and Docks and the Civil Engineering Corps, 1940–1945*, Chapter XXIV (Washington: U.S. Govt. Print. Off., 1947). "VPB" was a US Navy unit designator for a patrol bomber squadron.
42 Jersey, *Military Postal History*.
43 Command Summary of Fleet Admiral Chester W. Nimitz, USN, Nimitz "Graybook," Vol. 1, Feb. 19, 1942, 296. As for strengthening the Allied positions on Samoa, that task would be left for the second of the Navy's Construction Battalions. Like the 1st Construction Battalion (CB), the 2nd CB was also

split: half to Upolu (*Strawhat*), and half to Wallis (*Strawboard*). The two detachments sailed together, leaving the U.S. on April 9 and arriving at the Samoan Group in early May.
44   Steven J. Stasick, *A Study of the Naval Construction Force Project Material Supply Chain* (Massachusetts Institute of Technology, 2004).
45   *Building the Navy's Bases in World War II*; and Kennard R. Wiggins, "The 198th Coast Artillery (Antiaircraft) in World War II, Operation Bobcat Island"; and Glen Williford, *Racing the Sun: The Reinforcement of America's Pacific Outposts, 1941–1942* (Annapolis: Naval Institute Press, 2013).
46   Reports on the staffing of a construction battalion differ slightly. The above figures are taken from a document prepared by the commander of the Task Force. See: H. N. Wallin, "The Project Was Roses," *The Navy Civil Engineer*, Naval Facilities Engineering Command, May/June 1967. Among other sources is Naval History and Heritage Command, U.S. Navy Seabee Museum, Naval Construction Battalion, https://www.history.navy.mil/content/history/museums/seabee/explore/seabee-unit-histories/ncb.html). Last accessed March 23, 2024.
47   The 2nd Detachment of the 1st Construction Battalion departed Norfolk on April 10 and arrived at Tonga on May 9. The detachment remained at Tonga until February 24 when it was split, with most of the unit assigned to Efate and a smaller contingent retained at Tonga to work on the still-incomplete tank farm. The main contingent arrived at Efate on February 28 and, on its arrival, essentially two-thirds of the 1st CB was reunited. The smaller contingent of *Bleacher* left Tonga for Wallis Island on August 20, 1943, where it worked on the bomber field. It then left Wallis on December 4 and arrived at Efate on the 8th. With that unit's arrival at Efate, the 1st CB was effectively reunited for the first time in 20 months. Truesdale Fife, *History of the 1st Battalion of CBs*, unpublished manuscript, 1966; *Building the Navy's Bases in World War II*, Chapter VI.
48   Wallin, "The Project was Roses." The CB Detachment would later complete a fighter airfield at Quoin Hill. The base hospital would be enlarged to 100 beds in mid-1943.
49   Ritchie Garrison, *Task Force 9156 and III Island Command: A Story of a South Pacific Advanced Base During World War II, Efate, New Hebrides* (Waban, MA: 1983). The author refers to the Pacific Islands Sailing Directions, Hydrographic Office Publication No. 164 (1938), which give basic geographical, demographic, topographic, and hydrographic information about the islands.
50   Wallin, "The Project was Roses."
51   Garrison, *Task Force 9156 and III Island Command*.
52   *History of the 1st Battalion of CBs.*
53   Periodic Intelligence Report, 1–28 Feb 1943, to CO of the 5th and 11th Bombardment Groups, USAF, Major Frank S. Owen, S-2. Contained in History 98th Bomb Squadron, AFHRA IRIS No. 00044983, Roll A0575, 1231.
54   Lamont Lindstrom, "The Vanuatu Labor Corps Experience," paper for the Cultural Encounters in the Pacific War Conference, University of Hawaii Manoa Center for Pacific Island Studies, May 1988.

Chapter 4

1   William Bradford Huie, *Can Do!: The Story of the Seabees, 1942–1967* (Washington, D.C.: Naval Facilities Engineering Command, 1967).
2   Truesdale Fife, *History of the 1st Battalion of CBs*, unpublished manuscript, 1966.
3   H. N. Wallin, "The Project Was Roses," *The Navy Civil Engineer*, Naval Facilities Engineering Command, May/June 1967.
4   Op. cit. *Can Do!*
5   Lamont Lindstrom, "The Vanuatu Labor Corps Experience," paper for the Cultural Encounters in the Pacific War Conference, University of Hawaii Manoa Center for Pacific Island Studies, May 1988.; and Wallin, "The Project Was Roses."
6   Op. cit. *Fighter Squadron at Guadalcanal.*
7   Kent Brown, ed., "War Diary of Harold W. Bauer Dec. 1, 1941 to Oct. 13, 1942," 2011, in *Acepilots.com* and Op. cit. *Fighter Squadron at Guadalcanal.*

278 • SURVIVAL IN THE SOUTH PACIFIC

8 Ibid "War Diary of Harold W. Bauer"; and Op. cit. Advanced Bases South Pacific, Inspection Report.
9 *Fighter Squadron at Guadalcanal.*
10 Wesley Craven and James Cate, eds., *The Army Air Forces in World War II, Vol. One: Plans and Early Operations* (Chicago: University of Chicago Press, 1983).
11 Navy squadron VS-5D14 (later designation VS-55).
12 The Royal New Zealand Air Force had built a seaplane base at Vila Harbor prior to the arrival of Task Force 9156. This facility was taken over by Navy squadron VS-5D14 (later designated as VS-55). Lt. D. W. Kralovec, Base Historian, *A Naval History of Espiritu Santo, New Hebrides, 1945*, NARA Record Group 0313, ARC #5927775, 1945.and History of Air Center Command on Espiritu Santo, History of Pallikulo Airfield, National Archives RG 0313, Arc # 5923148.
13 "National Geospatial Intelligence Agency," *Geographical Names.org*, https://www.geographic.org/geographic_names/name.php?uni=-).
14 Lindstrom, "The Vanuatu Labor Corps Experience."
15 Matt Wells, *Pacific Paradise Lost*, unpublished, 1945. Cited in Op. cit, *Kralovec, Naval History of Espiritu Santo*.
16 Ritchie Garrison, *Task Force 9156 and III Island Command: A Story of a South Pacific Advanced Base During World War II, Efate, New Hebrides* (Waban, MA: 1983).
17 Command Summary of Fleet Admiral Chester W. Nimitz, USN, Nimitz "Graybook," 7 December 1941–31 August 1945, Vol. 1 (Newport, R.I.: U.S. Naval War College, 2013). Msg 19 1759, May 19, 1942, 485.
18 Ibid, 500.
19 Command Summary of Fleet Admiral Chester W. Nimitz, USN, Nimitz "Graybook," Vol. 1, May 13, 1942, 480.
20 Command Summary of Fleet Admiral Chester W. Nimitz, Nimitz "Graybook," May 19, 1942, 485. Also see Admiral Ghormley's endorsement of the plan, Command Summary, entry for May 20, 1942, Msg 20 0943, 500.
21 Command Summary of Fleet Admiral Chester W. Nimitz, Nimitz "Graybook," May 23, 1942, Msg 23 0333, 526.
22 War Diary, USS *Whipple*, June 7, 1942, for period 1–31 May, 1942; S. D. Waters, *The Royal New Zealand Navy* (Wellington: Historical Publications Branch, 1956); and, War Diary, USS *Whipple*, 1 May 1942 to 31 May 1942, NARA Micro Serial 41040, Catalog ID 4697018, RG 38, Roll 0038.
23 Op. cit. Kralovec, *A Naval History of Espiritu Santo*.
24 Order of Battle of the United States Army Ground Forces in World War II, Pacific Theater of Operations (Washington: Office of the Chief of Military History, 1959); and Stanley C. Jersey, *Military Postal History of the United States Forces 1942–1946, New Hebrides Islands*, Collectors' Club of Chicago; and History 182nd Infantry, 16 January 1941 to 11 Nov. 1942, Hq, 182nd Infantry, Americal Division, 21 October 1943; See Brad Peters and Jan Ross, "History of the 300th Combat Engineers, 1943–1945," for a brief description of the composition of an Engineer Combat Battalion.
25 Matt Wells, "The American Invasion," in Op. cit. Kralovec, *A Naval History of Espiritu Santo*.
26 Date of arrival June 14, 1943. These two aircraft were a detachment of VS-5-D14, the Naval Inshore Scouting Squadron that arrived at Efate with Joint Task Force 9156 on May 4. H.E. Lewis Priday, *The War from Coconut Square, The Defence of the Island Bases of the South Pacific*, A. H. & A. W. Reed, Wellington, 1945, and History of Commander Fleet Air, Alameda, 30 Dec. 1944, A3-1/05-gk, NARA Microserial no. 156199, Catalog ID 4697018, Group record 38.
27 On Espiritu Santo, General Rose got a lot busier after June 17, when his commanding officer, General Chamberlin, became ill and was returned to the United States. General Rose temporarily assumed his command and became responsible for the combined forces on both Efate and Espiritu Santo.
28 Interview of Capt. M. B. Gardner, USN, Chief of Staff, ComAirSouPac (Air Information Branch), 13 January 1943; memo for record, Security of New Caledonia and Efate, New Hebrides, 20 May 1942 in OPD 381, PTO, 29.
29 By November, the airfield would be lengthened to 6,000 feet, and would be surfaced with steel Marston matting.

30 Interview of Capt. M. B. Gardner, USN.
31 Lamont Lindstrom, "The American Occupation of the New Hebrides (Vanuatu)," Macmillan Brown Working Paper Series No. 5, Macmillan Brown Centre for Pacific Studies, 1996.
32 Jersey, *Military Postal History.*
33 Interview, Tom Harris, "Twenty Years on Santo," in Op. cit. Kralovec, *A Naval History of Espiritu Santo,* but original source is *Santonian* newsletter, Vol. 1, No. 1, 15 May 1944.
34 Frederick Shaw, "Locating Air Force Base Sites History's Legacy," Air Force History and Museums Program, United States Air Force, Washington D.C., 2004; and Thomas Manning, "History of Air Education and Training Command, 1942–2002," Office of History and Research, Headquarters, AETC, Randolph AFB, Texas, 2005. The numbers of cadets processed through SAAAB reflected the enormous demand for trained pilots by all branches of the service. By the end of 1942, nearly thirty-five hundred cadets had completed the Preflight program at Santa Ana; in 1943, the total was 57,895 cadets. See: http://www.militarymuseum.org/SantaAnaAAB.html.
35 *The War Experiences of Arthur R Driedger Jr, Radio Operator Mechanic, C 47, 13th Troop Carrier Squadron, 403rd Troop Carrier Group, 13th Air Force* (unpublished manuscript).
36 Wesley Craven and James Cate, eds., *The Army Air Forces in World War II* (Washington, D.C.: Office of Air Force History, 1983), Chapter VI, Men and Planes.
37 Information related to the role of American intelligence is taken from *A Priceless Advantage, Series IV: World War II,* Vol. 5, Center for Cryptologic History, 2017; and Craig Nelson, *Pearl Harbor—from Infamy to Greatness* (London: Weidenfeld & Nicholson, 2018).
38 Still, the intelligence produced was far from complete. Nimitz himself reported: "Generally speaking our present intelligence is mainly the decoding of 40 percent of the messages copied, and only 60 percent of possible messages are copied." They were accessing just 24% of the Japanese communications traffic. Command Summary of Fleet Admiral Chester W. Nimitz, Nimitz "Graybook," entry for May 26, 1942, 543; Battle of Midway, 3–6 June 1942, Composition of Japanese and American Naval Forces, Naval History and Heritage Command.
39 Command Summary of Fleet Admiral Chester W. Nimitz, Nimitz "Graybook," entry for June 4, 1942, 571.
40 Command Summary of Fleet Admiral Chester W. Nimitz, Nimitz "Graybook," entry for June 3, 1942, 570.
41 *A Priceless Advantage.*
42 Ernest J. King and Walter Muir Whitehill, *Fleet Admiral King, A Naval Record* (New York: W. W. Norton & Co., 1952).
43 Robert Leckie, *Challenge for the Pacific: Guadalcanal—the Turning Point of the War* (New York: Doubleday & Co., 1965).
44 Statistics on losses vary. The present figures are based on the work of Jonathan Parshall and Tony Tully, *Shattered Sword: the Untold Story of the Battle of Midway* (Dulles: Virginia Potomac Books, 2005).

Chapter 5

1 Pontus Skoglund, Stuart Bedford, Matthew Spriggs, et al., "Genomic Insights into the Peopling of the Southwest Pacific," *Nature,* Vol. 538, October 27, 2016.
2 *The Voyages of Pedro Fernandez de Quiros,* 1595–1606, Vol. I (of II), translated and edited by Sir Clements Markham, Hakluyt Society, London, 1904.
3 Margaret Jolly, et al. (eds.), *Oceanic Encounters, Exchange, Desire, Violence* (Australian National University, Canberra, 2009). The name of the island archipelago changed over time, from Terra Australis del Espiritu Santo (Quiros) to Archipel des grandes Cyclades (Bougainville) to New Hebrides (Cook). There was no indigenous name for the entire archipelago and no indigenous sense of its unity until the mid-20th century in the colonial and postcolonial periods.
4 John Reinhold Forster, *Observations Made During a Voyage Round the World on Physical Geography, Natural History, and Ethic Philosophy* (London: G. Robinson, 1778).

280 • SURVIVAL IN THE SOUTH PACIFIC

5 Cook and his party made detailed observations on the people, environment, and natural history of the three islands on which reprovisioning landings were made. Interested readers are referred to James Cook, *A Voyage Towards the South Pole and Round the World* (London, 1777).
6 Op. cit. *A Voyage Towards the South Pole.*
7 Jane Resture, "Jane's Oceania," at www.janeresture.com.
8 John Boyd Coates, Editor in Chief, *Preventive Medicine in World War II, Vol. VIII, New Hebrides* (Washington, D.C.: Office of the Surgeon General, 1963).
9 Felix Speiser, *Two Years with the Natives in the Western Pacific* (London: Mills & Boon, Ltd., 1913).
10 Beatrice Grimshaw, *From Fiji to the Cannibal Islands* (London: Eveleigh Nash, 1907).
11 James A. Michener, *Return to Paradise*, Random House, New York, 1951. Michener suspended his distaste for the jungle of Santo when he penned *Tales of the South Pacific* in 1946, and renamed the nearby island of Ambae—little different from Santo—"Bali Hai" and ascribed to it Edenic qualities.
12 Op. cit. Kralovec, *A Naval History of Espiritu Santo.*
13 Ibid.
14 *The Voyages of Pedro Fernandez de Quiros.*
15 Ibid.
16 Martin Johnson, *Cannibal Land* (Constable & Co., 1922).
17 John R. Baker, *Man and Animals in the New Hebrides* (London: G. Routledge & Sons. Ltd., 1929).
18 Jeremy MacClancy, *To Kill a Bird with Two Stones. A Short History of Vanuatu*, Vanuatu Cultural Center Publications No. 1, 2002.
19 Ibid.
20 *Voyage Around the World by the King's Frigate La Boudeuse & the Supply Ship L'Etoile In the Years 1766, 1767, 1768 & 1769*, translated from the French by John F. Fegan (Royal Navy, 2013).
21 MacClancy, *To Kill a Bird with Two Stones.*
22 Ibid.
23 Cited in Charlene Gourguechon, *Journey to the End of the World, A Three-Year Adventure in the New Hebrides* (New York: Scribner, 1977).
24 Tom Harrisson, *Savage Civilization* (A.A. Knopf, New York, 1937).
25 Maj. Robert D. Heinl, Jr., USMC, "Palms and Planes in the New Hebrides," *National Geographic*, Vol. LXXXVI, Number Two, August 1944.
26 Grimshaw, *From Fiji to the Cannibal Islands.*
27 Ibid.
28 Edward Jacomb, *France and England in the New Hebrides* (G. Robertson Pty. Limited, 1914).
29 Op. cit. *Savage Civilization.*
30 Op. cit. *Oceanic Encounters.*
31 Kastom, or variably Custom, is a pidgin word referring to complex social and spiritual patterns that comprise the tribal universe, subsuming religion, economics, art, magic, and more.
32 MacClancy, *To Kill a Bird with Two Stones.*
33 Stephen H. Roberts, *History of French Colonial Policy, 1870–1925* (London: King Publishers, 1929). In 1910, the French population had increased to 566, and Brits to 288. By 1939, the French would outnumber the British settlers by ten to one. "Vanuatu (New Hebrides) had become a French colony in all but name." MacClancy, *To Kill a Bird with Two Stones.*
34 Felix Speiser, *Ethnology of Vanuatu: An Early Twentieth Century Study* (University of Hawaii Press, 1996). Originally published in German in 1923. Speiser's estimate is the product of a careful review of nine separate population estimates between 1774 and 1910; and Op. cit. Kralovec, *A Naval History of Espiritu Santo.*
35 Alan John Marshall, *The Black Musketeers* (William Heinemann Books, 1937).
36 Speiser, *Ethnology of Vanuatu.*

Chapter 6

1. Jeffrey Cox, *Morning Star, Midnight Sun: the Early Guadalcanal–Solomons Campaign of World War II, August–October 1942* (Oxford: Osprey Publishing, 2019).
2. Soon to be called "the Slot" by Allied combatants, this central passage would be the site of brutal naval battles, and most of the 67 capital ships lost during the Guadalcanal Campaign sank in the waters that came to be called "Ironbottom Sound."
3. King to Nimitz, Msg 151830, February 1942, Cited in *The Amphibians Came to Conquer, Vol. 1, The Story of Admiral Richmond Kelly Turner*, George Dyer, Fleet Marine Reference Publication 12-109-1, 1991.
4. King to Nimitz, Msg 122200 Feb 1942. Ibid.
5. Unattributed Draft Report, contained in AFHRA 750.057, 1944-1945, IRIS A7635, Operational Material Misc.
6. Op. cit. Craven and Cates, *The Pacific*.
7. "Pacific Counterblow: the 11th Bombardment Group and the 67th Fighter Squadron in the battle for Guadalcanal, an Interim Report," *Wings at War Series*, No. 3, Air Force History Support Office, Bolling AFB, 1992.
8. Charles Robert Anderson, "Guadalcanal," *The U.S. Army Campaigns of World War II*, Center for Military History Publication, CMH Pub 72-8, 1993; Maurice Matloff and Edwin Snell, Strategic Planning for Coalition Warfare, 1941–1942, Center for Military History Publication, CMH Pub 1-3, 1953.
9. James A. Smith, "The U.S. Navy and the Tokyo Express at Guadalcanal, August–December 1942: A Battle That Required 'Every Conceivable Weapon'," Norwich University, 2014.
10. H. P. Willmott, *The War with Japan: The Period of Balance, May 1942–October 1943* (Wilmington, DE: Scholarly Resources Books, 2002), 90.
11. Op. cit. "War Diary of Harold W. Bauer."
12. Command Summary of Fleet Admiral Chester W. Nimitz, Nimitz "Graybook," entry for June 22, 1942, 599, and Messages 23 1256 (June 23, 1942), 24 2303 and 24 2306 (June 24, 1942).
13. Command Summary of Fleet Admiral Chester W. Nimitz, Nimitz "Graybook," Msg 24 2306, 24 June 1942, page 603; and entry for June 25, 1942, 670.
14. Memo, King for Chief of Staff (Marshall), 25 Jun 42, sub: Offensive Opns in S and SWPA, OPD 381 SWPA, 80.
15. Letter, King to Marshall, ser. 00555, 26 June 1942, sub: Offensive Opns in South and Southwest Pacific Area, OPD 381(SWPA) case 80.
16. Joint Directive for Offensive Operations in the Southwest Pacific Area, 2 July 1942; and George Dyer, *The Amphibians Came to Conquer, Vol. 1, The Story of Admiral Richmond Kelly Turner*, Fleet Marine Reference Publication 12-109-1, 1991; and Glossary of U.S. Naval Code Words (NAVEXOS P-474), Naval History and Heritage Command; and Operation WATCHTOWER: An Analysis in Operational Design, Naval War College, Scott Stewart, unpublished manuscript, March 1994.
17. Ghormley to Nimitz et al. Command Summary, Msg 16 0612, July 16, 620.
18. Ibid; *Guadalcanal and the Origins of the Thirteenth Air Force*, Army Air Forces Historical Studies: No. 35, Historical Division, July 1945.
19. Command Summary of Fleet Admiral Chester W. Nimitz, USN, Nimitz "Graybook," Msg 02 2314, July 2, 1942, 605.
20. Command Summary of Fleet Admiral Chester W. Nimitz, USN, Nimitz "Graybook," Msg 04 2144, July 4, 1942, 682.
21. Ibid; COMAIRSOPAC TO COMSOPAC, July 5, 1942, Msg. 05 0325; and Op. cit. "War Diary of Harold W. Bauer."
22. Op. cit. "War Diary of Harold W. Bauer." H. N. Wallin, in "The Project Was Roses" (*The Navy Civil Engineer*, Naval Facilities Engineering Command, May/June 1967), has July 4 as the date of this conference. The entry of July 5 in the contemporary Bauer Diary is the preferred date.
23. Op. cit. Wallin, "The Project Was Roses."
24. On May 27—just over three weeks after Task Force 9156 began its work on Efate—and while General Rose's small force was developing positions on Santo, the airfield on Efate became ready for

282 • SURVIVAL IN THE SOUTH PACIFIC

fighter operations and the "Hell Hounds" of VMF-212, under the command of Maj. Harold Bauer, began flying their Grumman F4F fighters from the new airfield—later known as Bauer Field. Brown, Op. cit. "War Diary of Harold W. Bauer."

25 Truesdale Fife, *History of the 1st Battalion of CBs*, unpublished manuscript, 1966; and Op. cit. Wallin and Op. Huie.
26 NavSource Naval History, Photographic History of the US Navy; and CINCPAC War Diary for the month of July 1942, NARA Microserial No. 42140, File A16-(4)/05, Serial No. 02474; and Ibid Truesdale Fife.
27 Ibid, Truesdal Fife and Op. cit. Wallin and Huie.
28 Op. cit. "War Diary of Harold W. Bauer."
29 Op. cit. Wallin.
30 Op. cit. *Can Do!*; and *Hell's Island: The Untold Story of Guadalcanal* (Stanley Jersey, College Station: Texas A & M University Press, 2008); and Material of General Interest in Connection with Some Phase of Aviation, Interview with M. Pascal Michel, contained in [A12] Airfield Data #1 [History of Air Center Command at Espiritu Santo and Appendices, Vol. I][Folder 1 of 2], NARA RG 0313, Naval Operating Forces, ARC# 5923148.
31 Op. cit. *Can Do!*
32 Joe Baugher, Chicago, Ill. See: www.joebaugher.com; Boeing B-17E Fortress. The range of the B-17 could be increased with a lighter bomb load, but at a cost of reduced effectiveness.
33 David R. Hinton, *Letters from the Dead: Guadalcanal* (Trafford Publishing, 2005); See also *The AAF in the South Pacific*, US Air Force Historical Study No. 101, AFHRA., IRIS No. 00467685, and *History of the US Army Forces in the South Pacific Area During World War II, 30 March 1942 to 1 August 1944*, Vol. I, Part I, Historical Section USAFISPA, US Army Center of Military History, Call No. 8-5.7 BA.
34 Vern Haugland, *The AAF against Japan* (New York: Harper, 1948); and Stanley C. Jersey, *Military Postal History of the United States Forces 1942–1946, New Hebrides Islands* (Collectors' Club of Chicago).
35 *History of the US Army Forces in the South Pacific Area During World War II*, Part 1.
36 Command Summary of Fleet Admiral Chester W. Nimitz, USN, Nimitz "Graybook," Entry for July 5, 1942, page 707.
37 COMSOWESPACFOR TO COMINCH CINCPAC COMSOPACFOR, Command Summary, Msg. 08 1018 Part 5, July 8, page 612.
38 Information confirmed on the basis of a captured enemy diary. *The AAF in the South Pacific*.
39 John Miller, United States Army in World War II, Guadalcanal: The First Offensive, Center of Military History, CMH Pub 5-3, 1949; and Op. cit. Craven and Cate, *The Pacific*.
40 13th AF Special Studies "Extract from Division Commander's Final Report on Guadalcanal Operation," Maj. Gen. A. A. Vandergrift, First Marine Division, 24 May 1943, AFHRA IRIS 750.04-1, Reel A7635.
41 Command Summary of Fleet Admiral Chester W. Nimitz, USN, Nimitz "Graybook," July 27 and 28, 1942, 782.
42 Jersey, *Hell's Island*; Fife, *History of the 1st Battalion of CBs*, 42.
43 Lieutenant Mathis's comments are included, Camp Endicott Naval Construction Training Center, U.S. Navy Seabee Museum, 1945.
44 Command Summary of Fleet Admiral Chester W. Nimitz, USN, Nimitz "Graybook," Vol. 1, McCain Msg 10 1143 of July 10, 615; and McCain Msg 13 0021 of July 13, 1942, 618.
45 Op. cit. "War Diary of Harold W. Bauer," entry for July 15 and 18.
46 Fife, *History of the 1st Battalion of CBs*.
47 Wallin, "The Project Was Roses."
48 Marston Mat was a perforated steel planking system used to provide rapidly installed, durable, but temporary runways and landing strips. Camp Endicott Naval Construction Training Center, U.S. Navy Seabee Museum, 1945.
49 Gene Salecker, *Fortress Against the Sun* (Conshohocken, PA: Combined Publishing, 2001).
50 *The AAF in the South Pacific*; primary sources include individual 11th BG squadron reports: History 26th Bomb Squadron May–Dec. 1942; 42nd Bombardment Squadron (H) Missions: 18 July 1942–7 February 1943, AFHRA 44028; History of 98th Bombardment Squadron (H) (16 Dec. 1941 to 1 Apr.

ENDNOTES • 283

1944), SQ-Bomb-98-Hi, AFHRA IRIS 0044984, Reel A0575; History 431 Bombardment Squadron, AFHRA IRIS No. A0613, IRIS Ref. 00046721.
51 Operation Plan No. 1-42, Aircraft South Pacific Force, A4-3/A16-3, Serial 0016, July 25, 1942, in: AFHRA Sq-Bomb-Sq (H), History of the 98th Bomb Squadron (H), 16 Dec. 1941–1 April 1944. Also see W. M. Cleveland, *Grey Geese Calling, Pacific Air War History of the 11th Bombardment Group (H), 1940–1945* (Portsmouth, NH: W. M. Cleveland, 1992).
52 History 26th Bomb Squadron.
53 Command Summary of Fleet Admiral Chester W. Nimitz, USN, Nimitz "Graybook," McCain to Nimitz, Msgs 28 0539 and 28 1440, May 28, 1942.
54 Command Summary of Fleet Admiral Chester W. Nimitz, USN, Nimitz "Graybook," King to Ghormley, Msg 28 1830, July 28, 1942, 627.
55 Command Summary of Fleet Admiral Chester W. Nimitz, USN, Nimitz "Graybook," McCain to Comsopac, Cincpac, Msg 29 0041, July 29, 1942, 628.
56 Op. cit. "War Diary of Harold W. Bauer," entry for July 28; and Op. cit. *Hell's Island*, p. 106. Wallin's small Seabee Detachment would return to Efate in mid-August after being relieved by the 7th Naval Construction Battalion on August 11. In October, the 15th Naval Construction Battalion would also arrive at Santo to join in the construction program. Histories of the 7th and 15th Naval Construction Battalions, Naval History & Heritage Command, Washington Naval Yard.
57 The date of the arrival of the first B-17 is reported in some sources as July 30. The date cited above, July 29, is per Brown, "War Diary of Harold W. Bauer," History of the 26th Bombardment Squadron, and in Salecker, *Fortress Against the Sun*, 217. The first-arriving B-17 was piloted by Maj. Allan Sewart. Re Garrison's inclusion, see Ritchie Garrison, *Task Force 9156 and III Island Command: A Story of a South Pacific Advanced Base During World War II, Efate, New Hebrides* (Waban, MA.: 1983).
58 Command Summary of Fleet Admiral Chester W. Nimitz, USN, Nimitz "Graybook," Rose to McCain, Msg 29 0800, July 29, 1942. Garrison's inclusion in the flight was a great relief to the flight crew. Newly arrived in the South Pacific, the navigator had not previously flown to Santo, and was grateful that Garrison knew the way. Narrative History of Task Force 6814 and Americal Division, Jan. 23, 1942 to June 30, 1943, World War II Operational Documents (Fort Leavenworth, KS: Ike Skelton Combined Arms Research Library).
59 Cleveland, *Grey Geese Calling*.
60 Op. cit. Air Force Historical Study 101.
61 Source is Ltr, Gen. Harmon to Gen. Marshall, 9 Sep 42, Secret, cited in: Louis Morton, *The War in the Pacific*.
62 Operations in Pacific Ocean Areas—July 1943, ComInch, U.S. Pacific Fleet and Pacific Ocean Areas, Pac-J5-1p, A16-3/July, Serial 001349, 21 October 1943, NARA micro serial No. 65300.
63 History 26th, 42nd, and 98th Bomb Squadrons.
64 *Pacific Counterblow: the 11th Bombardment Group and the 67th Fighter Squadron in the battle for Guadalcanal: an interim report* (Washington, D.C.: Center for Air Force History, 1992).
65 *The Windsock*, Aviation Cadet Yearbook for Class 43-B (published by the Aviation Cadets of Class 43-B, Eleventh Army Air Force Flying Training Detachment, Tucson, AZ, September 1942).
66 The following paragraphs are taken from Robert Richardson, *Spying From the Sky: At the controls of US Cold War Aerial Intelligence* (Havertown, PA: Casemate Publishers, 2020) and are used here with permission of the author.
67 Students' Manual: Primary Flying book, United States Army Air Forces, Training Command, Date unknown.
68 Students' Manual, Primary Flying School, Army Air Forces Training Command, 1943.
69 Fagen Fighters WWII Museum, Granite Falls, Minnesota, https://fagenfighterswwiimuseum.org, March 24, 2024.
70 Op. cit. *The War Experiences of Arthur R Driedger Jr.*
71 Craven and Cate, *The Army Air Forces in World War II*.
72 Samuel Hynes, *Flights of Passage: Recollections of a World War II Aviator* (New York: Penguin, 2003).
73 Ibid.

74 Aviation Archaeology Investigation and Research, 7644 S. 15th Ave. Phoenix, AZ 85041; and Anthony J. Mireles, *Fatal Army Air Forces Aviation Accidents in the United States, 1941–1945* (London: McFarland & Co, 2006).
75 Data was obtained from Fold3, and was cross referenced with the databank at Aviation Archaeology Investigation & Research, at https://www.aviationarchaeology.com/src/db.asp.
76 Senior Pilot Log, L. G. Richardson, July 28, 1942.

Chapter 7

1 Admiral E. J. King, "Our Navy at War: A Report to the Secretary of the Navy Covering Our Peacetime Navy and Our Wartime Navy and including Combat Operations up to March, 1944," *US News,* March 1944), 34.
2 *History of US Naval Operations in World War II, Vol. V, The Struggle for Guadalcanal, August 1942–February 1943,* Samuel Eliot Morrison, Little, Brown and Company: 1949.
3 "Operation Watchtower: An Analysis in Operational Design", Scott D. Stewart, Naval War College, Newport, R.I., March 9, 1994.
4 Op. cit. Air Force Historical Study Study 101; and Gene Salecker, *Fortress Against the Sun* (Conshohocken, PA: Combined Publishing, 2001); and Craven and Cate, *The Pacific.*
5 Op. cit. "War Diary of Harold W. Bauer."
6 Periodic Intelligence Report, 1–28 Feb 1943, to CO of the 5th and 11th Bombardment Groups, USAF, Major Frank S. Owen, S-2.
7 W. M. Cleveland, *Grey Geese Calling, Pacific Air War History of the 11th Bombardment Group (H), 1940–1945* (Portsmouth, NH: W. M. Cleveland, 1992).
8 Ibid, Air Force Historical Study Study 101, and Op. cit. *The Army in the South Pacific.*
9 Op. cit., Air Force Historical Study 101; and Op. cit. "War Diary of Harold W. Bauer."
10 The 11th Bomb Group would be relieved of duty in the South Pacific in April 1943 and was replaced by the 307th Bomb Group, flying the longer-range B-24 heavy bombers. The 11th would be re-equipped with B-24s and return to combat in November.
11 Apologia. American libraries contain over 9,000 titles related to Guadalcanal, including books related to early American or Japanese strategic planning, firsthand accounts, and many retrospectives. How many more titles have been written but not acquired by library systems? Surely five times that number. The present work does not attempt to provide a narration for the exhaustive but ultimately successful ground campaign by the U.S. Marines and later the Army's Americal Division. Interested readers are referred to endnotes in this chapter, or to www.worldcat.org, keyword "Guadalcanal."
12 David E. Quantock, *Disaster at Savo Island, 1942* (United States Army, US Army War College, 2002).
13 Marine Corps Maj. Lofton Henderson commanded a dive bomber squadron during the Battle of Midway, and was the first naval aviator killed in that engagement.
14 History of the Sixth US Naval Construction Battalion, May 1942–March 1943, Battalion, Historical Information, Naval History & Heritage Command, Washington Naval Yard; and History of the 26th Bombardment Squadron, contained in AFHRA Reel A0544, 1144 and ff.
15 Op. cit. Vandergrift Summary Report: "During the First Marine Division's stay on Guadalcanal, aviation based there (Marine and Air Force) destroyed 416 Japanese planes and sank 21 enemy vessels against a loss of 78 planes in combat; the crews of about 50% being saved." Also see Guadalcanal and the Origins of the Thirteenth Air Force, Army Air Forces Historical Studies No. 35, Assistant Chief of Air Staff, Intelligence, July 1945.
16 Op. cit. *The Struggle for Guadalcanal.*
17 Command Summary, Ghormley to Nimitz and King, 17 0230, August 17, 1942.
18 Command Summary, entry for October 15, 1942, 1093.
19 Eventually, over thirty-six thousand Japanese ground forces and over sixty thousand American troops would be committed to the campaign. They would launch attack and counterattack in bitter and protracted jungle fighting that would continue for six months. Op. cit. The U.S. Navy and the Tokyo Express at Guadalcanal.

20 Op. cit. Vandergrift Summary Report.
21 Op. cit. Craven and Cate, *The Pacific*.
22 Op. cit. Narrative History of Task Force 6814. The Americal Division remain on Guadalcanal for the duration of the campaign, and left the island on April 6, 1943.
23 Capt. Robert Allen and 1st Lt. Otis Carney, "The Story of SCAT," *Air Transport* magazine, December 1944 (Pt I) and January 1945 (Pt II); and History of the 13th Troop Carrier Squadron, Dec 1940–Sept 1943, AFHRA IRIS No. 00073461; and Timothy L. Clubb, Cactus Air Power on Guadalcanal, US Army Command and General Staff College, 1996; History 13th TCS Oct 42–July 43, AFHRA 73464; and "Guadalcanal and the Origins of the 13th AF." The historical records for the 13th TCS, like many aviation units that operated in the South Pacific in the early months of the war in the Pacific, are occasionally inconsistent. The air echelon was the first element of every aviation unit to arrive in a theater of operations, which included flight crews and a handful of key ground and administrative personnel. Clerks were typically not included, with the result that until the arrival of the ground echelon, record keeping was often not of the first order. For example, even reports written by the intelligence officer of the 13th TCS and by the 403rd Group historian provide different dates for the arrival of the 13th TCS into the South Pacific theater of operations. Five primary sources and three secondary sources were consulted with the result that three different dates are reported for the arrival of the 13th TCS. Given the lack of consistency among several primary and secondary sources, the official squadron report written most proximal to the unit's arrival in the South Pacific will be used as the date of arrival; that date, taken from the September 3, 1943 Squadron Report, AFHRA IRIS No. 00073464, is October 10.
24 William H. Armstrong, *Marine Air Group 25 and SCAT*, Arcadia Publishing, 2017.
25 Ibid.
26 Robert C. Owen, *Air Mobility, A Brief History of the American Experience* (Potomac Books, Washington, D.C., 2013).
27 Letter, Gen. Harmon to Gen. Arnold, 2 Nov. 1942. Also see Memo, Harmon for Hanley, 8 Dec. 1942.
28 Op. cit. Guadalcanal and the Origins of the Thirteenth Air Force.
29 Cited in *Combat Crew Rotation, World War II and Korean War* (Historical Studies Branch, USAF Historical Division, January 1968).
30 Ibid. Policies governing crew rotation often changed during the war. In April 1943, the War Department gave each theater commander the authority to establish rest and rehabilitation policy for aircrews in their theaters. This led to a high degree of variability between the theaters, and ranged from fixed-mission (General Spaatz, Northwest African Air Force: 150 hours and 50 sorties for fighters, recce and light and medium bombers; 250 hours and 50 sorties for heavy bombers) to complex formula that considered number of months in theater, hours of flying time, and number of missions (General Twining, Thirteenth Air Force).
31 Periodic Intelligence Report, Joint Headquarters 5th and 11th Bombardment Groups, Office of Intelligence Officer, 1 March 1943, contained in Records of the 98th Bombardment Squadron, AFHRA IRIS No. 00044983 and ff, Reel No. A0575.
32 Major General Kiyotake Kawaguchi, IJA Commander, 35th Infantry Brigade at Guadalcanal, cited in many sources.
33 Casualty statistics and *matériel* losses are taken from Wikipedia ("Guadalcanal Campaign"). Information there is based on data from several reputable sources, and is considered reliable.
34 Operation Providence was MacArthur's plan to garrison the northeast coast of New Guinea, areas he would later have to fight hard to capture from entrenched Japanese forces.
35 Henry I. Shaw, Jr, *First Offensive, the Marine Campaign for Guadalcanal* (Marine Corps History and Museums Division, Supt. Docs, USGPO, 1992).

Chapter 8

1. Henry I. Shaw, Jr, *First Offensive, the Marine Campaign for Guadalcanal* (Marine Corps History and Museums Division, Supt. Docs, USGPO, 1992).
2. Based on the experiences of Marshall Stelzriede, a young cadet who had also washed out of pilot training and became a navigator. His training was almost exactly contemporary with Richardson's, and he underwent the same training programs and training stations as Richardson. Stelzriede served with the 96th Bomb Group, 338th Squadron, operating B-17 heavy bombers out of Snetteron Heath in England, with whom he completed a full tour of 25 combat missions. At that time in the war, the chances of completing a tour of duty with a heavy bomber unit were not good. See *The Experiences of a B-17 Navigator During World War II*, www.stelzriede.com/warstory.htm.
3. Craven & Cate, ed., *The Army Air Forces in World War II*, Volume Six, Men and Planes (Office of Air Force History, Washington, D.C., 1983).
4. 11th Army Air Force Flying Training Detachment, Ryan School of Aeronautics, Special Order No. 24, 14 Sept. 1942.
5. Flexible Gunnery Training in the AAF, Army Air Force Historical Study No. 31, Asst. Chief of Air Staff, Intelligence, Historical Division, March 1945.
6. A BB gun is a single shot, unrifled, air-powered gun that fires a steel projectile roughly the diameter of BB-sized lead birdshot—about .18 inch. Many of the aircrew cadets would have never fired a weapon of any kind and this small training firearm introduced them to the practice of shoulder mounting, aiming, leading, and firing.
7. Craven and Cate, *Men and Planes*.
8. SMSgt R.W. Holley "The Radio Operator-Gunner Enlisted Crewmember During WWII," Air Force Enlisted Heritage Research Institute File 100.104, February 19, 1992.
9. Headquarters, Las Vegas Army Gunnery School, Special Order No. 18, Jan. 18, 1943.
10. The Chiefs reaffirmed that Germany was the principal enemy, and defined the scope and intensity of the Allied war effort in the Pacific, to include in part: Preventing Japan from further expansion, and from consolidating and exploiting its current holding; maintaining the vital Midway–Hawaii line, and the critical Southern Supply Line; and attaining positions which menace enemy lines of communication with the Dutch East Indies, the Philippines, and the South China Sea. Conduct of the War in the Pacific Theater in 1943, Memorandum by U.S. Joint Chiefs of Staff, 22 January 1943 (CCS 168).
11. Craven and Cate, *Men and Planes*.
12. Stelzriede, *The Experiences of a B-17 Navigator During World War II*.
13. Individual Training of Navigators in the AAF, Army Air Forces Historical Studies: No. 27.
14. Craven and Cate, *Men and Planes*.
15. Ibid.
16. Special Orders No. 112, Army Air Forces Advanced Flying School, Mather Field, 7 May 1943.
17. Headquarters, Army Air Forces West Coast Training Center, Santa Ana, CA. 8 May 1943, Thos. Al. Lee, Major, AC, Acting Asst Adjutant General.
18. This program normally led to a commission into the AAF, but by October 1943 the AAF requirements for meteorological officers had been met, and the Grand Rapids program was closed. Norman Richardson reverted to the enlisted ranks, was assigned to the 75th AAF Base Unit, and served the balance of the war 'Stateside, He was discharged in November 1945 at the rank of sergeant.
19. Shipping Ticket, AAF Navigation Training School, May 5, 1943, Kit Navigation Celestial, per T.O. 00-30-6.
20. Document reference not available. Date of issuance May 8, 1943. Also included were B-4 and A-3 bags, sunglasses, winter gloves, goggle assembly, an A-10 oxygen mask, a 24-inch seat-type parachute, a winter vest, a B-4 life vest, and a sweater.
21. 430522 letter, Richardson to parents. (Personal correspondence from Richardson is labelled in the YYMMDD format.)
22. Immunization Register, Leonard G. Richardson.

23 Special Orders No. 125, AAF navigation School, Mather Field, 22 May 1943. The other eight navigators were: George W. Bamberger, Railey G. Boydston, Carl M. Gonder, Jack W. Hauan, Richard O. Kraemer, Bryce E. Sammon, Edward J. Seliga, and Philip M. Smith.
24 Station Hospital, Basic Training Center (No. 5), AAF Technical Training Command, May 26, 1943.
25 Special Orders No. 146, HQ, Basic Training Center (No. 5), AAF Technical Training Command, Kearns, Utah, May 26, 1943.
26 Special Order No. 152, Headquarters, Basic Training Center (No. 5), AAF Technical Training Command, June 1, 1943, Assignment to Shipment AJ-707-E.
27 Bruce A. Ashcroft, et al., *History of Air Education and Training Command, 1942–2002* (Office of History and Research Headquarters, Air Education and Training Command, Randolph Air Force Base, Texas, 2005).
28 Base Facilities Summary, Advance Bases, South Pacific Area, 30 June 1945, Commander in Chief, US Pacific Fleet and Pacific Ocean Areas, 6 August 1945.
29 Op. cit. *The Logistics of Advance Bases.*
30 Operations in Pacific Ocean Areas–July 1943, ComInch, U.S. Pacific Fleet and Pacific Ocean Areas, Pac-J5-1p, A16-3/July, Serial 001349, 21 October 1943, NARA micro serial No. 65300.
31 Op. cit. Building the Navy's Bases; and 6th Naval Construction Battalion, Historical Information, Naval History and Heritage Command; and George Syer, *The Amphibians Came To Conquer, The Story of Admiral Richmond Turner*, Chapter 11, U.S. Dept. of the Navy, 1972.
    The arriving Navy Convoy PW2111 included the vessels USS *Wharton*, SS *Del Brazil*, SS *President Polk*, and SS *Santa Anna*. See: War Diary, USS *Gamble*, August 11, 1942, NARA 4697018, Micro Serial No. 42944.
32 7th Naval Construction Battalion, Historical Information, Naval History & Heritage Command.
33 Op. cit. *Military Postal History.*
34 Op. cit. *Naval History of Espiritu Santo.*
35 War Diary, U.S. Acorn (Red) Two, 9 Oct 1942–31 Oct 1942, NARA 4697018, Micro Serial No. 44554, Fold 3 image 267831861; and 15th Naval Construction Battalion, Historical Information, Naval History and Heritage Command; op. cit. Naval History of Espiritu Santo; and Building the Navy's Bases in WWII: History of the Bureau of Yards and Docks and the Civil Engineer Corps, 1940–1946, Dept. of the Navy; and op. cit. War Diary, U.S. Acorn (Red) Two.
36 War Diary, Twelfth Naval District, 8 September 1942, NARA 4697018, Serial No. 3280-06; and War Diary, U.S. Acorn (Red) Two, 9 Sept 1942–8 October 1942, NARA 4697018, Micro Serial No. 44036.
37 The Station List for Base Button, August 15, 1943, includes the 5th Construction Regiment, with the 7th, 15th, 36th, 40th, 11th, and 57th Construction Battalions and a Detachment from the 1007th CB. Op. cit. Military Postal History.
38 Op. cit. *History of the 7th CB*. Sixteen months after its arrival at Santo, and with its work done, the 7th departed Santo on November 20, 1943, for a much-deserved rest back in the States. Op. cit. *Building the Navy's Bases.*
39 In World War II, the Seabees were organized into 151 regular construction battalions, 39 special construction battalions, 164 construction battalion detachments, 136 construction battalion maintenance units, five pontoon assembly detachments, 54 regiments, 12 brigades, and under various designations, five naval construction forces. Roughly 80% of the Seabees deployed to the Pacific Theater. In the North, Central, South and Southwest Pacific areas, the Seabees would eventually build 111 major airfields, 441 wharves and piers, 2,558 ammunition magazines, 700 square blocks of warehouses, hospitals to serve 70,000 patients, tanks for the storage of 100 million gallons of fuel, and housing for 1,500,000 men. Op. cit. Building the Navy's Bases.
40 Op. cit. *Military Postal History*. See also: *Naval History of Espiritu Santo*, New Hebrides, D. W. Kralovec, Base Historian, 1945.
41 Pacific War Online Encyclopedia, Kent Budge, 2010, see: www.pwencycl.kgbudge.com/E/s/Espiritu_Santo.htm.
42 Enemy Action Against Base Button are recorded on October 15 and 22 and November 18, 1942, then in 1943 January 21–22, 22–23, 27–28, February 21–22, May 23–24, 41, June 17, 24, August 10,

24, 31, September 14–15, October 14. Notes from the Army History of Espiritu Santo as compiled in the S-2 Office of the IV Island Army Command, History of Air Center Command Espiritu Santo, contained in Secret General Administrative Files, 1942–1946, Airfield Data #1, ARC#5923148; War Diary, US Acorn (Red) Two, 9 Oct 1942–31 Oct 1942, NARA 4697018, Micro Serial No. 44554; Op. cit. Kralovec; Air Force Historical Research Agency. U.S. Air Force. Maxwell AFB, AL. Unit history. *29 Air Service Group, Palm Tree a Historical Record of the 29 Air Service Group*. Chester J. Jansen. Franklin Printing, Grand Haven, MI. 1983; Historical Record of Headquarters 4th Photographic Group, Quarterly Report, 1 April 1943–30 June 1943; 430918 Report on Bombing of Espiritu Santo USNR 615.
43   Op. cit. *29 Air Service Group, Palm Tree.*
44   Op. cit. *To Kill a Bird.*
45   Op. cit. *Naval History of Espiritu Santo.*
46   James Michener, *Tales of the South Pacific* (Macmillan Publishing, 1947).
47   Ibid.
48   Op. cit. *Naval History of Espiritu Santo.*
49   Ritchie Garrison, *Task Force 9156 and III Island Command: A Story of a South Pacific Advanced Base During World War II, Efate, New Hebrides* (Waban, MA., 1983).
50   At the age of 18, William I. Rose enlisted in the 9th Infantry Regiment (Mass.) and served under General Blackjack Pershing against Pancho Villa in the 1916 Mexican Punitive Expedition. The 9th was soon redesignated the 101st Infantry and would become the first National Guard unit of the American Expeditionary Force to arrive in France, and the first to enter frontline combat. During the war, the 101st fought in several major battles along the Western Front, including the second Battle of the Marne, and the Battle of Saint-Mihel, and Rose received a field commission just before the massive Meuse-Argonne Offensive. At war's end he had been promoted to 1st lieutenant and accepted a commission with the peacetime Massachusetts National Guard. In January 1937 he was in command of the 51st Infantry Brigade (Mass) when it was ordered into Federal Service in January, 1941 and was in overall command of Task Force 6814, including the 51st, during its assembly and transit to New Caledonia. Following his assignment as commanding general at Efate and later Espiritu Santo, General Rose commanded the invasion of Woodlock Island during America's Northern Solomons Campaign before returning as Island Commander at New Caledonia. Gen. Rose returned to the States in 1944 and after his promotion to major general, commanded the 26th Infantry Division (Mass.) until his retirement in 1951. He died on June 9, 1954.

Chapter 9

1   "A Declaration of Rights &C, Constitution of North Carolina, December 18, 1776."
2   The organization of state militias, and the president's authority to "call out" the militias were first established by Congress with the Militia Acts of 1792. All free, able-bodied male citizens between the ages of 18 and 45 were required to enroll in the militia of their respective states. The extent to which these state militias, also referred to as state National Guards, were subject to federal control—the subject of decades-long debates—was resolved in the Military Act of 1903. That act created the United States National Guard, predecessor to the National Guard of the modern era, and codified when the state National Guards could be federalized. The National Guard became the administrative organization for military reserves in the United States, with each state continuing to operate state National Guards. The National Defense Act of 1916 allowed the president to draft state Guard troops into the regular Army, and with the passage of the National Guard Mobilization Act in 1933, Congress mandated that all federally-funded soldiers accept a dual enlistment or commission into both the state National Guard and the National Guard of the United States. The modern National Guard effectively dates from that act.
3   Record of the Services of Illinois Soldiers in the Black Hawk War, 1831–1832; and, The Mexican War, 1846–8," Appendix, by Isaac H. Elliott, 1882; and Levering Family History, Col. John Levering,

ENDNOTES • 289

1897, part of the Nelson R. Tennis Family Tree, ref. wc.rootsweb.ancestry.com. According to author Curtis Craver, this group was the original 129th Infantry Regiment, and was designated at that time as the 3rd Regiment, Illinois Militia. Craver is the uncredited author of *The 129th Infantry in WWII* (Infantry Journal Press: Washington, 1947).

4   Ibid; and, Record of the Services, Orders No. 302, May 28, 1847, Headquarters, Brig-Gen. Wool. Craver disagrees, writing that on July 2, 1846 at Alton, Il; Illinois Adjutant General's Report, Regimental and Unit Histories, Containing Reports for the Years 1861–1866; http://civilwar.illinoisgenweb.org/battles/index.html and http://www.civil-war.net/pages/troops_furnished_losses.html; Army Lineage Book: Infantry, Vol. 2, US Dept. of the Army, Office of Military History, U.S. GPO 1953; Illinois Adjutant General's Report, Regimental and Unit Histories, Containing Reports for the Years 1861-1866; Historical Lineage, Illinois National Guard and Illinois Naval Militia, Military and Naval Department, State of Illinois, July 1953.
5   Executive Order No. 8633, History, 129th Infantry Regiment (Rifle) from March 5, 1941 to October 1, 1942, Headquarters 129th Infantry, Vatukoula Area, Fiji, 2 October 1942.
6   Holdridge O. Collins, *History of the Illinois National Guard* (Black and Beach Press, 1884); and Inventory of the Illinois National Guard, 3rd Regiment, 129th U.S. Infantry, Regional History Center, RC 204.
7   Regimental Staff, *The 129th Infantry in World War II* (Infantry Journal Press, 1947), unattributed author Curtis Craver.
8   Colonel Morris John Naudts, *Memoirs*, US Army Infantry, 1914–1994, unpublished, undated.
9   US Census for 1940; In 1942, the 129th Infantry Regiment was organized under Table of Organization 7-11 dated 1 April 42. By the time the 129th would be stationed at Espiritu Santo, a new Table of Organization would be in place, dated 15 July 1943. The new TO significantly increased the number of officers and enlisted men, "to absorb expected combat losses." Virgil Ney, *Evolution of the US Army Infantry Battalion: 1939–1969*, Combat Operations Research Group, CORG-M-343, October 1969.
10 Robert R. Palmer, et al., *Procurement and Training of Ground Combat Troops*, Center of Military History, Washington, D.C., 1991; and Roger K Spickelmier, *Training of the American Soldier During WWI and WWII*, Fort Leavenworth, KS: US Army Command and General Staff College, 1987.
11 Op. cit. Naudts, *Memoirs*.
12 Op. cit. *The 129th Infantry in World War II*.
13 ROTC = Reserve Officers' Training Corps; OCS = Officer Candidate School.
14 Op. cit. Naudts, *Memoirs*.
15 History, 129th Infantry Regiment (Rifle) from March 5 to Oct. 1, 1942, HQ 129th Infantry, 2 October, 1942.
16 Op. cit. *The 129th Infantry in World War II*.
17 Op. cit. Naudts, *Memoirs*.
18 The U.S. Army owned or controlled a vast naval fleet. Some vessels were Army owned, others were allocated by the War Shipping Administration, and others were "bareboat" or "time" charters. Included were 1,557 troop and cargo transport ships that were designated United States Army Transports (USAT). In total, the Army operated almost 128,000 vessels of all types and designs, which, in addition to the USAT ships, included hospital ships (108), freight and supply ships (511), tugs (4,300), launches (over five thousand), and nearly twenty-six thousand amphibious assault craft. David Grover, *U.S. Army Ships and Watercraft of World War II* (Naval Institute Press, 1987).
19 One of its regiments—the 147th—had been sent to Tonga as part of that island's defensive force, and the assignment of the 129th returned the division to a three-regiment, "triangularized" organization; For a history of the 37th Infantry, see Tyler R. Webb, *The Battling Buckeyes of the 37th Infantry Division*, Ohio State University, 2018, unpublished.
20 Table of Organization 7-11, Infantry Regiment, April 1, 1942, War Department; note that there would have been some discrepancies from the T/O due to last-minute reassignments, illness, etc.
21 Op. cit. *The 129th Infantry in World War II*.
22 John Kennedy Ohl, *Minuteman, the Military Career of General Robert S. Beightler* (Boulder, CO: Lynne Rienner Publishers, 2001).
23 Op. cit. *The 129th Infantry in World War II*.

24 Op. cit. *The 129th Infantry in World War II*.
25 War Diary, USS *Hunter Liggett*, from 1 October 1942 to 30 Sept. 1943, National Archives catalog ID 4697018; and 182nd Infantry History, 1942–1944, Eisenhower Library, Project 735035, Box 1420. In April, the remaining elements of the 37th ID would depart Fiji and take up station on Guadalcanal in preparation for a combat assignment as part of the Munda Campaign.
26 Op. cit. *The 129th Infantry in World War II*.
27 Command Summaries, Vol. 2, Msg 11 1802, 919; and Command Summaries, Vol. 2, August 29, Msg 1304, 814.
28 K. Graham Fuschak, *The 43rd Infantry Division: Unit Cohesion and Neuropsychiatric Casualties* (Fort Leavenworth, KS: 1999, unpublished).
29 Op. cit. *The Army in the South Pacific*.
30 Command Summaries, Vol. 2, 964, October 28, 1942, Msg 0921 from Commander Naval Unit Button to COMSOPAC; Command Summaries, December 3, 1942, COMSOPAC to COMINCH, Msg 2127, Volume 2, 1193.
31 Cited in Fuschak, *The 43rd Infantry Division*, and elsewhere.
32 The figure 591 pounds is cited frequently, as for example, in Dennis Cline, *Skeeter Beaters: Memories of the South Pacific, 1941–1945* (DeForest Press, 2002); and Peter Stone, *The Lady and the President: The Life and Loss of the S.S. President Coolidge* (Yarram, Vic: Oceans Enterprises, 1997). Sources are not provided in these, and many other postwar documents. It is also reported that the loss of the shipment of quinine led to a hastening of the introduction of atabrine as a quinine-substitute. Stone, *The Lady and the President*.
33 Op. cit. Louis Morton, *The War in the Pacific*.
34 Op. cit. War Diary, USS *Hunter Liggett*.
35 Op. cit. *The 129th Infantry in World War II*.
36 Ibid.
37 Op. cit. Naudts, *Memoirs*.
38 Ibid.
39 Op. cit. *The 129th Infantry in World War II*.
40 Ibid.
41 Observer Report of Lt. Col. Louis A. Walsh, Infantry (Parachute) Covering the South Pacific Area, March 13, 1943, HQ Army Gound Forces, 319.1/38.
42 Op. cit. Naudts, *Memoirs*.
43 Ibid.
44 Ibid.
45 Op. cit. Naval History, Chapter XXX, Base Malaria and Epidemic Control; and Robert J. T. Joy, "Malaria in American Troops in the South and Southwest Pacific in World War II," *Medical History*, Vol. 43, 1999, p.192.
46 Op. cit. *Naval History*.
47 Director General of British Army Medical Services Sir Neil Cantlie, cited in Maj. Peter J. Weina MC USA, "From Atabrine in World War II to Mefloquine in Somalia: The Role of Education in Preventive Medicine, *Military Medicine*, 163, 9:635, 1998.
48 Op. cit. Naudts, *Memoirs*.
49 Op. cit. *Malaria in American Troops*.
50 Op. cit. Naudts, *Memoirs*.
51 Epidemiological Observations On the Trend of the Dengue Fever Epidemic, August 1943. Contained in NARA, RG 0313, SOPAC Force Med. Officer/Malaria & Epidemic Disease Control, NARA ARC record no. 5722964NARA, ARC #5722964.
52 Dengue was hardly unknown to American epidemiologists. It first was described in 1780 during an outbreak in Philadelphia, erupted again in the United States in 1922 with more than 1 million cases, and flared again in 1924.
53 On average, the number of days spent in hospital or confined to quarters for admissions or readmissions due to malaria in 1943 was 25 days.

54 Internal Medicine in World War II, Vo. II, Infectious Diseases, John Coates, Ed. In Chief, Office of the Surgeon General, Dept. of the Army, Washington, D.C., 1963; Op. cit. 29th Air Service Group, *Palm Tree*.
55 Op. cit. 129th Infantry in World War II; and Entomological Aspects of the Dengue Epidemic, contained in NARA, RG 0313, SOPAC Force Med. Officer/Malaria & Epidemic Disease Control, NARA ARC record no. 5722964.
56 Sources include: D. W. Kralovec, *Naval History of Espiritu Santo, New Hebrides* (1945); *Preventive Medicine in World War II, Vol. VI, Communicable Diseases* (Office of the Surgeon General, 1963); Robert Gibbons, et al., "Dengue and US Military Operations from the Spanish-American War through Today," in *Emerging Infectious Diseases*, Vol. 18, No. 4, April 2012; Franz H. Stewart, Lt. Cdr, USNR, "Dengue—Clinical Syndrome," Medical Staff, US Naval Base Hospital #6, NARA, ARC #5722964; and Op. cit. *Entomological Aspects of the Dengue Epidemic*.
57 Op. cit. *Preventive Medicine in World War II*, p. 425.
58 Op. cit. *Naval History*, p. 431; and Op. cit. "Current Research Activities and Monthly Malaria Report." Base Malaria & Epidemic Disease Control Unit, Espiritu Santo, August 1943.

Chapter 10

1 *New York Times*, January 11, 1942; and, NavSource Naval History, http://www.navsource.org/archives/30/13/13052.htm; and Troopships of World War II, Roland Charles, Army Transport Association, 1947.
2 Log Book, USS *Lawrence*, June 1–June 30, 1943, NARA Micro Series 51844, Reel A428.
3 US Merchant Ships Sunk or Damaged in World War II, American Merchant Marine at War, see: http://www.usmm.org/shipsunkdamaged.html) On the night of 22/23 June, the Liberty ships *Aludra* and *Deimos* were torpedoed while en route from Guadalcanal to ports south. Both ships were lost.
4 NavSource, Naval History, US Navy Losses World War II, Dec 41–October 45, see: http://www.navsource.org/Naval/losses.htm#bb; and War Diary USS *Woodworth*, 6/1–30, 1943, NARA Catalog ID 4697018, micro serial number 52138.
5 War Diary and Operational Record of USS *Kenmore* (AP 62), 1–30 June 1943, NARA Identifier 4697018.
6 Log Book, Operational Remarks, USS *Warrington* (DL 383), 1–30 June 1943, NARA Micro Serial No. 53006, Reel A467).
7 Pocket Guide to New Caledonia, Special Service Division, Services of Supply, US Army, US Government Printing Office, 1943.
8 Officially the "Army Micro Photographic Mail Service, V-mail was a process in which letters were written on a standardized sheet of stationery supplied free of charge by the Post Office.

The page was photographed on 16 mm film and shipped overseas in film canisters where it was developed, printed back to paper and delivered. All major overseas bases, including New Caledonia and Espiritu Santo had V-mail processing units. Welcome as it was, V-mail was imperfect. The single 7×9 inch page limited the size of the message to 300 words or so, and the reproduced photo prints delivered to the addressee were just over 4×5 inches in size, making some V-mail unreadable. V-mail initially could not include an enclosure – no family photos! – and lipstick kisses on the original – termed the "scarlet scourge – would jam the machines used to film the letters. And it was censored. But even with these limitations, over 1 billion V-mails were processed in the three-and-a-half years of its use and the space savings were enormous: A single bag containing V-mail film would replace 37 mail bags of regular letters.

9 430627 V-mail, Richardson to parents.
10 George Bamberger, interview by Eric Tenbus, transcript June 6, 2000, Reichelt Oral History Program, Item 44, HPUA-2015-00R. Florida State University Special Collections & Archives.
11 430707 V-mail to family.
12 Op. cit. Bamberger.

13 War Diary, USS *Lawrence*, NARA Catalog Item 4697018; War Diary of USS *Warrington* (CL 383), 5/1/43 to 7/31/43, NARA 4697018. After discharging its contingent of troops at Noumea, *Puebla* continued to Espiritu Santo where it underwent a month of repairs. *Puebla* continued to be a challenge for the Navy because of the need to fabricate large components for its foreign-made engines. Just a few months after its repairs at Espiritu Santo, the ship would report to Hawaii for additional repairs that would take a year to complete. See Roland W. Charles, *Troopships of World War II* (Washington, D.C.: Army Transportation Association, 1947).

14 As a general reference, see: Narrative History of Task Force 6814 Americal Division Jan. 23, 1942 to June 30, 1943.

15 Op. cit. Pocket Guide; and Op. cit. *From Fiji through the Philippines*.

16 The 1936 census of New Caledonia includes 2,872 French (born in France), 12,600 French (born in New Cal), Aussie and British 32, Indo-Chinese and Javanese 6,666, and 32,883 New Cal natives. Op. cit. Advanced Bases South Pacific, Inspection Report of.

17 Op. cit. *From Fiji Through the Philippines*.

18 4th Photo Gp and 17th PRS: AFHRA 00098913, Historical Record of Headquarters 4th Photographic Group, 24 July 1942–31 Dec 1942; and Maurer Maurer, ed., *Air Force Combat Units of World War II* (Washington, D.C.: Office of Air Force History, 1983); and Maurer Maurer, ed., *Combat Squadrons of the Air Force, World War II* (Washington, D.C.: Office of Air Force History, 1982).

19 The construction work at PDG had been started by a civilian contractor, but had been completed by the 810th Engineer Aviation Battalion. The 810th was also responsible for the later rebuild of Carney Field on Guadalcanal. Op. cit. *Operations of Aviation Engineers*. Op. cit. *From Fiji through the Philippines*.

20 Building the Navy's Bases in World War II: History of the Bureau of Yards and Docks and the Civil Engineer Corps, 1940–1946, Department of the Navy, Ch. 24; and Op. cit. Advanced Bases South Pacific, Inspection Report of, and Operations of Aviation Engineers in the South Pacific, AFHRA Iris No. 753.01-1, Reel A7711, records of the XIII AF Service Command. The upgrading of Tontouta was largely the work of the 811th Engineer Aviation Battalion, which had arrived at New Caledonia with Task Force 6814. See Craven and Cate, *The Army Air Forces in WWII*, Vol VII, Services Around the World, Chapter 10, Aviation Engineers in the War with Japan; and Ulysses Lee, *The Employment of Negro Troops*, Center of Military History, CMH Pub 11-4-1, Washington, 2001.

21 Weekly Status and Operations Report, 13th Troop Carrier Squadron, contained in AFHRA SQ-TR-CARR-13-SV, IRIS 00073495.

22 The airfield was nearly 10 square miles in extent, and had been leased by the Army from its owner, Mr. August Creugnet, less than a year earlier at a monthly cost of 12,000 Francs—slightly less than $120. Op. cit. Operations of Aviation Engineers, Contract no. W 60 qm 340, 263.

23 Special Report for the Assistant Secretary of War for Air, Headquarters, Thirteenth Air Force, Office of the Engineer, 13th Air Depot, 14 Dec. 1943, contained in Reel A7711, AFSC Historical Monograph No. 17, Airfields of New Caledonia).

24 United States Army Air Forces, *The Crusaders, A History of the 42nd Bombardment Group (M)* (Army & Navy Pictorial Publishers, Baton Rouge, LA, 1946).

25 David R. Dresser, *World War II, A Veteran's Cartoon Diary*, Library of Commerce, Veterans History Project, October 26, 2011.

26 Op. cit. *The War from Coconut Square*.

27 Ibid.

28 New Caledonia was a malaria-free island and it was the Army's intention to keep it that way. Accordingly, all incoming flights, except those originating from aircraft carriers, were required to undergo a thorough insecticidal treatment after landing. Also excepted were aircraft that had been properly sprayed while en route to New Caledonia. The treatment applied to cargo, equipment, and baggage. Personnel exited the aircraft, which was treated and then closed for a period of not less than twenty minutes. Local Security Plan for Tontouta Air Base, 361st Base Headquarters, 30 August 1943, Contained in Records of the XIII Air Force Service Command, AFHRA document 753.01-2.

29 Op. cit. *From Fiji Through the Philippines*.

30 *Cairns (Australia) Post*, Wed 6 January 1943, 2.
31 Ibid.
32 Sean Brawley and Chris Dixon, *Hollywood's South Seas and the Pacific War, Searching for Dorothy Lamour* (Palgrave MacMillan, 2012).
33 Ibid, Pocket Guide.
34 43-0718 Letter, Richardson to parents.
35 430707 V-mail, Richardson to parents.
36 430707 Letter, Richardson to parents.
37 430709 V-mail, Richardson to parents.
38 Available records do not indicate if these flights were for the purposes of training and orientation, or were operational missions.
39 Date of incident June 8, 1943. Joe Baugher.com/navy_serials/thirdseries2.html, accessed March 26, 2024 See also https://aviation-safety.net/wikibase/340949 and William H. Armstrong, Marine Air Group 25 and SCAT (Arcadia Publishing, 2017).
40 Special Order 150, Headquarters, Sixth Replacement Depot, APO 502, July 25, 1943.
41 Thirteenth Air Force, Organization and Changes, Period 13 Jan 1943–30 June 1944, Historical Section, HQ Thirteenth Air Force, 24 July 1944. In Air Force Special Studies, Thirteenth Air Force Organizations & Changes, AFHRA Iris No. 00260882.
42 Op. cit. *From Fiji Through the Philippines*; and Thirteenth Air Force Losses of Aircraft, 1 July 1943 through 31 December 1943, AFHRA IRIS No. 00261207.
43 Op. cit. *From Fiji Through the Philippines*.
44 Thirteenth Air Force, Organization and Changes, Period 13 Jan 1943–30 June 1944, AFHRA Ref. 750.05-3; and General Order 135, Headquarters USAFISPA, June 6, 1943, Contained in Records of the XIII Air Force Service Command, AFHRA document 753.01-2; and General Order No. 9, June 6, 1943.
45 Special Order 180, Headquarters, Thirteenth Air Force, APO 719, August 1, 1943. On 19 Aug, the 403rd TCG and the 63rd and 64th TCS were assigned to the 13th AF Service Command, with station at Espiritu Santo, per General Order GO 27. Op. cit. AFHRA Iris No. 00260882.

Chapter 11

1 "Troop Carrier Groups of WWII," see http://www.troopcarrier.org/groups.html.
2 By the end of the war, the Army Air Force would operate 28 troop carrier groups and four combat cargo groups—in round numbers, 80,000 officers and enlisted men and 1,100 aircraft. Table of Organization and Equipment, No. 1-317, Troop Carrier Squadron, War Department, 16 August 1943; and Maurer Maurer, *Air Force Combat Units of World War II* (Washington D.C.: Office of Air Force History, 1983); and Troop Carrier/Tactical Airlift Association, at www.troopcarrier.org.
3 Marine Air Group 25, Official History, USMC, Washington, D.C., The DC3 Aviation Museum. See also Mae Mills Link and Hubert A. Coleman, *Medical Support of the Army Air Forces in World War II* (Washington: Office of the Surgeon General, USAF, 1955) for a second, and somewhat contrasting commentary on the date on which air medivac from Guadalcanal began.
4 *Two Years Pacific: Sandman: 403rd Troop Carrier Group*, by the Public Relations Staff, undated, contained in AFHRA Reel No. B0489.
5 Craven & Cates, editors, *The Army Air Forces in World War II* (University of Chicago Press, 1948–58), Vol. VI, Ch. 18, Combat Crew and Unit Training.
6 Narrative History of Headquarters, 403rd Troop Carrier Group from Activation thru 31 Dec. 1943, dated 8 May 1944, GP-403-HI (Tr Carr), AFHRA IRIS no. 00090198, Roll # B0489.
7 History of Organization from date of activation through 31 December 1943, 64th Troop Carrier Squadron, 403rd Troop Carrier Group, 1 June 1944, AFHRA IRIS 74682. Quotation is from Two Years Pacific Sandmen, 403rd Troop Carrier Group.
8 Biography of Brigadier General Harry J. Sands, Jr., contained in AFHRA IRIS No. 01105623.

9   Ibid, IRIS 74682.
10 Ibid, IRIS 74682; and Anthony Mireles, *Fatal Army Air Forces Aviation Accidents in the United States, 1941–1945*, Vols 1–3 (McFarland & Company, North Carolina, London).
11 Col. Jack Roessell, USAF, *Notes from the Pacific*, unpublished family memoir, 2007.
12 News accounts of the time reported 16 glider pilots were lost, but subsequent research confirms the correct number of losses was twelve glider pilots plus the crew of four.
13 Biography of Brigadier General Harry J. Sands, Jr.
14 Table of Organization and Equipment, T/O & E 1-317, Army Air Forces Troop Carrier Squadron, War Department document, 16 August 1943.
15 Dwight Eisenhower, *Crusade in Europe: A Personal Account of World War II* (Doubleday & Co.: 1948).
16 *Scientific American*, January 1935.
17 Irving B. Holley, *Buying Aircraft: Material Procurement for the Army Air Forces* (Center of Military History, 1964). As with many WWII statistics, production figures are reported variably. The DC-3/Dakota Historical Society reports 10,632 military versions of the DC-3 (C-47 et al) were built at Douglas factories in the United States, another 6,157 built under license in Russia, and 487 under license in Japan. See: DC-3/Dakota Historical Society, Sacramento, CA. and http://www.dc3history.org/home.html. Jennifer M. Gradidge reports 10,048 military C-47 and C-53 derivatives and 608 civilian variants of the DC-3 built at the three Douglas plants, with 4937 built in Russia and 487 in Japan. *The Douglas DC-1/DC-2/DC-3: The First Seventy Years, Volumes One and Two* (Tonbridge, Kent, UK).
18 Op. cit DC-3/Dakota History Society,
19 Ibid.
20 Michael Williams, "How health and safety rules have grounded the Dakota, the war workhorse," *Daily Mail*, February 25, 2008.
21 The ground echelon of the 65th and 66th Squadrons would depart San Francisco on/about July 26, aboard the vessel *Maui*, arriving at Brisbane on August 16. While afloat, the two squadrons had been assigned to the 54th Troop Carrier Wing, and were initially based at Port Moresby, New Guinea. In November 1943, they were reassigned to the 433rd TCG, and these two squadrons were reunited briefly with the 64th TCS when all were station at Nadzab, New Guinea. See: Interview with Joe Drastata, 65th Troop Carrier Squadron, Admiral Nimitz Historic Site, National Museum of the Pacific War, Center for Pacific Was Studies, Fredericksburg, Texas, August 5, 2002; and *Combat Squadrons of the Air Force in World War II*; and History of the 64th TCS, March 1944, AFHRA Iris No. 74685.
22 History of Organization, 64th Troop Carrier Squadron, undated, AFHRA document 00074681, SQ-TR-Carrier-64-Hi.
23 The older aircraft were the C-47-DL version. The main difference between these two variants is that the C-47A featured an upgraded, 24-volt electrical system. Op. cit. Joe Baugher.
24 Special Order No. 181, Headquarters, 403rd Troop Carrier Group, Baer Field, Ft. Wayne, Ind. 12 July 1943; and 90198 403rd TC Gp History.
25 Op. cit. Joe Baugher.
26 Roessell, *Notes from the Pacific*.
27 Op. cit. History of Organization, AFHRA 74681; and, Squadron Morning Reports, July 18–24, 1943, 64th Troop Carrier Squadron.
28 Historical Data, Headquarters, 403rd Troop Carrier Group, AAF, 30 September 1943, AFHRA IRIS no. 90199; Information related to ship sailing included in War Diary for August 1943, Commander, Western Sea Frontier, 28 October 1943, NARA archives 4697018.
29 Historical Data and Record of the 63rd TCS, 12 Dec. 1942 to 31 Dec. 1943, AFHRA Iris No. 74648.
30 Ibid; and Morning Report, September 3, 1943, 64th Troop Carrier Squadron.
31 Historical Data, 63rd Troop Carrier Squadron, AFHRA 74649; and War Diary, Month of September 1943, from Commander Destroyer Division Twelve, National Archives, NARA Identifier 4697018, Micro Serial No. 57259; and War Diary, US Naval Advance Base Nay 140, Ship Movements—15 September, 1943, J. E. Boak, Commanding, contained in RG 38 Records of the Office of the Chief of

Naval Operations; and Report on Activities of the 403rd Troop Carrier Group, Ltr, Hq 403rd Troop Carrier Group, 11 November 1943, F. A. Quinn, Lt. Col, Air Corps, AFHRA Iris No. 90200.
32 Op. cit. *Two Years Pacific: Sandman.*

Chapter 12

1 History of Organization, 64th Troop Carrier Squadron, 403rd Troop Carrier Group, 1 June 1944, AFHRA document SQ-TR-CARR-64-HI, IRIS No. 00074682; and Special Order No. 181, Headquarters, 403rd Troop Carrier Group, Baer Field, Ft. Wayne, Ind. 12 July 1943.
2 Historical Data, 63rd Troop Carrier Squadron, July 31, 1943, AFHRA Iris No. 74649, 12 Dec. 1942–Sep 1943. Note that a different report has them arriving on Aug 8. See XIII Air Force Service Command Unit Movement Data, contained in AFHRA Reel 7712, 733.
3 The 13th ADG was originally assigned to the Services of Supply, South Pacific Area (SOS SPA). On June 6th 1943 it was reassigned to the Thirteenth Air Force with no change of station. General Order No. 135, Headquarters, USAFISPA. Also see History 403rd Troop Carrier Group, AFHRA Iris No. 90198.
4 Special Orders No. 180, Thirteenth Air Force, August 1, 1943.
5 History of the 63rd TCS, SQ-TR-CARR-63-HI, AFHRA Iris Nos. 74649, and 74648; it is regrettable, and exceptional, that the records of the 64th TCS held by the National Archives have gone missing. But it is gratifying that the squadron's records at the Air Force Historical Research Agency are intact. The records of the 63rd squadron are quite intact at both the National Archives and the Air Force Historical Research Agency.
6 430728 Letter, Richardson to parents. Personal correspondence from Richardson is labelled in the YYMMDD format.
7 Col. Jack Roessell, USAF, *Notes from the Pacific*, unpublished family memoir, 2007.
8 430805 Letter, Richardson to parents.
9 430810 Letter, Richardson to parents.
10 "Duties and Responsibilities of the Navigator," excerpt from the *Pilot Training Manual for the B-17 Flying Fortress.*
11 XIII Air Force Service Command, Historical Monographs, Number 25, History XIII Air Force Service Command, organizational and Administrative History, 31 Jan. 1946, Contained in Records of the XIII Air Force Service Command, AFHRA document 753.01-2.
12 General Orders No. 27, Headquarters, Thirteenth Air Force, August 19, 1943. AFHRA Reel A7644, 13th AF Messages, Bulletins, Circulars, Letters, Memorandum,General Orders, 1133; Also, *Two Years Pacific: Sandman*, 10; and Sam McGowan, *Anything, Anywhere, Anytime: Tactical Airlift in the US Army Air Forces and US Air Force from World War II to Vietnam* (Authorhouse, 2012); And Special Studies, Thirteenth Air Force Organizations & Changes, AFHRA 650.04-3, 13 Jan 1943–20 June 1944.
13 Vanuatu is an archipelago, defined as a group of islands, interconnecting waters, and other natural features that are closely interrelated and form an intrinsic geographical, economic, and political entity. The Archipelagic Claim is the land and sea area roughly encompassed by the outermost points of each island in the archipelago. For Vanuatu, the scope of its Archipelagic Claim is 31,163 square miles, of which 4,706 square miles is land. International Law Studies, Archipelagic States, Stockton Center for International Law, Vol. 97, 2021; and, Limits in the Seas, No. 137, Vanuatu, Archipelagic and other Maritime Claims and Boundaries, United States Department of State, Bureau of Oceans and International Environmental and Scientific Affairs, 2014.
14 "National Geospatial Intelligence Agency," as presented in *Geographical Names.org*, at https://www.geographic.org/geographic_names/name.php?uni=-).
15 Op. cit. Speiser.
16 The 64th arrived at Santo before the hard copy of orders assigning it to the XIII Air Force Service command were received—a common situation at that time in the war. See Unit Organization and Administrative History, XIII Air Force Service Command, AFHRA Reel No. A7712, 398; and History 403rd Troop Carrier Group, AFHRA IRIS NO. 90198.

17 War Diary, USS *Colorado*, 1 August 1943, NARA 4697018; War Diary, USS *Maryland*, 1 August 1943, NARA 4697018; War Diary, U.S. Naval Advance Base, Espiritu Santo, New Hebrides Island, August 1943, NARA 4697018; War Diary, U.S. Naval Advance Base, Navy 140, contained in RG 38 Records of the Office of the Chief of Naval Operations, Box 465.
18 Op. cit. Kralovec, *A Naval History of Espiritu Santo*.
19 For an identification of facilities in place on Santo at the time the 64th TCS arrived, see documents contained in NARA RG 0313, Naval Operating Forces, South Pacific Area & Force (SOPAC)/(Red 179), Secret General Administrative Files; 1942–1945.
20 Report on Observations in the South Pacific Theater of Operations, 15 January 1944, Merrill E. DeLonge, Major, Technical Staff, The Engineer Board, Fort Belvoir, VA.
21 Weekly Activity Report, 31 July to 7 August 1943, 394th BS, 5th BG, AFHRA Iris No. 77497; WSOR 394th BS, Feb 43–March 45, AFHRA Iris No.46193; WSOR, 23rd Bomb Squadron, 5th Bomb Group, July 26–August 1, 1943 and Aug. 9–Aug 15th, 1943; and WSOR Sept. 6–Sept 12, AFHRA Iris No. 43687.
22 Like many other aviation units, the 18th Photographic Squadron was new in the theater. Still, between April and mid-June its aircraft had mapped the New Hebrides Islands, a good portion of the Solomons, and New Caledonia and the Loyalty Islands. In '42 and '43, the 18th was equipped with various aircraft, including the recon versions of the P-38, B-24 and B-25 aircraft. But when the 403rd arrived at Pekoa, the 18th had no planes. It's three B-25 heavy recon aircraft, and their crews had been on loan to the Fifth Air Force in Australia, but by the end of August, all three were back with the 18th, flying mapping missions out of Pekoa.
23 Report to the Commanding Officer, 5th BG, Special Search Missions, 8 Sept. 1943, 8 Sept 1943, and Weekly Status and Operations Reports for July–October, 1943, contained in AFHRA 43686. Also, XIII Air Force Service Command Unit Movement Data, contained in AFHRA Reel 7712, 733. See also Maurer Maurer, *Air Force Combat Units of World War II* (Washington, D.C.: Office of Air Force History, 1983).
24 History of the 307th Bomb Group, 15 Apr 1942 to Dec 1943, AFHRA 81874 and July–Sep 1943, AFHRA 81878.
25 Kralovec, *Naval History of Espiritu Santo*.
26 Location of U.S. Naval Aircraft, 17 August 1943, Op-40-A-KB (SC) A4-3/VZ.
27 History of Naval Air Transport Service, Pacific, NATSP/A12(2), AT-2.2/h1, Serial 0267, NARA RG 0313, Micro Serial No. 158913, https://www.fold3.com/image/302079582 and ff. The NATS facility at Santo was the destination of a large percentage of South Pacific cargo and was the terminus of southbound flight schedules. From Santo, short-haul flights to established South Pacific stations would complete the final distribution of personnel, cargo, and mail.
28 Kralovec, *Naval History of Espiritu Santo*; and Location of U.S. Naval Aircraft.
29 History XIII Air Force Service Command, Historical Monograph No. 21, Air Service Operations, South Pacific, to Dec. 31, 1943, AFHRA Reel No. A7712, 347. See also, *The Army Air Force in the South Pacific*, to October 1942, and Op. cit. US Air Force Historical Study No. 101, Historical Division, December 1944.
30 Among many useful sources are: Narrative History Thirteenth Troop Carrier Squadron, 11 May 1944, AFHRA IRIS NO. 00073462; Interrogation of Officer Returned from Overseas Theater of Operations, I Troop Carrier Command, 23 July 1943, AFHRA IRIS No. 00073496; and Historical Record of the Thirteenth Troop Carrier Squadron, 10 October 1942 to 31 July 1943, 3 Sept. 1943, Thirteenth Troop Carrier Squadron, in AFHRA IRIS NO. 00073464.
31 War Diary, Commander Aircraft South Pacific Force, from Nov. 1, 1942 to Nov. 30, 1942, Msg 232219, 24 Nov. 1942, page 111, NARA Micro Serial No. 45304, Fold 3 Image 267852800; War Diary, Commander Aircraft South Pacific Force, November 1, 1942–November 30, 1942, NARA Record Group 38, Micro Serial No. 45304, Catalogue ID 4697018; and Maurer Maurer, *Combat Squadrons of the Air Force, World War II*, Albert F. Simpson Historical Research Center, 1982; and Historical Record of the Thirteenth Troop Carrier Squadron from 10 October 1942 to 31 July 1943, AFHRA SQ-TR-CARR-13-HI, IRIS 00073464.

32 Stanley C. Jersey, *New Hebrides Islands, Military Postal History of the United States Forces, 1942–1946* (Collectors' Club of Chicago, 1994).
33 Ltr, Hq 403rd Troop Carrier Group, APO 708, 11 Nov 1943, GP-403-HI (Tr Carr), AFRA Iris Ref. IRIS 00090200; and Historical Record of the Thirteenth Troop Carrier Squadron, 10 Oct 1942–31 July 1943, AFHRA SQ-TR-Carr-13-Hi, IRIS Ref. No. 00073464.
34 History 63rd TCS Dec 1942–Dec. 1943, and General Order #38, Hq 13th AF, 10 October 1943. See Records of the XIII Air Force Service Command, AFHRA document 753.01-2, 66; and Robert Allen, Otis Carney and Pen Johnson, "The Story of SCAT," Parts I and II, *Air Transport*, December 1944/ January 1945.
35 In June 1944, SCAT was officially disbanded. Air Transport Command began taking over air transportation from Guadalcanal to points *south*, leaving the missions to the north and west to the Combat Air Transport units. SCAT was reorganized and redesignated the Solomons Combat Air Transport Command, thus continuing the acronym SCAT. See William M. Armstrong, *Marine Air Group 25 and SCAT*, Arcadia Publishing Inc., 2017; and, Morning Reports, 64th TCS, Maj. Jack Roessell, commanding.
36 Informal Notes Re: South Pacific Combat Air Transport Command (SCAT), July 1943, Air Transport Command files, Air Mobility Command History Office, Scott AFB, Il.; and Op. cit. Military Postal History of the New Hebrides.
37 Ibid.
38 Further confounding the historical record, later in the war, when SCAT closed its offices at Espiritu Santo and moved first to New Caledonia and finally to Bougainville, some of the records of the 801st were permanently lost. OP.Cit. Historical Data 801st MAES, and Op. cit. Informal Notes.
39 Interview with Major General Harry J. Sands, Jr. by Mark Cleary, April/May 1990, USAF Oral History Program, AFHRA Iris No. 01105623.
40 Allen, Carney and Johnson, "The Story of SCAT."
41 Ibid.
42 Report of Activities, 801st Medical Air Evacuation Transport Squadron, 26 September 1943, in AFHRA Reel A0321, 572.
43 Historical Data, October 1, 1943 to December 31, 1943, 801st Medical Air Evacuation Transport Squadron, December 31, 1943. In History 801st Med, 25 May 42–Feb 44, AFHRA Reel A0321 page 603. In the same source, also see Historical Narrative of the 801st Medical Air Evacuation Transport Squadron, May 25, 1942 to June 1, 1944, Maj. Wilbur Anderson Smith,563, and 1st Camp Site 801st Medical Air Evac Trp Sq, Tontouta Camp; New Caledonia, 572.
44 Assignment of Unit, HQ Service of Supply, South Pacific Area, AG 370.5, February 25, 1943. In History of the 801st Med, 25 May 1942–1 June 1944, AFHRA A0321, 589.
45 Air Evacuation, Headquarters Air Evacuation Transport, March 20, 1943, in AFHRA Reel A0321; and, Annual Report, Jan 1 1943 to Dec 31, 1943, dated 31 Dec. 1943, 801st MAETS, A0321 636.
46 Summary of the Work—Air Evacuation of the Sick and Wounded, South Pacific Theatre—801st Medical Air Evacuation Trsp. Sq., in AFHRA A0321 570; Between Jan 1943 and Oct 44 when the squadron left the South Pacific to follow the advance of the tactical units of the Army Air Force into the Southwest Pacific, the 801st (using Thirteenth AF, Navy and Marine Skytrains, evacuated more than 40,000 patients from the forward areas. From Oct 44 to April 45 the squadron evacuated nearly fifteen thousand patients from Allied bases in the Philippines, the Netherlands East Indies, and Palau. Fight nurses averaged 50–90 hours per month in the air, with flights averaging from 4–8 hours flying time. L. Col. Benjamin E. Lippincott, Historian, Thirteenth Air Force, *From Fiji Through the Philippines with the Thirteenth Air Force, the History of the 13th Army "Jungle" Air Force in WWII* (San Angelo, TX: Newsfoto Publishing Co., 1948); Op. cit. Annual Report, AFHRA A0321, 636. Jan 1 1943 to Dec 31, 1943, dated 31 Dec. 1943, 801st MAETS, A0321, 6360.
47 Allen, Carney and Johnson, "The Story of SCAT."
48 Op. cit. Report of Activities, 801st MAET, 173; and Technical Memorandum No. 2, 11 January, 1944, United States Army Services of Supply, in AFHRA Reel A0321, page 26; and Op Cit Report of Activities.
49 Kralovec, *Naval History of Espiritu Santo*.
50 Ibid, for a detailed station list.

Chapter 13

1. SOPA Instructions, Commander Aircraft South Pacific, Espiritu Santo, New Hebrides, dated 21 August 1943, Secret.
2. Report on Activities of the 403rd Troop Carrier Group, Ltr, Hq 403rd Troop Carrier Group, 11 November 1943, F.A. Quinn, Lt. Col, Air Corps, contained in AFHRA Iris No. 90200, GP-403-HI (TR CARR).
3. Public Relations Staff *Two Years Pacific: Sandman: 403rd Troop Carrier Group* (contained in AFHRA Reel No. B0489, undated).
4. Author n.d., *64th T.C. Sq* (Sydney: Waite & Bull, undated, but assumed between 1945 and 1950). The plane reference "6305" presumably refers to 43-16305, which was delivered to the USAAF on 20 July 1944. At the time, the 64th was stationed at either Guadalcanal or at Biak.
5. CQ was the designation given to the person in charge of quarters where military personnel were billeted—tents in the case of the 64th TCS at Santo. Aircrews assigned for the day's missions were awakened by the CQ in time for the mission briefing. The CQ had the only alarm clock allocated to an Army troop carrier squadrons. See Table of Organization and Equipment, No. 1-317.
6. History, Air Center Command, Navy 140, NARA Catalog ID 4697018, Micro Serial No. 156743. Also see 1944 Approach Map, NACI Hydrographic Office, No. 12-20-12-1, 2, 3, 4 & 7A.
7. Correspondence, Roger Connor, Smithsonian National Air & Space Museum, Jan. 11, 2021.
8. Oak Leaves, August 12, 1942, Oak Park River Forest Museum, Historical Society of Oak Park & River Forest; When fully staffed, the unit would include 47 officers, 52 nurses and 318 EM. Gilmary Andrews, ed., *A Service Remembered* (Bloomington, IN: AuthorHouse, 2009); and, United States Army Table of Organization, T/O 8-580, 2 July 1942.
9. Andrews, *A Service Remembered*.
10. Ibid.
11. *Building the Navy's Bases in World War II: History of the Bureau of Yards and Docks and the Civil Engineer Corp, 1940–1946*; and Andrews, *A Service Remembered*.
12. Mary Ellen Condon-Rall and Albert E. Cowdrey, *The Medical Department: Medical Service in the War Against Japan* (Center of Military History Publication 10-24, 1998).
13. Ibid.
14. World Bank Group, 2022, see https://data.worldbank.org/indicator/AG.LND.TOTL.K2?locations=S2.
15. Op. cit. 430810 Letter.
16. For the delivery date of aircraft: Aircraft History Card, National Air and Space Museum, provided by Elizabeth Borja, October 2020. For unit cost: U.S. Army Air Forces in WWII, Statistical Digest, Table 82, Average Unit Cost of Airplanes, Office of Statistical Control, December 1945.
17. 430820 Letter, Richardson to parents.
18. Report of Activities of the 403rd Troop Carrier Group, 11 November 1943, AFHRA IRIS Ref. No. 00090200.
19. Individual Flight Records, Leonard G. Richardson, National Personnel Records Center, St. Louis, Mo.
20. 430830 Letter, Richardson to parents.
21. Op. cit. *From Fiji*.
22. Op. cit *Naval History of Espiritu Santo*.
23. Report on Activities of the 403rd Troop Carrier Group, 11 Nov. 1943, AFHRA Iris No. 90200. In September, their first full month of operations, the 13th, 63rd, and 64th TCS combined to carry over two million pounds of freight, and over sixty-six hundred passengers, including 336 wounded, logging over ½ million miles and nearly thirty-five hundred flying hours. Op. cit. AFHRA Iris No. 90200.
24. Report on Activities of the 403rd Troop Carrier Group, T. H. Taylor, 11 November 1943, AFHRA Iris No. 90200.
25. Op. cit. *Army Air Forces WWII, Vol. Four: The Pacific*.
26. Records of the 801st Medical Air Evacuation Transport Squadron, in History of the 801st MED, AFHRA Reel No. A0321, 764.
27. Recommendations for Maintenance of 13th Troop Carrier Squadron, 801st Medical Squadron Air Evacuation Transport, March 20, 1943. In History of the 801st MED, AFHRA Reel No. A0321, 1532.

28 Col. Jack Roessell, USAF, *Notes from the Pacific*, unpublished family memoir, 2007.
29 Ltr, Hq 403rd Troop Carrier Group, APO 708, 11 Nov 1943, AFHRA Iris No. 90200.
30 Historical Data, 63rd Troop Carrier Squadron, May 10, 1944, Report of Activities from 12 December 1942 to 31 December 1943, AFHRA Iris No. 74648.
31 Historical Data, 63rd Troop Carrier Squadron, August (1943) Report, AFHRA Iris No. 74649; and History 63rd TCS Dec 1942–Dec 1943; and 403rd HQ unit movement incl air and ground echelons, AFHRA Iris Nos. 00262046 and 00262047, Reel A7712; and, Morning Report, 64th TCS, September 5, 1943, Roessell commanding.
32 Epidemiological Observations on the Trend of the Dengue Fever Epidemic, in Op. cit. Current Research Activities.
33 Secret to MacArthur, Eisenhower, Stilwell and Harmon from G. C. Marshall, July 13, 1943. Cited in Karen M. Masterson, *The Malaria Project: the U.S. government's secret mission to find a miracle cure* (New York: New American Library, 2014).
34 John Boyd Coates, Editor in Chief, *Preventive Medicine in World War II, Vol. VI, Communicable Diseases, Malaria* (Washington, D.C.: Office of the Surgeon General, Dept. of the Army, 1963).
35 NOAA, "What are the Doldrums," Ocean Facts, National Ocean Service, December 202, at https://oceanservice.noaa.gov/facts/doldrums.html.
36 Cited in John Fuller, *Thor's Legions: Weather Support to the U.S. Air Force and Army, 1937–1987*, American Meteorological Society, 1990. Credited therein to William C. Huyler, "The Military Weather Service and War Operations" (ca. 1960), text of briefing to Brig. Gen. E. Vourlakis, General Directorate, National Meteorological Service, Athens, Greece.
37 Robert Sherrod, *History of Marine Corps Aviation in World War II* (Combat Forces Press, 1952).
38 Commentary by Maj. Bill Kinney, cited in Clive Howard, *One Damn Island After Another* (Zenger Publishing, 1981).
39 Op. cit. AAF Against Japan; and B-17 Fortress Master Log, Dave Osborne, 1935–1945; and George Galdorisi and Thomas Phillips, *Leave No Man Behind: The Saga of Combat Search and Rescue* (Zenith Press, 2009).
40 George C. Kenney, *General Kenney Reports: A Personal History of the Pacific War* (New York: Duell, Sloan and Pearce, 1949).
41 W. M. Cleveland, *Grey Geese Calling, Pacific Air War History of the 11th Bombardment Group (H), 1940–1945* (Askov, Minnesota: American Publishing Co., 1981).
42 Op. cit. *The War Experiences of Arthur R Driedger Jr.*
43 G. Sam Piatt, "The Making of a Combat Pilot," subject Richard Jenkins, Ref No. 5342423, *Portsmouth Daily Times*, January 15, 2012.
44 Roessell, *Notes from the Pacific.*
45 *Two Years Pacific: Sandman.* The term "Sandman" is a reference to the commander of the 403rd, Col. Harry Sand.

Chapter 14

1 Brief of Narrative Report on the Development of the United States Army Forces in the South Pacific, Lt. Gen. Millard F. Harmon, July and August 1942, AFHRA Iris No. 251244.
2 *The War Experiences of Arthur R Driedger Jr, Radio Operator Mechanic, C 47, 13TH Troop Carrier Squadron, 403 Troop Carrier Group, 13th Air Force.*
3 Organizational History, XIII AF Service Command, 2 October 1943, AFHRA Reel A7716, 753.071, History 14 Apr–Sep 1943 Headquarters Squadron.
4 Keisan Online Calculator.
5 Integrated Surface Data (ISD), January 12, 2018, National Centers for Environmental Information, National Oceanic and Atmospheric Admin, Asheville, NC, January 12, 2018.
6 Op. cit. Kralovec, *A Naval History of Espiritu Santo*.
7 Col. Jack Roessell, USAF, *Notes from the Pacific*, unpublished family memoir, 2007.
8 Individual Flight Records, National Personnel Record Center, St. Louis, MO.

9. Leonard G. Richardson, *The Crash of '43*, unpublished memoir, 1980.
10. Integrated Surface Data (ISD), January 12, 2018, Station 915200, Honiara, National Centers for Environmental Information, National Oceanic and Atmospheric Admin, Asheville, NC, January 12, 2018.
11. The Thirteenth Air Force, March–October 1943, US Air Force Historical Study No. 120, AAF Historical Office, 1946, AFHRA Iris No. 00467704.
12. 64th T.C. Sq, 13th Jungle Air Force Sydney: Waite & Bull, Sydney, undated).
13. Op. cit. *The Crash of '43*.
14. Missing Air Crew Report (MACR) No. 466, Maj. Jack Roessell, Commander, 64th TCS, Sept. 7, 1943.
15. Data Documentation for Integrated Surface Data (ISD), Federal Climate Complex, January 12, 2018, National Centers for Environmental Information, NOAA, provided by Mark Seiderman, Meteorologist, NCEI, January 25, 2021.
16. Ltr, Maj. Jack Roessell to his mother, Mrs. Harry Hall, Oct. 2, 1943.
17. 64th T.C. Sq; Report on Activities of the 403rd Troop Carrier Group, 11 November 1943, in Reel B0489, Gp-403-HI; Correspondence, Dr. Roger Connor, Museum Specialist/Curator, Aeronautics Department, Smithsonian National Air and Space Museum.

Chapter 15

1. The crash site coordinates are: -15.379791, 167.04150.
2. Op. cit, Kralovec, *A Naval History of Espiritu Santo*.
3. Based on Army records, the crewman who survived the crash but died soon after was probably the pilot, Lt. Robert "Red" Healy.
4. Data Documentation for Integrated Surface Data (ISD), Federal Climate Complex, January 12, 2018, National Centers for Environmental Information, NOAA, provided by Mark Seiderman, Meteorologist, NCEI, January 25, 2021.
5. Leonard G. Richardson, *The Crash of '43*, unpublished memoir, 1980.
6. A. J. Marshall, *The Black Musketeers* (London: William Heinemann Ltd, 1937).
7. *Castaway's Baedeker to the South Seas*, U.S. Army Objective Data Section, Intelligence Center, Pacific Ocean Areas, December 1942. Printed at Fort Armstrong, Territory of Hawaii.
8. War History, Fleet Air Wing 17, 15 September 1943–30 September 1945, NARA micro serial no. 144646.
9. Adam Bartlett, "Men of Moresby," contained in the papers of John Williams, Australia War Memorial, Collection Ref 87/062, AWM, and cited in Judith A. Bennett, *Natives and Exotics, World War II and Environment in the Southern Pacific* (University of Hawaii Press, 2009).
10. Lost Plane Procedure for Aircraft Operating out of Espiritu Santo, COMAIRSOPAC, A16-3 Serial 00984, August 25, 1943, AFHRA Iris No. 751.314. The prior LPP was originally promulgated by IV Island Air Command on May 1, 1943, and had been amended twice in June.
11. Missing Air Crew Report (MACR) No. 466, September 7, 1943, Major Jack Roessell, Commander.
12. MACR 466.
13. James Michener, *Tales of the South Pacific* (Macmillan Publishing, 1947).
14. Information on each bomber mission were recorded on Weekly Status and Operations Reports (WSOR). Data included the date, time and type of the mission, the target or search area, the number of aircraft on each mission, the mission results, and many other operational details. All applicable WSOR were obtained from the Air Force Historical Research Agency.
15. Search missions were flown by B-17s of the 23rd BS and B-24s from the 72nd, 370th and 424th BS. Healy's C-47 was the only aircraft that went missing in the Pacific Theater (PTO) on September 5, but over a 10-day period from September 2 to 11, fourteen aircraft went missing in the PTO, including six bombers that went down in operations over New Guinea on the 2nd, and three fighters that went missing on the 6th.
16. Kent G. Budge, *The Pacific War Online Encyclopedia* (2008–2010).

ENDNOTES • 301

17 U.S. Radar, Operational Characteristics of Radar, Classified by Tactical Application, FTP 217, 1 August 1943. C-47s operating in September, 1943 were equipped with the SCR-595 airborne transponder. The range of the IFF was approximately the range of the radar. "… in operation, the set normally requires only turning on and off by pilot or operator," Erection and Maintenance Instructions for Army Models C-47, et al., manual AN 01-40NC-2, October 15, 1944.
18 Steven K. Dixon, *Photo Recon Became Fighter Duty: Marine Observation Squadron 251 in World War II* (McFarland & Company, Jefferson, N.C., 2016).
19 Budge, *Pacific War Online Encyclopedia*.
20 U.S. Radar Operational Characteristics of Radar Classified by Tactical Application, FTP 217, 1 August 1943.
21 Interview of Capt. M. B. Gardner, USN, Chief of Staff, ComAirSouPac (Air Information Branch), 13 January 1943.
22 *The Crash of '43*, etc.
23 Survival, Airlines War Training Institute, Washington, D.C., 1943.
24 Op. cit. *The Crash of '43*.
25 Ibid.
26 Report to the Commanding Officer, 5th BG, Special Search Missions, 8 Sept. 1943, 8 Sept 1943, contained in AFHRA 43686, SQ-BOMB-23-HI.
27 Richardson, *The Crash of '43*.
28 Survival, Airlines War Training Institute.
29 https://en-us.topographic-map.com/maps/sbjf/Espiritu-Santo. The Meno at -15.38333,167.01667 and the Melelo at -15.36667,167.03333. Mt. Turi is at also to -15.379791, 167.04150. Also see: Data Collection Survey on Power Sector in Espiritu Santo in Republic of Vanuatu, Final Report, Vanuatu Department of Energy, May, 2017, and Sustainable Management of Sarakata Watershed, Integrated Water Resource Management Demonstration Project, Department of Geology, Mines and Water Resources, Republic of Vanuatu, July 2007.
30 Op. cit. *The Crash of '43*.
31 Op. cit. *Man and Animals in the New Hebrides*.
32 Op. cit. Naudts, *Memoirs*.
33 Ibid.
34 Army Study Guide, Observation and Fields of Fire, Cover and Concealment, Obstacles (man made and natural), Key or Decisive Terrain, Avenues of Approach; and, Report of OPLR Reconnaissance Patrol, 11 June 1943, Headquarters IV Island Command, Lt. Col. Carl Westlund; and Naudts, Memoir.
35 Ibid Report of OPLR Reconnaissance.
36 Op. cit. Naudts, *Memoir*.
37 Op. cit. Report of OPLR Reconnaissance.
38 Op. cit. *The Crash of '43*.
39 Op. cit. Naudts, *Memoirs*.
40 Op. cit. *The Crash of '43*.
41 Interview, Curtis Craver, April 5, 2012. Roessell's request to the 129th Combat Team was made through IV Island Command on Sept. 13. See Certificate, Headquarters 129th Infantry, 5 April 1944, Capt. Morris J. Naudts.
42 Op. cit. Naudts, *Memoirs*.
43 Award of Legion of Merit, Chaplain Casimir W. Andruskevitch, ASN O-418208, 129th Infantry, 22 April 1944, Headquarters 129th Infantry.
44 Interview, James Moyle, March 22, 2021, Butte, MT.
45 Personnel selected for this patrol were identified in a newsletter clipping later found in the records of Lieutenant Richardson. Despite a thorough search, the source of his newsletter has not been found, but it is believed to have been from the 129th Combat Team.
46 Letter, Lt. Al McCreight to his mother, 25 Nov. 1943.
47 Op. cit. Naudts, *Memoir*.
48 Op. cit. *The Crash of '43*.

49. Sixteenth Census of the United States: 1940, Department of Commerce—Bureau of the Census; and Black Spokane: The Civil Rights Struggle in the Inland Northwest, Dwayne A. Mack.
50. Gilmary d. Andrews, *A Service Remembered* (AuthorHouse, 2009).
51. Certificate, 5 April 1944, Headquarters 129th Infantry, Capt. Morris J. Naudts, APO 37.

Chapter 16

1. https://en.wikipedia.org/wiki/Butmas.
2. From interviews conducted at the village of Fanafo–Kona, Espiritu Santo, on July 15, 2011. Interviewees included Assistant Chief Harry Job, Simeon Salier (Councillor of Sanma Province), Douglas Dick, Mark Tome, Jack Levus, Silas Tano, Hapraham (Abraham) Joseph, Remo Job and William Vira.
3. Op. cit. *The Crash of '43*.
4. Interview, Simeon Salier, Councillor of Sanma Province, July 14, 2011.
5. The dialogue between the villagers and Richardson is the only fiction in this narrative.
6. Op. cit. *The Crash of '43*. The fruit given to Richardson was likely is called nakavika, which has a pear-like quality.
7. According to the villagers at Fanafo–Kona, Kelly was actually "Kelliv" or "Kallif". Spelling uncertain.
8. Op. cit. *The War from Coconut Square*.
9. Op. cit., *The Crash of '43*.
10. T. H. Harrisson, "The New Hebrides People and Culture," *The Geographical Journal*, October 1936, Vol. 88, No. 4. Royal Geographical Society.
11. This style of cooking is called LapLap, and is considered Vanuatu's national dish. Manioc, taro or yams are grated into a doughy paste, then placed into taro or wild spinach leaves and soaked in coconut cream. Sometimes pork, beef, poultry, fish or flying fox is added. Leaves of the laplap plant are wrapped around the doughy mixture, tied up with strands of vine and then placed in a ground oven, with hot stones above and below.
12. Op. cit., *The Crash of '43*.
13. Report upon bombing of Espiritu Santo Island by Enemy Plane—15 September 1943, Maj. Walter C. Fuller, Headquarters IV Island Command, 18 September 1943.
14. Letter, Norman Richardson, Sept. 14, 1943
15. Op. cit. Naudts, *Memoirs*.
16. Op. cit. Interview, Curtis Craver, April 5, 2012.
17. Letter, McCreight to mother, 25 Nov. 1943.
18. Op. cit. Naudts, *Memoir*.
19. Op. cit. Naudts, *Memoir* and Interview, Curtis Craver.
20. The five accounts of the events that occurred atop Mt. Turi are remarkably consistent. McCreight's brief account was written two months after the events. Craver's similarly brief account was written four years after the events. The accounts of Richardson, Roussell and Naudts, all rich in detail, were written forty or more years after the events. While it is no longer possible to reconcile the slight differences in these accounts, they are of no significance to the narrative.
21. Op. cit. *The Crash of '43*.
22. Op. cit. Interview, Curtis Craver.
23. Op. cit. *The Crash of '43*.
24. Op. cit. Interview Simeon Salier.
25. Op. cit. Naudts, *Memoir*.
26. Op. cit. Naudts, *Memoir*.
27. Op. cit. *The Crash of '43*.
28. Op. cit. Naudts, *Memoir*.
29. In fact, McCreight would report that he and Sgt. Buchheit did most of the stretcher carrying, a point at variance with Naudt's memoir, and which is also not supported in Richardson's memoir. But recall that McCreight's commentary was written just a couple of months after the event. Naudts and Richardson's were written 40 years later.

30 Op. cit., *The Crash of '43.*
31 Interview, Raymond Buchheit Sept. 16, 2012.
32 Op. cit. Naudts, *Memoir.*
33 Op. cit. *The Crash of '43.*
34 Ibid.
35 Col. Jack Roessell, USAF, *Notes from the Pacific,* unpublished family memoir, 2007. No record of this radio call from the pilot to the tower has been located. The official record indicates the last contact with the aircraft was at 1:30 pm, when the aircraft was still 2½ hours from landing.
36 Op. cit. Interview, Curtis Craver.
37 Op. cit. Letter, McCreight to mother.
38 Op. cit. Naudts, *Memoir.*
39 Commendation, Col. J. D. Frederick, Commander 129th Infantry, 1 February 1944.
40 Western Union, Sept. 24, 1943, to Clifford Richardson.
41 V-mail, Norman Richardson, Sept. 30, 1943.
42 V-mail, Norman Richardson, October 7, 1943.
43 "US Marine Corps Squadrons of WW2," *Aircrew Remembered,* Great Yarmouth, England, Aircrew Remembered.com; and War Diary of Marine Torpedo Bombing Squadron Two Thirty Two, 1 July to 31 July, 1943, and 1 Aug–31 Aug 1943, Marine Air Group Eleven, NARA Catalog ID 4697018, Reel A547, Micro Serial Nos. 55523 and 55227.
44 Ibid. War Diary for month of August 1943.
45 All personnel from the forward echelon of VMTB-232 were transferred to Fighter Strip, Espiritu Santo. That included 30 pilots, 1 doctor, 1 Intel O, 37 Radio Gunners, 36 Turret Gunners, and 1 Corpsman.
46 Anders and his aircrew had been assigned detached service to APO 715 (Auckland) on 11 November, and were completing what is assumed to be his last leg under this assignment. Morning Report, 11 November 1943, Vincent J. Roesky, F/O. Morning Report, 64th Troop Carrier Squadron, 21 Sept. 1943 and 24 November 1943; and History 64th Troop Carrier Squadron, 27 December 1943, AFHRA Iris No. 00074683.
47 Missing Air Crew Report, Nov. 24, 1943, Major L. C. Messenger, commander. The men of the 64th lost were: Pilot Philip Anders, Copilot Richard Harpe, Navigator George Richardson, Crew Chief Carl Boeckmann, and Radio Operator Laurence Pitkus. Citing from the MACR: "Subject airplane was assigned to the 63rd Troop Carrier Squadron, 403rd Troop Carrier Group. The air crew was assigned to the 64th Troop Carrier Squadron, 403rd Troop Carrier Group. The Aircraft was performing a mission under the jurisdiction of the South Pacific Combat Air Transport (SCAT)" The date of the incident, Nov. 23rd, is cited in the War Diary of Marine Torpedo Bombing Squadron Two Thirty Two for the period 1 Nov–30 Nov, 1943.
48 George Bamberger, interview by Eric Tenbus, transcript Nov. 6, 2000, Collection WWII-1085, Reichelt Oral History Program, Florida State University, Tallahassee, FL.
49 Ibid.
50 War Diary of Marine Torpedo Bombing Squadron Two Thirty Two, 1 Dec. to 31 Dec. 1943, Marine Air Group Fourteen, NARA Catalog ID 4697018, Reel A824, Micro Serial Nos. 65312; and A History of the Marine Torpedo Bombing Squadron -232, Summary of Events from 1933 to 1943, MAG-45, 4th MAW, NARA micro Serial No. 156388.
51 Lost Plane Procedure for Aircraft Operating out of Espiritu Santo, COMAIRSOPAC, A16-3 Serial 00984, August 25, 1943, AFHRA Iris No. 751.314.
52 Lost Plane Procedure, HQ, IV Island Command, 452.05 (AG), 16 Oct 1943, by command of Major General Wallace.
53 Standard Operating Procedure, IV Isl. Air Command, Office of the Operations Officer, 15 October 1943. This SOP incorporated the revised Lost Plane Procedure that was promulgated by HQ, IV Island Air Command on 18 October 1943.
54 Aircraft Movement Reports and Lost Plane Procedure, South Pacific Force Headquarters of the Commander, Serial 01951, October 21, 1943, I. H. Mayfield, Actg Chief of Staff.

55 Radio Range Let Down Procedure, Espiritu Santo Island, Memorandum No. 2-43, Air Center Command, Espiritu Santo, 25 October 1943.
56 General Local Air Traffic Flight Rules and Approach Lanes for Airfields and Seaplane Bases Located at Espiritu Santo Island, Memorandum No. 1-43, Air Center Command, Espiritu Santo, 1 November 1943. These new regulations were further reinforced by the Headquarters of Pekoa Airfield on Santo in its Standard Operating Procedure Orders No. 1 of 15 Nov. 1943. Additional clarifications were issued by IV Island Air Command on 20 Dec. 1943. The Organization and Instructions, Air Center, were revisited and further clarified on 29 March 1944.

Chapter 17

1 Op. cit. *A Naval History of Espiritu Santo*.
2 Op. cit., *The Crash of '43*.
3 Gilmary Andrews, ed., *A Service Remembered* (Bloomington, IN: AuthorHouse, 2009).
4 Abstract of Clinical Record, McCornack General Hospital, Disposition Board Proceedings for Officers, 11 August 1947.
5 A Roger Anderson fixation involves surgically placing metallic pins to maintain position of a bone fracture, following which the affected limb is placed in a cast.
6 M. F. Harmon, *The Army in the South Pacific*, 6 June 1944, (Combined Arms Research Library, Fort Leavenworth, KS).
7 Special Orders No. 118, Headquarters Service Command, APO #708, 2 October 1943, A.R. Myatt, AGD, Adjutant General.
8 Tally Sheet, Incoming, Ebon Field Station, 64th TCS, October 8, 1943.
9 Op. cit. Special Orders No. 118. Data on total patients loaded aboard *Tabinta* have not been found. In its former life, *Tabinta* had been a Dutch cargo carrier operating in the western Pacific with a 65-man crew, mostly Dutch, but with a contingent of Indonesian engine room hands and stewards. In mid-June 1941, the ship was chartered to the Army Transport Service and underwent conversion to wartime use. It made its first voyage as a U.S. troop ship the following month, carrying 1,120 men of the 268th Infantry Battalion to Noumea and returning to San Francisco with general cargo and injured soldiers. Nedelands Instituut voor Militaire Historie, Londense Collectie Koorpaardij, 11.27 and 11.35, provided by Prof. Dr. B. Schoenmaker, Head, Public Information and Collections Division.
10 Ship specifications are somewhat variable. The definitive source is taken as Traces of War, Nederlandse troepentransportschepen in Amerikaanse Dienst, 2018, https://www.tracesofwar.nl/articles/4422/Nederlandse-troepentransportschepen-in-Amerikaanse-dienst.htm?c=gw. See also Roland W. Charles, *Troopships of World War II*, The Army Transportation Association, Washington, 1947; and War Diary of the USS *Helena*, 20 July 1942, NARA Micro Serial No. 42651, RG 38, Roll 0092, Fold3 image 267974992.
11 Processing of Baggage From Overseas, War Department, Adjutant General, AG 524, 29 August 1944.
12 War Diary, USS *Cleveland*, 24 October 1943, NARA Micro Serial Number: 59585, Fold3 Image 270566792.
13 War Diary, U.S. Naval Advance Base Navy 140, Ship Movements, 26 October 1943, NARA RG 38, Box 465; and, War Diary, SC 1047, 26 October 1943, NARA Micro Serial No: 59461, Fold3 Image 270574383.
14 War Diary, USS *Prometheus*, 28 October 1943, NARA Micro Serial Number: 58555, Fold3 Image 270596749; and Op. cit. SC 1047.
15 Op. cit. SC 1047, Fold3 Image 270574418.
16 War Diary, U.S. Naval Forces, Fiji Islands, 1 November 1943, NARA Micro Serial No: 62055, Fold3 image 270916350.
17 Richardson, *The Crash of '43*.
18 Op. cit. 1047, Fold3 Image 270776193; and War Diary, U.S. Naval Forces, Fiji Islands, Fold3 Image 270916360.

19   Op. cit., *The Crash of '43*.
20   Archives of the United Newsreel (U.S. Office of War Information), October & November 1943, and can be seen at https://www.youtube.com/watch?v=EcFAQ6Hi4Vw. In 2021, the Hunga Tonga undersea volcano, located about 350 north of Niuafo'ou in the Tonga Group, erupted with such force that water vapor reached an altitude of 93 miles—well into space.
21   CINCPAC War Diary for the Month of July, 1943, PAC-05-ses, A12/A12, 7 August 1943, NARA Micro Serial Number:53764, Fold3 image 269642994; Sailing Log *Tabinta*, Nedelands Instituut voor Militaire Historie, Londense Collectie Koorpaardij, 2376, provided by Prof. Dr. B. Schoenmaker, Head, Public Information and Collections Division.
22   Op. cit., *The Crash of '43*.
23   Ibid.
24   Special Orders No. 320, Hammond General Hospital, 3 Dec. 1943.
25   Op. cit., *The Crash of '43*.
26   Ibid.
27   Ibid.
28   Ibid.
29   Special Orders No. 287, 6 Nov 1945, Army Service Forces, McCaw General Hospital, Walla Walla, WA.
30   Op. cit., *The Crash of '43*.
31   Special Orders No. 240, Madigan GH, 11 Oct 1946.
32   Op. cit. Abstract of Clinical Record.
33   Disposition Board Proceedings for Officers, McCornack General Hospital, 11 August 1947.
34   Proceedings of Army Retiring Board for Officers, McCornack General Hospital, Pasadena, 28 Aug 1947, Testimony of Capt. William Berkeley, Personal records Leonard G. Richardson.
35   Proceedings of Army Retiring Board for Officers, McCornack General Hospital, Pasadena, 28 Aug 1847, Personal records Leonard G. Richardson.
36   Proceedings of Army Retiring Board for Officers, McCornack General Hospital, Pasadena, 28 August 1947.
37   HQ, AAF, Washington, Special Order Nos. 186 and 231.
38   Headquarters, McCornack General Hospital, United States Army, Pasadena, 2 Oct 1947, John Thayer, Maj, MAC Adjutant.
39   Oral interview, Leonard G. Richardson, Leonard Richardson, 1979, unpublished.

Epilogue

1   In the burst of South Pacific imperialism of the late 19th century, both France and Great Britain sought to extend control over the New Hebrides: France in order to provide greater protection for its New Caledonia colony; Great Britain because of its proximity to Australia and New Zealand. By 1906 both governments realized that some form of governance for the island was required and agreed to administer the islands in a joint custodianship – a unique form of governance termed the British-French Condominium. Under this arrangement, each power administered its citizens, but neither country exercised sovereignty. Within this "region of joint influence," Britain and France each established separate "Residencies" and enacted precisely parallel laws and regulations for their citizens. The two authorities came together only in a joint court that was, at least initially, ruled by a Spanish judge who spoke neither English nor French. Tom Fulton, *History of Santo and the New Hebrides*, The Fairmount Center, Novelty, OH.
2   R. C. Ratard, "Epidemiology of malaria in the New Hebrides," *Tropical Doctor*, 1979, vol. 9.
3   Development of "Olyset net" as a Tool for Malaria Control, TakaakiIto and Takeshi Okuno, SUMITOMO KAGAKU Vol. 2006-II.
4   World Health Organization (WHO), Global Health Observatory Data Repository/World Health Statistics (http://apps.who.int/ghodata/ and https://data.worldbank.org/indicator/SH.MLR.INCD).

P3?locations=VU; "Vanuatu leading the way on Malaria Elimination in the Pacific," *Vanuatu Daily Post*, April 28, 2021; "Eliminating malaria in Vanuatu," in Allison Phillips, Editor, *Country Briefing, Global Health Group Project Team*, April 2012; and National Malaria Strategic Plan, Vanuatu, 2015–2020.

5   Geoffrey White, ed., "Remembering the Pacific War," 1991, in Conference on the Cultural Encounters in the Pacific War, East-West Center, UH-Manoa Center for Pacific Islands Studies. Lamont Lindstrom *The Vanuatu Labor Corps Experience*, Chapter 5. See also James Gwero, "Olgeta Stori blong Wol Wo Tu" (The Stories of World War Two), Chapter 5, in John Taylor and Nick Thieberger, eds., Working Together in Vanuatu: Research Histories, Collaborations, Projects and Reflections, The Australian National University, 2011.

6   Geoffrey M. White and Lamont Lindstrom, *The Pacific Theater, Island Representations of World War II*, Pacific Islands Monograph Series, No. 8 (Melbourne: Melbourne University Press, 1990).

7   Tom Fulton, *History of Santo and the New Hebrides* (Novelty, OH: The Fairmount Center); John G. Peck and Robert J. Gregory, "A Brief Overview of the Old New Hebrides," *Anthropologist*, 7(4): (2005), 269–282.

8   Erik Victor McCrea, "An Introduction to the Coinage of Pseudo-Etats, Na-Griamel Federation," 2009, at www.oocities.org/erik_mccrea/.

9   In 1980, the sole country in the Commonwealth that was not a former British colony was Mozambique. The Commonwealth now includes 56 nations.

10 The CIA World Factbook 2019–2020, US Central Intelligence Agency, 2019.

11 UN General Assembly, Twenty-sixth Session, Article 2768, Identification of the least developed among the developing countries. The resultant list is found at the Dag Hammarskjold Library, at https://ask.un.org/faq/190378.

12 Commonwealth Innovation, 22 December 2020.

13 The Human Development Index (HDI) was developed by Pakistani economist Mahbub ul Haq in 1990 to "shift the focus of development economics from national income accounting to people-centered policies."

14 Worldometer.info, Dover, Delaware, USA, 2021; The World Bank; United Nations Development Programme.

15 World Risk Report 2013, United Nations University Institute for Environment and Human Security.

16 IMF Survey: With External Support, Vanuatu's Recovery Builds on Prudent Past, July 6, 2015; *Natural Disasters are the Shadow over Vanuatu's Development Progress*, Devyn Holliday, Research Officer, Economic, Youth & Sustainable Development Directorate, Commonwealth Secretariat, 16 August 2021.

17 Abdallah, S., Hoffman, A. and Akenji, L., The 2024 Happy Planet Index (Hot or Cool Institute, Berlin, 2024).

18 Worldometer. Data taken from United Nations, Department of Economic and Social Affairs, Population Division; and 2020 Vanuatu National Population and Housing Census.

19 Climate Change in the Pacific: Scientific Assessment and New Research, Pacific Climate Change Science Program, Australian Bureau of Meteorology and Commonwealth Scientific and Industrial Research Organisation, 2011.

20 Op. cit. *Bridging Mental Boundaries*.

21 Op. cit. *To Kill a Bird*.

22 Following account is based on recordings made by the author on July 21 and 22, 2011.

23 The first village I visited was at Fanafo–Kona, whose residents appeared to be most centrally involved in the rescuing my father. As events developed, I never did go to Butmas, though in retrospect, I deeply wish I had. I later provided Path's letter to Douglas and requested that he go to Butmas, present the documents to Chief Tas, and explain what I had done during my visit. At the end of my stay at Santo, I delivered a three-page report to the Secretary General Path confirming my search results.

24 Others met during my short time at Fanafo–Kona were: Jack Levus, Silas Tano, Hapraham (Abraham) Joseph, Remo Job and William Vira.

25 From the ground I saw very few of these garden areas. But in a later low-altitude overflight, I had very clear views of large gardens.

ENDNOTES • 307

26 A small piece of this strut was given to Curtis Craver, and to Madonna, Ron, Tom, and Denis Richardson, and to Ray Dickelman.
27 Lindstrom and White, *The Pacific Theater: Island Representations of World War II*.

Appendix 1

1   Squadron Order No. 42, 64th TCS, 403rd TCG, 24 May 1043.
2   Op. cit. Personal Correspondence Oct. 9th.
3   Sigma Kappa *Triangle*, Summer 1940; Barton Sensenig, *"The Sensiney" of America* (Philadelphia: Lyon & Armor, 1943).
4   Selective service registration cards, NARA, RG 147, Roll 44004_01)00010 and Phone Report, conversation with Linda Horton, August 26, 2012.
5   *Journal of the American Medical Association*, Vol. 122(8), June 19, 1943.
6   History 64th May 1944, and The Crusaders, A History of the 42nd Bombardment Group (M).
7   Personal correspondence, Linda Richwine Horton, August 27, 2012.
8   WWII Army Enlistment Records, Raymond N. Buchheit, Fold3 image 83654544.
9   Personal correspondence, Raymond Buchheit, September 16, 2012.
10 Op. cit. *Crash of '43*.
11 Raymond Buchheit, letter, Oct. 4, 2012.
12 Ibid.
13 *Spokane Daily Chronicle*, May 23, 1936, Empire Edition.
14 Col. Jack Roessell, USAF, *Notes from the Pacific*, unpublished family memoir, 2007.
15 Official Army and Air Force Register, Vol. II, Department of the Army: The Adjutant General's Office, January 1948.
16 Promotion dates per Official Army Register, Vol. 1, 1 January 1947, p. 954; Table of Organization and Equipment, No. 1-317, AAF Troop Carrier Squadron, 16 August 1943.
17 Letter, Jack Roessell to his mother, Mrs. Harry Hall, Oct. 2, 1943.
18 Op. cit. Roessell, *Notes from the Pacific*.
19 Ibid.
20 AFHRA Factsheet 10208 and cite: Official Army and Air Force Register, Vol. II, Department of the Army: The Adjutant General's Office, January 1948.
21 Telegram, War Department to Mrs. Irene F. Healy, 22 September 1943.
22 Much of what is known about the airmen who died on September 5, 1943, has been obtained from Individual Deceased Personnel Files provided by the US Army Human Resources Command on Jan. 21, 2011 for each individual. Additional information is taken from files of the National Personnel Records Center, Military Personnel Records, St. Louis.
23 Squadron Order No. 42, 24 May 1943, 64th TCS, Capt. Jack Roessell, Commanding.
24 Special Order No. 181, Headquarters, 403rd TCG, 12 July 1943, by order of Lt. Col. Sands.
25 Telegram, War Department to Mrs. Irene F. Healy, 13 September 1943.
26 Personal correspondence, Mrs. Roberta Healy, June 10, 2011, and with Mrs. Jane Correia, undated.
27 United States Census, 1930; and news articles in The *Avon Herald-News*, April 16, 1953 and in the *Rochester Times-Union*, September 25, 1943; and Personal Correspondence, Mrs. Nancy (Miller) Heuer, niece of Lt. Miller, 2012.
28 Enlistment Card, 101st Cavalry, October 1940; *Avon Herald-News*, September 30, 1943.
29 Individual Deceased Personnel File (IDPF), Augustus Miller, National Personnel Records Center, Military Personnel Records, St. Louis.
30 Letter provided by the family of Augustus Miller.
31 Enlistment Record, Fold3 Image 84131233.
32 Operations Order No. 67, Headquarters, West Coast Wing, AAF, Air Transport Command, Hamilton Field, 17 July 1943.

308 • SURVIVAL IN THE SOUTH PACIFIC

33 Biography of Joseph E. O'Connell, Dr. Regina Plunkett-Dowling, Iona College, Memorial Day, 2011, provided Nov. 9, 2011; Registration Card, Joseph E. O'Connell, Order No. 12665.
34 Operations Order No. 67, Headquarters, West Coast Wing, AAF, Air Transport Command, Hamilton Field, 17 July 1943; and Individual Deceased Personnel File, Joseph E. O'Connell.
35 Biography of Joseph E. O'Connell (1923-1943), Dr. Regina Plunkett-Dowling, Mission Integration, Memorial Day, 2011.

Appendix 2

1   Col. Morris John Naudts, *Memoir*, US Army Infantry, 1914–1994, unpublished, undated.
2   Interviews, Curtis Craver, Jan. 7, 2012; Jan. 15, 2012; April 5, 2012; April 30, 2012; and personal correspondence.
3   Ibid. "BAR" refers to the Browning Automatic Rifle.
4   33 Division Pictorial History, Camp Forrest—1941–1942, undated.
5   Interviews with Bulfer family, Oct. 8, 2012 and Oct. 30, 2012.
6   16th Census of the United Sates: 1940, April 22, 1940, City of Aurora, County of Kane, State of Illinois.
7   Sources for the life and service of Joe Gabriel include: Records of the Selective Service System, NARA WWII Draft Registration Cards; World War II Enlistment Records, NARA; Order to Report for Induction, April 10, 1941, Cook County Local Board No. 5; Report of Induction of Selective Service Man, April 13, 1942; US WWII Hospital Admission Card Files, 1942–1954; Individual Deceases Personnel File, Joseph Paul Gabriel, Army Serial No. 36 026 783, National Personnel Records Center, provided March 8, 2012.

Appendix 3

1   War Diary, Month of September 1943, from Commander Destroyer Division Twelve, National Archives, NARA Identifier 4697018, Micro Serial No. 57259.
2   *Two Years Pacific: Sandman: 403rd Troop Carrier Group*, Public Relations Staff, July 1945
3   Robert C. Owen, *Air Mobility, A Brief History of the American Experience* (Washington, D.C.: Potomac Books, 2013).
4   Vern Haugland, *The AAF Against Japan* (New York: Harper & Brothers Publishers, 1948). The initial commander was Navy Rear Admiral Charles Mason. Subsequent commanders over the 16 months of the command's existence rotated between the Navy, USAF, and Marine Corps.
5   Wesley Craven and James Cate, editors, *The United States Army Air Forces in World War II, Combat Chronology of the US Army Air Forces* (Washington, D.C.: Office of Air Force History, 1983).
6   History of Organization, 64th Troop Carrier Squadron, 31 December 1943, AFHRA Iris Ref. 75683; and *64th TC Sq., Jungle Air Force* (Sydney: Waite & Bull, undated).
7   Headquarters, 403rd Troop Carrier Group, Special Order No. 197, 20 October 1943; also see Morning Report, 64th Troop Carrier Squadron, October 20, 1943, and ff.
8   Morning Report, 64th Troop Carrier Squadron, November 24, 1943.
9   History of Organization, 64th Troop Carrier Squadron, 1 June 1943, AFHRA Iris Ref. 75682
10 Col. Jack Roessell, USAF, *Notes from the Pacific*, unpublished family memoir, 2007.
11 64th TC Sq, Jungle Air Force.
12 403rd TC Group History, AFHRA Iris No. 90198; and Report on Activities of the 403rd Troop Carrier Group, Ltr, Hq 403rd Troop Carrier Group, 11 November 1943, F. A. Quinn, Lt. Col, Air Corps, AFHRA Iris No. 90200; and History of the 13th TCS, Iris No. 73462; and *Two Years Pacific: Sandman*. In mid-December the 64th returned its 27 Glider pilots and 18 glider mechanics to the United States for reassignment. History 64th TCS Oct–Dec 1943, AFHRA Iris No. 74683.
13 History of the 64th Troop Carrier Squadron, Jan–Feb 1944, Iris No. 74684.

14 Report on Activities of the 403rd Troop Carrier Group, 12 May 1944, T. H. Taylor, AFHRA Reel B0489, 62.
15 History 64th TCS, April and May 1944, Iris Nos. 74686 and 74687.
16 History 64th TCS, AFRA IRIS No. 00074682.
17 Ibid.
18 History 64th TCS, AFHRA IRIS No. 00074683; and History 63rd TCS, AFHRA IRIS 00074648. Note that 00074683 indicates the downed aircraft was assigned to the 13th TCS, but 00074648 indicates it was assigned to the 63rd and is the preferred source.
19 See joebaugher.com/usaf_serials/1941_5.html.
20 History 64th TCS, AFHRA IRIS No. 00074684.
21 History of the 64th Troop Carrier Squadron, Jan–Feb 1944 (Iris No. 74684); and History of the 63rd TCS, Dec 42–43, AFHRA Iris No. 74648; and Troop Carrier Operations, XIII Air Force Service Command History for Jan–March 1944, AFHRA Reel No B0489; and Skytrain Vol. I Issue 8 and ff, AFHRA Reel B0489, 498; and www.joebaugher.com.
22 Other reports indicate that the losses sustained by the 403rd were greater. The report "The Thirteenth Air Force in the War Against Japan," The United States Strategic Bombing Survey, Military Analysis Division, 30 September 1946, indicates that from September 1944 to the end of the war, a total of 25 aircraft were lost. The report does not contain data for the months prior to September 1944.
23 Lt. Col. Benjamin E. Lippincott, Historian, Thirteenth Air Force, et al., *From Fiji Through the Philippines with the Thirteenth Air Force* (San Angelo, TX: Newsfoto Publishing, 1948).
24 74682 History 64th TCS Dec 42—Dec 43, AFHRA Iris No. 74682; and 64th TC Sq, Jungle Air Force.
25 AFHRA Reel A7712, page 1364, April 44 Missions flown 403rd.
26 Unit Organizational and Administrative History, XIII Air Force Service Command, A/6/whs, AFHRA Reel A7712, 333 and 341.
27 *Two Years Pacific: Sandman.*
28 64th TC Sq, Jungle Air Force; and Roessell, *Notes from the Pacific.*
29 Roessell, *Notes from the Pacific.*
30 *Two Years Pacific: Sandman.*
31 Roessell, *Notes from the Pacific.*
32 *Two Years Pacific: Sandman.*
33 Combat Squadrons of the Air Force, World War II, Maurer, Albert F. Simpson Historical Research Center, 1982.
34 64th TC Sq, Jungle Air Force.
35 Table of Organization and Equipment 1-317, Troop Carrier Squadron, War Department, 16 August 1943.
36 *Two Years Pacific: Sandman.*
37 Interview with Major General Harry J. Sands, Jr., by Mark C. Cleary, ESMC History Office, Patrick AFB, April-May 1990, United States Air Force Oral History Program, K239.0512-1924.
38 *Two Years Pacific: Sandman.*
39 Ibid. Date of departure of the air echelon from Hamilton Field, California: July 17, 1942. End of war: September 2, 1945.
40 Interview with Major General Harry J. Sands.
41 64th TC Sq, Jungle Air Force.
42 War Diary, Marine Air Group 12, NARA 4697018 Micro Serial NO. 141903, 13 August 1945.
43 Interview with Major General Harry J. Sands.
44 JoeBaugher.com Military Aircraft database. Re 23696, Baugher has: (MSN 9558) to USAAF May 19, 1943. Missing on flight form Yangkai, China to Chabua, India Apr 28, 1943. Crew of 5 presumed killed. This is incorrect. NASM queried and responded 10/27/22 to confirm the above details.
45 Op. cit. Combat Squadrons.
46 *Two Years Pacific: Sandman.*

Bibliography

33 Division Pictorial History: Camp Forrest 1941–1942. Atlanta, Georgia: Army Press, 1942.
"Analysis of DNA from Early Settlers of the Pacific Overturns Leading Genetic Model," Binghamton University, State University of New York, October 3, 2016. https://www.binghamton.edu/communications-and-marketing/media-public-relations/pr-archives/index.html?id=2436.
Bedford, Stuart. *Pieces of the Vanuatu Puzzle: Archaeology of the North, South and Centre*. Canberra: Pandanus Books, 2006.
Bedford, Stuart, Matthew Spriggs, Ethan Cochrane, and Terry Hunt. "The Archaeology of Vanuatu: 3,000 years of History across Islands of Ash and Coral." In Ethan Cochrane and Terry Hunt (eds.), *The Oxford Handbook of Prehistoric Oceania*, Oxford University Press, New York, NY, 2014.
Bouchet, Philippe, Herve Le Guyader, and Olivier Pascal (Eds). *The prehistory of Santo*. Paris: Muséum national d'histoire naturelle; IRD; Pro-Natura international, 2011
(COMAIRSOPAC), Message for Improvement of Combat Air Transport Services, SoPac, Area, November 24, 1942.
Combat Narratives, The Landing in the Solomons, 7–8 August, 1942, Solomon Islands Campaign: I, Office of Naval Intelligence, 1943.
"Enquete entomologique sur le paludisme aux Nouvelles-Hebrides." Commission du Pacific Sud, Document Technique No. 119, January 1959.
"First Ancestry of Ni-Vanuatu is Asian: New DNA Discoveries Published." Interview by Bob Makin, *Vanuatu Daily Post*, October 4, 2016.
Francillon, Rene J., *McDonnell Douglas Aircraft Since 1920*, London: Putnam, 1979.
Francois, Alexandre. "Shadows of bygone lives: The histories of spiritual words in northern Vanuatu." In *Lexical and Structural Etymology: beyond word histories*, edited by Robert Mailhammer. Boston, Massachusetts: De Gruyter Mouton, 2013.
Frankel, Stanley. *The 37th Infantry Division in World War II*. Washington: Infantry Journal Press, 1948.
Grimshaw, Beatrice. *In the Strange South Seas*. Freeport, New York: Books for Libraries Press, 1971.
Hays, Terence E. (ed.), *Encyclopedia of World Cultures, Vol II, Oceania*. New York: G.K. Hall & Co, 1992.
History of the 67th Fighter Squadron, Rough Draft of Manuscript, 1942, AFHRA IRIS No. 750.057.
Lineage and Honors, 130th Infantry Regiment (Fourth Illinois), Center of Military History, Department of the Army.
"Luzon, 15 December 1944–4 July 1945." In *Campaigns of World War II: A World War II Commemorative Series*. Center of Military History Publication 72-28, GPO 008-029-00301-5.
Macdonald, David. *Lives of Fort de Chartres: Commandants, Soldiers, and Civilians in French Illinois 1720–1770*. Carbondale: Southern Illinois University Press, 2016
Miles, William F. S. *Bridging Mental Boundaries in a Postcolonial Microcosm: identity and development in Vanuatu*. Honolulu: University of Hawai'i Press, 1998.
National Integrated Water Resource Management Diagnostic Report, Vanuatu, Report 648. Suva, Fiji: Pacific Islands Applied Geoscience Commission, November 2007. https://www.pacific-r2r.org/sites/default/files/2020-03/GEF-Pacific-IWRM-Diagnostic-Report-Vanuatu-part1.pdf

Naudts, Morris J. *The operations of the 129th Infantry Regiment (37th Infantry Division) in the Battle for Clark Field and Fort Stotsenburg, Luzon, Philippines Islands, 27 January–3 February 1945 (personal experience of a battalion executive officer)*. Fort Benning, Georgia: Academic Department, The Infantry School, 1948.

Ratard, R. C. "Epidemiology of malaria in the New Hebrides." *Tropical Doctor*, 1979, vol. 9.

Report After Action, Operations of the 37th Infantry Division, Luzon, P.I., 1 November 1944 to 30 June 1945. Headquarters 37th Infantry Division, AG 314.7 W, 10 September 1945.

Robin, Claude, et al. *The Geology, Volcanology, Petrology, Geochemistry, and Tectonic Evolution of the New Hebrides Island Arc, Vanuatu*. Canberra, Australia: Australian Geological Survey Organisation, 1993.

Smith, James A. The US Navy and the Tokyo Express at Guadalcanal, August–December, 1942: A Battle that Required "Every Conceivable Weapon." Masters capstone paper, Norwich University, 2014.

Spriggs, Matthew. "First People On Vanuatu and Tonga came from Taiwan." *New Archaeology*, October 2016.

Stanley, David. *South Pacific Handbook*. Chico, California: Moon Publications, 1993.

Taylor, John Patrick. *The Other Side—Ways of Being and Place in Vanuatu*. Manoa, Hawaii: Center for Pacific Islands Studies, University of Hawaii, 2016. https://search.worldcat.org/title/220419878

Tyron, Darryl. "Pacific Islands Stakeholder Participation in Development: Vanuatu, A Report for the World Bank." In Pacific Islands Discussion Paper Series No. 8, May 1999.

Wales, William. *Journal on the Resolution, 21 June 1772–17 Oct. 1774*. Mitchell Library, State Library of New South Wales. Accessed at: http://acms.sl.nsw.gov.au/_transcript/2013/D02369/a1800.htm#a1800089. Date accessed February 8, 2017

Wedgwood, Camilla H. "The Nature and Functions of Secret Societies." *Oceania*, Vol. 1, No. 2 (July 1930): 129–45.

West, Barbara A. *Encyclopedia of Peoples of Asia and Oceania*. New York: Facts on File, 2009.

World Culture Encyclopedia. "Countries and Their Culture, Vanuatu." Accessed at https://worldculture.medium.com/culture-of-vanuatu-849a156ac4ff.

Zimmerman, John L. *The Guadalcanal Invasion*. Historical Division Headquarters, US Marine Corps, 1949.

Index

Page numbers in italics denote photographs or graphics.

IV Air Center Command
IV Island Command 11
IV Island Air Command 210
1st Independent Company 26
4th Marine Defense Battalion *see* U.S. Marine Corps
6th Replacement Depot 122
25th Evacuation Hospital 148, 151, 197, 204, 211
57th Engineer Combat Battalion *see* United States Army units
129th Infantry Regiment (Combat Team)
  Bougainville 162, 212, 253
  Camp Forrest 104
  Espiritu Santo 107
  Fiji 106
  Philippines campaign 251–8
129th Infantry Regiment (Combat Team) personnel
  Andruskevitch, Chaplain Casimir 189, 200, 254, *254*
  Bulfer, Sgt. Harry 190, 255
  Craver, Capt. Curtis 109, 189, 199, *252*, 253
  Gabriel, Pvt. Joseph 190, 255, 256
  Naudts, Col. Morris 103, 105, 109, 112, 184, 186, 189, 251–2, *252*
403rd Troop Carrier Group
  13th TC Squadron 84, 122, 129, 155, 181
  63rd TC Squadron 132, 135, 147, 155, 260, 264
  64th TC Squadron 132, *133*, 137, 139, 142, 147, 150, 153, 162, 190, 241–50
  801st Medical Air Evacuation Transport Squadron 129, 147, 155, 261, 267
Alliance Field, Nebraska 132
Baer Field, Indiana 134, 136
Bowman Field, Louisville, KY. 132
Pope Field, North Carolina 132
403rd Troop Carrier Group personnel
  Bamberger, 2nd Lt. George 95, 118, 139, 208
  Buchheit, Cpl. Raymond 190, 200, 203, 243–5, *244*, 260, 302
  Gonder, 2nd Lt. Carl 95, 117, 127, 139, 212
  Healy, 1st. Lt. Robert 162, *163*, 165, 173, 247–8
  McCreight, Lt. Albert Noble 187, 190, 199, 203, 241–242, *242*, 244, 260, 266, 269
  Miller, 2nd Lt. Augustus 162, *163*, 165, 172, 248
  O'Connell, Cpl Joseph 162, *163*, 181, 249–50
  Richwine, Capt. Alfred 189, 199, 203, 242–3, *243*, 261–2
  Roessell, Maj. Jack 133, 139, 155, 180, 189, 197, *245*, 259, 264, 265, 266, 269
  Sands, Col. Harry 129, 139, 147, 155, 244, 259, 264, 266, 268, 269
  Seliga, 2nd Lt. Edward 95
  Smith, 2nd Lt. Philip 94, 95
  Wlodarsky, M/Sgt Harry 162, *163*, 248

Advance Naval Base 32, 97, 102
American-British-Dutch-Australia Command (ABDACOM) 17
African American/Black units 32, 222, 267
Air Crew Qualification exam 21, 89
Andruskevitch, Chaplain Casimir *see* 129th Infantry Regiment
Arcadia 12, 14, 17, 33, 62
Army Air Corps *see* U.S. Army Air Forces
Arnold, General Henry ("Hap") 14
Atabrine 29, 112, 156, 261
Auckland, New Zealand 85, 153

Aviation Cadet Program, Army Air Corps 21, 46, 75
Aviation Cadet Qualifying Examination (ACQE) 21, 89
Axis forces 5, 12, 16

Baker, John 53
Bamberger, 2nd Lt. George *see* 403rd Troop Carrier personnel
Bauer, Maj. Joseph ("Indian Joe") 39, 63, 65, 70, 73, 79
Biak Island 246, 261, 262, 264, 265, 266
Big Bay, Espiritu Santo island 49, 59, 87, 142, 168, 171, 178, 185
Bislama (language) 226, 227
Bismarck Archipelago 14, 26, 57, 86
Bleacher (codename for Tongatabu) 16, 20, 33
Bobcat (codename for Bora Bora) 33 f
Bomber 1 Airfield (Pallikulo) 73, 79, 144, 150, 196
Bomber 2 Airfield (Pekoa) 128, 141, *144*, 147, 150, 151, 164, 261
Bomber 3 Airfield (Luganville) 145, 151
Bora Bora Island 14, 18, 33
Bougainville Island, Solomon Islands 14, 26, 124, 162, 208, 253, *258*
Buchheit, Cpl. Raymond *see* 403rd Troop Carrier Group personnel
Bulfur, Sgt. Harry *see* 129th Infantry Regiment
Butmas village ix, x, 53, 193, 226
Button (codename for Espiritu Santo) 65, 72, 89, 97, 99, 102, 148
Byrd, Adm. Richard E. 96

Cactus (codename for Guadalcanal) 64, 81, 207
Canton Island 12, 14, 16, 18, 139
Cape Cumberland 165, 169, 178
Cape Quiros 164, 167
Chamberlin, Gen. Harry 35, 41
Christmas Island 139
CINC 14, 42, 108
CINCPAC–CINCPOA 23
Civilian Pilot Training Program (CPT)
 Civil Aeronautics Authority (CAA) 6, 75
 Preliminary 7, 8
 Secondary 7, 9, 20
Clark Airfield 268

Clarkston, WA 1, 3, 8
Clearwater River 1, 6, 8, 22
climate *see* weather
COMAIRSOPAC 23, 72, 175, 209
COMSOPAC 23, 64
Cook, Capt. James 49
Coral Sea, battle of 31, 45
Craver, Curtis *see* 129th Infantry Regiment
Crash of '43 243

de Quiros, Pedro Fernandez 49, 53
depopulation 59
Dick, Douglas 226, 230, *233*, *236*
Dickelman, Lt. Evelyn 215, *217*
diseases
 Malaria 21, 27, 38, 83, 98, 111, 113, 125, 151, 156, 221, 232, 261
 Dengue Fever 112, 152, 155
Driedger, Arthur 46, 77, 158
Douglas Aircraft Company 132, 134, 135, 137, 152
Dulag, Leyte, Philippines 246, 267

Efate Island, New Hebrides Archipelago 16, 20, 24, 27, 28, 32, 35, 37, 39, 41, 62, 67, 70, 73, 112, 141
Eisenhower, Gen. Dwight 16, 94, 134
Eliott Detachment, Lt. H. V. Eliott *also see* 57th Engineer Combat Battalion
 deployment to Efate 24
 deployment to Espiritu Santo 66
Espiritu Santo Island, New Hebrides
 biome 50, 67, 110, 183
 languages and communalects 50, 55
 map *100*

Fanafo village 193, 196, 199
Fanafo-Kona village 226, 227, *228*, 229, 230, 240
Fiji 12, 14, 16, 18, 20, 30, 47, 49, 106
First Construction Battalion, US Navy (Seabees)
 1st Detachment (Bobcat) 33, 37
 2nd Detachment (Bleacher) 33
 3rd Detachment (Roses) 33
Force A
 on Efate (Roses) 24, 28, 29, 38
 on Santo (Button) 42

INDEX

French-British Condominium 221, 233

Garrison, Lt. Ritchie 41, 73
Ghormley, Vice Admiral Robert 23, 41, 64, 79, 82
Gonder, 2nd Lt. Carl *see* 403rd Troop Carrier Group personnel
Grimshaw, Beatrice 29, 51, 56
Guadalcanal, Solomon Islands campaign 26, 44, 61, 64, *67*, 68, 72
Guam Island 11, 15, 96

Halsey, Admiral William ("Bull") *64*, 82
Hammond General Hospital 214
Harmon, Gen. Millard F 74, 84
Harris, Tom 25, 40, 195
Healy, 1st. Lt. Robert *see* 403rd Troop Carrier Group personnel
HYPO code breaking 30, 47

Japanese military operations
    advances in early December 1941: 12, *13*, 17, 20, 26
    Operation FS 30, 61
    Operation MI 47
    Operation MO 30
Job, Chief Harry 228, *230*
Johnson, Martin 53
Joint Chiefs of Staff (JCS) 14, 19, 23, 32, 61, 65
Joint Plan for the Occupation and Defense of Efate, New Hebrides 32
Joint Task Force 9156 32, 34, 35
Jungle, Bush, Rainforest 50, 51, 180, 184, 198

King, Admiral Ernest 14, 16, 19, 41, 47, *64*
Kralovec, Lt. Dalibor 52, 145

Las Vegas Aerial Gunner School 90, 95
Leahy, Admiral William 14
Lewiston State Normal School 6, 7
Lewiston, ID 1, 3, 6
Little Detachment, Capt. John Little 25, 38
Lost Plane Procedure
    in effect August 1943 175
    in effect October 1943 209
Luganville, Espiritu Santo 25, 40, 44, 145, 151, 226

Lunga Plain *68*, 74, 80, 163, 260

MacArthur, General Douglas 17, 23, 63, *64*, 69, 93
MacClancy, Jeremy 53, 55, 225
Marshall, General George 14, 16, 19, *64*, 65, 156
Mathis, Lt. Sam
    on Efate 37, 65
    on Espiritu Santo 66, 70
McCain, Rear Adminral John 23, 65, 70, 71
McCaw General Hospital 214, 215
McCornack General Hospital 216
McCreight, Lt. Albert Noble *see* 403rd Troop Carrier Group personnel
Michel, Pascal 40, 66
Michener, James 52, 101, 177, 251
Midway, battle of 46
Miller, 2nd Lt. Augustus *see* 403rd Troop Carrier Group personnel
Missing Air Crew Report 181, 197
mosquito
    Aedes (genus) 113
    Anopheles (genus) 111, 113
MS *Tabinta* 212, *213*, 214
Mt. Turi 142, 165, 169, 171, *172*, 180, 184, 199, 232

Naval Advance Base Button ("Buttons")
    attacks on 99
    facilities 101
Navigation, Aerial 84, 90, 92
New Britain 11, 162, 261
New Caledonia 12, 13, 16, 18, 24, 30, 42, 58, *120*, *123*
New Guinea Island 11, 15, 26, 30, 50, 86, 162
New Hebrides
    Blackbirding 57
    climate *see* weather
    depopulation 59
    European discovery 49
    European settlement 58
    history 49, 195
    people of *54*, *194*
    population 59, 225
New Hebrides National Party (NHNP) 223
New Ireland 11, 14, 26
New Zealand 12, 20, 26, 47, 85

Nimitz, Admiral Chester 23, 41, 47, 62, *64*, 65, 82, 97
Ni-Vanuatu 222, 225
Noumea, New Caledonia 24, 39, 62, 112, 120, 121, 124

O'Connell, Cpl Joseph *see* 403rd Troop Carrier Group personnel
Operation "Mo" *see* Japanese military operations
Operation *Cartwheel* 93, 161
　Operation *Chronicle* 161
　Operation *Toenails* 161
Operation FS *see* Japanese military operations
Operation MI *see* Japanese military operations
Outpost Line of Resistance, Espiritu Santo 184, *186*

Pacific Theater of Operations (PTO) 12, 18, 105, 139
Palmyra Island 16
Patch, Gen. Alexander 41, 83
Philippine Islands 11, 96, 257
Piper J-3c "Cub" 7, 9, 76
Poppy (codename for New Caledonia) 18, 41
Port Moresby 26, 30, 45

Rabaul (New Britain Island) 14, 16, 30, 61, 86
radar, SCR-595
　SCR-270 warning radar 178
　SCR-595 friend/foe radar 178
Renee River 44, 156, 184
Richardson, Evelyn *see* Dickelman, Evelyn
Richardson, Leonard
　crash 161, 171
　early years 1, 2, 4
　education 1, 3, 218
　embarkation to South Pacific 95
　Espiritu Santo 142
　marriage and family 216, 217, *219*, *220*
　navigator training 90, 91, *92*
　New Caledonia 119, 124, 126
　pilot training 8, *45*, *77* also see Civilian Pilot Training Program
　recovery and treatment 211, *215*
　survival 161
　teaching, Asotin 5
Richardson, Norman 1, 4, 5, 22, *92*, 93

Richwine, Capt. Alfred *see* 403rd Troop Carrier Group personnel
Roessell, Maj. Jack *see* 403rd Troop Carrier Group personnel
Roosevelt, Franklin D. 9, 12, 104
Rose, Brig. Gen. William I. 24, 40, 65, 70, 73, 108
Roses (codename for Efate Island) 24
Rose Detachment (1st Seabee) 33
Royal Australian Air Force (RAAF)
　#11 and #20 Squadrons 26
　Advanced Operating Base Vila 26
Royal New Zealand Air Force (RNZAF) 145, 148, 163

Samoa 12, 18, 20, 33, 49, 140
Sands, Col. Harry *see* 403rd Troop Carrier Group personnel
Saunders, Col. Laverne (Blondy) 72, 74, 80, 150
Santa Ana Army Air Base (SAAAB) *45*, 90, 93
Sarakata River 44, 110, 171, 182, 203
Segond Channel 25, 40, 43, 96, 108, 142
Selective Service ("draft") 6, 104
Seliga, 2nd Lt. Edward *see* 403rd Troop Carrier Group personnel
Smith, 2nd Lt. Philip *see* 403rd Troop Carrier Group personnel
Snake River 1, 6, 181
South Pacific (Southern) Supply Line 12, 13, 16, 18, 24, 33
South Pacific Combat Air Transport (SCAT) 145, 155, 260, 264
South Pacific Theater of operation (SOPAC) 41, 139
Southwest Pacific Theater of Operation (SOWESTPAC) 23, 30, 64, 65, 158, 161
Speiser, Felix 51, 59, 142
Straw (codename for Samoa) 20
stress, fatigue 83, 155, 266

Task Force 6814: 18, 24, 29
Task Force 9156: 32, 37, 38
Tavuli, Thomas 228, *230*, *233*, 236, 240
Tokyo Express 82
Tome, Mark *230*, *231*, *233*
Tome, Pascal 226, *230*, 232, *233*, *238*

Tulagi, Solomon Islands 26, 30, 37, 42, 61, 64, 68, 72

U.S. Army Air Forces Pilot Training Program 7, 21, 75
U.S. Army Air Forces and Navy Pacific airfields
  Bauer Field, Efate, New Hebrides 25, 71, 97
  Biak, New Guinea 246, 262, 264, *265*
  Henderson Field, Guadalcanal Island 81, 84, 146, 162, 166
  Kukum Airfield ("Fighter 2"), Guadalcanal Island 163, *166*, 260
  Tontouta Airfield, New Caledonia 39, 84, *121*, 125
  Turtle Bay Airfield (Navy), Espiritu Santo, New Hebrides 109, 145, 151, 165, 171, 178, 184, 196
U.S Army Air Force units
  4th Photographic Group (17th Photo Recce Squadron) 121
  5th Air Force 158, 264
  5th Bomb Group (23rd, 31st, 72nd, 394th Squadrons) 128, 163, 180
  11th Bomb Group (26th, 42nd, 98th, 431st Squadrons) 71, 80, 85, 128, 158
  13th Air Force 128, 131, 162, 178
  13th Troop Carrier Squadron 84, 122, 129, 141, 146, 155
  18th Fighter Group (12th and 44th Fighter Squadrons) 128
  42nd Bomb Group (69th and 70th Bomb Squadron) 71, 74, 121, 128
  307th Bomb Group (370th, 371st, 372nd, 424th Squadrons) 144, 163
  347th Fighter Group 121, 128
  403rd Troop Carrier Group 132, 136, 139, 141, 147
U.S. Army Air Force aircraft
  Beechcraft AT-7 twin engine trainer 91
  Bell P-39 Aircobra fighter 128
  Bell P400 Fighter 128
  Boeing B-17 Flying Fortress heavy bomber 65, 70, 71, 73, 79, 128, 177
  Consolidated B-24 Liberator heavy bomber 144, 177
  Douglas A-20 Havoc light bomber 158
  Douglas C-47A Skytrain troop/cargo aircraft 137, *146*, 152, 165

Lockheed AT-18 Hudson light bomber 90
Lockheed P-38 Lightning fighter 128, 163
Martin B-26 Marauder medium bomber 70, 72, 128,
North American B-25 Mitchell medium bomber 32, 158
Ryan PT-22 Recruit training aircraft *76*
U.S. Army units
  Americal Division 83
  4th Field Artillery Battalion 32
  6th Field Artillery Battalion 107
  24th Infantry Regiment 32
  57th Engineer Combat Company 24, 66, 70
  129th Infantry Regiment (Combat Team) *see* 129th Infantry Regiment
  172nd Infantry Regiment 108
  350th Engineering Regiment 151, 197
  822nd Engineer Aviation Battalion 144, 148, 151
U.S. Marine Corps units
  4th Marine Defense Battalion 24, 70, 99
  Marine Air Group 11 (MAG-11) 145, 207
  Marine Air Group 23 (MAG-23) 81
  Marine Air Group 24 (MAG-24) 25
  Marine Air Group 25 (MAG-25) 146
  VMF-124: 163
  VMF-212: 25, 38, 63
  VMJ-152: 84, 146
  VMJ-253: 84, 210
  VMTB-232: 207
U.S. military aircraft
  B-17 "Flying Fortress" 65, 70, 80, 128, 158, 177
  B-24 "Liberator" 144, 145, 158
  C-47 "Skytrain" 129, 133, 135, *136*, 152, 238, 269
  F4F "Wildcat" 39, 63, 145
  F4U "Corsair" 163
  J2F "Duck" 25, 39
  OS2U "Kingfisher" 40, 43
  PBY 40, 145, 178
  R4D 84, 121, 127, 131, 145, 146
  Ryan PT-22: 76
U.S. Navy and Marine Corps aircraft
  Consolidated PBY Catalina amphibious airplane 145, 40
  Douglas SBD Dauntless dive bomber 145, 207

Grumman F4F Wildcat fighter 39, 63, 145
Grumman J2F Duck amphibious airplane 25, 39
Grumman TBF Avenger torpedo bomber 145, 207
Lockheed PV-1 Ventura bomber/patrol airplane 145
Vought F4U Corsair fighter 145, 163
U.S. Navy units
    VS-5D14: 43
    1st Construction Battalion (Seabee) 32, 37
    6th Construction Battalion (Seabee) 81, 98, 99
    7th Construction Battalion (Seabee) 98, 99
    15th Construction Battalion (Seabee) 151
USAT Puebla 95, 115, *116*, 118
U.S.S. *President Coolidge* 108

Vanuatu *see* New Hebrides
Victory Plan 9

Vila Harbor, Efate Island 25, 29, 37
V-mail 127, 207

Wadke Island 264
Wake Island 11, 15, 96
Wallin, Lt. H. N. 37, 65
War Plan Rainbow Five 12, 14
weather 52, 80, 109, 157, 158, 159, 164
Whitworth College 3, 5
Wlodarsky, M/Sgt Harry *see* 403rd Troop Carrier Group personnel
Woolley, Sidney, Sgt. 25, 39

Yamamoto, Isoruku, Admiral 11, 30, 46, 94

Zimmerly Flying School 3, 6